Books by Nigel Nicolson

Alex: The Life of Field Marshal Earl Alexander of Tunis   1973

The Diaries and Letters of Harold Nicolson (editor)   1966–1968

Great Houses of the Western World   1968

Great Houses of Britain   1966

Lord of the Isles   1960

People and Parliament   1958

The Grenadier Guards, 1939–45   1947

ALEX

ALEX

THE LIFE OF FIELD MARSHAL EARL ALEXANDER OF TUNIS

NIGEL NICOLSON

ATHENEUM

New York

1973

CONTENTS

ILLUSTRATIONS

MAPS

AUTHOR'S NOTE

In February 1969 I asked Lord Alexander if he would allow me to write his biography. He consented, and promised me 'all the assistance I can'. It was arranged between us that in the autumn of that year we would meet for the first of many talks. In June he died.

His widow has done much more than honour the Field Marshal's undertaking. She allowed me to borrow for months on end all the surviving documentation of his life, recommended me to friends who had known him well at different phases of his long career, and cheerfully underwent many hours of questioning in her own home. It is therefore right that almost the first words of this book should express my gratitude for her hospitality and help.

It is not an 'authorized' biography: still less an official one. The term upon which Lady Alexander and I finally settled was 'accredited', meaning that she would allow me access to all the relevant papers, and I should feel free from constraint in writing what I wished, submitting the book to her for comment before publication. She has used that right sparingly and helpfully, for though there are inevitably passages which she would have phrased differently herself, she agrees that it would lose in authenticity if it were not an honest expression of my own opinions.

Alexander left a number of papers in addition to the official documents of his campaigns on which he based his despatches. As far as is known, he kept a diary on only one occasion (his visit to Korea as Minister of Defence in 1952), but he periodically wrote summaries of special incidents, such as an account of his childhood until he went to Harrow, a narrative of his experiences in Latvia in 1919, and a third dealing with his first campaign on the North West Frontier of India in 1935. From his childhood, the First War and the inter-war years, a number of his letters survive at Caledon, his family's home in Ireland, and I am grateful to Lord Caledon for permission to quote from them. During the Second War he was too busy to write more than purely personal letters to his wife and children, but it is fortunate that at the moment when the letters cease, the documents take over. They are very full, and the central part of this book is based upon them. They are now in the Public Record Office.

The third source has been the mass of published books and articles dealing with Alexander's campaigns, including his own despatches and the Official Histories, which are acknowledged in the Bibliography. The fourth is the memory of his friends and associates. I have interviewed many of them, and have adopted the device, new, I believe, in biography, of including in the text extracts from the tape-recordings of our conversations, in order to vary the pace and style of the narrative, and to preserve unparaphrased the recollections of people who knew Alexander best at decisive moments of his life.

In addition to Lady Alexander, I would like to thank the following for their help:

Other members of the Field Marshal's family, including his four children (Shane, the present Earl Alexander of Tunis; Rose Crossman; Brian Alexander; and Susan Hamilton); his surviving brother, Lieutenant-Colonel William Alexander; and the Earl and Countess of Caledon.

The Lieutenant-Colonel (Colonel J. A. Aylmer) and successive Regimental Adjutants of the Irish Guards.

Earl Mountbatten of Burma; Field Marshal Lord Harding; Field Marshal Sir Gerald Templer; Mr Harold Macmillan; General Sir William Morgan; Major General H. L. Davies.

In the United States: General Lyman L. Lemnitzer; General Alfred M. Gruenther; General Mark Wayne Clark; Mr John L. Sullivan; Mrs Calvert Carey.

In Canada: Major General H. F. G. Letson; Mr Justice Douglas Abbott; Major General Ernest Walford; Brigadier J. G. Gauvreau; Mr Nathaniel V. Davies; Mr Frank Delaute; Squadron Leader H. Keane.

Mr M. J. Babington Smith; Lieutenant-Colonel R. Baggallay; Rev J. H. Bradbury; Hon John Brooke; Rt Rev J. R. Brookes; Lord Bruntisfield; Brigadier E. G. Bull; Brigadier A. D. P. Campbell; Lord

Chalfont; Sir Rupert Clarke Bt; Lord Cornwallis; Major D. V. Fanshawe; Lieutenant-Colonel J. S. N. Fitzgerald; Sir Derrick Gunston Bt; Mr Denis Hamilton; the Headmaster of Harrow; Sir David Hunt; the late Sir Shane Leslie; Mr A. Mackinnon; Lady McCreery; Lady Alexandra Metcalfe; Brigadier C. J. C. Molony; Lord Nugent; Prince Serge Obolensky; Mr A. F. Phillpotts; the late Major A. R. Pym; Lord Rhyl; Mr Kenneth Rose; Mr Edward Seago; Lieutenant-Colonel G. A. Shepperd; Brigadier Sir John Smyth VC; Sir Norman Stronge Bt; Major George Thorne; Miss May Turner; Major P. V. Verney; and Mr J. Wells.

To Diana Crawfurd, my literary agent, and Tony Godwin of Weidenfeld & Nicolson, I am indebted for their encouragement, patience and advice. And to Mrs Robert Malins and Mrs P. Kilbane for typing the book.

Nigel Nicolson

Sissinghurst Castle, Kent
July 1972

ALEX

FOREWORD

This biography had its remote origin (or do I now romanticize it?) at about 6 pm on 12 May 1943. It was the day of the German surrender in Tunisia. The brigade of which I was the Intelligence Officer was leading the advance of First Army south from Tunis towards the rear of the German Afrika Korps, who were entrenched in the hills above Bou Ficha facing the Eighth. It was the classic situation of which Generals dream, a perfectly executed encirclement leading to the enemy's mass capitulation *en rase campagne*. On a map it looked beautiful. On the ground, the action took place on a scale small enough for every soldier in the three armies to comprehend its significance and design. There on one side was the Mediterranean, shore-sea green and deep-sea blue, the destroyers and fighter-aircraft making escape that way impossible; and inland, straight from the beaches, rose muscular hills already spotted with white flags of surrender. There was no fighting any more, but the sound of battle was maintained for a few hours longer as the Germans fired their ammunition dumps. Then they formed up to march down from the hills into captivity. Our leading tanks, their mission accomplished, had halted in the plain below.

I drove my jeep along the coast-road to a point where a demolished bridge delayed the final junction of the two British armies, and exchanged shouted congratulations across the stream-bed with an Eighth Army officer on the far side. I was not the first to arrive there. Engineers were already laying a Bailey bridge to span the gap and, as I waited to cross it, I noticed with pity blunted by familiarity the corpse of an Italian soldier beside the bridge-abutment, the belt of his machine-gun trailing like a serpent in the dust.

At that moment a staff-car drew up behind me, and out stepped Alexander. I had never seen him before, and I did not meet him then. I stood aside as he walked up to the lip of the *wadi*. For several minutes he stared at its sandy bottom. I wondered what could be passing through his mind at the moment when everything he had planned and done since reaching Africa nine months before had reached this ful-filment, at the moment (as he must have known) when the whole free world was acclaiming him, with hyperbole justified by his achievement, as Alexander Africanus. Which was dominant – a sense of triumph or a sense of relief? Then he did something which showed me what sort of man he was. He walked up to the Italian machine-gun, put the toe of his polished field-boot under the magazine, and toppled it, with a sharp jerk, into the ditch. It was a gesture of finality, but it was something more. It expressed all his loathing for the wastage of war, and his contempt for the adulation of which he was then the hero. He turned on his heel, walked back to his staff-car without a word or even a glance in my direction, and drove off. It was at that moment (or so I like to tell myself and others) that I conceived the ambition to write his life.

I saw him and talked to him, with the diffidence appropriate in a young Captain finding himself face to face with a Field Marshal, on half a dozen occasions during the campaign in Italy, and everything which I observed or learnt of his character confirmed my first impres-sion. Here was a man whom it would not be easy to know, and what made it difficult were his most obvious traits, his modesty and his reserve. How, I asked myself, could a man of so gentle a nature have chosen the life of a professional soldier? And how could a soldier ap-parently so undemonstrative have risen to the highest rank of field command, and gained the confidence and affection of a million men of mixed nationality who marched on his orders to possible death? What was the secret of that magnetism to which I was myself a victim without quite knowing why?

After the war I once saw him standing isolated but smiling in a ballroom; and again at the Victory Parade in London, where his place of honour seemed uncomfortable to him. He was absent in Canada for six years as Governor General, and it was not until his return in 1952 that I came to know him a little better. I was then on the Conservative backbenches of the House of Commons, and he was Minister of Defence in Churchill's second Government. He disliked politics, finding himself ill at ease in the company of people who struggled for power instead of waiting until it was thrust upon them, and he could never fully identify himself with the political party of which he was nominally a leader, speaking at party-committees of 'you', never 'we' or 'us', and once, in 1954, when we were debating in private the evacuation of the Suez base, declining to answer the question whether he thought it politically wise, on the grounds that such decisions belonged to his colleagues, not to him. Nothing of my early veneration for him had faded, but my wonder grew. His close friends would say that Alexander's success was due to his simplicity. I do not dispute that this was an element in it. But it does not explain much. There have been men of angelically simple natures who have done nothing with their lives. What lay behind? Henceforward I appear seldom in this narrative. I have set out these facts only to make clear how much I admired him, how slightly I knew him, and what questions are in my mind as I begin.

CHILDHOOD AND YOUTH

Alexander was born in London, but he belonged to Ulster, where generations of Alexanders had built up a reputation for public service in and out of uniform, and for an unfeignedly patrician style of living, maintaining with dignity and good humour their great estate at Caledon in County Tyrone, on the borders of Armagh. The family came originally from Scotland, a cadet branch of the Earls of Stirling, and reached Ireland as a Plantation family in the reign of James I. We can trace them first at Eridy in County Donegal, and in the early eighteenth century as Aldermen of Londonderry, where they owned a considerable house called Boom Hall. The shift from middle-class respectability to aristocratic affluence came with James Alexander (1730–1802), a second son who joined the East India Company to serve in Bengal under Clive and Warren Hastings. He returned to Ireland in 1772 having made the large fortune with which he built Caledon Castle, and became a Unionist Member of the Irish Parliament. He was an active supporter of Grattan's volunteer movement and raised the Aughnacloy Volunteers. In 1790 he was created Baron Caledon, in 1797 a Viscount, and in 1801 an Earl. At his death his estates were valued at £600,000.

James Alexander was known in the family as 'the Nabob'. He was succeeded by 'the Governor', his only son Dupre (1777–1839), who in 1806 became the first British Governor of the Cape of Good Hope, and thereafter devoted his time and fortune to the embellishment of his house, the care of his tenantry, and his seat in Parliament. Something of the flavour of the period is preserved in a testimonial presented to him in 1835:

An address from the tenantry of the Caledon estate to their landlord, the Rt Hon Dupre, Earl of Caledon, Knight of St Patrick, Lord Lieutenant of the County of Tyrone, and Colonel of the Royal Tyrone Militia. My Lord, we gladly avail ourselves of the occasion of your lordship's return to Caledon from attending your Parliamentary duties to express the joy with which that event is ever hailed by us, and to assure your lordship of the lively sense we entertain of the many benefits we derive from your constant residence amongst us, a residence ever marked by acts of liberality, munificence and kindness. . . .

And so on. Life was still undoubtedly very feudal and very grand.

The 3rd Earl of Caledon, James Dupre, Alexander's grandfather (1812–55), was overshadowed by his two famous predecessors. He followed them into Parliament as Member for Tyrone, and inevitably became Colonel of its militia, but the central experience of his life was when he served in Quebec as a Captain in the Coldstream Guards. He took the trouble, unusual for a British officer, to cultivate the friendship of the local Indians and made several trips into the interior. Some charming water-colours by his hand survive at Caledon, of Canadian scenes which a hundred years later, in 1946, his grandson also painted, as far as he could manage from the identical spots. The 3rd Earl died, probably of appendicitis, at the age of forty-three, leaving the earldom to his eldest son, Alexander's father, who was then only nine years old.

This ancestral catalogue, less remarkable in print than when ill-ustrated by the portraits at Caledon, explains something of Alexander's background. There was a military tradition, strong but not exclusive nor particularly distinguished; a tradition of political service; great wealth, with which went the luxury of living in a magnificent house and the habit of organization and command; and the preservation of blood and money by marrying into the right families. Alexander was never a rich man, being the third son in a family which took primogeniture for granted. But his pedigree is scintillating. It is studded with Earls. His grandfather, father and brother were Earls of Caledon. His paternal great-aunts became the Countesses of Craven, Clarendon and Radnor. His grandmother on his father's side was Lady Jane Grimston, a daughter of the Earl of Verulam. His mother's father was the Earl of Norbury, and her mother the daughter of the Earl of Lindsay. Alexander himself married the daughter of the Earl of Lucan. In other men such a lineage might have induced a lifetime of complacency, and encouraged an exaggerated regard for the titular great. To Alexander it simply meant an agreeable set of relations, and Caledon.

Ulster was very important to him. Protestant Ulstermen are patriotically British, but at the same time intensely Irish, and their dual nationality (a term which they would instantly dispute) involves them in no conflict of loyalties, particularly when Ulster is torn apart. Irish Protestants and Roman Catholics have shown themselves quite capable of sinking their differences. From the moment of their formation in 1900 the Irish Guards were never troubled by political or religious controversy within their ranks, which were filled by young volunteers, most of them Catholic, at the very moment when other British troops were standing ready to uphold Protestant supremacy in Ulster. Never at Caledon, in the 4th Earl's day a strongly Orange household, were there any difficulties between Protestant and Catholic members of the staff, who often intermarried. At no stage of his life was Alexander himself directly involved in Ulster's politics, but he was not in the least indifferent to them. He regarded Northern Ireland as his native land in a manner quite distinct, say, from a Yorkshireman's feeling for Yorkshire. Like Scotland or Wales, Ulster lay half-way between a country and a province. He looked upon Tyrone as the place where his roots were most firmly planted; and when the time came for him to choose a regiment, he unhesitatingly chose the Irish Guards.

It is impossible to explain satisfactorily the bouquet of high military talent which the northern part of Ireland has given Britain over the centuries. The record is extraordinary. To consider only the Second World War and the period immediately before and after it, the following Field Marshals were either born in Ireland or had strong Irish connections: Alexander, Alanbrooke, Montgomery, Dill, Auchinleck, Gort, Montgomery-Massingberd and Templer. To say that the mingling of Irish blood with Scotch or English breeds a martial temperament explains nothing, for these distinguished contemporaries had otherwise little in common than the simple fact that they were all soldiers, and Alexander's character was identical with that of a pure-blooded English gentleman. To say that Ulstermen are always spoiling for a fight is not only defamatory, but a characteristic more likely to produce crazy Majors than Field Marshals. Some will argue for family tradition, but it is no stronger in Ulster than in many English families who have never boasted more than Colonels. If Alexander had become Prime Minister, it would be as convincing to claim that he had inherited his political talent from the Nabob and the Governor, as to suggest that he became a Field Marshal because his grandfather was for a short time a Captain and his father a Major. We must look for explanations of his career elsewhere than in his ancestry or Ulster's traditional fire.

He was born at 1 Chesterfield Gardens, Mayfair, on 10 December 1891. This was a London house which the Caledons owned temporarily in addition to 5 Carlton House Terrace, and it meant so little to Alexander that in his later years he could only say, 'I have every reason to believe that I was born in London.' What mattered to him was that he was taken to Caledon when he was only a few weeks old. There he was christened Harold Rupert Leofric George, the 'Leofric' in recognition of the Scandinavian period through which his mother was passing when all her sons were born. The others were saddled with 'Erik', 'Herbrand' and 'Sigismund'. Alexander was never known by any of his given names, except to servants and nephews, to whom he became respectively Master and Uncle Harold. By his mother and brothers he was always called 'Tubby', a singularly inappropriate baby-name which he never managed to shake off but was able to conceal from his friends, who from his youth onwards called him Alex, as did his wife.

His father, the 4th Earl of Caledon, died in April 1898, when Alexander was six. He could remember him only as 'a kind and misty figure', but it is possible to fill in the outline because his life is reasonably well recorded, and he created around his name much affection which has still not completely faded. He was abnormally shy. Once his mother (who had been a Lady-in-Waiting) arranged for him to dine with Queen Victoria when he was on guard with his regiment at Windsor, but the prospect so appalled him that he did not turn up. The Queen dismissed the incident with a sympathetic murmur, 'Poor young man'. Less easy to explain away was his failure to attend his own twenty-first-birthday celebrations at Caledon, where a vast marquee had been erected on the lawn, banners of congratulation strung across the drive, and a battalion of tenants assembled to greet him, the more senior in top-hats. He joined the Life Guards, and later became a Major in the Royal Inniskilling Fusiliers, taking part in the battles of Kassasin and Tel-el-Kebir during the Egyptian campaign of 1882. On his return he married Lord Norbury's daughter, Lady Elizabeth Graham-Toler, and became a representative Irish peer and Deputy Lord-Lieutenant for County Tyrone. His greatest pleasures were yachting, hunting, and boxing. He owned several yachts, all named *Viking*, in which he sailed courageously as his own Master as far as the Albanian coast, Morocco, Murmansk and at least once to Canada. During one of these cruises, the Lutine Bell was rung at Lloyds when he was long overdue. His adventurousness at sea won him the unexpected friendship of the Kaiser, but normally Lord Caledon played little part in society, preferring his seamen or his tenants. When he died, one of the latter spoke of him as 'courteous, high-minded and easy of approach, a gentleman of great integrity who was much loved'.

In the year before their father's death, Alexander and Erik were taken by their parents on a European tour. Of this he remembered the hotel where they stayed in Paris, his first sight of the Alps, the doctor's house in Mentone where he was taken to recover from chicken-pox, and a small town in the Alto Adige called Merano, which fifty years later he revisited on his way to the Potsdam Conference to find it quite unchanged. There he had walked with his father a little way beyond the town, and when he grew tired Lord Caledon took him by the hand to lead him back. This tiny vignette of experience was the most vivid recollection which he retained of his father. Six months later Lord Caledon died in a London nursing-home at the age of forty-five, from an infection contracted abroad.

Alexander was too young to attend the funeral, and too young to miss greatly someone whom he had never really known. His father's place was taken by his mother and three brothers. Lady Caledon lived for over forty years a widow, dying in October 1939. This is how her grandson, the present Lord Caledon, remembers her:

She was an imperial old lady, rather than imperious. She had very great personality. She would never let her emotions get the better of her – in fact it was very hard to know where her emotions lay. She was never defeated in argument; she was never really defeated by anything. She wasn't naturally gentle, and yet she was capable of acts of very great kindness and generosity. There was a hint of sentimentality underneath, but she kept it well hidden. Children were to be seen and not heard, and to be seen at certain hours of the day, and then only when they were wanted.

Once when I was a boy I made a primitive wireless-set, and tuned it in to the local transmitter. After a hideous squeak one of Strauss's waltzes emerged. Before more than a couple of bars had been heard, she interrupted me: "My dear child, you are playing that much too fast." I was about to expostulate when she raised her hand and said, "Don't argue, child. Many is the time that I've danced to that tune in Vienna. It's much too fast." Of course I didn't argue, but dismantled the set and carried it back upstairs. To the best of my knowledge she never heard a wireless-set again. She wouldn't give in to anything, not even her own illness.

What was her illness?

It was a form of dropsy which swelled her feet, and it was not helped by her consumption of vast quantities of port. She never appeared drunk, nor the slightest bit tipsy. She simply drank port as other people might drink water.

She used to drink alone? She had very few friends?

She had very few friends as far as I remember. Sometimes an aunt or an uncle would stay at Caledon for a month. She passed her time running the estate (she was very interested in forestry, and knew a great deal about it, and kept the household accounts most meticulously), and reading trashy novels. She was vain to her dying day, poor thing, and wouldn't wear spectacles, so she read through a reading-glass.

Of her four sons, who was closest to her?

I would say Erik; she had a special regard for her eldest son, which she didn't have for the others. Next in order was probably her youngest, William. She was rather irritated by my father, Herbrand. She fairly well ignored the Field Marshal.

But surely she must have been pleased by his career?

It's hard to say. I never heard her mention it. She would never hold him up as anything exceptional. She was pleased when he got command of the 1st Division at Aldershot. "That's very good", she said: but that's about as far as it went. I remember my uncle saying that during the First World War she behaved quite unnaturally to her children. When they came home on leave from the trenches, she more or less ignored them. When Uncle William was on convalescence leave after being quite badly wounded, she reckoned that he had quite recovered, and should go back to the front and fight.

She was very conservative?

To a degree that is quite inconceivable today.

She was formidable and grand, but could be considerate. Once when the old butler at Caledon had too much to drink, he went to her and said, 'I'm very sorry, m'lady, but I'm drunk.' She knew that he had had a hard day, and ordered him some strong black coffee and sent him to bed. It was this sort of gesture which won her servants' devotion, and they rarely left her. She was tolerant of genuine mistakes, but would not endure sloppiness. The children were strictly disciplined in dress, cleanliness and good manners. On Sundays they were taken to church in stiff Eton collars and their best blue suits. Sometimes she would indirectly let slip her feeling for them, obliging them, for instance, to wear their hair long in order to postpone the day when they grew up and away from her. There is a photograph at Caledon of the young Alexander with hair hanging like a girl's to the level of his chin, and another of him in a lace eighteenth-century court-dress, both wholly out of character with the tough little boy he had become. She would not let him cut his hair until the day before he went to his first school. That was her sentimental side. But hers was not a shoulder to cry on; she would have called it whining. She was not indifferent to her children, but she held herself aloof, like Lady Randolph Churchill from the young Winston. 'My feeling for her', wrote Alexander in later years, 'was more respect and veneration than close intimate affection.' The only time she visited him during his schooldays was in his last term at Harrow, when she watched the Eton and Harrow match in which he played at Lord's. When she died intestate, the family was not greatly surprised. It was typical of her apparent lack of concern.

In the year of their father's death, Erik was thirteen, Herbrand ten, 'Tubby' six, and William (the boy who was also christened 'Sigismund', but known as 'Baby' in the family even when he was a Lieutenant-Colonel, retired) three. Despite their difference in ages, they formed a happy gang. Caledon was a wonderful place in which to grow up. The house stands on a flattened knoll above the River Blackwater only a mile from the present border with Eire, and you approach it through the park uphill to one corner, like the Parthenon. It is a classical eighteenth-century house, built by the Nabob and much enlarged by the Governor, who employed John Nash to create the most complete example that has survived in Britain of a large Regency country-house. Inside there are four great rooms on the ground-floor, including a famous library and an oval sitting-room, ornamented by Regency fire-places and friezes, and furnished with the spoils of the Governor's European tour soon after 1815. In the early part of this century the rooms were obscured but not destroyed by potted plants, cuddling Victorian cupids, and heavy tapestry and family photographs on inlaid table-tops. Upstairs there is a wide corridor between the main bedrooms, and above them the nursery storey where the boys slept and ate under the eye of their

Nanny, Mrs Harriet Harding. At basement-level there are cavernous kitchens, and innumerable semi-cellars for the servicing of the house and the storage of its fuel and junk. To the young Alexanders, the house was a sandwich, the nursery and basement where they were always welcome containing the two ceremonial floors where they wandered at their peril.

The park became their hunting-ground, a territory which still invites adventure. The river divides it, winding serpentine between rounded hills, some of which are grazed by deer and cattle and others covered by magnificent beech and oak, which fall away to leave flat meadows each side of the stream. It is a marriage of park and farm, of contrived scenery and pastoral utility. Here Alexander spent 'glorious, happy days'. He had his pony, his bicycle, his gun, his rod. The boys built themselves a hut in the wood, and if they spent a night there, not a reproachful word was said. Their mother did not care what they did out of her sight. If they lost their way on the moors and did not return until hours after sunset, no alarm was raised. There were never tearful partings when she left Caledon for her English houses, for it meant the removal of the last small disciplines which limited their perfect freedom. They rose before dawn to watch for duck and pigeons. In winter, when the river became a torrent, they would work their way upstream in birch-bark canoes, or skate on flooded meadows. Sometimes they were allowed to drive the engine of the Clogher Valley light railway which ran through Caledon village, putting horses, dogs, chickens and children to flight. It was a Tom Sawyer boyhood on an aristocratic scale. It taught Alexander initiative and basic skills, and gave him a love of country things that lasted all his life.

Caledon was an estate run in the nineteenth-century tradition, self-supported by its home-farm, laundry and dairy, its estate carpenters, stone-masons and painters, its gamekeepers dressed in dark-green jackets, porters in cockaded hats, farm-labourers, foresters, gardeners, and an indoor staff of thirteen. These men and their wives became Alexander's friends. When he was missing he would be searched for in the workshop of Robert Scott, the carpenter, or in Graham's, the painter; in the lovely eighteenth-century stables, or in Mrs Graham's cottage. There was a distinctly military air about the place. Many of the men, like the head-forester, Corporal-Major Robertson, had served with Lord Caledon in his squadrons, and older men were reminders of earlier wars, like Jem Wilson, the odd-job man, who had lost two fingers

in the Indian Mutiny, or Jack Rogers, the stockman, who could remember the troops returning from Waterloo, and claimed that his
father had told him from first-hand experience about the excitements of
the '45. From his small army of veterans Lord Caledon had formed a
drum, fife and bugle band, who sometimes played in the house after
dinner dressed in uniforms like those of the Zouaves, and six small
cannon from his yacht were fired on festive occasions. The boys soon
found themselves involved in this paramilitary activity. It was their
duty to raise and lower the house-flag each morning and evening, and
Alexander learnt to play the side-drums in the band. They would
charge each other on ponies with lance and shield, and evolved an
elaborate war-game, the Vaxa Nation against the Comba Nation, by
drawing battle-scenes in the form of strip-cartoons, with much fire and
movement, and ending in the triumph of the Vaxa Nation, who
invariably won (so his brother William remembers) because Alexander
was their commander and he was the better draughtsman.

Other talents were developing too. They made up their own plays,
and acted them. Alexander became adept at the Irish jig. He began to
carve, both in wood and stone, making Celtic crosses and tomb-stones
for favourite dogs and deer. But the hobby which gave him greatest
pleasure, then as throughout his life, was painting. It originated in the
hours he spent in the estate paint-shop, where Graham allowed him to
cover the walls with boyish frescoes, but soon he became more experi-
mental, painting portraits of his family or of Napoleon and other
historical figures on wood or canvas in a Van Dyck manner, joke-
pictures of snarling faces which he mounted on clothes-hangers and
rigged up in the windows to frighten the rare visitor, and finally landscape, for which he early developed a remarkable eye. Years later,
recalling his childhood at Caledon for the amusement of his own
children, he wrote:

One of the most beautiful effects of light which I ever remember was when
I crept out of the house very early one morning. There was a full moon
struggling against the light of dawn. It was neither a moonlit night nor a
sunlit day, just the two great sources of light struggling against each other.
I think it is these impressions which I gained in youth which drew me towards
painting, and especially towards landscape painting as interpreted by the
French impressionists.

When he first read Reynolds's *Discourses on Art* at an age when he could barely understand it, 'it gave me my first ambition, to become President of the Royal Academy'.

He spent the greater part of his childhood at Caledon, where these many activities jostled abreast of each other, and he drew closer to William as his older brothers went away to school. The two boys needed no other company than each other's. Only rarely did they visit the Leslie boys at Glaslough, two miles away across the border, or the Westenras at Rossmore. His acquaintance with Alan Brooke of Colebrooke was of the slightest, and with Montgomery non-existent, for the Montgomerys then lived in London and Tasmania. There were expeditions to other parts of Ireland, and occasionally to England. Their favourite was a fortnight's annual holiday at Derg Lodge, sixty miles from Caledon in the northern part of County Tyrone. It was a simple house of pink limestone which his father had built in the middle of some of the emptiest moors in Britain. It overlooks a little lake half a mile from the border, and is surrounded by sliding hills and bogs through which the children sloshed barefoot, until Alexander invented the perfect boot with a hole at one end to let the water in and a hole at the other to let it out. They returned to the lodge soaked to the skin after a day's shooting or fishing, and were immediately plunged into hot brown baths and set to dry before peat fires. Alexander loved Derg. He remembered always the wind in his gun-barrels, the plunk of falling snipe, the flapping of trout so small that three was the breakfast-ration, the simple pinewood rooms of the lodge and the all-pervading smell of peat. The Scottish border-country must have been like this in the Middle Ages, a wild and rather hostile land, a land of legend and superstition, where no fish would swim in certain pools because St Patrick had put a curse upon them, where a river could have a sea-dragon as its familiar, and strange stories were told to the boys by the keepers' wives.

In the early part of August Mrs Harding usually took them to the seaside, either to Newcastle in County Down, or flipping them over to the Atlantic coast, to Bundoran in Donegal. It was at Bundoran, when he was eight years old, that Alexander first came under fire. He wandered, unescorted as usual, along sand-dunes which were unsuspected back-stops to the local rifle-range, and for fifteen minutes crouched under a sudden cataract of bullets, emerging unscathed to tell his Nanny that he had found the experience 'interesting'. Occasionally the intrepid gang would also go to England, where Lady Caledon had two houses which she occupied for a few months in each year. These were Tyttenhanger near St Albans, one of the most graceful houses to survive from the mid-seventeenth century; and, in central London, 5 Carlton House Terrace, another Nash house, more spacious than convenient, more suited to debutante daughters than rusticated sons, and for that reason often let to strangers in the Season. Alexander's most delightful childhood memory is connected with it. Every day Mrs Harding would take him for a walk across St James's Park to listen to the band and watch the Foot Guards drilling in Wellington Barracks. He was fascinated by the guardsmen on sentry duty at Buckingham and St James's Palaces, and to his childish mind it was always the same man under the heavy bearskin, living permanently in the sentry-box. What puzzled him was the sentry's change of attitude. One day the guardsman would smile back when he said 'Good morning'. On the next he would pay no attention at all. 'Funny,' thought little Alex, 'he must be feeling grumpy today.'

When he left home for his first school Alexander was remarkable for the diversity of his interests and talents more than for precocious brilliance in any one of them. He was self-reliant, courageous, inquisitive and never bored. He had inherited a special characteristic of his family, their circumspection. Hand an Alexander an object like a small painting or a piece of machinery, and he or she will instinctively turn it round to look at its back and sides, to see how it is made and of what it is made, before examining the front. It is a craftsman's way of looking at things. If he had not become a soldier, he would have been an artist or an engineer. His boyhood could have branched in a variety of directions. The military influence in it was incidental, and only by hindsight can it be made to seem decisive. He was born and bred with many advantages which created many opportunities, and the lack of a father, sister or sympathetic mother turned out paradoxically to be one of them. He was thrown back on the company of two older brothers who loved him and fought with him, and of one younger whom he protected. The four of them, as Tennyson said of his boyhood with Hallam, 'rubbed each other's angles down'.

In the spring of 1902, when Alexander was ten, he was sent by his mother to a preparatory school in England, St Michael's, Westgate-on-Sea, near Margate in Kent. It was a colony of red-brick Victorian buildings connected by corrugated-iron tunnels, cold and a bit dismal, but not a penitentiary, for the Headmaster, Hawtrey, was a kind, fat, lame, red-faced man, nicknamed Bumble, who was deservedly popular, and his school was a happy one. All the Alexander boys went there one by one, Tubby's first term overlapping Herbrand's last. Erik, now 5th Earl of Caledon, had already left for Eton.

At first he was inevitably home-sick, and his letters are touchingly illustrated by imagined scenes at Caledon, of the deer and the carriages, and of 'Baby' still enjoying their familiar pursuits, but now alone. For the first time in his life he was subject to hourly discipline, and could not understand why the masters should consider that a minute or two either side of the ringing of the school-bell should matter so desperately. He stared out of the window from his desk, envying the passers-by who were free to go to London, even to Caledon, while he was a prisoner. Then things changed. He became a success. He made friends easily, and was good at games. Cricket was his favourite, and he was in the school teams for football and hockey as well. He sang in the choir (no great compliment to his voice), and his conduct was so impeccable that he was never once birched, an omission of which he later felt rather ashamed, like an infantry soldier who could not claim to have been under fire. For the first time he began to acknowledge heroines as well as heroes. Among them was Mrs Hawtrey, the Headmaster's wife, 'a very loveable lady'; the matron, Miss West, 'Pussy West', a handsome elderly woman with bright yellow hair, to whom he gave a silver-backed hair-brush which he could ill afford, only to discover that the hair which he had so much admired was a wig; Lady Westmorland, the mother of his friend Lord Burghersh, the most beautiful woman he had ever seen, whose portrait he painted from a photograph she gave him; and, above all, a Miss Hallowes (her first name has not been recorded) who could occasionally be seen, head gracefully bowed, in the crocodile of a neighbouring girls' school as it passed the Hawtrey crocodile going in the opposite direction. The Captain of the XI, Popham, smuggled notes to this enchanting girl, making much play with chivalrous phrases like 'None but the brave deserve the fair'. The notes were intercepted by Miss Hallowes's Headmistress, who passed them with appropriate distaste to Popham's Headmaster. 'Don't be silly', replied Hawtrey. 'The boy's only crime is that his approach was clandestine, and that is half the fun.'

It has been said that Alexander could neither read nor write until he went to school. This is only partly true. The earliest surviving letter in his handwriting was written in July 1901 from Bundoran, and there are dog-eared fairy-stories at Caledon which must precede the Conan Doyle, Merriman, Ainsworth and Wilkie Collins favourites of his school holidays. But Mrs Harding was no governess, and he received no tuition except from her, so that he was certainly backward on reaching school, though not quite illiterate. His early letters from Hawtrey's rely for their spelling more on the sound of words than their derivation. The boys had a lecture with 'a maget lanton'; 'their is going to be a football match tomorar; it is very exsitten to watch. We genly win.' When in doubt he illustrated his letters, or fell back on stuffing them with football and cricket scores or the Maths paper. To one important letter, the Headmaster, concealing his probable disgust, helped him compile a suitable reply. His Uncle Charles had seen him through London on one of his early journeys from Ireland to Kent and at the station had pressed half a sovereign into his hand. 'I made a mistake', wrote Uncle Charles next day. 'I thought it was 6d. Kindly return my 9/6.'

From Hawtrey's he went to Harrow, in January 1906. It had been his father's school, and was now his mother's choice for her three younger sons. Only Erik went to Eton. Again Alexander overlapped Herbrand by a single term, and William entered the school the term after his brother left, in the autumn of 1910. All three were in the Headmaster's house, which Winston Churchill had left with relief fourteen years before, complaining that it was 'a hell of a place' for someone like him who had never risen above the Fourth Form. Alexander was happier and more successful. He had never been awkward or shy or aggressive, and he began his career at Harrow with the knowledge that he was not an underdog, that he could succeed at work and had a natural gift for games, and that both boys and masters instinctively liked him. Harrow became for Alexander a fond memory, and he often revisited the school, but the same scene with its small variations was exposed too often on the plate of his adult mind for his first impressions to remain sharp. It does not in any case present the static picture of collegiate schools like Eton or Winchester. It is coiled round its hill without a still centre. Traffic splits what should be precincts, and Victorian buildings struggle for footholds on the slopes. The school has a hive-like quality. The boys pour in and out of a hundred orifices, and by their criss-cross flights create a unity of mood and style out of spinal ribbon-development. The cricket-pitches at the foot of one slope, the football-fields at the other, provide areas of calm or at least of flatness, but Harrow should be seen as a community in constant motion, and this exactly suited Alexander's temperament.

The Headmaster's house was the biggest, a pleasing nineteenth-century building near the centre of the school, where every boy except the very youngest had a room of his own. Hard-wearing stairs, mops stuck in pails, iron banisters for swinging on, a cavalcade of boots, the sudden change on the far side of the Headmaster's door from scrubbed boards to pile carpets, from chipped enamel to porcelain, from row-diness to apprehension – none of this varies much from age to age, nor from school to school. In Alexander's day the Headmaster was Dr Wood, a sweet-faced old gentleman, a classical scholar with con-ventional ideas of leadership and obedience, better as a preacher than administrator, who took no particular interest in Alexander, since he had chosen to follow the Modern Side and, within it, the Army Class. His academic career at Harrow was ordinary. He worked steadily up the school, ending in his last term in the Modern VI. His best subjects were history and geograp hy, and he won a school prize for drawing. He never became head of his house, and never a school monitor. But he did become a member of the Philathletic Club, the élite of the natural leaders, who were self-electing, unlike the monitors who were appointed by the Headmaster from among academic stars. The difference between Harrow then and Harrow now is that most boys today would prefer to become monitors. In 1910 they would have chosen the 'Phil'. They can and could, of course, become both, but it was asking too much of Dr Wood to make that judgement in Alexander's favour.

Of the friends he made at Harrow the one who remained closest to him was Walter Monckton, a scholar, diplomatist, advocate and politician, in whom one could still see, when he was over sixty, the boy to whom Alexander was immediately attracted at school, although they found themselves in different houses. In his own house there was an Indian boy named Jawaharlal Nehru. A group photograph hanging in the dining-hall shows him and Alexander one behind the other, Nehru looking the lonelier and more reflective of the two, for – as he confessed in his autobiography – he did not quite fit in, and thought Harrow a 'small and restricted place' where the English boys talked only cricket. He left young, and it was only in their later lives that he and Alexander came to know each other. Two of Alexander's closer friends were Ogilvie Graham and Guy Earle, who moved up the school to take over from their own heroes podiums of popularity and success. Alexander's career was launched by a slower-burning rocket. But nobody could have called him cautious. Once, with another boy called Stone, he played truant for a night in London. They were dining gaily at the Café Royal when across the restaurant they suddenly saw their tutor, Archer Vassall. It could have meant expulsion. Vassall waited until he had finished his own meal, and then sent a note to their table: 'I haven't seen you, but be back by midnight.'

It was at games and in the Rifle Corps that Alexander excelled. His sports were cricket, athletics, racquets, rugger, boxing, fencing and gymnastics. In 1910 he won the school cross-country race by over two hundred yards, and came second in the mile and half-mile. He was in the school rugger XV. He just failed to qualify for the racquets pair. He first played cricket for the XI in 1908 when he was sixteen and was awarded his Flannels in 1910. In that year, during his last few weeks at Harrow, he played a prominent part in Fowler's Match.

In the minds even of non-cricketers the very mention of Fowler's Match may arouse a faint movement, as of something rare and strange. To those who took part in it, the memory turns old men into boys. It was the match played between Eton and Harrow at Lord's on 8 and 9 July 1910, when Bob Fowler, the Eton captain, achieved almost single-handed a reversal of fortune unequalled in cricketing history.

Harrow expected to win this game. They had been undefeated the whole season. They won the toss, and in their first innings made 232, and then dismissed Eton for 67, Alexander taking with his leg-breaks three wickets in four overs. Eton followed-on to score 219, and Alexander took another two of their wickets. The situation was then nothing out of the ordinary. It was even rather dull. Harrow needed 55 runs to win, and had two hours in which to make them, a trifling task for a team of that quality with all their second-innings' wickets standing intact. The match was considered to be so much of a walk-over for Harrow that Etonians and even Harrovians began to leave the ground, and only heard what happened later when the newspapers were spread in triumph or dismay over the breakfast-table next morning.

Fowler had already saved the faces of the Eton side by making their highest score in each innings, 21 and 64. He now set about saving their bacon. He took an Harrovian wicket with his first ball, and two more in his second over. Three wickets had fallen for only 8 runs. Guy Earle, the Harrow captain, went in next, to make 13 before he was caught at slip. 4 for 21. It was now Walter Monckton's turn. At this turning-point of the match he faced Fowler confidently. 'Walter took guard', wrote Lord Birkenhead, his biographer, 'and played the first ball safely. Then Fowler, by an inspiration of genius, tried him with a slow full toss, and to the dismay of all his friends and of every Harrow supporter, Walter was clean bowled, and had to make a silent and terrible return to the pavilion.' Wickets then fell with panic-stricken rapidity. 9 for 32. Harrow still needed 23 runs to win a match which only an hour before had seemed theirs without question, and they had only one wicket left. That wicket was Alexander's. As last man in, he walked out to join his friend Ogilvie Graham in a desperate attempt to save the match. If he had succeeded, it would have been known in history as Alexander's match instead of Fowler's. 'Thirteen priceless runs were sneaked or stolen by the indomitable last pair', wrote C. P. Foley, an Etonian onlooker, in language legitimately smacking of Edwardian school-fiction. But it was not enough. When he had made 8, Alexander edged a ball into the slips, and all was over. Harrow was beaten by nine runs, and in this second innings Fowler alone had taken eight of their wickets. He died young in 1925, immortalized by the match which *Wisden* called 'without exaggeration, the most extraordinary ever played'.

In his last year at Harrow Alexander rose to the highest rank open to a boy in the Rifle Corps, becoming one of five cadet officers in a Corps which numbered about three hundred. Not much is recoverable of this earliest phase of his military career, for the Corps itself has no detailed records, his mother kept few of his letters, and the school magazine *The Harrovian* rated reports on Corps activities even lower than those on the beagles. One at least of their field days was enlivened by a joint exercise with the Irish Guards in an attack on a derailed munition train, and it is recorded that Alexander with four other cadets from Harrow attended the funeral of Edward VII. But the most remarkable evidence of his early interest in the Army is the painting by which he won the Yates Thompson Art Prize after he had been at Harrow only a year. It is described officially as a still life, but the picture, which is still in the possession of Lady Alexander, is a water-colour of a General's feathered helmet and sword, lying beside a Union Jack. More should perhaps be read into the painting than its subject. It is mature for a boy of fifteen, and his childhood ambition had still not faded when he was about to leave Harrow for Sandhurst. He did not intend to be a soldier, except temporarily. He wanted to paint, professionally. This was a serious ambition, not a passing caprice. He would enter the Army on a short-term basis, for it too fascinated him, and after a year or two he would probably retire to make his living as an artist. This carefully thought-out plan was upset by the First World War, which committed him deeply to the Army, and from then onwards there was no doubt which would be his pastime and which his career.

Meanwhile, Harrow was to be followed by Sandhurst. His mother wanted it; he wanted it. When he left school at the end of the summer term of 1910, he had already sat the London University Leaving Certificate for the Army and was accepted for the Royal Military College without further examination. He put his name down for the Irish Guards as his ultimate destination.

The course for Sandhurst cadets lasted less than a year. Discipline was far stricter than at Harrow, combining, as Churchill had found, 'the evils of the life of a private schoolboy with those of a private soldier'. Unpunctuality and untidiness were not tolerated. Reveille was at 6.30 and the first parade at 7. No cars were allowed, and not much leave. There was the same odd mixture of austerity and elegance, as there had been, in different circumstances, at Caledon, and to some extent still is at Sandhurst today. Splendid uniforms and regimental plate were accompanied by barrack-room food; belts and caps scintillated on rough army blankets; the cadets were called gentlemen, but were treated like delinquents. Sir John Smyth, who was a contemporary of Alexander at Sandhurst and wrote the history of the College, recalls a drill-parade under the terrifying Staff Sergeant Ham: 'Ham had a stroke just after he had called us to attention. He was not able to order us to stand at ease, and we all stood without moving until one or two cadets started to faint. The senior NCO then took charge and marched us back to barracks.' These 'barracks' lay within one of the most elegant Palladian buildings in the country, so closely resembling a magnificent country house that once a London taxi-driver, anxious to please his young passenger, turned to him as they drew up at the great portico and remarked, 'Nice little place you have down here, sir.' Inside, the illusion is at first maintained by arches forming graceful perspectives down the corridors, but off them open bleak rooms which, in Alexander's day, were curtainless and unheated. While he was there, the new buildings, which today form the centre of the RMC, were rising a quarter-mile away across the park, but they were still unfinished when he left. He learnt his soldiering on the old parade-ground and in the sand-and-pine country of military England. He learnt to make patterns of men upon the ground, neatly in ceremonial formation, or tactically disarrayed. He learnt that drill, like rowing, is a matter of rhythm and muscular control, and is only pleasurable when done well. He learnt the subtle social and disciplinary distinctions between on and off duty. He learnt that *Mens Sana in Corpore Sano* is not so foolish a formula after all.

Alexander's career at Sandhurst was one of no more exceptional promise than he had shown at his private and public schools. On passing out, he was placed 85th out of 172. Three years earlier, Bernard Montgomery had been 36th, a Corporal who had been reduced to the ranks for setting fire to the shirt-tails of an unpopular cadet. Alexander, in typical contrast, became Colour Sergeant of his company – the highest rank that a cadet could attain. Some of his marks were excellent, particularly in practical subjects: 388 out of a possible 400 for riding, 270 out of 300 for musketry, 193 out of 200 for drill, 199 out of 200 for signalling. The academic subjects let him down: Administration, 258/400; Law, 212/400; History, 315/600; French, 247/400. Yet Sandhurst to him, as to Churchill, was not a matter of marks. His place in the Irish Guards was already assured, and he could enjoy himself as far as regulations and time-tables allowed. He and his friend Earle formed the College racquets pair. In athletics he was first string for the mile and two miles. Of course he played cricket, partnering his old adversary Bob Fowler in a last-wicket stand of 78 against Woolwich, whom Sandhurst defeated in the most important match of the year. Fowler, in Alexander's year, won the Sword of Honour.

Sandhurst was a ten-month link between Alexander's boyhood and manhood. When he left in July 1911, he was nineteen. He had become what a housemaster would describe as 'well-balanced', which means that he cared for his work and pleasures in equal proportion. He was no intellectual, but he read for fun; a cricketer who rode, a soldier who painted. Caledon, school and now Sandhurst had sieved his mind. The debutant Alexander was in some ways an idealized product of the English public school, a youth who can turn with equal ease in either direction – to fame or insignificance.

2

THE FIRST WORLD WAR

Alexander and his closest friend Eric Greer joined the 1st Battalion of
the Irish Guards as Second-Lieutenants on the same day, 23 September
1911. At first they were stationed at Chelsea Barracks, then in the
Tower of London, where they remained for the next year. From 1913
until the outbreak of war the battalion's main base was Chelsea or
Wellington Barracks. They went on musketry courses or short manoeuvres to the area of Aldershot, where the metropolitan Army was
tidily and unobtrusively trained when they were not acting in the
capital as decorative reminders of the past.

These were happy days for young regular officers of the Brigade of
Guards. Alexander received his commission at a moment which might
have been chosen for him by providence. Not for him, as for born soldiers
like Douglas Haig, fifteen years of peacetime soldiering before he first
led men into action: nor a sudden translation from University or office
to the trenches, which was the lot of the great majority of young
officers in the First War. He had time enough in which to enjoy his
youthful manhood and acquire the art of junior command, before war
tested both.

In August 1914 Alexander was twenty-two, and he had advanced one
rank, automatically, to Lieutenant. The three previous years had not
been years of conscious preparation for the inevitable. The officers of the
Irish Guards, if politics meant anything to them at all, were more
concerned with the situation in Northern Ireland than in central
Europe. So stirred was Alexander by the possibility that British troops
might be ordered to crush rebellion in his native Ulster that at the time
of the Curragh incident in March 1914 he and Eric Greer informed their

Commanding Officer that they would resign their commissions rather than take part in such an atrocity. They were told sharply not to be such fools. With their tails between their legs they left the Orderly Room, but not the regiment.

Their duties were minimal. To those who have never been privy to the curious mystique of the Brigade of Guards, it may seem shocking that army officers in peacetime had so little work to do. Four months annual leave for Captains, five for Majors, six or more for Colonels, would be a reproach to any other profession. Even when on duty, the daily routine was derisory. Company Orders, which officers could attend in civilian clothes, were at 10, followed by Commanding Officer's Orders, and then a glass of Black Strap, a heavy vintage port, in the Officers' Mess at noon. They were then free for the rest of the day, for polo, cricket or lounging in the Guards Club or the boat-club at Maidenhead. Only the Adjutant and two or three newly-joined officers slept in barracks. The others led bachelor lives in the West End of London. The summer brought a little more activity, on the ranges at Pirbright or divisional exercises, and in London there were public duties at the palaces, where the guard-mounting was theatrical, the accommodation almost luxurious, and women could be entertained to lunch and men to dinner.

> The officers of the Brigade [wrote Peter Verney, historian of the Irish Guards] led essentially a gentleman's existence, and they deferred to a gentleman's code of conduct. Military activities were conducted with elegance, and a knowledge of parade-ground drill was of greater importance than proficiency in the field. Social graces were accepted as normal, and an officer in the Guards carried an open passport to the highest society.

Major Verney tells us that 'the Tower was a particularly popular station for the officers, for there was nothing whatsoever to do, and all the amenities of London were at their feet.'

The Army had no real function except in war. The notion of maintaining an army to prevent war was not then born: the soldier's purpose was to wage it, and the waging of war could not be taught except by war itself. Therefore the conscientious officer wanted war, just as an actor desires live performance not constant dress rehearsal, but he thought it unnecessary to do much to prepare himself for it. What the Brigade taught in peacetime was conduct. This meant two things. First, the importance of hierarchy and discipline. A guardsman will look at a man's shoulders before the face above them, to see what stripes or stars they carry. Obedience to the superior officer is laid down by regulation and accepted by habit. Drill is its most obvious manifestation. Moving together, halting together, shifting feet and rifles in exact synchronization and alignment, create the expectation of command and an instinctive response to it which hold together a body of men in the totally different situations of battle when everything else is confused. Careful attention to dress and routine strengthens their cohesion. It is no coincidence that uniform and uniformity are linked words. Drill and turn-out and punctuality give the Sergeants something to shout about on the parade ground and so establish their authority, but all three evoke a response which is less grudging than most guardsmen would admit. Perfection in something so simple as a polished boot or belt, or the kaleidoscopic change of a battalion on parade from one formation to another, induces satisfaction and ultimately pride. For centuries discipline of this kind has been an incentive for the regular soldiers of all armies. In the Brigade of Guards it became a point of honour.

Conduct also meant a standard of behaviour. Among officers the most important assumption was that one should not let another down. So basic was this rule that in the Brigade a special word was applied to any breach of it, to 'cart'. You could cart a brother-officer by leaving him all evening with a plain girl while you danced off with the belle of the ball (you could also cart the plain girl by abandoning her), and you could cart him by borrowing his polo-pony and laming it, or in battle by failing to relieve him on time. Betrayal at any level led to ostracism in the mess. You must not fail to repay a debt, nor cheat at cards, nor reveal a confidence, nor speak maliciously of women. There were certain rules of etiquette too. An officer must not be seen to carry a suitcase or even a parcel. He must not reverse in waltzing. He could smoke Turkish, but not Virginian, cigarettes. Some of these conventions survived until the opening year of the Second War, and may seem absurd, but there was also a tolerance in the Brigade which even sophisticated officers like Osbert Sitwell and Harold Macmillan came to admit as an influence on their whole lives. Privacy was respected, and variety of character welcomed. If you did not choose or could not afford to hunt or play polo, and preferred to paint or read, it was not held against you. While intellectual accomplishment was rare, it was not despised. Shyness was considered a drawback, not a deformity, and heartiness thought vulgar unless wit or adventurousness were allied to it. The importance of leadership was little emphasized, since there were so few opportunities to display it, the men living for most of the time apart from their officers. The serious study of war was almost unknown. All the qualities required of an officer in battle were assumed to be latent, fostered in peacetime by lively society and energetic sport, tempered by chivalry, comradeship, generosity and a certain decorum. It is best summed up by their definition of a gentleman as a man in whose presence a woman feels herself to be a lady.

The whole Brigade of Guards was of this character, and they knew themselves to be collectively an élite. The Irish Guards had in addition a special family feeling. It was a young regiment, formed in 1900 at the express wish of Queen Victoria in recognition of the valour of her Irish troops in the South African war, and it never saw action before the First World War. The character of the Irish made up for this lack of experience. Ninety-eight per cent of the men came from Ireland itself, or from the Irish communities of Glasgow or Liverpool, and over three-quarters were Roman Catholics. They were a band of brothers in an alien world. They were natural soldiers, loyal, exuberant, aggressive, hard to drive but easy to lead. Rudyard Kipling, who wrote the First War history of the regiment, said of them: 'They had all their race's delight in the drama of things; and whatever the pinch ... could be depended upon to advance the regimental honour. They needed minute comprehension, quick sympathy and inflexible justice, which they repaid by individual devotion and a collective goodwill that showed best when things were at their utter worst.' Alexander himself said in the last years of his life: 'They were my bosom friends. In the Micks there is a great feeling of matiness between officers and men. The Irish love their leaders, as I had found as a boy, and they have natural good manners.'

This was the setting in which Alexander found so natural a place. He was an aristocrat in disposition and appearance, an Irishman by upbringing. The slight chubbiness of his boyhood had disappeared, and he was extremely handsome in the conventional military way, 5 feet 10 inches tall, well-proportioned, athletic, buoyant and always perfectly dressed in and out of uniform. He did not work very hard. He did not need to. He carried out cheerfully the few duties demanded of him, and for the rest of the time enjoyed himself. His letters to his mother during the pre-war years reveal something of his character and manner of life.

26

5 October 1911. We have just moved to the Tower today. I like it awfully. I think it is a dear old place. I went to *Macbeth* the other night with Erik again, and enjoyed it just as much, if not better, than when we went.

14 April 1912. Can I send the little monkey over to Caledon? It is an awful nuisance here, it eats my collar studs, breaks and upsets everything. If it was at Caledon it would be absolutely happy and safe. It was very nice being down at Pirbright for a few weeks. We did our shooting on the ranges from 10 to 12, then we had the next day free. I have learnt to play golf with some skill. I have also started polo, which is the best game of the lot.

8 May 1912. In the afternoon I go up to London [from Pirbright] and play cricket one afternoon and polo the next. That brings it to about 6 in the evening. Then I go and have a good big bath in the Guards Club, and go out to dinner and then on to a dance. I feel awfully fit and well and am very keen on dancing. I gave the little monkey away to one of the servants who seemed very fond of it. I bought a dear little Irish terrier pup from a man in Leicester Square for only 5/-.

16 January 1913. There's a splendid place called the Cabaret in Regent Street where we go and dance and make an awful noise. They dance ragtime. Of course it's not very high class but quite respectable as they throw you out if you make too much noise. I am sending you a small drawing of it. [Drawing of Alexander by himself, sitting alone at a table smoking a cigar and watching a Spanish male-dancer.]

There were long leaves at Caledon, and skiing holidays in Switzerland. He stayed weekends in the country-houses of his family's and regimental friends. He went frequently to dances and the theatre, always in white tie and tails, and drove a car at Brooklands. By the standards of other young officers he was not extravagant, because he could not afford it. His pay was only £100 a year, supplemented by an allowance from his mother of another £400, out of which he was expected to buy his expensive uniforms.

His sports were hunting, polo, cricket, golf, boxing and athletics, and it was in athletics that he first gained for himself a reputation outside the ordinary. At Whitsun 1914 he won, almost casually, the Irish Mile. He had trained regularly with Greer at the Stamford Bridge Athletic Grounds under a famous old trainer called Henry Andrews, but it seems to have been on the spur of the moment that he decided to enter for the amateur championship of Ireland. The meeting was held in the grounds of the Royal Dublin Society at Ballsbridge. The programme had already been printed when the secretary received a telegram from Aldershot, 'Enter Harold Alexander for mile championship. Birth qualification, born County Tyrone', a statement which his birth-certificate does not support. Alexander caught the night-mail from London and reached Dublin on the morning of Whit Monday. There were seven runners in the race, of whom he was the only one totally unknown. He went to the front after a lap and a half. The holder, F. J. Ryder, retired 220 yards from the finish, and Alexander, according to the report in the *Irish Times*, 'experienced no difficulty in resisting the attention of J. Gamble of Ballymoney', and won the event easily. He then packed his bag, returned to Aldershot that same night, and appeared on parade on Tuesday morning as if nothing unusual had happened in the interval. He was regarded as a likely candidate for the Olympic Games, which were to have taken place in 1916.

Of his military activities there is less to record. He commanded 1 Platoon and was Battalion Signals Officer, which entitled him, alone among the subalterns, to ride a horse, but his signalling equipment consisted in nothing more than flags and shutters with a range of a few hundred yards. He supervised weapon-training in the empty dank moat of the Tower of London, and went annually to Purfleet for musketry, Pirbright for the ranges, and Aldershot or Marlow for manoeuvres. There was almost no tactical training, since (it was argued) if war came, three-quarters of the men would be reservists whom the officers had never seen before, so there seemed little purpose in it. In spite of their lack of opportunity, he and Greer had come to be regarded at the end of these three preparatory years as the most promising young officers in the regiment.

On 3 August 1914 Alexander was acting as Adjutant of a public school camp at Mytchett near Aldershot. He was dining that evening with the officers of a Coldstream battalion when towards the end of dinner the Commanding Officer was told that general mobilization had been ordered, and all visitors must report back to their own units immediately. Alexander returned to Wellington Barracks, where the only battalion of the Irish Guards was stationed, in a mood of great excitement. The reservists began to pour in next day and were soon equipped from the mobilization stores, marching through the London streets to break in their new boots. The officers were issued with pistols and sharpened their swords (which ruined them). On 11 August the battalion was inspected by Field Marshal Lord Roberts, Colonel of the Regiment, and at 5 am next morning they marched to Nine Elms

station *en route* for Southampton. On the troop-ship *Novara*, crossing
to Le Havre, Alexander said to the battalion's Quartermaster, who had
seen service in the South African war, 'What's it like being wounded,
Hickey?' 'Well, you'll soon find out.' But this was not his main fear:
it was that the war might be over before he reached it.

The strategy of 1914–18 was well beyond Alexander's knowledge, and
no attempt will be made in this book to place his actions in a context
wider than he comprehended at the time. Nor is it necessary to describe,
battle by battle, every part which he played in huge operations, nor
the rhythmic movements of his battalion from front line to support,
support to reserve, reserve to rest, and back again, for all this will be
found in general and regimental histories, particularly Kipling's. While
Alexander's First War career was outstanding, it is now mainly of
interest for its effect upon him psychologically and in reputation.
Examples of what he achieved, rather than a chronological narrative,
will illustrate better in what his great gifts of leadership consisted. But,
first, the factual record is worth setting out in this form:

	Rank	Command	Major Battles	Decorations	Wounds
1914 4 Aug.–1 Nov.	Lieutenant	1 Pl., 1st Bn	Retreat from Mons River Aisne (Oct.) 1st Ypres (1 Nov.)	Legion of Honour	
					Thigh and hand
Nov.–					
1915 March	Captain	(Recovering from wounds)			
April–Aug.		1 Coy, 2nd Bn			
16 Aug.–20 Oct.			Loos (25–30 Sept.)	MC	
20–31 Oct.	A/Major	A/CO 1st Bn			
23 Nov.					
1916 10 Dec.		1 Coy, 2nd Bn			
10–31 Dec.		2 i/c 1st Bn	Somme (15 Sept.)	DSO	
1917 Jan–March		2 i/c 2nd Bn			
3 Mar.–23 May		A/CO 1st Bn			
July–Sept.	Major	(Officers School)			
1 Oct.			Passchendaele (Oct.)		Back
	A/Lt-Col	CO 2nd Bn	Cambrai (27 Nov.)		
1918 22 March					
23–30 March		A/Brig. 4th Gds Bde	Retreat from Arras		
18 April–Oct.		CO 2nd Bn	Hazebrouck		
18 Oct.–Dec.		X Corps School	(13 April)		

To sum up: in little more than a year he rose from the command of a
platoon to the temporary command of a battalion. He became one of
the youngest Majors in the British Army, and then one of its youngest

Lieutenant-Colonels. For a few days in 1918 he commanded a Brigade. He was in action throughout the war, except when recovering from wounds or on courses. He was twice wounded (the first time seriously), and three times decorated. He was mentioned five times in despatches. He served alternately in each battalion of the Irish Guards, and reached his peak during his year in command of the 2nd Battalion, which made him indisputably the most highly regarded officer in his regiment.

His reaction to coming under fire for the first time was one of high exhilaration. In a letter to his mother of 28 August 1914 he thus described the beginning of the retreat from Mons:

We marched about seventeen miles and billetted in a certain village [Landrecies] which was nearly the death of us. We all expected a night's rest, but no sooner had we got settled down, the alarm went, and we all rushed out. We were informed that we were surrounded on all sides by thousands of the enemy, and there was only one Brigade, ourselves. Some companies were sent out to hold all the roads, while others were ordered to run up barriers. I had one road, or street, to defend, and tired as we were, having had no sleep for practically two nights, we worked like blacks, and my platoon of sixty-five men made the most enormous barricade by putting up piles of logs and picking up the street-cobbles. When completed it looked very formidable. By midnight we had finished it.

By 2 am the Germans had not succeeded in forcing their way in, and at that hour my Company was ordered to relieve another [Coldstream] Company which had held on to a road all night against several very strong attacks. When we got there, it was a death-trap, there being absolutely no cover at all. We had just to lie down on the open road. We crept up it on either side and relieved those other wretched fellows man by man. They were in an awful state, almost deaf from the continual firing and sort of silly from excitement and suspense.

Well, I got my fellows down all right and there we lay, twenty or thirty yards from the Germans face to face, only it was so dark that you could hardly see in front. The ground on which we lay was covered in cartridges, rifles and dead men. I lay for an hour next to a dead man whilst we could hear the wounded Germans moaning or talking just in front. Of course we expected a fresh attack immediately it got light. We were preparing to die on top of the mound when the orders came for us to retire gradually and noiselessly. This we did, and we were out of the town before light dawned. We had about 150 killed and wounded, and three officers.

In September, having survived the retreat of 160 miles in thirteen days to the south-east of Paris, the British Army advanced to the Aisne.

There Alexander won his first decoration, the Legion of Honour, for patrol-work, and a few weeks later, on 1 November, at the first battle of Ypres, he was wounded in the thigh and hand.

His wounds were serious, and he was invalided home. After nearly two months in a London hospital, he went to Caledon for Christmas, his arm still in a sling and stitches in his thigh, to be met at the station by a guard of honour composed of local volunteers. He was in the best of spirits, determined to return to the front as soon as possible. To give the cautious army doctors evidence that he was fit enough, he proposed to the gamekeeper at Derg, Peter Taylor, that they should walk from Derg to Donegal and back, a distance of twenty-eight miles, without food or drink. This they did, returning to Derg late in the evening. Then Alexander sprung his surprise. They would start off again before dawn next morning, and walk the sixty-four miles to Caledon in a single day. Leaving Derg at 4 am, they rested after thirty-two miles at Omagh for tea and sandwiches. 'I would not put my hand on a donkey-cart for help', he said to Taylor during this halt. 'This walk has to be done. If I can't do it, you go on. It's do or die. I am going to do it if I have to crawl on my hands and knees.' They halted again at Bally-gawley for twenty minutes, and reached Caledon at 9 pm, seventeen hours after leaving Derg. Alexander was in considerable pain during the last half of the walk, but when he came to the high park gates and found them locked, he climbed over them, and on entering the house did a step-dance on the pantry floor, to prove to himself as much as to Taylor, his sole witness, that he was incapable of fatigue. Next day he wrote to the War Office a full account of his exploit, and the local doctor, shocked but convinced by his folly, removed his stitches a few days later.

In February 1915 he was promoted Captain, and went to Warley Barracks, near Chelmsford, where the 2nd Battalion of the Irish Guards was being formed from the regiment's reservists. In August he returned with it to the front in command of a company, and within a few weeks was leading it into action at the battle of Loos.

During the war Alexander won a reputation which was only equalled by that of his friend Eric Greer. If he had not survived, like Greer, who was killed in 1917 at Passchendaele, he would still be remembered. Greer was a more reflective man, more mature, less ebullient, accepting his ordeals philosophically, without Alexander's love of adventure and ambition for personal glory. Alexander's qualities were his courage, his resilience, his imperturbability, his power of quick decision, his ingenuity, and his capacity to make friends of the men he led. Kipling wrote of him:

He had the gift of handling the men on the lines to which they most readily responded. At the worst crises he was both inventive and cordial and, on such occasions as they all strove together in the gates of death, would somehow contrive to dress the affair in high comedy. Moreover, when the blame for some incident of battle or fatigue was his, he confessed and took it upon his own shoulders in the presence of all. Consequently his subordinates loved him, even when he fell upon them blisteringly for their shortcomings; and his men were all his own.[1]

An Irish-guardsman, Robert McShane, confirmed this view to Norman Hillson, Alexander's first biographer:

We saw at once that he was an extraordinary young man. There was originality in everything he did. He appeared to be able to lead and control men by the power of his personality. He was entirely free from fear, superior airs or snobbery. Being an athlete who knew how to train and look after himself, he was fitter than anyone else in the Regiment. He was the most perfect man, morally, physically and mentally, that I have ever met. These things enabled him to be superb in face of danger and tight corners. For his own safety he never gave a thought.[2]

'He was entirely free from fear.' This cannot be true. If it were, he could not be called courageous. One of his junior officers, Major A. R. Pym, remembered that during the battle of Loos the Company were being shelled by heavy guns as they were digging in, and a bursting shell carried a man's body to twice the height of the surrounding trees. 'There was a look of fear in Alex's face then.' He overcame it by his strong sense of duty and honour. He was a romantic. He had a cavalier's view of war. In an interview with Major Verney shortly before his death, he came as close as he ever did to analyzing his emotions in battle:

On the whole it was a very gentlemanly war. One just accepted the danger and discomfort. But towards the end I felt, 'I just can't go on being so lucky, if we are always being asked to attack.' But I argued to myself, 'There is an awful lot of space around you, the whole universe. And even if you are hit,

---

[1] The notes will be found at the end of the book. They are only references to publications, and add nothing to the text.

it doesn't necessarily mean that you'll be killed. You might get a cushy one. And what's the alternative? To stay behind in the trench and rat? If you're found out (and you're bound to be found out), you'll be shot for cowardice.' One was very fit, tough and screwed up with patriotism and desire for glory. It was a terrific adventure. We were very young. It was all very intriguing and exciting, and all your friends were around you, and the men.

Alexander enjoyed the First World War, and was not ashamed to admit it. He was happy doing what was expected of him, and knowing that he could do it well. To his mother he wrote in April 1916, 'There's something terribly fascinating about it all, the starlights at night which one shoots out of a pistol to light up the ground, the rattle of musketry, and then the sound of big guns. I wouldn't miss it or be out of it for anything.' A year later he wrote to the Colonel of his regiment, 'I don't want to go home. I have been out here so long now that I should like to see the end. I am very happy here and need no rest, as I have never been fitter or happier in my life. In fact I shall be almost sorry when it is all over.' On Christmas Day of the same year he wrote from the trenches to his Aunt Margaret, 'I'm afraid the war will end very soon now, but I suppose all good things come to an end sooner or later, so we mustn't grumble.'

These sentiments, which now seem to us strange and even shocking, were not peculiar to Alexander. What Harold Macmillan has described as 'a sense of teamship and a sense of triumph' excused the bestiality of war, and preserved the sanity and self-respect of men who were wrenched from civilized life to do terrible things to an enemy who were doing terrible things to them. Brutality was reciprocal and therefore guiltless. The excitement of battle, the planning and sudden execution, survival and retrospect, had their parallels in the hunting field and even on the track. It was sport magnified into drama. Showmanship and vanity had their part in it, particularly for officers who were on stage in a way the men seldom were, the observed of all observers, apprehensive of disgrace more than wounds, impelled by orders which originated with unseen Generals and were then handed down rank to rank, becoming at each stage more particularized, sharper, until the moment came when an officer ceased to receive orders but gave them, and the commitment of having given them carried him over the top, a leader now, across a No Man's Land that had suddenly become everyman's. He moved automatically, buoyed up by responsibility, friendship, audacity and a determination to reach the objective as quickly as possible, for that is what he had said he would do, and there, with any luck, he could rest. All successful officers felt this, even one who ultimately rebelled against it, Siegfried Sassoon, who wrote of 'the honour and glory which made the War such an uplifting experience for those in close contact with it'; even Duff Cooper, who in his life of Haig, wrote of 'the glory of battle, the thrill of the race across No Man's Land, the sudden carelessness of life that comes as a revelation, and the heart-filling triumph of standing on the captured position and witnessing the flight of the foe'. Glory, thrill, triumph – the words occur in every account of every battle, and Alexander thought these moments among the most wonderful of his life.

Never did he question that war was necessary or this one right. It was more important to him that the enemy was 'worthy' than that it was Germany. To the origins of the war he gave hardly a thought. There is no indication in his letters from the trenches that it ever struck him as dreadful that millions of young men should suffer so abominably at each other's hands. The stench of the dead and unwashed living, or so abhorrent an activity as shovelling aside the remains of corpses under shellfire, were inseparable from his chosen profession, as bloodshed is from surgery. The detail was horrible, but the cumulative effect of their common suffering was exalting. Far from coarsening him, war developed his innate sympathy.

I only once saw him really angry [wrote Sir Derrick Gunston many years later] and that was in one of the Passchendaele battles. I was acting as his second-in-command. When we had achieved our objectives, I walked back to see him about something, and came across three badly wounded Germans calling for water. I asked some officers from another unit to fetch some water, and they refused. I went on and told Alex. He came back at once and was shocked at what he saw. In justifiable rage he told the officers what he thought of them and ordered them to carry water to the dying Germans. (Letter to Lady Alexander. 1969)

Alexander did not see the enemy as fellow victims of a universal tragedy, but as opponents who ran the same risks as he did, and deserved from him the treatment which he would expect from them, merciless-ness in battle, compassion in defeat. The war was a contest, not a massacre. He felt no hatred. All through his life he liked and admired the Germans. They were the designated enemy, and he did his duty by killing them before they killed him.

34

It was not his nature to reason why. He was a-political, and in religion a conventional Protestant. He accepted Tory-Christian attitudes because he was brought up to respect them, much like the standing orders of an army. His Christian goodness was displayed in his genuine love of people, his care of his soldiers, the trouble he took over other men's personal problems. Among those closest to him were the Roman Catholic chaplains in his battalions. He admired the ritual of their Church, perhaps with his natural chic envied them their vestments. Their throw-away humour and fatalism made a great appeal to him. They never raised awkward moral questions about the war. 'Why do the men have to go to Mass, father?' he once asked. 'I never heard that it did them any harm', was the reply that delighted him. As he stood by while Mass was celebrated, he was seen to nod approval when the priest told the men not to pray for their own preservation, but for courage.

His brother-officers at first accepted, and then demanded, his leadership because they saw in him all their own aspirations magnified. There is no occasion, no place, except the House of Commons, where false charm and weakness of character are more rapidly exposed than by active warfare. He had extraordinary calm, which is both an element of courage and inspires it. He could produce a high gloss on the poorest of human material. He had in his mind a complete picture of what he intended to do. He thought positively of what could be achieved, while others thought negatively of what they might suffer. He was, and felt, responsible. But he was also an optimist, which means that he was personally convinced that nothing is so desperate as it first appears, and he could transmit this optimism to his men. The enemy, too, are suffering. Their will can crack, their capabilities have a limit. Hold on for a few hours more, and gradually the tide will turn. Some of us will die, but most will survive. Therefore take it easily. Fill the time of waiting by doing something else. Valentine Williams, then a junior officer in his battalion, gives this instance:

One cold day an order had come through that the brigade must be ready to move at a moment's notice for a critical part of the line. While we were experiencing the usual uneasiness in waiting for transport – the distance being long – we were surprised and indeed stimulated to see Alexander and a few other enthusiasts in running kit – and running through the snow. He had guessed correctly that the lorries would be late. Instead of sitting down and fussing, he was using the time profitably, showing the men the value of control and discipline.[3]

Alexander's experience gave him a complete knowledge of the small tactical variations possible in this strait-jacket type of war. He knew his men's weapons intimately. He was an excellent map-reader, and had an instinctive sense of direction which told him when the maps were wrong. He insisted that any danger or discomfort could be mitigated by self-help. No conditions were beyond some remedy. If the ground was too wet to dig downwards, parapets must be raised upwards, and the morass floored by duckboards. His battalion's dugouts were always the strongest and cleanest, and he was the leader of their improvisations. If he doubted the battle-worthiness of a neighbouring unit, he would convert his own sector into a fortress by wiring it down both sides, however much offence the precaution might give. Every attack, every patrol, was planned and rehearsed in complete detail, but with a flexibility that was only possible because of his quick reaction to the unexpected and the confidence which he inspired.

Alexander's professionalism explains why he was trusted, but it does not explain why he was loved. When guardsmen were asked who commanded their battalion, they would reply, 'The Honourable Alexander.' 'And your brigade?' 'The Honourable Alexander.' 'And the division?' 'The Honourable Alexander.' No more senior officer existed for them. He never asked them to do the impossible, nor to endure any ordeal which he did not share. His relationship with them was well attuned to their character. They knew him to be just, and the first to spot the distinction between an explanation and an excuse. His standards of honesty, courage and discipline were high but not beyond reach. He was always prepared to give a second chance. When he first arrived at Warley Barracks in April 1915, he had his company paraded in field-service marching order. He inspected each man carefully, and found fault with almost every one of them, for careless shaving, dirty boots or cap-star, a bruised face or rusty rifle. He told them, 'I am not at all satisfied with this. I wish to see the whole company in the barrack-room at 2 pm.' There he addressed them: 'The turn-out this morning was disgraceful, far below the standard I expect. I believe that a really smart turn-out means a tremendous lot to the morale and discipline of a company. I am determined to improve it, and it is up to you how I do it. I can do it by punishment. I don't want to do it that way. Or you can do it yourselves by striving to make this the best company in the battalion. At the parade this morning I took a lot of names. You deserved it. Now I am going to cancel the lot. Let's start again.' Next morning the parade was impeccable.

He was the ideal of a commander, but he was not typical. His minor eccentricities increased the affection in which he was held. Most obvious was his individuality of dress. Even in the trenches he preserved a faint air of dandyism. He had special marching-boots made for him with a strap across the instep. He wore a Sam Browne belt over his greatcoat. Once on leave he was walking down St James's Street and saw a Russian officer wearing a high-peaked cap, its visor dropping almost vertically over his eyes. Alexander stopped him and asked whether he might examine it. Then he went straight to a hatter and had an identical cap made for himself. He continued to wear a cap of this type throughout both World Wars, not because it was more comfortable, not because he admired the Russians, but because it had style. In winter he wore a heavy sheepskin coat, and asked his aunt to send him a fur muff, which he used alternately as bearskin, a pillow, to keep his hands warm in the trenches and his feet warm in bed. In conversation, too, he was different from the others. Nobody would tell a dirty story in his presence. He never swore. Although he was not an abstainer, nobody ever saw him drunk. He used words like 'tiresome' and 'gentle' which were not in the average officer's vocabulary. He could be seen sketching the battlefield under fire, not for military record but because he liked to draw. In his dugout he studied German and Russian from textbooks which he had sent out from home. He modelled from putty, wire and paint ghastly corpses to entice German patrols. He could take these small risks of ridicule because he was so clearly unridiculous, and his unconventional manner became an extra asset. But the more percipient of his officers observed that in spite of his bonhomie he was reticent and wished to remain slightly aloof. He had few intimate friends after Greer was killed, possibly because he feared to become too attached to men who might soon die, or because he bore his worries so lightly that he had no need of a confidant. The role of a Commanding Officer in a battalion which held no other of equal rank was in any case a lonely one.

With the guardsmen he was completely at ease. He would tolerate in them the small breaches of convention that he claimed for himself. Once, in an off-moment, he took a favourite Corporal to visit the ruins of the Cloth Hall at Ypres. When they were challenged by a French sentry, Alexander found that he had left behind his identity-card. The sentry turned to the Corporal: 'Do you know this officer?' 'Never saw him before in my life', he replied. Few incidents illustrate better the egalitarianism of the Irish Guards, the impertinence of their pride in themselves, the nice judgement with which they could tease their commanders. Alexander encouraged it. He would read to his company in the early days of the war the exploits of Brigadier Gerard, partly to amuse them, partly to stimulate their love of glory, but partly, one suspects, to deepen their devotion to their own gay and gallant young Captain. Off-duty he was more than companionable. He excelled at step-dancing and jigs, and at battalion concerts no performance was awaited more eagerly than the Commanding Officer's. After one of the Somme battles, when spirits were low, he acted an encounter between himself and Hindenburg, playing both roles with remarkable impromptu and mimicry. In battalion-sports he was the instigator and chief participant, playing football and cricket with his men, and carrying off every athletic prize for which he entered.

There was much in the First War which was repetitive and wearisome (the more usual word 'boring' does not express adequately the constant strain, the half-dread, half-longing, for more energetic action), and Alexander's reputation was made as much in the long intervals between battles as in the battles themselves. But no record of his early days would be satisfactory without giving some account of his moments of greatest stress. A description of four battles, told, as he would have wished, as adventure stories, will illustrate his daring and his luck. They are: Loos, where he won the Military Cross; the Somme, where he won the DSO; Cambrai, when his battalion came nearest to total disaster; and Hazebrouck, when he first tasted higher command.

Loos (25–30 September 1915)

When the 2nd Battalion left Warley Barracks on 16 August, with Alexander commanding its 1 Company, they had little idea that they were destined within a few weeks to take part in what Sir Douglas Haig described in his diary on the opening day as 'the greatest battle in the world's history'. 800,000 men of the Anglo-French armies were to breach the German front in the west before the Germans could crush the Russians in the east. There was a four-day preliminary bombardment by 1,000 guns. For the first time gas was to be used in an Allied offensive. The objectives were unlimited. Five days later the operation was written off, having gained something under a mile at the cost of 45,000 British casualties alone.

Alexander's battalion formed part of the Guards Division. For both the battalion and the division it was their first action, and they lay in GHQ reserve, directly under the control of the Commander-in-Chief, Sir John French, and did not take part in the opening phases of the battle. This was one cause of the bitter controversy which developed between French and Haig, the latter commanding the actual battle area. Haig claimed that he would have broken through at Loos if he had had the reserves under his command at the start or immediately at hand. As it was, the Guards Division and two others were held far back, and came up too late to exploit the early successes. The first German trench had been crossed: the enemy had then been able hurriedly to occupy the second. Only fresh troops could break this new line, and it took two days for them to arrive. The momentum had been lost.

Something of this situation must have been known at the level of company commanders as the Guards Division forced its way forward up cluttered roads. They reached the old German front-line having marched for forty-eight hours with very little rest or food. They expected an order to attack immediately into the scrub and mine-workings ahead of them, just north-east of Loos itself. But there was further delay, a further shift of position, and zero hour was put back till 4 pm on 27 September, after another sleepless night. What happened then can be told in Alexander's own words in a letter which he wrote to his brother William a few days later:

We were told to attack a bit of wood and some chalk pits about 1,000 yards from where we were. At 4 pm after a fair bombardment we started off. My Company was in support. We came under heavy fire from the German artillery but the men were quite magnificent and never wavered once. They marched in perfect order with rifles at the slope and in step. We reached the wood and started to dig ourselves in on the other side under perfectly appalling machine-gun fire.

Then the Grenadiers and Scots Guards attacked across about 1,000 yards on our right with their objective a pit-head 200 yards in front of us. They came in for machine-gun fire the whole time and it was dreadful to see how they were mown down. They reached the pit, but somehow something went wrong, and they all came streaming back and through our fellows, who also thought that everyone had to retire. But I managed to rally all the men on the right of the line and got them dug in. The Commanding Officer, who was on the other side of the wood, thought the whole situation was lost, not knowing that a few of us were still hanging on, but he got my message just in time and rushed up reinforcements on my left. We stayed there for three nights and were then relieved, having been very heavily shelled. Our losses were about eight officers and 300 men.

This exactly corroborates the account given by Rudyard Kipling with his wider view and subsequent knowledge. It was a particularly poignant passage of the regimental history for Kipling to write, for it was in this very battle that his own son was killed, a fact which he records in a single unemotional line. But in writing of Alexander he did not conceal his admiration:

A runner came back with a message from Captain Alexander saying that he and some men were still in their scratch-trenches on the far side of Chalk Pit wood, and he would be greatly obliged if they would kindly send some more men up, and with speed. The actual language was somewhat crisper, and was supplemented, so the tale runs, by remarks from the runner addressed to the community at large.

Reinforcements were sent, and in this way the mile gained was a mile held. But the brigade could advance no further.

Alexander was awarded the MC. More significantly, he was put in temporary command of the 1st Battalion less than a month later. Jubilantly he wrote to his aunt, 'This time last year I commanded No. 1 Platoon, and now I have the whole battalion! What a change in less than three hundred days!'

The Somme (*15 September 1916*)

'Alexander', wrote Valentine Williams, 'was the only man I knew who appeared to enjoy the battle of the Somme.' If Williams was right, it was the enjoyment of a light-footed boxer who knew that at any moment he might stop a knockout blow. Alexander was still a Captain, having reverted to the command of his old company in the 2nd Battalion. The Guards Division was ordered to renew the offensive in which three Allied armies had been engaged since 1 July. The carnage had been appalling. 'It was magnificent,' wrote Kipling in a rare ironic aside, 'for the whole Press said so; and it was also extensively advertised as war.' Now the idea – but this had always been the idea – was to punch a hole clean through the German lines, and the place chosen was Ginchy, where in the previous month's fighting the British had advanced to a depth of three miles on a front of ten.

Kipling's account of this battle was among his most brilliant. His prose began to throb:

Long before the Brigade was anywhere near their first objective, companies and battalions were mixed up in what with other troops would have been hopeless confusion.... In due time, and no man saw anything coherently, their general advance reached the German trench which was their first objective. Its wire had not been properly cut by our guns, and little gasping, sweating parties dodged in and out and round the wings of it, bombing enemies where they sighted them. There were many Germans, too, in the shell-holes that they overpassed, who fired into their backs, and all the while from their right flank, now wholly in the air, came the lashing machine-gun fire. So the wrecked trench of the first objective was, as one man said, 'none too bad a refuge even if we had to bomb ourselves into it'.

Alexander found himself with 120 men of all units of the brigade and about five other officers, among them Greer. They began to bomb right and left to clear the trench. The Germans further off machine-gunned their own men who tried to scuttle back. Though they scarcely knew where they were, and both flanks were wide open, they thought they had 'a sporting chance' of pushing on. Captain Oliver Lyttelton (later Lord Chandos) of the Grenadiers, and Alexander, were among those who favoured the attempt. They collected about a hundred men and advanced half a mile to a point where they overlooked standing crops, a sight as unfamiliar to front-line soldiers as mown lawns, so deeply had they penetrated the battlefield. They halted in an unoccupied trench and sent back a message for reinforcements. 'As they were utterly detached from an already detached force', commented Kipling, 'they might as well have indented for elephants.' The Germans crept through the tall corn and rushed them. The attack was repulsed, but being beyond all support, the guardsmen made their way back to the main body with surprisingly few casualties. The day's work had resulted in a net gain of 800 yards, at the cost of 300 men. Alexander and one other were the only officers to escape unhurt.

The citation to the DSO which Alexander won that day said that he was 'the life and soul of the attack, and throughout the day led forward, not only his own men, but men of all Regiments'. We do not have his account of the action, but this letter from his brother Herbrand to his mother, written on 18 September, showed that Brigadier Gerard had indeed been reincarnated:

I have just met Tubby, who has come out of the line after a big attack in which he has done splendidly. I had him in our camp [Royal Irish Lancers], and luckily one of our fellows had some grouse sent to him, and we were able to give him a real good dinner for his first meal out of the trenches. He is more than splendid, and talks so well, and with so much confidence and enthusiasm, that we all felt like rushing over and taking on the Bosch ourselves, then and there. Everyone was spellbound. I might have met him for the very first time in my life, I was so impressed by his clearness of vision and grasp of everything, and the quiet confidence with which he spoke. The Guards all swear by him. He now has a great breast full of medals, and thoroughly deserves them. I get reflected glory from him, and feel quite proud. Fellows say, 'Oh, are you a brother of Alexander in the Irish Guards?', and when I say I am, I become quite a distinguished person.

Cambrai (27 November 1917)

Alexander had commanded his 2nd Battalion since early October and first led them into action at Passchendaele, where he was wounded in the back by a shell-splinter, which the Medical Officer picked out with a scalpel. He was able to remain with his men, 'though it was a bit sore at the time', he wrote to his aunt, 'especially as I had nothing but a hard floor or a piece of board to lie on at night'.

As usual, the Guards Division was kept in reserve at the beginning of the battle, and Haig repeated French's mistake at Loos by holding them too far back. So when the battle opened on 20 November with the success of the tanks, now used for the first time in massed formation, in overrunning three parallel defences of the Hindenburg Line, there was nothing with which to extend the breach once the tanks and their accompanying infantry were exhausted. By the time the Guards were called forward, the Germans had rallied. It was a familiar story. The 2nd Guards Brigade were required to march all night to their start-line. Orders were given, then changed, and it was not until midnight 26/27 November that Alexander could give his company commanders details of the attack which was due to start within a few hours, at dawn. The

Irish Guards were to capture Bourlon Wood, a 100-acre plantation lying west of Cambrai aslant a low ridge which dominated the whole northern part of the salient, and which had already twice changed hands in the fighting of the last few days. Until the wood was captured no further progress could be made. But the battalion could not see it in the dark. They were to march by compass-bearing across torn ground into the wood and consolidate on the far side. William Alexander, who was then a Company Commander in his brother's battalion ('It was awkward for him to send me into action, but more awkward not to') subsequently wrote this account for the Irish Guards records:

It was bitterly cold and snowing hard. We formed up in dense under-growth. The attack never looked like anything except a failure. The barrage was thin, and advanced too quick. The Germans retaliated strongly. We captured four hundred prisoners in the wood, but two hundred of them escaped by attacking their guards, or when the escorts were killed by shelling. Then the enemy counter-attacked round our left flank, and the Battalion was almost surrounded. The state of things in and around the chalet where Battalion H.Q. was located cannot adequately be described. There was no place for a dressing station. Nearly all the orderlies were killed or wounded. The whole place was stacked with dead, dying and wounded, and it is no exaggeration to say that the floor of the chalet was running with blood, and still this merciless shelling continued, aided by low-flying aeroplanes. In the midst of this pandemonium an orderly rushed in to say that the Germans had broken through and were streaming down the wood, and were even now behind Battalion H.Q.
Where thousands would have given up in despair, there was one man who stood head and shoulders above everyone else. The Commanding Officer [Alexander], calm, cool, and collected, never lost his head for one moment, but seemed to affect everyone with his courage, steadiness and determination. We all looked to him for support, having absolute confidence in his skill and foresight.

The battalion emerged from the wood eighty strong, out of the 400 who had gone in. It was the first reverse that the Guards Division had suffered, and in the next week the Germans took back almost all the ground won. It was a war of attrition, and the men accepted it, but it was humanly impossible – and they were very human – for them to excuse the mistakes, the false optimism and the missed opportunities which marred their every fresh effort. Alexander never allowed himself publicly to blame the higher command, except their refusal to see the fighting for themselves ('Throughout my service as a regimental soldier from 1914 to 1918', he wrote in his Memoirs, 'no commander above my Brigade Commander ever visited my front-line sector'), and his coolness in the crisis of Bourlon Wood was founded on confidence in himself more than in his superiors.

Hazebrouck (12–14 April 1918)

His last battle in the First War was the most desperate, and ended in the extinction of his battalion as a fighting force. Hazebrouck was the culmination of the three weeks mêlée which followed the German offensive of 21 March 1918. The Irish Guards were then out of the line near Arras, and on the day of the attack were holding their divisional sports. From the make-believe of boxing and tug-of-war they were hurried into actual combat. The Allied retreat had begun, but it was not so orderly as it had been in September 1914. There were disgraceful scenes of panic. Lord Ardee, commanding 4th Guards Brigade, was gassed, and Alexander took over from him until the brigade came into reserve. Sir John Hall wrote from the Irish Guards' Headquarters in London to Alexander's family on 6 April:

We now have definite news that our beloved Alex is resting with his Battalion and that he is all right. You know that after Ardee was gassed, it devolved upon him to command the 4th Guards Brigade. We all knew that he was a fine soldier, but the critical situation in which the Brigade found itself gave him an opportunity of showing, at a time when even the coolest men were at a loss to know what to do, that he was possessed of powers of leadership, and of correctly judging the situation, such as are vouchsafed to few. It is said that it was due to him alone that the situation was saved.

That was just the beginning. On 9 April the brigade was called upon to deal with a new crisis. A Portuguese division covering Hazebrouck had collapsed. Hazebrouck was a road and rail junction on the only lateral road which remained between the Germans and the coast. The brigade was told to plug the gap, and Alexander gave out his orders, 'almost seductively' in Kipling's percipient phrase (for the battalion was filled with young recruits who had never seen action before), to find the enemy and any flanking troops of our own. The position of neither was known. They scratched for themselves a line in open country south of the village of Vieux Berquin, and next morning found themselves overlooked by a fence of observation-balloons which had sprung up overnight. The Irish Guards were split into two halves, two companies to assist the Grenadier battalion, two the Coldstream, both in the front line, and there they were drenched in fire, by artillery frontally, by machine-guns laterally, and after attempting to attack, were themselves attacked.

That was the day, 13 April, when Haig issued his famous order, 'There is no other course open to us but to fight it out. Every position must be held to the last man: there must be no retirement. With our backs to the wall, and believing in the justice of our cause, each one of us must fight on to the end.' When the message reached Alexander, he commented grimly, 'It's not backs to the wall for us: it's backs to back.' The enemy had broken through the remnants of the Grenadiers and Coldstream. Alexander sent in a company to mend the breach, and it was never seen again. The brigade's position was that of 'a crumbling sandbank thrust out into a sea whose every wave wore it away'. They held on just long enough for the Australian Division to come up to their support. Haig wrote in his despatch, 'No more brilliant exploit has taken place since the opening of the enemy's offensive'. Hazebrouck had been the point of the Germans' maximum effort, and the brigade had saved the Channel ports almost single-handed. The Irish Guards lost 250 men, the Grenadiers and Coldstream many more. The brigade in all but name was disbanded, the survivors acting as reinforcements to other battalions. Though the 2nd Battalion Irish Guards remained in being at Criel Plage, near Dieppe, Hazebrouck was their last battle.

Alexander went to Paris for the celebrations of 14 July, and then on leave to London. On 18 October, with less than a month of the war to run, he was posted to command X Corps School, where young officers were instructed in battle-drill. His departure released an unusual demonstration of pent-up affection, of which these awkward verses, given to him by a Guardsman on behalf of hundreds, express the spirit:

Our C.O.

Now you've gone we miss you so,
In truth a friend and staunch C.O.,
We live in hopes 'tis but for a while
That once again we'll see your smile.

The love we've always born for thee
Each and everyone can see.
In fight or sport t'was all the same,
You taught us to uphold our name.

Glory be unto that day
When we'll depart upon our way.
But no matter where we wander,
We shall *never* forget you, brave Commander.

Alexander himself took the end of the war calmly, almost sadly, but was already looking ahead. To his Aunt Margaret he wrote on 22 November from X Corps School:

It must have been wonderful in London. We took everything very quietly out here. I am marking time for the present. It all sounds very attractive 'marching to the Rhine', but I am an old enough soldier to know it isn't as much fun as it sounds, and therefore I am not over-anxious to get myself tied down to anything definite. Garrisoning some German town where the people are bad-tempered and you are not allowed to do anything, and all this in the middle of winter – I am not sure that it will be very attractive. I should imagine that I could go back to the Battalion tomorrow if I applied, but I want to see what's going to turn up before. I was rather thinking of trying to get sent to one of the Russian expeditions – there's bound to be some fighting over there. I have had a good weathering in this war, and I am going to get the fruits of it if I can. You can bet your life that I shall have a good try.

3

THE BALTIC

The First World War had been 'a good weathering'. The nautical metaphor (the language of the military being stiff and arid in comparison) was well chosen. Alexander was toughened by the tempest, and had learnt to ride with the seas as they came at him. He had acquired a taste for war – the taste for adventure had always been there – and nothing more was heard of his ambition to become President of the Royal Academy. He was now a Lieutenant-Colonel. The ascending steps drew him upwards. The reasons why he had accepted command of X Corps School were because 'I have always been interested in instruction' but more 'because it is half-way between a Lieutenant-Colonel's command and a Brigadier's'. He was ambitious, still young, and unmarried. No family obligation attracted him home. His three brothers had also survived the war (Herbrand and William with DSOs), and his mother's interest in her sons wavered between intense pride and total indifference. He found the prospect of a barrack in Germany or England 'too dull for words'. He looked for another war, any war, like Churchill at a slightly earlier age, and in 1919 there were plenty for a British officer to choose from.

At first he considered joining one of the Allied expeditions on the periphery of Russia, at Murmansk, Archangel, Vladivostok or in Siberia, some of which had been launched during the war to stiffen the Russians and remained after the Armistice as anti-Bolshevik crusades. But when his chance came, it was initially for something tamer. He was invited to join the Allied Relief Commission in Poland. The invitation came to him from a brother-officer in the Irish Guards, Stephen Tallents, whom Alexander had known but slightly. Tallents was nearly ten years older, and their paths had seldom crossed during the war, for Tallents was severely wounded early in 1915 when Alexander was recovering from his own wounds, and he then returned to the Civil Service, where he was responsible for food rationing. After the Armistice he volunteered to help the organization of relief supplies to Poland, and applied to the Irish Guards for some suitable officers to help him. Alexander and one other (Captain Hamilton) responded.

He travelled overland to Poland via Paris, Italy and Austria, and reached Warsaw at the end of March 1919, reporting to Tallents at the Allied headquarters in the Hotel Bristol, where the Prime Minister, Paderewski, and Carton de Wiart VC, head of the British military mission, were also staying. Tallents told him that his first task was to tour the Polish provinces and report on conditions there in preparation for the distribution of food, medicine, clothing and other supplies which were soon expected to reach Poland from the Allies. Alexander was therefore first involved in eastern Europe in a quasi-civilian role, but as the country was in turmoil and the southern part of it still a battleground between the Poles and nascent Czechs, a uniform commanded more respect than a brief-case. Even Tallents had been given the rank of Lieutenant-Colonel. Alexander set out at once.

Hamilton and I first went to the Teschen district [he wrote home]. We travelled down to Cracow in a sleeper, and spent the day there. It is a beautiful old town and has a wonderful picture gallery. We motored through the Carpathians, just over the frontier into Hungary. The Poles and Czechs are still at variance although there is an armistice. It's great fun motoring through the lines. Men dash out and point their rifles. Then you say, 'Commission Angelski', and there is much saluting and heel-clicking, and you glide off.

They are such nice people, the Poles. We went to a little farm owned by a very fine-looking young soldier who had been in the Austrian army. Such a dear little house, very clean and beautifully decorated. The women wear such picturesque clothes. The people are very nice looking, clean, happy and healthy: some of the peasant girls are lovely. They insisted on giving us milk and bread to eat, and when we left, such magnificent salutes, salaams and bows. They have perfect manners.

They went on to Vienna, where Alexander was shown the Imperial stables with their magnificent Andalusian-Arab greys, and then returned to Warsaw. He had seen much poverty in Poland, much unemployment, many refugees and long queues at the soup-kitchens. In the country districts, which rival armies had stripped of food and farm-implements, Tallents reported that the peasants were living on roots, grass, acorns and heather. But in Warsaw there was another life of insensitive extravagance and gay parties at which officers of many nationalities sank their past differences in mutual toasts. Alexander saw something of this too:

All officers salute each other and bow when coming into restaurants. There is a wonderful collection of uniforms here, as the Poles have not got any of their own, and they wear their old ones, according to the army they were in, Russian, Austrian or German. I sat at dinner the other night, and there we were, four officers all in completely different uniforms, and we had all fought against each other during the war. Really war is very silly. I am learning Polish, and am now as good as I was at Russian. In the evening when I get well warmed up, I am quite fluent in a sort of mixture of Russian and Polish.

Carton de Wiart asked him to join his staff, and he was tempted to accept 'as the work is more in my line', but at the end of May 1919, two months after his arrival in Poland, he was attached to Tallents's new mission to the Baltic, and that was the real beginning of his remarkable adventure.

For centuries the Baltic Sea and its littoral have been contested between Russia, Germany, Poland and Sweden. The smaller countries of Estonia, Latvia and Lithuania were territories for the great powers to cross in their marches and counter-marches against each other, and nations to subjugate, divide and absorb. The three Baltic states had been under Russian rule since the eighteenth century. But earlier history had left upon them an even deeper mark, which is important to an understanding of Alexander's role in 1919–20. This was the gradual German colonization of Latvia from the twelfth to the sixteenth centuries. At first the Germans came as conquerors (Knights of the Teutonic Order) and divided the land into great estates, reducing the native Letts to serfdom. They were followed by Hanseatic merchants and industrialists who gained as firm a grip on trade as the Teuton barons had on the land. These Germans never became Letts, as the Normans became English, and even after Latvia became wholly Russian in 1795, they continued to regard the country almost as part of Prussia, just as the Prussians regarded it as a lost province to be regained.

For six centuries the Germans retained their estates, their language and their culture, and asserted their rights against the Czars as a feudal and alien minority in a population of two million people. The Letts hated the Germans. At first the Russians allowed the Balts (as the Latvian Germans were commonly called) to have their way, but were soon obliged to pay some attention to the clamour of the Letts. Serfdom was abolished in Latvia in stages during the nineteenth century, and laws were passed to limit German schools, courts of justice, police and other privileges, replacing them by new institutions on the Russian model. The Balts deeply resented these encroachments on what they still call 'our historic rights and spiritual traditions'. Their *Deutschtum* was intensified by the attempt to 'russificate us'. At the same time the increasing nationalism of the Baltic peoples threatened the German Balts from a new direction. They saw themselves destined to lose their powers and even their identity to their previous serfs. They hoped for a German victory in the 1914–18 war. They would have been happy to see Prussian rule extended along the whole south-eastern coast of the Baltic, and live under its protection. These were the people whom Alexander was to weld into a small army and command in action against the Bolsheviks.

Early in 1919 the situation in the Baltic countries was therefore extraordinarily confused. So little was known about it in Western Europe that the leader of the first French Mission to Latvia, on appealing to his Government for funds, was authorized to draw up to a thousand *yen*, the official at the Quai d'Orsay explaining later that he imagined Latvia to be a Japanese island. There were six groups manoeuvring for control of the Baltic countries: the Bolsheviks, the White Russians, the Germans (Balts and Prussians), the Baltic peoples themselves, and the Allies. The Bolsheviks wished to reassert Russian rule over territories which had been ceded to Germany by the Treaty of Brest-Litovsk but which they regarded as historically their own, and to restore to northern Russia its only outlet in winter through Latvia's ice-free ports. The White Russians, with their different motives, had the same idea. The Germans were anxious to redeem their defeat in the West by creating a strategic base in the East, and at the same time protect the frightened German Balts. The nationalists saw in the break-up of Russia by revolution and of Germany by military defeat an opportunity to strike for their independence of both. The Allies supported the nationalist movements, not only because independence was the watchword at Versailles, but because they saw great advantage in the emergence of three small buffer-states between Russia and Germany on the southern Baltic shore.

The Allies were not however dealing with people who awaited a decision from Versailles. All other parties to the dispute had already acted by the time Tallents and Alexander arrived. The Bolsheviks had invaded both Estonia and Latvia. The Germans had occupied Lithuania and were advancing to contest Latvia from the south. The White Russians were grouped in armies on the Russian frontiers, poised to overthrow the revolutionary Government. The Balts had formed a little independent army known as the Baltic Landeswehr, and it was uncertain on whose side they would fight. The independence of Estonia had been declared by the nationalists in November 1918, and that of Latvia a month later. The Supreme Allied Council of the Allies, sitting at Versailles, made it clear that they did not intend to intervene with an expeditionary land-force to restore order, but the British sent a fleet in November 1918 to show their support for the nationalists and to contain the Russian fleet at Kronstadt.

As the Allies could spare no troops for the liberation of the Baltic states from the Bolsheviks, they had no choice but to invite the German eastern army, an integral part of the forces of an enemy who had just capitulated to them, to act in the Allied interest. Curzon called it 'a necessary evil'. If the Germans withdrew from the Baltic, the Bolsheviks would flood in. The Germans must fight the Allies' battle for them, on the understanding that as soon as their task was completed and the Bolsheviks expelled, they would go home, leaving the Baltic peoples to enjoy their independence. The Germans had very different ideas. They intended to conquer the Baltic states, and stay there. They would settle German veterans as colonists in Baltic lands. They reinforced their eastern army by 10,000 volunteers, enticed by this very promise. Their commander, General Rudigen von der Goltz, saw himself as the saviour of German honour and future master of the Baltic. As he admitted in his Memoirs, 'Why should we not revive our old Eastern policy [*Drang nach Osten*] under the flag of an anti-Bolshevist crusade?'

The Baltic Landeswehr had an important role to play in von der Goltz's calculations. The Balts felt themselves to be German, but they had the additional advantage of having lived in Latvia for 600 years. However much the indigenous Letts might hate them, the Balts could be represented as fighting for the survival of their adopted country. The Landeswehr (which means a militia or home-guard) had been raised initially by the Balts themselves from among the Baltic Barons and their retainers in Latvia and Estonia, and had been taken over by

Map 1 The Baltic in 1919

von der Goltz to stiffen the retreating Lettish army. The force was
equipped and paid by him, and led by officers from his own command.
They numbered about 6,000 men. Alexander grew to love them. 'It was
an honour', he said, 'to command a force consisting of nothing but
gentlemen', and in later life he remarked that they were the best troops
whom he had ever had under his orders. But in the early stages of the
Baltic war they gave the Allies much trouble. While nominally acting

in conjunction with the Lettish army, they threw into the sea the military equipment which the Allies had landed for the Letts, and in April 1919 attempted to overthrow the Lettish Government of Ulmanis and executed thousands of Letts with the excuse that they were collaborating with the Reds. Many of them perhaps were. Von der Goltz feigned ignorance of this coup, pretending, as occasion suited him, that the Landeswehr were independent of his command, while using them as an instrument and front for his own ambitions.

Tallents and Alexander left Warsaw at the end of May 1919 by train for Danzig. It was a special train, an engine drawing a single coach. 'Have you ever driven a train?' Alexander asked his companions. 'Get in.' They mounted the cab, and Alexander, whose only previous experience of locomotives had been on the Clogher Valley railway when he was aged ten, drove them across the Polish corridor to Danzig, where the German staff officer vainly looked for the British party in the coach, only to find them descending behind him from the engine, without any explanation, as if this was their normal means of travel. From Danzig they went by destroyer to Latvia. They could not land at Riga, the capital, because it was occupied by the Bolsheviks. They landed at the lesser port of Libau, then the seat of the provisional Government of Ulmanis, but in effect under the control of von der Goltz. Such was the insolence of the Germans, who were behaving like an army of occupation, that Ulmanis and his ministers had taken refuge aboard a British warship in the harbour.

In early June 1919 the Germans advanced with Allied consent to capture Riga from the Bolsheviks. The Landeswehr were in the van of the attack, supported by a mixed force of White Russians and Letts. The assault succeeded, and von der Goltz drove on into Estonia to complete his Baltic conquest, only to find himself opposed by Estonian troops, nominally on his own side, but even more anxious to save their country from German occupation than Bolshevik. Tallents sent Alexander (who was still 'Relief Adviser' to the mission, but was used by Tallents as a political and military scout) to see what was happening. He landed at Riga on 5 June, and set up an office in the Ritterhaus, the great hall of the Baltic Barons and the symbol of their power. On notepaper headed 'Central Committee of the Communist Party of Latvia' he wrote home:

I have been living in Riga under German rule for about a fortnight, making reports secretly on all conditions of life and the pulse of the people. It is not particularly pleasant, as the Germans are anything but the beaten Hun as we knew him. I nearly got into some proper rows with German officers in cabarets – revolver-drawing and all that type of thing. The Germans would come to sing patriotic songs outside our windows. Finally I had to leave the town at an hour's notice in a motor, travelling from Riga to Libau in five hours.

From Libau he went by sea to Revel (now Tallin) in Estonia, and was attached for a week to the White Russian army of some 16,000 men under General Yudenitch, who was planning an advance on Petrograd with arms supplied by the Allies. With Yudenitch he visited the whole front, and then left him at Helsingfors (Helsinki) to return to Revel. During his absence, the British mission had moved to Riga, and was engaged in an attempt to restore peace between the Estonians and Germans, who were still fighting a dozen miles outside the town. Tallents could not allow this war-within-a-war to continue. Estonia was clear of Bolsheviks, and the German advance had no legitimate purpose. So, accompanied by Alexander, Tallents set out to arrange an armistice. We have Alexander's own account:

We set off in a special train at midnight and reached a point about five miles behind the Estonian lines. Here once again we heard the rat-tat of the machine guns and the music of the artillery. We crossed the lines in a motor flying the Union Jack and a white flag, and stopped at a school-house about 100 yards behind the German lines at Strasdenhof. Here we met representatives of the Estonians, the Landeswehr, the Letts and Russians. The conference started at 9 p.m. and at 3.30 next morning the armistice was signed.

It was a terrific struggle to get the different sides to agree, but Tallents was marvellous and pulled it off, although several times I thought it was impossible. The whole proceedings were very dramatic. We all sat round a table in a bare room with candles flickering in the draught. On our side, Tallents, tremendously alert and businesslike; Victor Warrender of the Grenadiers, cool and correct; Harrison, our shorthand typist, rather journalistic; Colonel du Parquet the Frenchman, obviously not understanding a word of the discussion in English, but looking frightfully formal and severe; Colonel Dawley, the American, making long-winded speeches entirely off the point, and getting rather snubbed by the Germans; the Estonian, frightfully suspicious and not at all anxious to sign an armistice but longing to get at the throats of the Germans.

Then the Germans: three typical officers, one Major von Westenhagen, with an iron face; Captain von Jagow (spokesman for the Landeswehr), a typical diplomatic soldier; and Count von Donach, who was formerly personal ADC to the Crown Prince.

By the terms of the Strasdenhof armistice, the Estonians agreed to stay their ground, and the Germans to withdraw from Riga within forty-eight hours, and from the whole of Latvia by the end of October. It was a great triumph for Tallents's diplomacy. The Germans left the city for Mittau, twelve miles away, within the stipulated time, their withdrawal supervised by Alexander, and a few days later he was at the quayside in Riga to welcome Ulmanis back to the capital. Now that the German threat was at least temporarily removed, nothing remained but to clear the remaining Bolsheviks out of Latvia and to make certain that von der Goltz kept his word by withdrawing his entire force from the country.

To deal with the Bolsheviks three antagonistic forces must be induced to cooperate – the White Russians, the Lettish national army, and the Landeswehr. The first two presented little problem, so long as the future status of Latvia was not raised. But what should be done with the Landeswehr? They were willing enough to fight the Bolsheviks, but were known German sympathisers, and at the first sign of trouble might desert the Letts to rejoin von der Goltz. It was to forestall this possibility that Tallents decided that the Landeswehr must be removed from von der Goltz's control, and placed under the command of an Allied officer. The only alternative was to disband them, but they were the most experienced anti-Bolshevik force available. So Tallents, in consultation with Sir Herbert Gough, head of the British military mission in Riga, decided to dismiss the German commander of the Landeswehr, a Major Fletcher (whose unlikely name was said to come from a Scottish ancestor), and appoint a British commander in his place. They chose Alexander.

Gough and I talked the question over [Tallents wrote in his autobiography] and decided that Alexander was the right, indeed the only, man for this particularly difficult command. He was already well-liked and trusted by both Balts and Letts. Irish blood and Irish experience both helped him. . . . So I agreed to spare Alex, and we arranged a meeting for him with the leaders of the Landeswehr. This seemed promising. Major Fletcher, I heard, behaved very well in the background at this point. He discouraged all suggestion of opposition, and urged his men to accept the new régime with good heart.[1]

It was an astonishing twist in Alexander's career. He had been sent first to Poland, then to Latvia, to distribute Allied alms to the victims of war. Instead, he found himself employed in military reconnaissance deep in Baltic lands, a solitary British soldier sandwiched between Germans, White Russians and Bolsheviks, and was then thrown into intricate political negotiation, of which he had had no experience, between hostile groups of whom he had never previously heard. Now he was to command the equivalent of a brigade, officered for the most part by his ex-enemies of the Western front, whose loyalty to him and to the remote country which they were jointly serving was in grave doubt. He was to campaign in the Latvian hinterland, cut off from his base at Riga by over a hundred miles, and expel the Bolsheviks. He was only twenty-seven.

Of course he was delighted by the opportunity. His very eagerness was one reason why he was acceptable to the Balts. Another was his obvious military professionalism. A third was that, like them, he was born and bred in the aristocratic tradition. One must add a fourth – the personal attraction he had for soldiers of all nations. He possessed this quality in an unusual degree. He had already given proof of it when he commanded his own Irishmen in the First War, and it was to hold together a great Allied army in the Second. Alexander's charm consisted partly in his capacity, as Kipling had said, to dress every crisis in high comedy. He was amused by difficulties, conveyed his amusement, and so dissipated them. It was partly the combination of modesty and audacity in his demeanour, his instinctive regard for other men's feelings, his willingness to give credit when it was earned. It was partly his innocence. Victor Warrender (later Lord Bruntisfield) has given me this instance of it. When he and Alexander entered Riga, they went to the city-gaol to release the political prisoners. Among them were two fine-looking girls. Alexander suggested that they should take them into the British Mess to cook and serve. His brother-officer remarked that this might be misunderstood. 'Oh surely not,' replied Alexander. 'Nobody would ever imagine that.' 'He never really grew up', commented Lord Bruntisfield long afterwards. 'He was a knight in armour, a paragon of chivalry, and he imagined that everyone else was too.'

Never were these qualities put to a greater test than when he took over command of the Landeswehr on 25 July 1919. He arrived at their headquarters at Tuckhum, west of Riga, and was received with great courtesy. Major Fletcher handed over the force with good grace, requesting him 'to take the German Baltic people and German Baltic culture, as far as lies in your power, under your protection'.

My orders [Alexander later recollected] were that all pure Germans were to leave the Landeswehr immediately. When I got to Tuckhum, I found that my chief of Staff [Baron Woffert von Rahden] was a German, and all three battalions were commanded by Germans. If all the Germans left the force, it would just break up. So I didn't answer my orders from higher authority, and said, 'Any Germans who want to stop and fight with me against the Reds can do so, provided that they will let me replace them by indigenous Balts when I can.' A lot went back: some stayed, and I ended up with a force of about 6,000, paid by the Letts, and under Lettish supreme command, but retaining some of their German officers and most of their German equipment.

There was no language difficulty. Alexander could speak good German and some Russian. The Balts were educated country gentlemen, equally fluent in English, German, French and Russian, but mostly they spoke German.

Relations between the Balts, Letts and Estonians were still very bad. They had been fighting each other until a few weeks before Alexander assumed command, and his task, as the neutral commander, was extremely difficult. At first many obstacles were put in his way. Pay, and supplies of food and clothing, did not arrive as the Letts had promised, and the Allies had nothing with which to make good the deficiencies. The German army still in western Latvia showed no sign of leaving. Von der Goltz's camp at Mittau was only thirty miles from Tuckhum. Some of Alexander's German officers were in secret communication with him, and the entire force was exposed to incessant German propaganda.

Alexander dealt with this problem in three ways. First he removed from the Landeswehr the Germans known to be in close touch with von der Goltz. Secondly, he reorganized it into manageable units, forming three battalions and a cavalry squadron, to occupy his officers' minds with administration and leave less room for politics. Thirdly, he moved the Landeswehr as far as possible from German influence by requesting the Lettish high command to allot him a sector on the Bolshevik front in southern-central Latvia, where they would be divided from the Lettish forces by the River Dwina but faced by a common enemy. The Landeswehr were not easily persuaded to move.

They suspected that the Letts might order them into a suicidal battle, and missed the comforting proximity of von der Goltz. Alexander told them that so long as he was in command, the Letts would never dare harm them. He had a private talk with each officer individually, and put to them the alternatives of resignation from the Landeswehr or a pledge of loyalty to himself. The great majority gave the pledge. His Adjutant, Baron Joachim von Hahn, has given this description of Alexander's methods:

He was intelligent and understood quickly and instinctively, and thought things out with exceptional clarity and logic. His education had been typically English and, therefore, pragmatic. . . . For Germany he had sympathy and a high opinion of her army. . . . Politically he believed in democracy. I often discussed it with him, and he explained to me the system of democracy in Britain and North America. He stressed the need for us to reckon, in the circumstance in which we found ourselves, with this form of government, if we expected support from the West. . . . It was no good, he thought, to insist on ancient rights to property, to be guided by former political privilege and to live on the memories of past services rendered in the history of one's country. This way of thinking was out of date.[2]

At the end of August 1919, the Landeswehr moved from Tuckhum by train and bullock-cart to the area of Kreutzberg (Krustpils), where they took over twenty-five miles of the Lettish front. At that stage there was very little fighting. The Bolsheviks were on the defensive, holding a series of fortified villages, and the front lines were separated by as much as three or four miles. Alexander put the Landeswehr through an intensive course of training, forming a battle-school for his NCOs, and then tried out his ideas in a series of small-scale patrols and raids against enemy lines. The Landeswehr soon proved that they were the most professional force in Latvia, on either side. The staff were efficient, the men German-equipped and German-trained. It was compact and highly organized. The battalions were respectively 1,200, 950 and 850 strong, still under their German commanders, and each was divided into three infantry companies and a machine-gun company, with its own cavalry detachment and a battery of four field-guns. They were supported by a headquarters unit of signallers, engineers, medical services, a horsed supply-column, and a squadron of eight light 'planes. In the British Army it would have been called a Brigade Group. Alexander called it 'a very nice commando'.

By 3 October the Landeswehr were sufficiently well prepared and cohesive for serious operations, and Alexander led them into a major raid against the fortified village of Lievenhof. Following an artillery barrage, they attacked the position frontally and captured it, penetrating ten miles beyond and holding off a three-day Bolshevik counterattack. This operation had a double purpose: to raise the morale of the Landeswehr and confidence in his own leadership; and to restore some degree of unity between them and the Lettish army which attacked alongside them. All had gone very well. But then two disasters struck almost simultaneously. On 7 October 1919 the Germans and White Russians, commanded by an adventurer called Count Avolov-Bermondt, but under the secret orders of von der Goltz, attacked Riga in force, and having occupied a large part of the town were only driven out by the Letts in a three-week battle supported by British naval gunfire. The loyalty of the Landeswehr was put under its greatest strain. Their Lettish allies of the Lievenhof battle were now fiercely engaged with their German allies of the Riga battles in June, and there was no doubt on whose side the Landeswehr's sympathies lay. There was a serious danger that a great number of them would desert. Alexander's personality, and the affection which he had already gained, won the day. One of his officers said to Walter Duranty, then a correspondent of the *New York Times* in Riga:

We wanted to march on Riga, and perhaps we ought to have done it in our own interests, because those damned Letts had seized our estates and it was not likely that the British or French would do much for us to get them back, as the Germans would have done. But in that case we should have had to knock Alexander on the head, and we liked him far too much, so we stayed quiet in our trenches, and von der Goltz retreated.[3]

Tallents confirmed this tribute in a despatch to the Foreign Secretary, Lord Curzon:

The fact that the Landeswehr was commanded by Alexander, firstly at the time when it was separated from General von der Goltz's troops, and later during the Bermondt attack, prevented, in my opinion, possibly civil war in Latvia, and certainly a dangerous and inflammable situation.

Two days later, during this critical test of his control, Alexander was wounded, for the third and last time in his career. He was approaching the captured village of Lievenhof when one of his own sentries challenged him, and without waiting for a reply, fired at a range of sixty yards. The bullet entered his side and came out in his back. He was in hospital in Riga for a fortnight while the battle raged about him. It was a fortuitous opportunity for the Balts to abandon him. Their loyalty held despite his absence, and he returned to the front in late October to resume command. In the same month one menace was removed when von der Goltz's troops finally left Latvia.

Winter was coming, and with it the planned general offensive against the Bolsheviks. Alexander appealed to his Aunt Margaret in England:

My men have only got old torn uniforms, years old, no gloves, no scarves, no greatcoats, just the old worn-out clothes they stand up in, and the weather is getting bitterly cold. Today, 11 November, it is ten degrees below zero, with biting winds. I am sure there must be stacks of woollen clothes left over from the Great War if one knows where to lay one's hands on them. Anything and everything is acceptable. I myself know of no actual organisation, but I am sure that you do. It means so much to our poor fellows.

A shipload of clothing was sent out from England to Latvia, but Alexander wrote back sadly:

It had to fit out the whole of the Lettish army of about 30,000 men, and there was very little left over for us. My little army was at war with the Letts in last July, and so you can imagine that now we get very little from them in the way of comforts. Still, I have managed to collect, by every means, enough to keep them more or less from being frozen to death. We have taken a lot off the Bolshevik prisoners whom we have taken lately.

It was in these conditions that the general offensive was launched on 11 January 1920.

The Landeswehr advanced on a front of fifteen miles, flanked by the much larger forces of the Letts on their left, and the Poles on their right, and were themselves under the command of the Courland Division of the Lettish army. Their object was to free from Bolshevik control the whole of Lettgallen, the eastern province of Latvia. The Landeswehr sector included the capital, Rjeshiza (now Rezekne). Alexander had by then raised his force to a pitch of great efficiency and high morale, and while the claim that the Landeswehr 'liberated Latvia singlehanded' is not true, there is no doubt that their contribution was the major one. Step by step throughout January they advanced against sporadic resistance and gradually drove the Bolsheviks back over the Latvian frontier into Russia. Rjeshiza was captured on 21 January 1920, and the frontier was reached on the last day of the month. They had advanced 100 miles in twenty days, captured over 800 prisoners, at the cost of only twenty-nine casualties, eight of whom were killed.

These statistics may suggest that the fighting was not very severe, nor the enemy very stubborn. It is true that the young Communists opposing them were home-sick and ill-organized, and that at no stage was there a pitched battle of any great intensity. But it was the only successful offensive against the Bolsheviks in the whole history of Allied intervention. It was won by the superior skill of the Landeswehr in their coordination of all arms, and by following the Bolshevik retreat before they could regain their balance. Weather conditions were more severe than the fighting. Alexander found time to write home this description:

January 25th 1920. We are in the middle of our offensive just now, and have covered about fifty to sixty miles since the beginning of the month. We find it extremely difficult to get forward, as the snow is so deep that all the roads have disappeared, and the guns get stuck in the snow. Everything has to be carried on sledges, even the men, as it is impossible to march more than a few miles. It is now the coldest time of the year, and the temperature is 28 degrees below zero. It is so cold that you get frostbitten unless you cover up everything.

His men suffered terribly from the cold and poor diet, and there was much sickness in their ranks. But the conditions had been familiar to them since birth, and they were hardy. The country was very open, snowbound and icebound. All transport was by sleigh. The lakes and rivers were frozen hard enough to support the movement of artillery, but Alexander's few aircraft were unusable. As they approached the railway-line at Rjeshiza there was the novelty of a Russian armoured train, which withdrew, after bombardment, trailing blood. Usually the troops were required to attack against machine-guns up ridges devoid of cover and knee-deep in snow. Their extreme hardships were made more endurable by Alexander's own example. He was seen everywhere, by car when the roads were passable, on horseback when they were not, on foot when even the horses were exhausted. Late at night he would attend divisional conferences to receive his orders, and early next morning interpret them to his front-line troops. Daily he confirmed his verbal orders in writing, by himself in English, then in German translation by his staff. The advance was always resumed at dawn. He seemed tireless. But it was his precision, his good humour, and his courage under fire, that won the unhesitating acceptance of his orders by men who had as great an experience of war as himself.

The drawing reproduced at the foot of this page was made by one of his officers, and was kept by Alexander among his papers to remind him of one of the most exhilarating months of his life. It illustrates in semi-caricature, which is not inappropriate, the nature of the campaign. The sufferings of the Landeswehr were mitigated by their sense of comedy. Every contemporary account speaks of the day's battle as if it were a hunting expedition. They were all friends, united by kinship and danger, and by a lighthearted attitude to the enemy and even to the desperate cause for which they were fighting. It was a serious business, but it was not serious warfare. The enemy was untrained and un-certain, a crowd of peasants for whom the aristocratic Landeswehr felt emotions of mingled affection and contempt.

Alexander shared their mood. Typically he designed for himself a special uniform: a soft, peaked cap with the Landeswehr rosette set

prominently over the visor, a blouse-like tunic with a simple high collar, breeches and jack-boots. On his shoulder-straps he wore the insignia of a Colonel in the German Army. In the coldest weather he threw a heavy sheepskin coat over this strange medley of Polish, Russian and German military dress. He was often to be seen thus attired in the van of the advance, firing his rifle from horseback or from a borrowed sleigh, leading a small party through the pine-forests to appear behind a nest of sharp-shooters, or directing with his cane the attack of an entire battalion. As resistance lessened, his daring increased. Once he marched for a whole night with a handful of followers to intercept a munition-column. He took his prisoners to a peasant's house for rest and warmth, and waited with them until his own men caught up with him. They had given him up for lost. They found him sketching the scene inside the house, a drawing which he later copied for his mother. 'There is a great brick stove along one wall', he explained in a caption, 'and they never open the windows. The stove is a huge thing, on which

the whole family sleeps – wives, children and all – because it remains warm for twenty-four hours after the fire has gone out. Very unhealthy, but undoubtedly pleasant.'

When the campaign was over the Landeswehr settled down on the Latvian-Russian border to await the result of the political negotiations that followed. On 2 February Alexander wrote to his Aunt Margaret:

We are in a beautiful piece of country here, the borders of Latvia and Russia. The country is quite hilly and dotted with fir forests and lakes. I am going everywhere on skis. One can go twenty miles a day easily. Since our offensive, the Bolsheviks have become quite tame. I and four other officers rode up to one of their villages and they just stood and looked at us and never fired a shot. We are only waiting for the moon to rise to go wolf-hunting.

Sometimes I go to Riga. The military mission gave a dance at the Ritterhaus. There was an international crowd of people – Balts, Letts, Russians, Poles and English. This sort of war is ideal. Fancy fighting a battle yesterday in the snow, and next evening dancing in a brilliant gathering in Riga, then back again to the front next day! I should love to come back and see you all, but I want to go to the Caucasus if I can. What an opportunity for people who are fond of adventure! I think I was born just at the right time.

To his Uncle Norbury he wrote:

February 22nd 1920. I have men serving as private soldiers here under the most terrible conditions, who were immensely wealthy before the war and owned hundreds of thousands of acres and a castle. But it was all destroyed in the Big War or by the Bolsheviks. Amazing. The same fellows are now quite cheerful, but after this country, England seems like a garden, so small, compact and beautifully cultivated.

More seriously he wrote to Lady Jane van Koughnet:

March 15th 1920. I think I am going to try to buy an estate here. A couple of thousand pounds would get a place of several thousand acres and a nice house. I really think it is worthwhile, as the country is very rich, especially in timber.

Alexander was a romantic. Every new experience stimulated his appetite for more. With his capacity to identify himself with the troubles of others he felt compassion for the men he led, for the men he defeated, for the peasants whose land he ravaged. It stemmed from his boyhood intimacy with the families on the Caledon estate. He understood peasant simplicity and respected their work and homes. He had a

64

feeling for landscape – as a painter, as a countryman, as a humanist – and comprehended the deep truth that

> Nature, tender enemy, harsh friend,
> Takes from them soon the little that she gave.

Latvia had meant to him a people's fumbling, inarticulate struggle for independence – independence from the Russians whom he fought, from the Balts whom he commanded, from the Germans with whom he had briefly fraternized. Politically he was uncommitted; militarily he had given all his skill and experience to the Balts; but emotionally his deepest ties lay with the peasant Letts. He felt for Latvia something of what Byron had felt for Greece. He saw himself as 'Oberst Alexander, Baltic Baron' (as he once signed jocularly to his mother), and he could conceive, if only for a moment, settling in this distant land to create a Baltic Caledon where people would work for him in freedom and happiness. Soon he recognized the idea as ridiculous. He had no money to buy an estate, and the dream, if realized, would not have satisfied his ambition. The two strands in his character are illustrated by a final quotation from his Baltic letters:

I hope to get home on leave soon, but I very much want to come back and fight against the Reds. I love this country, and I should like to live here.

In March 1920 Alexander gave up his command. By the terms of the Armistice with the Soviets, Latvia was given her independence. The Landeswehr was converted into the 30th Tuckhum Regiment of the Latvian Army. Alexander's farewell to his troops was marked by unforced and unrestrained tributes to his achievement. The three leaders of the German Baltic political parties wrote to him a joint letter:

In July last year you undertook the command of the Baltic Landeswehr. At that time the political and military situation was very confused, which made your task no easier. In a few months you captured the hearts of all our people by your friendliness and chivalrous attitude, by your courage and your skill. You led the Landeswehr in a successful campaign against the Bolsheviks, and the troops under your command won undying laurels in the fight to liberate Lettgallen.

The assembly of German Baltic parties in Latvia, who represent all our people, convey to you our profound thanks for your unselfish leadership, and assure you that so long as Balts inhabit Latvia, your name and achievement will never be forgotten among us.

At a farewell dinner on 20 March 1920 Alexander addressed the Landeswehr for the last time. His final gesture was to send his combat-flag to Major Fletcher, with the characteristic message, 'This combat-flag should be in the hands of one who has led the Landeswehr from victory to victory.' Latvia awarded him the Baltic Cross of Honour, and General Yudenitch, whose attack on Petrograd had been as great a failure as Alexander's offensive had been a success, gave him the Order of St Anne with Swords. 'Just between you and me', he wrote to his mother, 'I have grown to like the Landeswehr just as much as my own regiment. It is very sad to leave such nice fellows. Still, life is full of bitter partings.'

It is not quite the end of the Baltic story. In later years Alexander attended several reunion dinners of the Landeswehr, and often corresponded with its officers. Then the Second War separated him from them. Many fought again on the German side, and without great surprise recognized in the opposing Field Marshal their Colonel of the Landeswehr. He met at least one of them in a prisoner-of-war camp in Italy. When the war was over he received pathetic appeals from survivors among them. Their country was once more destroyed by war, their independence once more lost. Alexander did what he could for them. As Governor General of Canada he managed to secure immigration visas for a handful of Balts who had served with him. But most remained in exile, and looked back to the days of 1919–20 as their happiest and most glorious, when Alexander was their commander.

4

CONSTANTINOPLE AND
INDIA (1921-38)

Alexander returned from the Baltic in May 1920, having been away for just over a year. He had avoided what he had most dreaded, the anticlimax of occupied Germany, and had stored away the memory of a concentrated experience which must have been the envy of his brother officers. The only remaining battalion of the Irish Guards was then stationed at Aldershot. He became its second-in-command, under Colonel T. E. Vesey, with the rank of Major. In such ways does the Army remind its most successful officers that eccentric adventures are no short-cut to regimental advancement, and that it is only in the higher ranks and in wartime that merit can leap-frog mediocrity.

The inter-war years were for Alexander no flatter than for most regular officers. He had enjoyed, and was still to enjoy, more than his fair share of opportunity. The First War came at exactly the right time to make full use of his youthful energies, the Second to coincide with his prime. Of the twenty years between, he spent eight on active service abroad, and rose in rank from Major to Major-General. Meanwhile he was content to have two years in regimental duties with his original battalion, first at Aldershot, then at Windsor. He had a great deal of leave. He went to Caledon, Switzerland and Scotland, pursuing his many sports and interests. There are few records of this period. There is no need for them. His activities can be presumed.

In April 1922 the battalion was sent to Constantinople under Alexander's command. He succeeded Colonel Vesey only a few days before their departure, at a parade in Windsor which was inspected by the King. A week later, in the train travelling to Southampton, he restored to his shoulder-strap the crown and star of a Lieutenant-

Colonel. He was now at last entitled to the substantive rank which he had held temporarily and at intervals since 1915.

Constantinople was not a peace-station, nor was there openly a state of war. The dangerous situation which had suddenly arisen had its origins in 1915, when the Allies promised Greece, in return for her participation in the war, a slice of Turkey. That slice was Smyrna, on the Aegean coast. When peace came, the Greeks cashed their voucher, and with Allied encouragement occupied Smyrna in May 1919. The Turks, who had hitherto reacted calmly to their defeat and accepted without trouble Allied occupation of Constantinople and the straits, strongly resented the annexation of a Turkish town by the most hated and despised of their enemies. Mustapha Kemal, their hero of Gallipoli, raised in Asiatic Turkey a formidable army of veterans, supported by a National Assembly at Ankara which he declared independent of the Sultan. There were thus two Turkeys: the Sultan's Government in Constantinople which the Allies recognized, and the breakaway Kemalists in Anatolia. Just as the Allies in the Baltic had used the Germans to overthrow the Bolsheviks, now they encouraged the Greeks under Venizelos to crush the dissident Turks. Venizelos was only too willing. In June 1920 the Greek forces advanced from Smyrna to attack Kemal, guaranteeing that 'within a few weeks they will sweep the Kemalists from the zone of the straits, both in Europe and Asia'.

It seemed at first that they would succeed. By July they had taken Adrianople in Thrace and joined forces with the tiny Allied garrison on the Ismid peninsula across the narrow strip of the Bosphorus. Lloyd George told the House of Commons, 'The Turks are broken beyond repair.' Then King Constantine of Greece, who had collaborated with the Germans throughout the war, returned to Athens, and Venizelos fell from power. The Greeks lost their dynamic leader, the Allies their friend. The morale of the Greeks dropped sharply, while Kemal's army was constantly growing in strength by desertions from the Sultan. Winter came, bringing terrible sufferings to the Greeks on the Anatolian steppes, but in the early summer of 1921, they again advanced against Kemal, and at the Sakarya River fought a battle which lasted twenty-two days and nights. In the end it was the Greeks who retreated, but they were able to maintain their positions in central Turkey throughout a second winter. In the spring of 1922, when the war was still in the balance, the Irish Guards joined the Allied forces in Constantinople.

At that stage the Allies were uninvolved in the Graeco-Turkish war.

They were in Constantinople as an occupying force pending a final peace-treaty, and their role was to keep order in the city and defend it against attack from any quarter. In 1920 there had been no enemy in sight. In 1922 there were potentially two. Mustapha Kemal might at any moment threaten the capital from the east. The Greeks might try to forestall him by advancing on it from the west. Within months of the battalion's arrival, each did so.

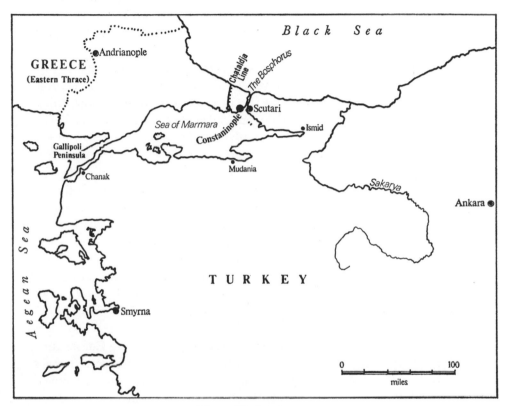

Map 2 Turkey in 1922

When the Irishmen landed at Constantinople on 12 May 1922, there was no atmosphere of panic in the city. The war was simmering 100 miles away, and Kemal's immediate objective was Smyrna, not Constantinople. The battalion marched peacefully through the streets to the Tash Kishla barracks in the European quarter of Pena, and the inaugural salute was taken by General Sir Charles Harington, the

Allied Commander-in-Chief. They found the barracks filthy, and their first task was house-cleaning. The men were lodged in permanent buildings, their officers in Nissen huts. To compensate for the poorness of their quarters the weather was lovely and the view superb. They looked from their heights across the Bosphorus to the Asiatic shore, and in the historic half-mile strip of water below them lay six battle-ships of the Allied fleet. The ships were the most impressive demonstration of Allied power, for on land there were only ten infantry battalions, three British, six French, and one Italian, with some gunners and engineers, and a handful of RAF 'planes, a total of 7,600 men.

The Irish Guards soon made their presence felt. Ceremonially they held public parades; tactically they guarded various vital points like the Turkish armoury, to prevent the weapons and ammunition falling into rebel hands; socially they began to discover the attractions of the town. It contained a polyglot population, for among the $1\frac{1}{2}$ million inhabitants were 400,000 Greeks and some 90,000 White Russians, survivors of General Wrangel's defeated army evacuated from the Crimea. The soldiers on the whole preferred the Turks. The officers, especially Alexander, sought the company of the Russians. Both disliked the Greeks. They knew that at the slightest provocation the three communities would be at each other's throats. There was a spice of danger, but it did not prevent officers and men from enjoying themselves. For the veterans of the First War it was not serious soldiering. During their sixteen months in Constantinople, the Irish Guards had only a single fatal casualty, a guardsman drowned while bathing in the sea.

At two moments it looked like war. In August 1922 King Constantine informed the British Ambassador in Athens that 'the only way to restore peace was to occupy Constantinople by Greek forces', and he moved two divisions from the Anatolian front to join those already in eastern Thrace. If the Greeks could take the capital from this new direction, they would have outwitted Mustapha Kemal in Asiatic Turkey. The large Greek minority in the city would certainly help them. General Harington, a soldier with marked political gifts who distrusted politicians, immediately issued a proclamation that any attack on Constantinople by any army would be opposed by the Allies. To make clear that he meant what he said, he moved part of the Constantinople garrison to the Chataldja lines which lay between the Black Sea and the

Sea of Marmara some thirty miles from the Bosphorus, and units of the fleet in support of them. Among them were the Irish Guards, who on 27 August occupied the eastern end of the line, near the Bunar fort.

The Chataldja line has been described as the strongest natural defence line in Europe. During the Balkan wars of 1912 it had been fortified and held by the Turks against the Bulgarians, and there were still some relics of this battle on the ground, but contemporary accounts and photographs show that the main defences of 1922 were trenches which the guardsmen newly dug. They looked confidently across a great waste of treeless rolling country, awaiting a Greek attack by six divisions which never came. There can be little doubt that the Greeks would ultimately have broken through and captured Constantinople if they had tried. Opposing them were only six British battalions and some French colonial infantry on a front of thirty miles. But pawns have their role in war as well as in chess. They stake a claim, and if threatened, the stronger pieces move rapidly across the board to their support, and both opponents know this. In London, in Paris, in Athens, the Greeks were warned to consider carefully the consequences of an attack. Was the possibility of capturing Constantinople worth the certainty that it would bring three major powers into the war against them? King Constantine withdrew. Not a single Greek soldier had appeared in the sights of an Irish rifle. The battalion were absent from their barracks for only two weeks, and even in the field they were able to sleep under canvas. 'To some extent', wrote Alexander, 'it has been a boon, for it has given the men something else to think and talk about.'

It was now September 1922. In that month there was a dramatic change in the fortunes of the Greeks. Mustapha Kemal took advantage of the withdrawal of their two divisions to launch a major offensive against the Greek Army in Anatolian Turkey. On 9 September he entered Smyrna. The fate of the Greek soldiers and civilians was terrible. They lost 30,000 dead and 40,000 prisoners. The town itself, except for the Turkish quarter, was razed by fire. Allied warships in the harbour, though officially neutral, took off what Greek survivors they could, and landed them in Athens, a beaten army fit only to disperse to their homes. It was the end of Greek ambitions for a new empire on the far side of the Aegean. More seriously, it released Kemal's troops for the conquest of the parts of his country still in the Sultan's hands and under Allied protection – Constantinople itself and the neutral zone which extended each side of the narrows. 'I shall be obliged to march on Constantinople with my army,' said Kemal, 'which would be an affair of only a few days.'

Half the Irish Guards battalion remained in Constantinople, where there were known to be 20,000 armed Turks waiting to support Kemal, while the other half moved across the Bosphorus to hold the ridge of hills above Scutari. They were not quite alone. Two other battalions were already in position, attempting to hold a line fifty miles long, and the fleet was behind them, but Kemal had at his disposal victorious troops twenty times their numbers. Alexander took this threat as calmly as he had taken the very similar threat at Chataldja, even when the message reached him that the Turks were advancing with 30,000 cavalry and 20,000 infantry. His brother William was in local command across the narrows, and having but two companies to defend a front which needed a whole division, he posted his sections at intervals to keep watch on the ground ahead and secured his line of retreat by commandeering barges on the Scutari waterfront. A photograph of Alexander shows him supervising the digging of trenches on the new line, dressed in peacetime uniform and accompanied by the wife of one of his officers. In the background on the grass is a lunch-hamper. Harington was equally unruffled. When he was asked by the War Office to explain why he thought it necessary to occupy the Asiatic shore when the Bosphorus lay between it and Constantinople, he replied, 'Because I swim the Bosphorus every morning before breakfast.' There was a real danger that the Turks would slip across in small boats to be welcomed by their army of supporters on the far side.

The crisis did not, however, develop at Scutari. There the Turks kept their distance. It developed at Chanak, on the south shore of the Dardanelles facing Gallipoli. Here the British held a small base, a token of their claim to control both sides of the narrows. Kemal sent troops from Smyrna to grimace at the British through the wire and for two weeks seemed on the point of attacking them. The threat created the most dangerously explosive crisis during Alexander's whole tour of duty in the Middle East. If Chanak had been attacked, Britain would once again have been at war with Turkey, and the Constantinople garrison exposed to the greatest peril. The British Cabinet were convinced that the narrow sea-route from the Mediterranean to the Black Sea was a vital British interest and Chanak a test of their determination to safeguard it. They ordered General Harington to tell Mustapha Kemal that if he did not at once withdraw from Chanak,

British troops would open fire. Harington did not deliver the ultimatum. He kept it in his pocket, and telegraphed to London for permission to use his own judgement. Without waiting for an answer, he arranged a conference with the Kemalists at Mudania, at which an armistice was signed on 11 October. The terms were that the Kemalists should withdraw fifteen miles from Chanak and the British their line above Scutari. Kemal would be permitted to occupy eastern Thrace. The Greeks would stop fighting the Turks. The Allies would remain in Constantinople only until a peace-treaty was signed, and it was implicit in the armistice that Kemal would soon be allowed to enter the capital as its master.

Alexander was now able to reunite his battalion on the European shore. There was only one further incident, the fall of the curtain on 500 years of Ottoman rule. The Sultan Mehmed Vahid ed Din abdicated. Alexander had seen him once only, when he made his weekly royal procession from the Dolma Bagtche Palace to prayers in the Great Mosque, and described him as 'terribly ill, very old, very unimpressive, a pathetic figure'. His ministers had condemned Mustapha Kemal to death in absence, but after the Mudania armistice the pretence of the Sultan's authority could be maintained no longer. The Sultan appealed to the Allies to save him from assassination by removing him furtively from Constantinople to a safer place. The Grenadiers (who had arrived with a Coldstream battalion in October) took the old man by ambulance to a waiting battleship, and he was given temporary asylum in Malta. At Alexander's suggestion the Irish Guards looked after members of his staff for a few weeks, since they had nowhere else to go.

For nine months more the battalion remained in or near Constantinople, through a bitter winter and a glorious summer. Paper-plans were drawn up to take over the Turkish police stations in case the need arose, but it never did. At the regulation intervals the colours were trooped and the shamrock distributed. The Irishmen came to love Constantinople. There was excellent bathing and boating. Cricket, tennis and athletics occupied the summer, and in winter they played football on a levelled Turkish cemetery. Alexander ran in the brigade mile, which he won easily. There were night-clubs for the officers, beer-gardens and a private cinema for the men. Alexander kept a firm hand on a fairly loose rein. The relaxed atmosphere and the temptations of the city ('filthy drink and filthy women', he reported to his Regimental Lieutenant-Colonel in London) caused him a little trouble at first, but the discipline of the Brigade of Guards and organized games and expeditions soon cured it. Alexander himself took things easily. He spent most evenings in a favourite White Russian restaurant, the Black Rose, and enjoyed the hospitality of the seaside villas of senior officers. For a fortnight he was the guest of the Royal Navy on HMS *Benbow* in a cruise round the Aegean, visiting Troy, Athos and Athens.

He left to his subordinate officers all detailed administration. ('Just tell me at what time I'm supposed to be on parade.') This came to be a well recognized characteristic. He was never greatly interested in the paper-shuffling and automaton stiffness of orderly room routine, and took for granted the logistic arrangements by which his men were fed and clothed, just as he reacted with mild indifference to the political negotiations which would ultimately determine his orders. He had a keener eye for what lay beyond the barrack gates. He was intellectually more curious than the average officer about the countryside, the life of oriental peoples and the monuments of their past. He would wander off alone or with one companion for hours on end. One day, when his battalion were manning the Chataldja lines, he left them to walk with a Dutchman to the Black Sea. By nightfall they had not returned, and a mounted search-party failed to find them. Alexander strolled into the mess at breakfast-time having spent the night in a remote Turkish police-post, and seemed quite unconcerned that within a few hours the battalion were expecting an official visit from their Regimental Lieutenant-Colonel. It was this sort of incident which puzzled his officers and deepened their affection for him. He was unpredictable in small matters, utterly dependable in big. He emphasized his seniority in rank by a capriciousness which he would not tolerate in others. He could appear to mock what he held most dear.

In July 1923 the Treaty of Lausanne was signed, which confirmed Turkish independence under Mustapha Kemal. The Allied garrison was to withdraw in October from Constantinople and the straits. The final scene of embarkation was carefully stage-managed to preserve Allied dignity in face of a Kemalist triumph, but by that time the Irish Guards, except for a colour party left behind to represent them, had sailed for Gibraltar.

'We get sadder and sadder as the days move on to our departure from Constantinople', Alexander had written to his regimental head-quarters. But in Gibraltar there was a new experience, new people, new interests. Families were sent out from England to join their men. There were expeditions to Tangier to buy horses, which they hunted in Spain.

The present airfield was a polo-ground. Alexander went on a long leave to Caledon and skied in Switzerland. There were no political troubles, no threat to the Rock from any direction. They remained there for six months, and then returned to England, to barracks first at Woking, and then in London.

It is only in the biography of a soldier that one is likely to find the years between the ages of thirty-two and forty-two summarized in a few pages. 1924–34 were the bleak years of Alexander's career, but bleak only in the sense that they were spent unadventurously in England on regimental and staff duties, and though he gained some valuable experience from them and edged forward his career by an inch or two, it was not for staff-work nor his conduct at ceremonial parades that he gained in 1934 a prize command in India, but for the reputation he had previously won.

For the first two years he continued to command his battalion of the Irish Guards. One glimpses him bicycling with two friends over his old battlefields of the First War, and noting with amusement that the steep hills and precipitous escarpments which he remembered were in reality nothing but faint swellings in the agricultural scene. In the General Strike, to his great pleasure, he drove another train, between Peterborough and London. Then in 1926 he went to the Staff College at Camberley.

The Staff College had already been suggested to him in 1920, but he had preferred the Baltic; and again in 1924, when he was not admitted. One difficulty was his comparatively advanced age and rank. In 1926 he was thirty-four, and entry into the Staff College was normally at thirty or younger. He was a full Colonel. No other officer on the course ranked higher than Captain, and the instructors were Majors or temporary Lieutenant-Colonels, among them Montgomery, Alan Brooke and Paget. Only the Chief Instructor, Robert Gordon-Finlayson, outranked him. So Alexander was temporarily reduced to the rank of Major, which he thought justified, and paid as such, which he thought mean. He sat the competitive exam, and passed it respectably if not with honour.

There is no surviving account of this first association between the three great commanders of the Second War, Alexander, Montgomery and Alan Brooke, but Gordon-Finlayson has left this impression of Alexander:

I had never met him before, but like all others who met him, I was soon struck by his natural gift for leadership and his uncanny instinct for obtaining quickly and without apparent effort a solution to the many military problems given him to solve. The reason was that he is gifted with a mass of common sense, knows exactly how soldiers react in war, and is entirely practical in everything. He simply cannot be rattled.

A fellow-student, later Major-General Douglas Wimberley, wrote of his 'simplicity, directness and kindness. . . . A lesser man might have been excused for showing some signs of being pleased with himself. But Alex showed no trace of his success in war and peace, and we all respected him enormously.' It is unnecessary to quote other opinions, for they all say the same. There was reserve in his character but no duplicity: he appeared the same person to an intimate friend or a chance acquaintance, and he never changed. He was good-tempered, good-mannered and always believed that the best qualities in a man were his real qualities, an assumption that was certainly true of himself.

Life at the Staff College was lived on two levels, on and off duty. Alexander was particularly well endowed to enjoy the latter. He had natural social gifts, a charming presence and appearance, and a fund of good stories. There was no restriction on leave after working-hours, and his mantelpiece, it was observed with some envy, was crowded with invitations from London hostesses, and at least one from Windsor Castle. At Camberley he rode to the drag-hounds, and played tennis and cricket. Of his work less is now known, for his confidential report is not yet available for publication, and there was no exam at the end of the two-year course to place him in order of merit among his fellows. The purpose of the Staff College was to fit officers for appointments up to the rank of Brigade Major or the equivalent. Instruction was given partly by lectures, partly by tactical exercises on the sand-table or (without troops) on the ground, and partly by acting as umpires in divisional manoeuvres. In the first year much was taught about army organization; in the second there were higher studies, including strategy and cooperation with air and naval forces. From all this Alexander derived much benefit.

When he had passed the Staff College late in 1927, he was appointed to the command of the Irish Guards and the Regimental District, an appointment which demanded from him even less than when he commanded its single battalion. In 1930 he was sent to the Imperial Defence College, where he gained an insight into the broader aspects of strategy, including economics and foreign affairs, and was then posted to the War Office, in the department which dealt with military training.

In the next year he married.

He was thirty-nine. He had been in and out of love several times, and there are women alive today who remember how eagerly they awaited his letters or his arrival, and how disappointingly intermittent were both. When he finally made up his mind to marry, his decision was firm and lifelong. He first met Lady Margaret Bingham, younger daughter of the Earl of Lucan, in May 1931, only five months before their marriage, at the house of Colonel Vesey, his predecessor in command of the 1st Battalion. She was twenty-six. Lord Lucan was a delightful, conventional country gentleman who had commanded a brigade in the First War and for two years was a Conservative Member of Parliament. His family was a happy one. They lived at Laleham in Surrey, and spent occasional holidays at his Irish house, Castlebar in County Mayo. Margaret was sent to school at Notting Hill and then, at seventeen, for a year to France. She was a shy girl, too shy to enjoy the vulnerable role of a débutante, but she was determined to make her way. At the age of nineteen she announced to her astonished parents that she was taking a job. First it was in a hat-shop, where she not only sold hats but made them. Then in an antique-shop. Finally in Mrs Charles Paravicini's estate-agency in Bond Street, where she was one of three girls in charge respectively of houses in London, flats in London, and houses in the country. Margaret took the London houses. It was then that she met Alexander.

He used to find out where my car was parked, and often there would be a lovely bunch of flowers in it when I came out – rather a good way of telling me that he wanted to see me again.

What did you think of him when you first met him?

He was an extremely original person: he was unexpected. He was very easy – and I wasn't. He was a good talker, and had a great sense of humour. He was fun: not in the least like a conventional soldier.

Was he very good-looking?

I suppose he was. I've never really thought about that. He was always very well turned-out in uniform, otherwise he simply didn't mind what he put on. He had style. He wore things at different angles from other people.

How much did you know about his career?

Not a thing. Such was my ignorance of the Army that it wasn't until we were engaged that I read about him in the newspapers and realized that he'd already made a name for himself. He would never talk to me about that sort of thing. I didn't marry Alex because he was a soldier. I married him because he was Alex.

The wedding was in the Guards Chapel on 14 October 1931. There was a Guard of Honour supplied by the regiment, six pages and four bridesmaids, and the Irish Guards pipers. Erik Caledon was best man. But although the wedding was mounted in style, there was no reception, since it was a time of acute unemployment and as a gesture of patriotic self-denial, no more than a small family party saw them off on their honeymoon. They spent a few days in Ashdown Forest at Lord Norbury's house, and then motored to Dartmoor, where fog enveloped them. They went on to Caledon and Derg, and stayed two nights at Tyttenhanger on their way back.

Very soon afterwards Alexander was posted to York as the senior General Staff officer in Northern Command. Few appointments could seem less appetizing to an aspiring soldier. But Alexander was adept at marking time. He accepted as the natural and not unwelcome phenomenon of a military career the slow pace of peacetime soldiering. He had none of Montgomery's ambition to master his profession in an office when service in the field was denied him. He did his duty superbly when opportunity offered, and made no complaint when it didn't. He could be indolent when nothing of much consequence depended upon his industry. Gerald Templer (later Field Marshal Sir Gerald Templer) was his GSO2 at York:

I worked like blazes. I had to. Alex wouldn't do any work, except when he had to, and when he had to, it was on big exercises. Then he'd work like a black. On smaller exercises he used to say to me, 'This is the general object of this exercise, and the main lines of carrying it out. Now draft it.' He would then disappear to his charming house for weeks on end, and paint imaginary portraits of the opposing commanders. Once he produced a newspaper, distributed down to soldier's level while the exercise lasted, called *The Lion of Beverley*. There's imagination for you. It made every soldier on that exercise take an interest.

Was he ambitious?

He was ambitious to do his duty. He was lazy, but not over the essentials. He relied on his staff. If they did something wrong he would pull them up.

The Earl and Countess of Caledon, Alexander's parents

(*above*) Alexander at Caledon as a child

(*below*) Caledon Castle, Co. Tyrone, Northern Ireland

(*above*) The Harrow School Rugger XV in 1910. Alexander is seated on the extreme right. His close friend, Guy Earle, was Captain of the XV, holding the ball
(*below*) The painting with which Alexander won the drawing prize at Harrow when he was aged fifteen

MUTUM EST PICTURA POEMA

(*above*) The First World War. Left to right: Eric Greer, J. S. N. Fitzgerald, and Alexander

(*opposite*) Alexander (right) with a brother officer in the Irish Guards in 1912

How does this look?

(*above*) Commander of The Landeswehr in Latvia, 1919

(*opposite*) Two drawings by Alexander illustrating letters to his family. (*above*) To thank his aunt for sending him a muff to the First War trenches; (*below*) from Latvia, February 1920

Alexander with his wife, Margaret, at Nowshera, India, in 1936

His laziness was a virtue. It meant the capacity to delegate, and in wartime it became a tremendous asset, because it meant that he could relax and unhook.

So York was a period of relaxation. He and Margaret at first lived south of the city at Sandisfield and then moved into the northern suburbs. Sometimes they went to London. They spent a summer's holiday with the Lucans in Suffolk. Alexander hunted, and York was very hospitable. It was a happy time for them both. Their first child was born in October 1932. 'She is the dearest little baby that you have ever seen', wrote Alexander to his mother, as sons have written to their mothers ever since sons could write. They christened her Rose Maureen.

Then came India.

Alexander was appointed early in 1934 to the command of the Nowshera Brigade on the North West Frontier. It was very rare for an officer from the Army in England to be given such a pearl of a command, and for a guardsman it was unprecedented. Nowshera was one of the most coveted appointments for officers of the Indian Army who had spent their whole careers in the Punjab. It was proof that Alexander had been marked many years earlier for quite exceptional promotion. His rapid rise had been for a time an embarrassment to the War Office. He had been too young to command what he was fit to command, and too senior in rank for appointments to which his age suited him. For this paradoxical reason, unparalleled in civilian life, his career had at one moment been in actual jeopardy. But he was too good to waste. Every officer in England and India had heard of Alexander, as at that time they had never heard of Montgomery or Alan Brooke. His career had been not only impeccable, but brilliant. 'We all felt in those days', said Templer, 'that the two up-and-coming men in the Army, one on the British side and one on the Indian, were Alex and Claude Auchinleck. And now they found themselves commanding brigades side by side.'

The two brigades were based respectively on Nowshera and Peshawar, twenty miles apart, at the edge of the uppermost limit of the north Indian plain. Alexander arrived there in April 1934, and his wife followed with Rose in September.

Nowshera [he wrote in his first letter home] is a sort of oasis of trees and gardens in a flat open plain, through which runs the Kabul river. Right round us, and rising straight out of the valley, are the mountains of the North-

West frontier. When the visibility is clear, as it is most mornings, the snow-capped mountains of Afghanistan and Kashmir are clearly visible. Most of them are, I suppose, a hundred miles away. The weather is beautiful, cloudless blue skies, but it is beginning to get almost too hot.

Then immediately, instinctively, having dealt with the landscape, he comments on the life of the people, before saying a word about his brother-officers or his command:

It is most picturesque to see the Indians with their camels and old-fashioned bullock-carts. Probably life hasn't changed in the least during the last two thousand years. One is seeing human existence just as it was in Biblical days.

The Brigadier's official residence (like many others throughout the Empire, and for an obvious reason) was called Flagstaff House. It was a large, cool and airy bungalow built on a Palladian scale, with arched porticos and a garden of six acres. The Alexanders were provided with a dozen servants. They had never lived more grandly, and were expected to maintain a certain style. Every night, whether they were alone or not, they changed for dinner, since the servants would have been shocked by any departure from the code. Margaret's nature was gentle, affectionate, domesticated and undemonstrative. She did her social duty as first lady of the cantonment without any of that self-satisfaction or paramilitary posturing which has turned so many Army wives into skirted replicas of their husbands. 'It is very difficult to meet a lot of new people all in a bunch', she wrote to Alexander's Aunt Jane. 'There are endless horse-shows and dances, of which I manage to avoid all but our local ones.' Her reticence, her unfailing good manners, soon won respect and the privacy she craved. They could not, and did not, hold themselves aloof from the Officers' Club, with its tennis, card-games, golf, polo, bars and dining-room, around which the social life of the cantonment revolved. But they could escape. Alexander painted, and played with his daughter. Sometimes they went to Peshawar; once to stay with the Viceroy in New Delhi. Their life, between manoeuvres and campaigns, was easy and pleasant.

Alexander took his military duties seriously. He knew that he was once again on trial, this time in a country and in circumstances of which he had had no experience while all his subordinate officers were bred to them. There were four battalions in his brigade, three Indian and one British (from the Duke of Wellington's Regiment), a field brigade of artillery and the usual supporting troops. He immediately took a liking to the Indian soldiers:

They are very fine-looking men [he wrote to his brother Erik], very well turned out and smart as paint, and as keen and as quick as lightning in manoeuvre. It is all so different from our soldiers at home, where the men are bored stiff by training. Here a soldier's career is the most honourable profession there is, and a man will almost murder his best friend to gain a lance stripe. The Gurkhas (of course they are not Indian) are grand little men with a tremendous sense of humour, especially as regards the ridiculous.

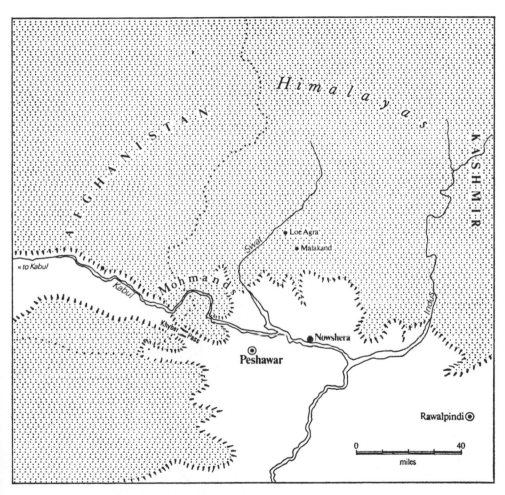

Map 3 The North West Frontier of India

His manner was friendly and natural with all ranks, British and Indian, on and off duty. One of his staff, Geoffrey Bull, recalls two instances of his original approach. Alexander found that the camp reservoir was overflowing, the water running to waste because the men in married quarters were obliged to pay a heavy water-rate, and so rationed themselves. He suggested to the Government of India that the water-meters should be replaced by a flat-rate based on five years' normal consumption. Delhi demurred. Alexander paid no attention, declaring that only two people knew about the Nowshera water-supplies, himself and the Almighty, and as the authorities could not appeal to the Almighty, they should leave the decision to him. He did what he wanted, and thereafter the water flowed. The second incident was more remarkable. Alexander would disappear from his brigade office for hours on end, and his staff at first assumed that 'here was a young Guardee who had never been in India before, and was obviously affected by the heat'. Not at all. Alexander, with the help of a native teacher, was secretly learning Hindustani. Two months later he was required to make a speech at the presentation of cups to victors in the brigade sports. To Bull's astonishment he made his speech in perfect, indeed flowery, Hindustani, a language which no previous commander had ever mastered. The whole parade broke into applause. 'What's the use of my coming to a first-class Indian Brigade', he explained to Bull afterwards, 'and not be able to talk to the men in their own tongue?'

Under the cloak of apparent lethargy he was learning hard the whole time. He was too wise to find fault with methods which a century of experience had proved viable; too tactful to challenge a tradition of which the Indian NCOs were as jealous as their British officers; too appreciative of the orderliness which he found to apply a new broom. He allowed his battalion commanders to train their men according to time-honoured routines, riding round the field-exercises to observe and study more than to supervise or correct. He was consciously preparing himself for the day when he would have to take command of them in action.

For beyond the hills there was an enemy. The tribes of the North West Frontier were not very numerous, nor normally very aggressive, nor well-armed. But they were there, and because they were there, the British had been compelled for over a century to maintain an army in the northern plains. Alexander's attitude to the tribesmen was mixed:

All this part of the country [he wrote to Erik] is populated with Pathans, a fine fighting race of men who look like brigands, which of course they are. Proud independent devils, who would probably shoot you in the back. But not because they dislike us. They are just primitive men, three thousand years behind our civilization.

Although he was sympathetic to a people's yearning for liberty, Alexander was torn by no moral scruples in leading an imperial expedition to crush them. He had carefully read Winston Churchill's *The Malakand Field Force*, and recommended it to all his young officers. Churchill had campaigned over the identical country for five weeks in 1897, and there had been little change since then. In his book he painted a picture of bloodthirsty tribesmen who 'torture the wounded and mutilate the dead. It is a war without quarter'. In a letter to his grandmother Churchill described those few weeks as 'the most glorious and delightful that my life has yet contained'. Alexander was not given to such hyperbole, but he, too, had not come to India to play polo, and was elated when in June 1934, only two months after his arrival in Nowshera, he was woken early one morning by a telephone call from Peshawar to say that the tribes between Malakand and the Afghan border were on the march southward under a new leader, the Fakir of Alingar. Alexander scribbled on the whitewashed wall of his bedroom the names of villages which the staff officer at Peshawar read out. Among them was the name of Loe Agra.

The story of the Loe Agra campaign of 1935 has often been told before, most recently and excellently in General Jackson's book on Alexander as a military commander, and need not be repeated in detail here. Alexander himself left a manuscript account of its opening phases, as well as an official report. He describes how the scare in June subsided almost as quickly as it arose, with the deployment of few aircraft and a single company from his battalion at Malakand, but higher command decided that the Fakir (who, Alexander heard, was 'small in stature, and with feet so soft and delicate that he could cross over sand without leaving a trace of his footfall') was a menace whose mythical reputation must be destroyed. A major expedition was to be mounted in February 1935 to enter the territory which he had occupied south of the Swat river and establish British rule over it. Loe Agra lay in its very centre, and was the main objective of the campaign.

Alexander, having been given this long notice of what was required, made his preparations with great care. His manuscript account narrates:

83

When the plan was first tabled, I flew over the Loe Agra salient. It was instructive from several points of view. I gained a fairly accurate knowledge of the ground we were about to fight over, but the track by which the column was to move, although clearly marked on the map, was almost invisible from the air, which made me doubt whether it really existed. What was more noticeable was the size and difficulty of the gorges. Loe Agra was surrounded on all sides by a huge rim of mountains – clearly visible, and looking like tea-leaves in a teacup.

He was told that the operation would be little more than a flag-march, to overawe the natives. It turned into a minor campaign. The tribesmen fought fiercely on ground ideal for defence. Alexander was obliged to lead his force back into Loe Agra twice after its first capture to quell the revolt which flared up again behind him. On 11 April he deployed all four of his battalions to clear the passes surrounding the village. When they descended into it for the third time, the political agent, Leslie Best, who accompanied Alexander throughout, was killed a few yards from him. A stray bullet was responsible, reckons Geoffrey Bull, who was present, not a deliberate ambush, for the tribesmen knew well that to kill the political officer would mean severe retribution. Best's escort returned with his body. It was a sad end to a successful campaign. The tribesmen dispersed, and a road was built from the south as far as Loe Agra which effectively added the salient to British dominions. Bull returned six years later, and there had been no trouble since 1935.

In the autumn of the same year, Alexander took part in a second and larger campaign, against the Mohmand tribes on the India-Afghanistan border. Both brigades, his and Auchinleck's, were employed, and Auchinleck, as the senior of the two, was in command. It was again a 'pacifying' operation, and again the ultimate intention was to make a road into the Mohmand country, as the people, it was optimistically assumed, 'want cars, not war'. In a temperature of 102 degrees Fahrenheit the two brigades advanced into the hills to clear the snipers from their hiding-places, while the RAF sealed off their escape routes. Tanks were used operationally for the first time in India. The battalions leap-frogged through the mountains, ridge to ridge, piqueting the nodal peaks as they went, and taking it in turns to guard the communications. A few weeks before the end Alexander fell sick with malaria and was obliged to return to Nowshera. The campaign was entirely successful. On 1 October the Mohmands submitted, and the road was built as planned, deep into their mountains. Alexander recovered in time to lead his brigade back to their base.

From these two operations he emerged as a commander who had surpassed in his leadership and tactical invention the veterans of the Frontier. He was made a Commander of the Star of India, a much coveted decoration; and to his delight the 2nd Punjab Regiment invited him to become their Colonel.

What pleased my ears [recalls his chaplain, J. H. Bradbury] was what the troops said about him after their return. They had always respected him: now they could not speak too highly of him. They said that he had never ordered them to go anywhere where he had not first been himself. At daybreak they had watched him crawling along a ridge where they would later have to follow; and they boasted how he had marched with them along the valleys.

It was a tribute to which he had grown accustomed, for leadership by example had always been the hallmark of his military style. Now, with his regimental battles behind him and on the eve of generalship, he could look back on the first major phase of his career. He was forty-four. His remarkable record in the First War, when he had risked his life again and again as if he had not expected to survive it, had placed his courage beyond question and beyond envy. It would be impossible for anyone to say, as they had said of First War Generals, that Alexander did not know what a battlefield was like. To his courage he had added the capacity to think quickly and ahead. Alexander's was not a brilliant mind. It was too deeply nurtured in tradition, too stable for intellectual adventurousness. Some of his friends have remarked with affectionate admiration that all through his life he remained at heart a subaltern. His attitude was intensely practical. He could see the foreground very clearly, the middle-ground better than most, the distance only hazily. He was a pilot, not a navigator. He was fascinated by the variety of local circumstances. No two battles were the same. So he put himself in the place of the company and platoon commanders who had to make the immediate decisions, as once he had to make them himself under the orders of less considerate men.

That he was an optimist was partly due to his equable nature, but also to his success. Alexander never had a major failure. It could be said that in the Second War he made a few mistakes, but all were remediable. Before 1942 there were no mistakes at all that are now remembered.

His command of the Landeswehr had proved that his success had not been due to luck, though he had his share of that, because a more crippling combination of difficulties would be hard to imagine. Constantinople had put him to no equivalent test, since the crisis was resolved by diplomacy, not by war, but there again he had twice faced impossible odds with intelligence and indestructible calm. He was a man for tight corners.

The 'bleak decade' had done little to change his character. He arrived in India very much the same man who had led the Landeswehr. There was the same boyish pleasure in his 'nice little commando'. The same sudden concentration upon problems which interested him, whether cooperation with the Air Force or the organization of a brigade athletics meeting. The same determination to learn the language. The same withdrawal within himself to focus his mind upon a task which he could foresee. Then, as when the cameras begin to turn in a studio, sudden action, quick improvisation, complete absorption, the assumption of success. Alexander was confident in his own powers. At no moment did he feel himself unready for the command immediately above him. He saw his career like a flight of hurdles, the last of them visible from the start-line. The commander of the Peshawar District, General Dashwood Strettell, wrote in his final confidential report: 'He is qualified for the highest commands or appointments in the Army.'

It was therefore with no surprise, and certainly without alarm, that he heard in the autumn of 1937 that he was to be promoted Major-General, in command of the 1st Division at Aldershot. During the two years since the conclusion of his two Indian campaigns, he had lived quietly at Nowshera. He had flown home to England for the birth of his eldest son Shane in June 1935, between the Loe Agra and Mohmand operations, and he was to return once more for the Coronation in 1937, when he was appointed ADC to the King. The Alexanders spent two holidays in Kashmir, and visited Kabul. On 1 January 1938, after spending Christmas with the Governor of Bombay, they sailed for home. Alexander wrote from the ship as they approached the Suez Canal: 'Once we leave Port Said, it is goodbye to the East. Although we are delighted to get home, we are very sorry to leave India, where we have spent four very happy years.'

5

THE 1st DIVISION (1938-40)

Alexander's appointment to command the 1st Division was announced on 16 October 1937. Only Freyberg had won more rapid promotion, and now his temporary retirement through ill health made Alexander, at forty-five, the youngest General in the British Army. The 1st Division was one of the only four regular divisions in England. Montgomery, on the eve of war, was given command of the 3rd. The neat pattern of the British Expeditionary Force in September 1939 is interesting for two reasons: it reveals the smallness of Britain's initial contribution to the defence of France; and it contains the names of the five soldiers who (apart from Wavell and Slim) were to make the greatest contribution to our survival and victory in this war:

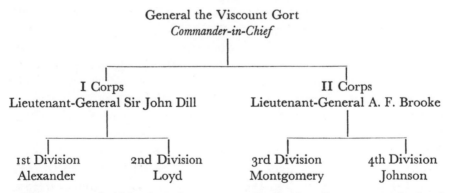

General the Viscount Gort
Commander-in-Chief

| I Corps | II Corps |
| Lieutenant-General Sir John Dill | Lieutenant-General A. F. Brooke |

| 1st Division | 2nd Division | 3rd Division | 4th Division |
| Alexander | Loyd | Montgomery | Johnson |

The area of Aldershot is not among the loveliest, nor typical, of English scenes. It was willingly surrendered to the Army, who found it conveniently accessible to London and the south-coast ports, and a strangely sandy scrubby land in which most forms of warfare could be simulated. Alexander lived in the GOC's official residence, Wellesley House, on the town's outskirts. He had few social obligations, since the Munich crisis had induced a more serious attitude to military preparation, and even the Aldershot Tattoo, a minor diversion in London's Season which took place in Ascot week, was regarded as excellent practice for administrative officers and advertised the Army to our own people and representatives of many different nations. He could devote his whole time to making his division first not only in name but in reputation.

His chief staff officer was Richard McCreery, a cavalryman, the winner of many riding trophies, who had never previously served with infantry. He had not met Alexander before, and confessed that he was slightly unnerved by his legend. He need not have worried. In a fragmentary autobiography McCreery wrote: 'At quite an early stage I realised that my divisional commander was a man who liked to decentralise. Although he gave the directions, he expected me to do most of the detailed work. . . . He was a charming and versatile man.' His diary reveals the process by which mutual confidence grew. 'Alexander', he wrote a week after his arrival in Aldershot, 'is quick and good.' They travelled much together by car, and while Alexander would never interrogate him, he probed McCreery's character by throwing out suggestions in handfuls and watching for the reaction. He always carried a pad of paper in his pocket (like Lutyens, the architect) on which he would illustrate his ideas, whether of a tactical problem or a change in the soldier's battle-dress. His ADC, George Thorne, the other usual occupant of the car, confirms this impression of Alexander's eagerness and universal curiosity. He spent little time in the office, and most of it inspecting troops, often on horseback. He was particularly insistent that his men should learn the skills of minor tactics. The English, he told Thorne, are not natural soldiers like the Germans, Russians or Gurkhas. The German soldier would regard it as an honour to carry the platoon mortar or anti-tank rifle, the British as a penance. Therefore, they must be taught – taught to site their positions for all-round defence, to look over the hedge before settling down to brew their can of tea, to put their eye to ground-level before they started to dig. 'Never', he said, 'reprimand a soldier for his first mistake, only for repeating it.' His interest in all things practical made him equally at home with the sappers, the signallers, the gunners, the mechanical engineers. He would inspect barracks conscientiously. He had an uncanny gift for memorizing names and faces. He was always superbly dressed, wishing without arrogance to be known as the smartest soldier in the smartest division.

In May 1939 Alexander went to France with his Corps Commander, General Dill, to meet the French and visit the Maginot Line. On his return he told McCreery that it seemed impregnable. The brigade and battalion exercises at Aldershot seemed child's-play in comparison, and he was privately conscious of the inadequacy of British preparations for the type of war which he foresaw. When war came in September, his second-line transport was composed entirely of requisitioned tradesmen's vans, though the 1st and 2nd Divisions were the only ones which the War Office considered to be properly equipped.

Mobilization went very smoothly. Reservists flooded in to complete the 1st Division's strength, and the King visited Aldershot to inspect them before they left for France on 19 September. Alexander himself crossed from Southampton to Cherbourg that day, taking with him as his entire luggage a small suitcase, a new battle-dress, two pairs of field-boots and a small collapsible bed and chair. By 27 September 150,000 men of the BEF were ashore, without suffering a single casualty in transit. They assembled round Le Mans and Laval, and then by easy stages moved to the Franco-Belgian frontier to take up their agreed positions. On 4 October the 1st Division was in the front line at Cysoign, a few miles south-east of Lille.

The words 'front line' were used almost satirically. They were facing a neutral frontier. The nearest German was more than 100 miles away, the rearmost guard of an army which was then completing the conquest of Poland. The whole of Belgium lay in between. But it was obvious that the Maginot Line could be outflanked between its northern terminus on the Luxemburg frontier and the sea. As in the First War, the German offensive, if it came, would be likely to violate the neutrality of Belgium, and possibly of Holland too. French strategic planning, in concentrating upon the defence of the Franco-German border, had ignored the longer and more vulnerable frontier to its north-east, and this was the gap which the BEF was to hold in part, by defence-works which they were to construct as fast as possible. They had longer to prepare them than they had dared to hope. For seven months, between October 1939 and May 1940, the BEF were left undisturbed to fortify a line in expectation of a Second War which would repeat, with few variations, the strategy and tactics of the First.

The battalions set to work at once. The border country was very slightly undulating, well wooded and intersected by small streams. The Belgian frontier was not marked by any visible signs on the ground, but it was patrolled by Belgian guards, who had strict instructions to prevent any infringement of their country's neutrality, and a shopping or shooting expedition near the border might end in sudden internment. But from the Belgian side there was a constant traffic of civilians, who either worked legitimately in French fields or factories, or had come to spy out the land with treacherous intent. Of all the front-line troops, Field Security Police found that they alone were engaged on the duties for which they had been trained. The infantry spent their whole time digging, draining and revetting, day after day. They soon discovered that as the water lay very close beneath the surface, and their trenches became untenable after every shower of rain, they must dig deep sump-pits and shore up the crumbling trench-walls by wattle hurdles, and in many places replace the trench-system by a series of breastworks. Simultaneously, progress was made on the construction of two reserve-lines lying in rear of the Gort Line proper. A series of concrete pill-boxes sprang up, and a second anti-tank ditch was dug by mechanical excavators. By the end of the winter the Gort Line was more or less complete. It was still not strong by Maginot Line standards, and tactically its chief drawback was the lack of any dominating ground from which the artillery could observe or which could shelter reserve troops forming up for counter-attack. But at least there was a continuous triplicated obstacle, and a trench, a pillbox or a breastwork from which every man could fire his rifle or his gun.

There is no need to dwell on this twilight opening of the war. Alexander's experience was that of a score of other senior commanders. His headquarters was a little four-square moated château called Bersée, which belonged to a French businessman who remained in the house with his wife. Alexander lived very frugally, sleeping on a camp-bed in a room which had a turret-room off it for his ADC. Every day he toured his battalions. Whatever misgivings he had about the Gort Line he kept to himself. How could these petty entrenchments be defended against tanks and intensive bombardment from the air? The men half-realized it, and grew tired of digging trenches in the rain against an enemy whom they never saw. There was no training for the new type of war which the Polish campaign had demonstrated, because, the French said, it would ruin the countryside. Alexander, by attention to detail, convinced everyone that he thought the line important. There was not much more a divisional commander could do. The line was fixed, his sector of it unaltered from October to May, and the method of its construction determined by higher policy and the ground. So, as at Aldershot, he would make unheralded appearances in a platoon position, inspect their simple arrangements, and ask sudden stabbing questions: 'If a squadron of tanks broke through there, what would you do?' He was already making his private assessment of the capabilities of his subordinate commanders. Once when he arrived at a battalion headquarters in mid-morning he was offered a glass of sherry, which he refused. 'I wish to inspect the battalion's positions', he said shortly. 'Very well,' replied the Commanding Officer, 'I'll send my tactical adviser with you.' Alexander sacked the Colonel next day. On another occasion when he was on his way to a GHQ conference in Arras he noticed a queue of officers and men. 'Is that a football match?' he asked McCreery. 'I'm afraid not, sir. It's a brothel.' Alexander was furious, and ordered the provost-marshal to take the name of every officer in the queue.

He received visitors of eminence: the King, the Commander-in-Chief, the French President, the British Prime Minister, all of whom radiated the confidence which Alexander did not share, asking the obvious questions of detail, ignoring the strategy. When his brigades were moved in rotation to the Saar front, he visited them there, and formed new conclusions about the Maginot Line, contrasting the professionalism of the French engineers who had constructed this underground warship with the complacency of their Generals who (as he was quick to note) had no strategic reserve. Alexander never openly questioned the decisions of higher commanders. He gave his views when asked, but did not volunteer them. He accepted orders, even when he was a Field Marshal, on the assumption that no organization can operate, particularly in wartime, on any other principle than the chain of command, and in any case 'they' probably knew better, or at least more, than he did. He therefore never put on record his reactions when he was told in November 1939 that the line which his men were so laboriously constructing would not be defended if the Germans attacked through Belgium. It would be abandoned immediately for a new and unprepared line in Belgium itself.

This decision was not as illogical as it appeared. The Belgians were neutral, but not so neutral that they failed to foresee an attack on their country by the Germans or the need for Allied help if it came. Belgium at one end of the Maginot Line was not like Switzerland at the other. It was the traditional invasion route. But the Belgians could only accept Allied help when that help became urgent. They could not invite it in advance without impairing their neutral status. It was tacitly agreed with them that as soon as a German invasion began, the Allies would flood into Belgium from the opposite direction and hold a line

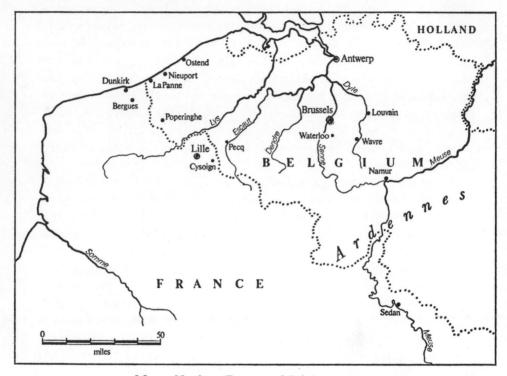

Map 4 Northern France and Belgium, 1939–40

as far east as possible to halt the Germans at least before they reached Brussels. For the Allies there were obvious advantages in this plan. By fighting in Belgium they would save northern France from becoming once again a battlefield. They would involve the Belgian and perhaps the Dutch armies on their side. And a line east of Brussels would be shorter than their present frontier-line, and based upon water-obstacles, the Meuse and the Dyle.

In 1939 both Brooke and Dill, the two Corps Commanders, had protested to Gort that it was madness to leave a prepared position for one totally unprepared. Gort replied that it was a political decision on which he had no right to comment. Even in May 1940 the BEF was only ten divisions strong compared to 100 in the French Army, and it was natural, in Churchill's words, 'that we should place ourselves under French command, and that their judgement should be accepted'. Throughout the winter preparations were made to advance to the support of the Belgians should the Germans attack them. While the men dug for one purpose, the staff planned for its opposite. It gave both something to do, but the work of one or the other was bound to be wasted.

At the beginning of April 1940 Hitler invaded Norway. On the 11th the Germans were reported to be massing on the Belgian and Dutch frontiers, and the BEF was put on four hours' notice to move. On the 16th tension relaxed and Alexander went on leave to England. He was back before 9th May, when Gort's Chief of Intelligence told him that he could guarantee forty-eight hours' notice of a German attack. It came less than twenty-four hours later, without notice. The first that the little group in the Bersée château knew of it was at 6.30 am on 10 May, when they heard the distant explosion of bombs falling on Arras.

Everyone knew exactly what to do. The whole force was to swing forward sixty miles into Belgium as far as the River Dyle. They rejoiced in the spectacle, the game, the action, after a winter of wet and cold. They were, after all, advancing, as every army wishes to do, between women and children at the roadside holding out flowers of welcome. There was almost no interference with their movement by the German Air Force. East of the plain of Waterloo, the country became more wooded, and there were some deep valleys lined by the prosperous villas of Brussels commuters. When they reached the Dyle, they might have crossed it unawares, for it was little more than a brook. This was the first unpleasant surprise. Although the little river was certainly an anti-tank obstacle, strengthened by marshes on each bank, and better than any which they had managed to construct on the Belgian frontier, no commander would from choice have sited his main defence line where it could be approached through thickly wooded country and was overlooked from the German side. It was a thin blue line chosen off a map because it happened to run conveniently north and south level with the

Meuse and at the right distance from Brussels. Was it intended to become a permanent line? There was no plan to advance from it into Germany. What, Alexander might have asked himself if he had the time, what sort of war did 'they' envisage?

It was hoped that the Belgian army ahead of them would hold the Germans off the Dyle for at least seven days. All British accounts allege that Belgian morale broke much sooner. 'Streams of refugees were coming through', reads the I Corps diary, 'but they were outnumbered by Belgian troops. The latter were marching, or came in cars and waggons or on bicycles. Many were without boots, apparently happy to get behind our lines. The villages in our rear were soon packed with Belgian soldiers.' Alexander's division was the central one of the three holding the seventeen miles of the British sector between Wavre and Louvain. Brussels lay twelve miles behind them. Once the retreating Belgians had been disentangled from the BEF, they blew all the bridges on their front, and on 14 May were in contact with German patrols along its entire length. No fight developed, except briefly at Louvain, where Montgomery's division threw back small enemy penetrations. From the German records we now know that they planned a major attack on the 17th which would have fallen mainly on Alexander's front. But on the night of the 16th/17th the whole British line was withdrawn.

The reasons for this withdrawal are now well known, but at the time, when information about the flanks of the BEF was very scanty, the order created consternation. The Allies had expected the main attack to come through the Belgian plain. They had seen it come. They watched 'with interest' (I Corps diary) the deployment of the German divisions on the far bank of the Dyle, and awaited their assault. The first great battle of the war was to be fought here. It was at that moment that Reynaud, the French Prime Minister, was telephoning to Churchill: 'We have been defeated. . . . We are beaten. We have lost the battle. . . . The front is broken near Sedan: they are pouring through in great numbers with tanks and armoured cars.' A gap of fifty miles had been punched through the Ardennes, and German spearheads were already in rear of the unbroken British line and meeting almost no resistance further west. When Churchill asked Gamelin, the Commander-in-Chief, when and where he intended to counter-attack, Gamelin replied, ' "Inferiority of numbers, inferiority of equipment, inferiority of method", and then a hopeless shrug of the shoulders.'

This major threat was still remote from the BEF, but on their immediate right the French First Army had been pressed back between Wavre and Namur, and on their left the Dutch had surrendered on 15 May. Alan Brooke wrote in his diary that night, 'The BEF is therefore likely to have both flanks turned, and will have a very unpleasant time extricating itself.' Thus a withdrawal developed into a retreat. Forced by pressures on either side, but itself intact, they began to climb down the ladder which they had so recently ascended, of which the rungs were river-lines, the Dyle, the Senne, the Dendre, the Escaut, pausing twenty-four hours on each, marching by night, digging by day. The Escaut was to be the final stop-line.

Alexander's role at this period was more exhausting than exacting. At divisional level the retreat was more the concern of staffs than Generals. The 1st Division, still in the centre of the line, were to some extent cushioned on each side by troops whom they knew and on whom they could rely, and frontally the German pressure was not yet very great. But the strain was beginning to reveal the depth of men's reserves. The Corps Commander, Michael Barker, who had taken over I Corps from Dill in April, was proving under stress to be incompetent to command. 'He lacked the physical strength and resilience', wrote Arthur Bryant, 'to cope unperturbed with the succession of contradictory reports and rumours, the continuous lack of sleep, and the appalling shock and pace of the blitzkrieg', to all of which tribulations Brooke and Alexander were equally exposed. It was only by chance that Alexander heard from his neighbouring division of their orders to retreat to the Dendre, and withdrew his own divisions on his own initiative and in conformity. On the night of 17/18 May he had received no orders of any kind for forty-eight hours. He sent his chief staff officer, William (later General Sir William) Morgan to Corps headquarters, and Morgan was fortunate to find that an army conference was about to begin, at which Gort himself was present. During the conference, Morgan took a wise but unprecedented step. Finding himself sitting next to Brooke, he whispered, 'Couldn't you get us transferred to your Corps?' Brooke agreed, with the excuse that I Corps had too many divisions, and II Corps too few. When Alexander's division reached the Escaut, they therefore came under the command of a man in whose judgement he had utter confidence, and his feeling was reciprocated.

At such moments the bearing of senior commanders is watched with anxiety by troops and staff. Alexander seemed refreshed by only a few hours' sleep, and was careful to remain clean and tidy. He told his men that they must shoot back at German aircraft, even with revolvers, and at every halt they must send fighting-patrols back along the route they had covered, for this was good for our morale, and bad for the enemy's. He tried to give an intelligible role to every man in his division. 'It was comforting to hear him say', recalls George Thorne, 'that it "does not matter in which direction you move, forwards or backwards, provided that you march on a route of your own choosing and at a time of your choice. This is not a rout. It is a military manoeuvre. We are conforming to the movement of troops on our right and left." ' Brooke's own recollected impression of Alexander is striking:

In taking over the 1st Division I was for the first time having the experience of having Alexander working under me. It was a great opportunity . . . to see what he was made of, and what an admirable commander he was when in a tight place. It was intensely interesting watching him and Monty during those trying days, both of them completely imperturbable and efficiency itself, and yet two totally different characters. Monty with his quick brain for appreciating military situations was well aware of the very critical situation that he was in, and the very dangers and difficulties that faced us acted as a stimulus on him; they thrilled him and put the sharpest of edges on his military ability. Alex, on the other hand, gave me the impression of never fully realising all the very unpleasant potentialities of our predicament. He remained entirely unaffected by it, completely composed, and appeared never to have the slightest doubt that all would come right in the end. It was in those critical days that the appreciation I made of those commanders remained rooted in my mind and resulted in the future selection of these two men to work together in the triumphal advance from Alamein to Tunis.[1]

Before his division stumbled back to the Escaut line, Alexander had made a careful survey of it and of a divisional reserve line further back. The ground on each side of the river was a flat plain except for one dominant hill, Mont St Aubert, which he could not occupy for lack of sufficient troops. The country was free from dykes or hedges but thickly cultivated in fifty-acre farms. Short lines of poplars and willows led to the many farm-houses. The river, which was much wider than the Dyle, had no prepared defences, but by 19 May the division was entrenched behind it, and on the following day they were once again spectators to the massing of a large German force on the far bank. Impotently they watched the arrival of battalions of German lorried infantry, the assembly of bridging materials, the conferences of German officers with flapping maps. A heavy mist lay over the fields and water when at 7.30 am on 21 May the Germans attacked.

It was the only serious battle in which the 1st Division were engaged until they reached Dunkirk, and it was on no great scale. The enemy forced a crossing over the river at Pecq, but all their bridgeheads were eliminated in two days' fighting. A renewed and stronger attack seemed imminent, and the Escaut had been declared the final line. But once again events in a wider field determined their fate. The southern gap was still open. The Germans had reached the sea, and the Allied command was cut in two. Seven of Gort's nine divisions were holding the Escaut line, two were improvising a flank-guard in rear. Gort was ordered by the Cabinet to attack southwards across the gap to join the French in the area of Amiens. 'How was he', writes Gort's biographer, 'with neither ammunition nor food in plentiful supply, to disengage on his front and while fighting a rear-guard action against the strong German forces which would pursue him across the Scheldt [Escaut], do battle with the armoured divisions blocking his retreat?'[2] By his decision to disobey, Gort saved the BEF. He saw the position of his force as that of a beleaguered fortress, whose only salvation lay in its retreat to the coast and then evacuation. Alexander had no fault to find with Gort's manoeuvres. A few days before his own death he said to Colville, 'Gort was the ideal commander of a British force', and then added, astonishingly, 'He was the British Rommel, with the same dash and same resourcefulness, but with a thorough staff training which Rommel lacked. . . .' But this is true: 'With the equipment available to the BEF in 1940, nobody, in my opinion, could have done better than Gort.'

On 22 May the BEF were ordered to withdraw from the Escaut to the positions on the Franco-Belgian border which they had prepared during the winter. It could be nothing but another delaying line, for the enemy was behind them as well as in front, their communications temporarily protected by a scratch British force, but their northern flank exposed by the imminent capitulation of the Belgian army. Five German armoured divisions threatened the only two remaining ports, Ostend and Dunkirk. Brooke told them that the situation was 'serious but not desperate', but in his diary he wrote, 'Nothing but a miracle can save the BEF now, and the end cannot be very far off.' To Alexander's great regret the 1st Division reverted that night (2 am 24 May) to command of I Corps.

So once again they withdrew. The long roads were crowded with vehicles, sometimes moving even slower than the infantry, sometimes halted for hours on end in paralysed blocks. Drivers fell asleep as soon as they stopped. On one side of the road was the military traffic, two or three vehicles abreast; on the other, all moving in the same direction, long lines of civilian refugees. Old men and women pushing prams and wheelbarrows loaded with their worldly goods, small farm-carts crammed with twenty people apiece, fought for a place among the cars of the well-to-do. In and out of the thin lanes left between them marched the British infantry, footsore and immensely tired. From time to time German aircraft would streak overhead, bombing and machine-gunning the column, soldiers and refugees alike, but the refugees were the more common victims. Children were lost, born, killed, by the way-side. To one officer the chief memory of these marches is the sight of an old woman, blood-stained and with a dead baby in her arms, rising from the ditch to shake her fist at the disappearing bombers. Another tells of a field where hundreds of crowded refugees had been cut to pieces by a dozen Dornier aircraft.

When they reached the Gort Line they had a few days' rest. There was heavy shelling but no serious attack. The threat developed further north, where a gap opened between the BEF and the Belgians, now rapidly disintegrating. It was hastily plugged by Brooke, who borrowed three of Alexander's battalions, and then by Gort, who again without orders cancelled all plans for an offensive southwards, and switched his only two remaining divisions, the 5th and the 50th, to hold the line.

On 26 May the British Government issued the formal order that the BEF must retreat to Dunkirk and embark. 'I must not conceal from you', Gort replied, while accepting the policy as the only one possible, 'that the greater part of the BEF and its equipment will inevitably be lost.' The most optimistic forecast was that 45,000 men might get away. Alexander decided to thin out at once. His rearguard marched all through the night of 27/28 May to Poperinghe and onwards to an intermediate line on the River Lys.

We spent the whole night on the road [wrote Morgan] and I must say it was a very unpleasant night. The refugees were still there, but the French forces were the main trouble. Some of them were going backwards and some of them were coming forwards, for reasons that we couldn't quite under-stand. However we struggled through and by about lunchtime we had arrived west of Poperinghe. As far as we could get news, our Brigades were coming back steadily. . . . That night the weary infantry, who had been marching for about eighteen hours, finally came into bivouack west of Poperinghe, and the crisis was over. We had got through the gap. . . . I remember General Alexander and myself discussing how we could evade capture and try to get out of France. We made a sort of plan to go down to the south and lie up in the marshes at the top of the Somme river, which we knew pretty well from the first war.

Late on 28 May the headquarters of the 1st Division crossed the canal between Bergues and Nieuport to enter the Dunkirk perimeter. The division was ordered to defend its central part, south of La Panne. All British transport was to be dumped outside, to prevent congestion in the bridgehead. Alexander destroyed his own car by holing the tank with revolver shots, and then firing it with incendiaries. For the remainder of the battle his only possessions were a spare uniform, his revolver, his field-glasses and his brief-case.

His division was safe. In considering how this extraordinary operation had succeeded, Morgan was in no doubt that Alan Brooke's character and achievement had been decisive. Then he went on: 'Of course, another supreme reason was the courage of the British soldier. He never panicked. He never worried. He always fought honestly and truly, and nothing would rattle him.' This was true of Alexander too. At such moments he epitomized the best qualities of the British infantry. *Aliis licet: tibi non licet.* Let others behave supinely, but not you.

6

DUNKIRK

The purpose of this chapter is not to retell the detailed story of the evacuation from Dunkirk, but to describe Alexander's role as commander of the British rearguard. Dunkirk made him for the first time a nationally known figure, and the successful evacuation of all the remaining British troops was among the finest achievements of his life. But the events of those few days are seen differently by British and French. Visit the war museum in Dunkirk today and you will be treated to a forty-minute *son et lumière* account of the battle which amazes an Englishman brought up on his own version of the story. Examine a French history of the period, and you will find that the French still bear resentment against the British for what they regard as the 'betrayal' of Dunkirk, claiming that we let them down by insisting that they form the rearguard to allow the BEF to escape. It is only now possible, by quotation from the contemporary records, to explain how the misunderstanding arose.

Early on 29 May 1940 Alexander left the perimeter to reconnoitre the beaches from which his troops were to embark when the word was given, and established the headquarters of his 1st Division at Bray Dunes on the coast, eight miles east of Dunkirk. For the next five days, first as Divisional Commander and then as Corps Commander, he had a dual role: to defend the front line, and organize the embarkation. It was to the latter task that he first turned. As the road to the front was so clogged with French traffic that even soldiers on foot could not pass along it without great difficulty, he ordered it to be cleared by throwing the stationary vehicles into the ditches. On the beaches the embarkation was proceeding with alarming lethargy. So gradual was the slope of the shore that the few rowing-boats were grounding well out to sea, and of the thousands already waiting to embark only a hundred or so were being taken off in each hour. Alexander ordered his divisional engineers to drive lorries into the water and lay planks along the roofs to form a jetty about 150 yards long at the head of which the boats could float at all but the lowest stages of the tide. Each boat held ten or twenty men, two of whom were ordered to row it back to the jetty when the others had embarked on the transports lying off-shore. 'I was not very pleased with the response', Alexander later admitted. Several of the boats were cast adrift when they reached the ships. But the scene was then quite tranquil. The bombing of the beaches had not started in earnest. Those who awaited their chance dug themselves slit-trenches among the dunes.

The beaches east of Dunkirk are flat and wide, dirty-grey in colour and striped in black. Off-shore there are frequent sand-bars. A few low breakwaters stretch over the sand and at intervals streams spin across it. The dunes behind the beach are in places half-a-mile wide and heavily contoured, tufted with marram-grass. The first firm soil behind the dunes is heavily and tastelessly overbuilt with mean houses of red and yellow brick. It is very ugly, a poor northern frontier for France. Beyond the coast-road the fields stretch flatly to the horizon in a landscape more Dutch than French. There are few trees apart from wind-breaks round the farm-houses, and the ground is sliced up by canals and irrigation ditches, the roads running on embankments alongside them to provide the only ridges in a polder-land. It is easy to understand why the Germans thought it impossible country for armoured attack, for there is no cover, a water-obstacle every quarter-mile, and in May 1940 the fields were slowly flooding through breaches blown in the dikes. The half-bowl of the sky covered almost exactly the area of the bridge-head. From the front-line the tower, chimneys, cranes and spires of Dunkirk were clearly visible. Shellfire arched overhead from canal to beach, beach to canal. The proximity of the sea was comforting, but a reminder of how quickly a single breakthrough could split the bridge-head in half. On a marked map the disposition of the Allied forces resembled the situation which a General would wish to see five days after a successful landing from the sea, with a firmly held perimeter, a captured port, seven divisions ashore, and a vast amount of landed stores. Instead, it was the situation of a beleaguered army five days before its retreat.

Gort was still in command. By 30 May all his men were safely within the perimeter and the policy of evacuation was firmly decided upon. The bridgehead was to be reduced in two stages by narrowing it from east to west by the progressive withdrawal of his two remaining corps. III Corps had already gone. II Corps was beginning to embark its rear elements, and General Brooke, its commander, having appointed Montgomery to succeed him, was under orders to leave for home. I Corps (Barker), in which was Alexander's 1st Division, was to form the rearguard. At 6 pm that evening Gort held a conference of his senior commanders in his headquarters at La Panne, four miles east of Bray

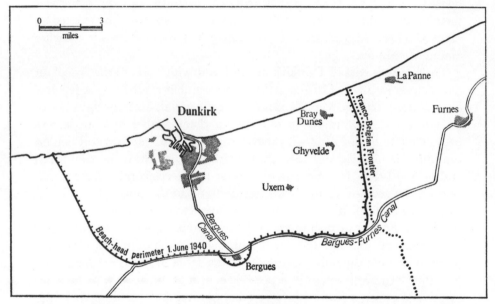

Map 5 Dunkirk

Dunes. Present were Gort, Brooke, Barker (who arrived late), Montgomery and three staff officers, one of whom subsequently made this record:

The Commander-in-Chief read extracts from a message he had received from London, saying that he had been ordered home, much against his will, and was instructed to hand over the BEF to a selected Corps Commander, as the Germans must not be allowed to catch such a prize of the C-in-C. There was also the need for the rearguard to leave either *pari-passu* with the French or, if needs be, surrender with them.*

* The full text of the telegram is given in Churchill, *Their Finest Hour*, p. 95.

The latter, said the C-in-C, seemed to be the more probable contingency, as the French evacuation arrangements were bad and there was still much of the French First Army to come back. The C-in-C said that he considered that the Commander of I Corps would have to remain. General Barker arrived at that moment. The C-in-C then outlined his proposals and told General Barker that he was to be the Corps Commander to remain. General Brooke then asked leave to withdraw, as his destroyer was waiting. . . . The C-in-C then told General Barker to get in touch with Admiral Abrial, the French commander in Dunkirk, and if and when the time came, to arrange with him the terms of capitulation. He was to retain one divisional commander, and the C-in-C was very anxious that General Alexander should be sent home if possible.

Gort did not choose Alan Brooke or Montgomery to command the rearguard, since their corps was already embarking. He did not choose Alexander, who was still only a divisional commander, and he wished to save him for future high command. Barker commanded the largest body of remaining troops, and Barker was expendable. Gort regarded Barker's capture together with a large part of I Corps as more or less inevitable, because the British must make sacrifices equal to the French and he thought it almost inconceivable that the entire bridgehead force could get away. Then he decided to appoint Alexander in Barker's place. Montgomery describes in his Memoirs why Gort changed his mind:

The conference broke up. I stayed behind when the others had left and asked Gort if I could have a word with him in private. I then said that it was my view that Barker was in an unfit state to be left in final command. What was needed was a calm and clear brain, and given reasonable luck, such a man might well get I Corps away, with no need for *anyone* to surrender. He had such a man in Alexander, who was commanding the 1st Division in Barker's Corps. He should send Barker back to England at once and put Alexander in command of I Corps. I knew Gort very well; so I spoke very plainly and insisted that this was the right course to take.

Alexander had not attended the conference, and Barker did not pass on his orders to his divisional commanders that evening. Next morning, 31 May, still in ignorance of what was intended beyond the general policy of evacuation, he was ordered to report to GHQ at La Panne about noon, and was then told by Gort that he was to take over command of I Corps from Barker immediately. Barker was going home.

The orders which Gort gave Alexander, first verbally, then in writing, were as follows:

1. You have been selected to command the I Corps of the British Expeditionary Force and to assist our French allies in the defence of Dunkirk.

2. The responsibility for the defence of Dunkirk rests with the French Admiral Commanding-in-Chief the Naval Forces of the North [Abrial]; you will act under his orders, but should any orders which he may issue to you be likely, in your opinion, to imperil the safety of the Force under your command, you should make an immediate appeal to His Majesty's Government, through the Secretary of State for War, at the same time notifying the Admiral du Nord that you are doing so.

3. In addition to any sector of the defence of Dunkirk for which you may assume responsibility, you will also occupy yourself with arrangements for the evacuation of the Force under your command. This you will do in collaboration with the Admiral du Nord and also in accordance with the policy which may be laid down from time to time by H.M. Government.

It is important that the troops of the French Army should share in such facilities for evacuation as may be provided by H.M. Government. The allotment of facilities for evacuation in accordance with this policy will be made by the authorities at home; if at any time you consider that the allotment is unreasonable, you should represent the matter to the Senior Naval Officer, Dunkirk, without delay.

4. If at any time in your judgement no further organised evacuation is possible, and no further proportionate damage can be inflicted on the enemy, you are authorised in consultation with the Admiral du Nord to capitulate formally to avoid useless slaughter.

Before leaving Gort's headquarters, Alexander spoke on the telephone to the War Office in London. 'I was informed by Major-General Percival on behalf of the CIGS that my duty was to hold the Dunkirk area as long as possible, provided the safety of the BEF was not imperilled.' (From a report which Alexander wrote for the War Office on 10 June 1940.) He then returned to his headquarters and handed over the command of the 1st Division to his senior Brigadier. Barker was waiting at Bray Dunes when Alexander arrived, and heard the first news of his supersession from Alexander himself. He broke down and wept.

That afternoon, 31 May, two conferences assembled almost simultaneously. One, in Paris, was at the highest level, between Churchill and the French Prime Minister, Reynaud, accompanied respectively by the CIGS, Sir John Dill, and the Allied Commander-in-Chief,

Weygand. The other was at Dunkirk, between Alexander and Admiral Abrial. The conclusions of the Paris conference were not communicated to Alexander because the only telephone link between the bridgehead and London was broken when the Germans occupied La Panne later in the day. The different emotions generated at the two conferences, the fact that they were coincident, the ignorance in Paris of the situation in Dunkirk, and the ignorance in Dunkirk of the precise agreement reached in Paris, resulted in the successful evacuation of the BEF, and the French charge of betrayal.

First, Paris. A brilliant account of the conference was written after the war by Sir Edward Spears, Churchill's personal representative with the French Government, who was himself present. The statesmen were engaged in drafting a telegram to Abrial:

> The third paragraph stated that as soon as it had been ascertained that none of the troops outside the Dunkirk perimeter were able to reach it, the units defending the bridgehead would embark, the British forces first.
>
> The Prime Minister jumped on this. 'Certainly not', he boomed. . . . '*Nong*', he roared, '*Partage – bras dessus, bras dessous.*' The gesture he made, effectively camouflaging his accent, conveyed better than the words, that he wished the French and British soldiers to leave Dunkirk arm in arm. . . . 'The three British divisions will form the rearguard', he said; 'as so few French have got out so far, I will not accept further sacrifices from the French.'
>
> Again he was under the strain of a strong and generous emotion. I suddenly, and for the first time, felt out of sympathy with him. His emotions were leading him too far, I thought, he was being too generous. . . . We ought not to sacrifice our chance of survival to the French, who certainly would not do so for us. The idea that we might be invaded because we had absolutely no troops to resist even a weak landing was unbearable.[1]

At another stage of the talks, Churchill said to the French, 'There are four French divisions in the Dunkirk perimeter, also three British divisions. The three British will stand and allow the French to escape. We will do this in honour. It will be our contribution to comradeship.'

Quite unaware of these appalling commitments being made on his behalf in Paris, Alexander went to meet Abrial in the citadel at Dunkirk. Abrial had been pitchforked into supreme responsibility by the chance that the coasts of France were divided into sectors, each under the command of an admiral. Abrial's stretched from the Belgian frontier to Le Havre. If an enemy landing occurred within his sector, he was responsible for repelling it, and for this purpose he was given command of some local units of the French fleet, the coastal artillery, and a small body of troops. At Dunkirk the evacuation was an invasion in reverse. It was unthinkable, even in this unforeseen situation, to transfer his authority to a French General, though several were available, senior to Alexander. Abrial was *chef amphibie*. Therefore he must command. This paradox was entirely acceptable to the French, but seemed illogical to Alexander. He had heard that Abrial had never left his headquarters to visit the perimeter, and had little knowledge of military matters or the crisis he was supposed to deal with. Alexander come to like Abrial personally, but he found himself at a critical moment under the orders of a naval officer in whose judgement he had little confidence. He went to the conference with many misgivings.

Four accounts of their discussion survive. One, by Alexander himself, is dry and factual, and confirms the essential points of the other three.

The second was written by his Brigadier General Staff, later General Sir William Morgan:

We first got hold of Captain Tennant [the Senior Naval Officer in Dunkirk] and went into the citadel, a quarter of a mile from the base of the mole. We went a long way downstairs into an underground headquarters. When we sat down, Abrial was very pleasant, but made it quite clear that he didn't know anything about this evacuation idea. His idea was that only specialists, technicians etc were being evacuated, and the troops were to remain. Of course we knew this was impossible. The British troops were absolutely finished. It was a very difficult thing for Alexander to represent this. However, he did.

He pointed out to the French that they were living in a false world, that the situation was such that it was merely to invite a collapse to try and hang on any longer than was necessary. In any case, his instructions from Gort were to evacuate as many troops as possible. He added, 'Of course, all our facilities are available to evacuate your troops too.' It was rather sticky to start with. We had to be very careful because all Abrial had to say was, 'I'm afraid the port will be closed.' That would not allow any British ships in. Alexander said, 'What you are asking is an impossibility', to which Abrial replied, 'Those are my orders.' He was a very decent fellow and didn't panic at all.

The third account is from the French point of view, written after the war by Jacques Mordal, who fought as a junior officer at Dunkirk and

based his story on what he heard from the Frenchmen present on
31 May:

The discussion was most painful. Alexander declared that his divisions
were not in a fit state to hold their front. Besides Gort had not ordered him
to hold a sector of their bridgehead with the French troops, but to embark
the British force completely. This declaration conflicted with the sense of
Gort's letter to Abrial. Alexander, very upset, declared that in any case he
was going to withdraw at midnight, that Dunkirk would fall in 24 hours,
and that the German artillery was approaching so close that the enemy
could very soon prevent all embarkation. . . . The French argued in vain.
Then Abrial said he intended to go to La Panne to see Gort. Alexander
said that Gort had already left. A long silence followed this remark. 'I must
point out', Abrial said eventually, 'that the last British troops will only
escape because the French are still fighting.' He then declared the meeting
closed, saying that because he could no longer count on the cooperation of
the British, he would carry on the battle with the French alone.[2]

The fourth account, written immediately after his return to England,
is by Captain Tennant:

On 31st May I returned to Dunkirk with General Alexander and discovered
that totally different instructions had been given to General Alexander by
Lord Gort, and by Lord Gort in writing to Admiral Abrial and General
Fagalde [Abrial's military deputy]. Lord Gort had told the French authorities
that General Alexander would assist in holding the perimeter for the French
to embark, and that he was to place himself and his three divisions under
General Fagalde's orders. General Alexander, however, was told by Lord
Gort in my hearing that he was to do nothing to imperil his army and was
ultimately responsible for their safety and evacuation.

This throws important new light on the matter. Reluctant to demoralize
the French and uncertain what to do, Gort told Abrial one thing,
Alexander another. The French were never informed that the safety of
the BEF was to be Alexander's prime consideration, and Alexander
never saw Gort's written message to Abrial. When he was told about it,
he could scarcely credit it, because it conflicted with the orders he had
received from Gort himself and from the War Office.

All accounts agree that Alexander then decided that he must put the
controversy to higher British authority, since a situation had arisen
which was envisaged in the second paragraph of Gort's written orders.
He drove to La Panne and telephoned to Anthony Eden, Secretary of

State for War. It was the last communication between GHQ and London before the line was cut, and La Panne was dive-bombed as they spoke. The exact words used in this conversation with Eden are of some importance. Alexander, in his report of 10 June, records them as follows:

At 8.15 pm on May 31st the Secretary of State gave me the following verbal instructions: 'You should withdraw your force as rapidly as possible on a 50–50 basis with the French army, aiming at completion by night 1st–2nd June. You should inform the French of this definite instruction.' In reply to my enquiry as to the exact meaning of 'a 50–50 basis with the French army', the S of S informed me that it meant equal numbers of French and British soldiers from that time on.

The War Diary of the 1st Division reports the decision:

He was given a policy by the Secretary of State, which was that the security of the BEF was the first consideration, and that embarkation was to be carried out on a 50–50 basis with the French.

Finally, Eden's own version:

Alexander told me of the extreme danger which threatened his force. I agreed to immediate evacuation, but asked him to give French troops equal facilities with our own to get away.[3]

Alexander now had instructions which confirmed the intention which he had expressed to Abrial. On his way back through Bray Dunes he said to Morgan that he had never been in such a terrible position, and wished that he had been knocked out by a shell. He returned to Abrial in the citadel and told him what Eden had said. He was willing to delay the evacuation of his corps until the following night, 1/2 June, but implied that if the French did not choose to conform, they would be left on their own. 'They agreed', Alexander wrote in his report ten days later, 'that in view of my instructions, no other plan was possible.'

That was the turning point. Although Alexander carried out his orders from Gort and Eden to the letter, and even improved upon them to the benefit of his allies, his attitude seemed to the French quite different from Gort's and Churchill's. Gort, they considered, had been prepared for an equal sacrifice. He had expected the capitulation of a joint Anglo-French rearguard. In Paris, as they soon heard, Churchill had gone much further: the British were to hold the line while the French withdrew. Eden's orders to Alexander had not reflected this spirit of self-sacrifice because at the time of their conversation Eden in London had not heard from Churchill in Paris, and communications with La Panne were cut soon afterwards. Nothing had been said by Eden about the composition of the rearguard, and (according to the contemporary War Diary of the 1st Division) 'the security of the BEF was the first consideration', echoing the words which General Percival had used to Alexander on the previous day. Alexander was wholly in sympathy with this attitude. He considered the salvation of three of the best divisions in the British Army more important than amity with the French, whose fortunes already seemed to him beyond repair. He thought, with some reason, that he had at most forty-eight hours in which to get his troops away. He never asked the French to hold the perimeter meanwhile, but took natural advantage of their decision to do so.

He was, however, mindful of the second part of his instructions. The French must be offered facilities for escape fifty-fifty with the British. This apparently clear directive concealed an ambiguity. Did it mean that honour would be satisfied if for every English soldier who embarked, a French soldier must embark too? Or did it mean, as Abrial had understood from Gort, that French troops must from now onwards embark with the British in such numbers that at each stage the proportion of French to British left in the bridgehead would remain constant? The two interpretations would have widely different results. On 31 May Alexander took over command of approximately 20,000 British troops. The French had more than 120,000 in the bridgehead, and more were still entering it from the shattered First Army around Lille. If the troops of both nations were to withdraw in proportion to these numbers, six Frenchmen must be embarked for every Englishman, and if 30,000 men were left when the Germans eventually broke through the perimeter, at least 5,000 of them must be British. If Churchill had had his way, they would all have been British. As it turned out, they were all French.

Alexander made a carefully calculated compromise. When one considers the strain, exhaustion and continual danger to which he was exposed, one must admire the 'calm and clear brain' to which Montgomery had drawn Gort's attention. If he could prevent it, not one of his men would be captured. Meanwhile the French must be given every chance to get away whatever troops they did not retain for the perimeter defences. Hitherto the evacuation had been heavily weighted in favour of the British, and the French in Dunkirk had made no protest because they had received no orders to embark. By noon on 31 May 144,000 British troops had been landed in England, and only 15,000 French. 'The French staff at Dunkirk', Tennant reported to the Admiralty on 29 May, 'feel strongly that they are defending Dunkirk for us to evacuate – which is largely true.' But between 31 May and dawn on 3 June (the three days when Alexander was in command) the numbers evacuated were 20,000 British and 98,000 French, a proportion of nearly one to five. This was a great deal better than fifty-fifty or even *bras dessus, bras dessous*. Why then did the French harbour such resentment against their allies?

Fundamentally it was because until the last moment the French saw no reason to abandon Dunkirk at all. They regarded this British passion for the sea as a strategic eccentricity. On 29 May, when Gort told Abrial of his hope to extricate the entire force, 'Abrial expressed great surprise. . . . He had, it seemed, imagined that only rearward elements would be withdrawn, and that British troops would stay and defend the perimeter to the last, side by side with the French.' (Gort's Dunkirk despatch, 1941). Very few French ships had arrived to assist the embarkation. The French considered that the bridgehead round Dunkirk (as round Tobruk two years later, or at Anzio in 1944) might be held indefinitely, and a breakout in the direction of the Somme front or at least as far as Calais must be the long-term strategy. Besides, there were still the French divisions cut off at Lille, who must be assured of an ultimate refuge in Dunkirk. Now, when Alexander replaced Gort, the withdrawal was becoming indecently precipitate. 'I am ordered home myself', Gort had told Abrial, 'but I am leaving you my best General, who will be under your orders.' Before Gort had even left the bridgehead, this best General was refusing to accept orders and showed every intention of leaving the French in the lurch, with the humiliating excuse that his troops were too exhausted to fight on. Were not the French equally exhausted? When Abrial received the report of the Paris discussions late on the 31st, Alexander's attitude seemed even more incomprehensible. Mordal wrote in retrospect:

When Weygand insisted that the bridgehead be enlarged towards Calais, the British merely shrugged their shoulders; and when Abrial and Fagalde suggested that the bridgehead be held for the four or five days necessary for the evacuation of the entire French force, Alexander could only reply that the enemy artillery was already trained on the beaches, without considering for a moment whether a superhuman effort might not throw the

Germans back out of range for the few hours required. In fact the British had already made up their minds and thought only of saving the BEF. . . .

Strategically Alexander may have been right, and tactically it must be admitted that the evacuation was admirably executed. But one would have preferred to read in Gort's despatch a single phrase to indicate that the fate of the French First Army meant something in British calculations. . . . Inevitably some of our people felt rancour.[4]

The Navy could have taken off thousands more Frenchmen, if only the French had appeared at the right time and place. Crowds of French troops assembled on the beaches on the nights of 1/2 and 2/3 June to find no ships awaiting them: a dozen British ships, having waited in vain until dawn, sailed empty back to Dover. This fruitless risk of ships and sailors' lives made a deplorable psychological impression on the British. Anglo-French relations were already strained by stories of Frenchmen crowding out of turn on to British ships, and by rumours that the British intended to abandon their allies. It should be remembered that during the last few days the evacuation could only be carried out in the hours of darkness, that the beaches and harbour were under constant shellfire, that there was no Anglo-French staff to make joint arrangements, and that men sheltering in daylight in the dunes and cellars could not easily be marshalled at nightfall for orderly embarkation. So the men missed the ships, and the ships missed the men. Nor was the behaviour of the troops as irreproachable as the published accounts suggest. There are British manuscript records which tell a very different story, particularly of the early days of the evacuation, and French hints that the British troops looted the drink-stores of Dunkirk. Alexander later confessed privately that he was shocked by incidents of indiscipline which he witnessed.

By his own demeanour he did everything possible to restore confidence and calm. Only once did Brigadier Morgan see him lose his temper, and that was when a senior British staff officer said that all was lost. His ADC, George Thorne, wrote afterwards:

On the beach at Malo-les-Bains, and later at the entrance to the fort at Dunkirk, he was cool and confident. Never for a moment did he reveal that disaster was just around the corner. This was one of his special gifts. He was saddened by seeing a number of dejected stragglers without rifles shuffling down the mole, but when the Grenadier Guards marched past the fort and gave Alex an eyes-right, he returned their salute as if he had had a week's leave.

III

His driver, Corporal Wells, has told the author that he picked up a big Humber limousine in which Alexander made frequent visits to the perimeter, always under heavy fire. Once, when Wells drove too fast, Alexander slowed him down: 'They'll get you, Wells, whether you drive fast or slow. Better not add another hazard.'

The British and French lines on the canals held until midnight on 1/2 June. There were some local penetrations, particularly at Bergues, held by the 1st Loyals, but they were sealed off on reserve lines some thousand yards back. That night the entire British force withdrew according to plan behind the shorter line which the French had manned through Uxen and Ghyvelde to the sea just west of the Franco-Belgian frontier. All were clear by 11.40 pm, and the Germans, who disliked fighting by night, did not follow up immediately. It had been the intention that the whole British rearguard would embark that night from the mole at Dunkirk and the beaches just east of it. Alexander established his headquarters in a concrete emplacement at the root of the mole, and sent his staff home. According to Admiralty records, 26,256 men were landed at Dover early next day, the majority of them British, for it was 'a British night' just as the 31/1 had been a 'French night'. Movement was halted at 3 am because the shelling and dive-bombing made daylight evacuation too hazardous, and the remaining British troops, now about 4,000, were dispersed in the dunes and town to await the return of darkness.

'They held the outskirts of Dunkirk throughout June 2nd', reads the Appendix to Lord Gort's despatch. It is true that seven British anti-aircraft guns and twelve two-pounder anti-tank guns were deployed at the rim of the town, for there was a serious risk that German tanks might advance along the beaches at low tide from east to west. But this was a pitiful inner line of defence. The main line, three miles beyond, was held in strength by the French against the Germans, and there was fierce fighting all day. At 3.38 pm on 2 June Tennant reported to the Admiralty, 'The French still maintain their front line except east of Bergues', where they had just counter-attacked. No wonder that Alexander could report that apart from shelling and bombing, 'the British troops were not interfered with'.

As soon as it was dark on 2 June, the remnants of the BEF began to embark on destroyers at the mole. 'There was to be no embarkation by the French until the British were finished', the War Diary of the 1st Division states unequivocally. The arrangements worked without a hitch. All the men were aboard by 11.40 pm. When the destroyers had sailed for Dover, Alexander with Brigadier Parminter (the military embarkation officer) and half a dozen others including Corporal Wells, boarded a motor-boat in the harbour, ordering a single destroyer to await them at the mole. There was no shelter on the boat from the incessant gunfire. They zig-zagged out of the harbour, and then turned east parallel to the beaches for about two miles, as close inshore as the draught of the boat would allow. Twice they grounded on sand-bars. The sea, Wells remembers, was covered by a film of oil, in which were floating the corpses of many soldiers. Alexander took a megaphone and shouted over and over again, in English and French, 'Is anyone there? Is anyone there?' There was no reply. They returned to the harbour, shouted the same question round the quays, and then boarded the waiting destroyer. At about 2 am on 3 June they left the harbour for England. The wide wake of the ship attracted the attention of the Luftwaffe, and they were bombed and machine-gunned for half the journey homeward. Unharmed, they reached Dover as dawn was breaking, escorted over the last few miles by an RAF patrol.

There was, of course, somebody there. There were 80,000 Frenchmen. Some 50,000 of them were holding the line to cover the British with-drawal. The others were waiting their turn to embark. The 1st Division's order that the British were to be given priority is itself proof that the presence of the waiting Frenchmen was known, though Alexander had no idea that they were in such great numbers. Why then did he receive no reply when he shouted his question in French? It is certain that about 20,000 Frenchmen were embarked that night after he had left, mostly in French ships, for the Admiralty reported their arrival at Dover next morning. But 10,000 Frenchmen for whom there would have been room in the ships were left behind. Mordal suggests that 'the only possible explanation is that these men were delayed and reached the mole too late'. Elsewhere he says, 'It is a fact that there were no troops on the east mole, but there was a vast crowd in the dunes nearest the west mole.' Alexander's motor-boat had turned east out of the harbour, not west. This may be why he failed to see or hear them. But there was a profounder reason. He was under no obligation to enquire whether any French soldiers were left. He had already given them more facilities for embarkation than his orders required, and Abrial had consented to the manoeuvre which saved the BEF. When Alexander toured the beaches, it was as the British, not as an Allied, commander. He was searching for British survivors, not French. By then the French had their own quays, beaches, ships, generals, and naval and embarkation officers. Alexander had accomplished the task given to him far more successfully than Gort or Churchill had dared to hope. He had achieved for the Army what Dowding a few days later achieved for the Air Force, by refusing to sacrifice to the lost battle in France the means of defending his own country against German invasion.

Nevertheless, in London there was a sense of guilt towards our ally. All through 3 June the French rearguard continued to defend the perimeter, four days longer than Alexander had initially conceived to be possible. The German records show that the French fought for every house and every foot of ground, but the line was forced back to the Dunkirk-Furnes canal, two miles from the beaches. The Royal Navy determined to make one last effort to save them. Fifty vessels sailed from Dover that night, and nearly 53,000 Frenchmen were brought away, including Abrial himself. He refused the Navy's offer to return the following night, 'for the enemy is now closing in on every side'. On the morning of 4 June the French remaining at Dunkirk surrendered. The British official history estimates their number at 40,000. Mordal says 'nearly 30,000'. More exact (suspiciously exact) is the tally of those who were saved from Dunkirk and its beaches between 26 May and 4 June. 338,226, said the Admiralty, of whom 198,315 were British and 139,911 French.

When Alexander landed in England he went immediately to see Anthony Eden at the War Office. 'After he had given me an account of what had passed', Eden wrote in his Memoirs, 'I congratulated him, and he replied, with engaging modesty, "We were not pressed, you know." '

7

ENGLAND (1940-41)

Following his return from Dunkirk Alexander had two or three days' leave. He did not appear to his wife to be exhausted, and she noticed that one invariable sign of mental strain, a loss of appetite, was absent. It was one of the few occasions during the war when he was united with his family. When the war was over they calculated that during those six years he saw them on only forty-six days. His youngest son Brian, born shortly before the war started, was almost a stranger to him in 1945.

He was retained in command of I Corps, the same which he had brought back from Dunkirk, and soon received orders that he was to take over the defence of Lincolnshire and the East Riding of Yorkshire, from Scarborough to the Wash. His headquarters was near Doncaster, at Hickleton Hall, a house belonging to Lord Halifax which was stripped of its furniture but not of its pictures. It was to be his base for the next six months.

He had three divisions under him, one on the Lincolnshire coast (his old 1st Division), one on the Yorkshire coast, and one centrally in reserve, which could move in an emergency either north or south of the Humber. His sector, one of two in Northern Command, was not of course the most threatened part of the English coastline. It soon became clear that if, as seemed probable, the Germans attempted an invasion of Britain, it would come in the south-east where the sea-passage was shortest, London most vulnerable, and the Luftwaffe could give air-cover from their bases in northern France. The location of the German troop-concentrations, and the gradual assembly of barges in the nearer Channel ports throughout the summer, confirmed this assumption. But there remained the possibility that subsidiary attacks might come across the North Sea, and the east coast north of the Wash could not be left undefended. On 15 August there was a false report that the Germans had embarked a force in Norway and were heading in that direction. What role I Corps would have played in the event of an invasion in the south was never settled. It was enough for the moment that Alexander should position his meagre and ill-equipped forces to best advantage over this great stretch of coastline, and retain in his hands a sufficiently mobile reserve to influence any battle that might develop on his front.

When he arrived at Doncaster he discovered that existing plans were based upon nineteenth-century conceptions of linear defence of the coastline, and on the first map which was shown to him the most prominent defence-works dated from Napoleonic times. He soon changed all that. The coast was to be held thinly by section-posts which would keep every beach under observation, and the beaches were to be obstructed by scaffolding erected below high-tide mark and hung with mines. Some six miles inland each brigade was to hold a battalion in local reserve which would move on foot or in buses to the point of attack, and behind them were massed the divisional and corps reserves which were to move forward as the battle-plan became clearer, or be available to recapture any coastal airfields which airborne troops might seize.

Obvious as was the inadequacy of the corps and its equipment to meet any serious attack, morale was high. The situation seemed unreal. The British Army campaigns in other people's countries, not our own. The villages and fields of the deep-bosomed Lincolnshire wolds were training-grounds perhaps, but not battlefields. The continued ordinariness of life, the calm traffic of our own civilians, soon blunted any sense of anxiety or even of emergency. So appalling was the idea of a German armoured division attacking our pitiable defences that it became unthinkable, absurd. The author was then a subaltern under Alexander's remote command. One day, we thought, we would tell our children what it was like to watch the dawn rising over the beaches at Mablethorpe in the summer of 1940, or to patrol through wet corn in search of parachutists dropped during the night, but we knew even then that our recollections would be coloured by invented emotions. We did not understand what was happening. We were corralled by lines on a map which separated us from our immediate neighbours. It is true that we felt important, for the newspapers said that we were, and once our battalion was inspected by Winston Churchill himself, whose only comment was on reading the names of battleships which we had painted on our carriers in his honour, 'You've spelt *Indomitable* wrong.' Our repetitive routines, the attention we gave to drill and to cleaning boots and rifles, trivialized our role. Yet we were happy. It was a lovely summer and we had good billets in the farms and small towns of Lincolnshire. There was nothing much more we could do than wait.

Such must have been the attitude of the larger part of Alexander's command. He himself radiated confidence. He toured his sector incessantly. The corps war-diary shows that having given his divisional commanders general instructions on defence-works and dispositions, he left them to make their own detailed arrangements, and his visits were in the nature of spot-checks and morale-boosters, or to watch exercises and familiarize himself again with the topography of a part of the country which he already knew well from his three years in Northern Command before the war. A large variety of support troops had passed under his command, and he was careful to give them a full share of his attention, knowing that they felt even more isolated from hard news than the regular brigades. The special circumstances created responsibilities which would not usually fall to a Corps Commander. He must make preparations for defending and if necessary demolishing the ports of Hull and Grimsby; for controlling the five-mile strip along the coast which was closed for 'all holidays, recreation or casual wayfaring'. He must settle the roles of the Home Guard and village invasion-committees. The digging of trenches in cemeteries was forbidden, and soldiers must not ask innocent civilians for their identity-cards, because the first gave offence to the bereaved and the second frightened the women. People painting cryptic signs on telegraph-poles will immediately be arrested. Finally, this, signed by Alexander himself: 'As regards the ringing of church-bells as an alarm signal, it is pointed out that nearly everybody who rings a bell for the first time pulls the rope too hard and finding that the bell does not ring, pulls it harder. The result is not to make the bell ring, but to carry the would-be ringer up into the roof. The Archbishop of York is kindly arranging that there should be a competent person always available.'

Gradually new arms flowed to the divisions. When Alexander first arrived, he had armed his gunners, who had no guns or vehicles, with cudgels and bicycles, and told them to learn quickly how to use both.

A month or two later some of his artillery regiments were equipped with old French 75-mm guns. This was better than nothing, but the old-type wheels broke up if the guns travelled at more than six miles an hour, and the commercial vans hired to tow them soon burnt out their engines at that speed. One of his regimental commanders (M. J. Babington Smith) accordingly devised a trailer for carrying the guns behind the vans, and had some prototypes made by a manufacturer of agricultural machinery at a cost of £80 each. As this expenditure was quite unauthorized, and Babington Smith's offer to pay for them himself was regarded as unprofessional, the facts were adversely reported to Alexander. He was delighted. He demanded a demonstration in the presence of the commanders of the other regiments equipped with '75s, and a month later arranged a point-to-point at which each regiment was to put its own model through its paces, the best of them to be recommended to the War Office for universal adoption. The ingenuity and improvisation which the times required were endemic to his own nature.

The most memorable and influential of his innovations at this period was the I Corps school. He had always emphasized the importance of tactical drills to save time in training young officers and to evolve methods recognized by all. In organizing the X Corps school in 1918, and similar schools in the Landeswehr, at Constantinople and Nowshera, at Aldershot and in France, his ideas had gradually taken shape, and now he was ready to reduce the most common situations of infantry battles to a few basic rules. He drew annotated sketches to explain how best to defend a bridge or capture it, to search a village or a wood, to loop-hole a wall, deploy a patrol, and so on, and had these printed in York as a booklet for distribution to every infantry officer in the corps.

As a nation of games-players [he wrote in the Introduction] we all know the necessity of teaching young people the orthodox techniques of sport. . . . Surely a soldier on the battlefield, beset by fear and doubt, is far more in need of a guide to action than any games-player at Lord's or Wimbledon? Better to know instinctively some orthodox line of conduct than to be paralysed by the uncertainty of what to do. Let us, therefore, study and draw up lines of conduct – simple guides for the simple soldier – so that we may ensure that our soldiers when faced with problems on the battlefield will have an answer to them.

Alexander's little red book was in the pocket of every subaltern, and one by one we were detached from our battalions for a fortnight's course at his school in Lincoln to practise these drills under expert guidance and spurred on by thunderflashes and live bullets. The idea was taken up throughout the Army. Montgomery bought 5,000 copies of the red book for his own corps in the south of England, and the CIGS, General Dill, set up battle-schools on the Lincoln model in every Command.

The Battle of Britain was remote from I Corps. On one day only, 15 August 1940, was there a serious air-attack on northern England, and it fell on the Tyne, to be repulsed with such heavy loss to the Germans that they never repeated it on that scale. Every soldier in the corps was conscious that all depended upon the air-battle in the south. Preoccupied as Alexander was with plans that never materialized, he was now able to lift his eyes to horizons which the Battle of Britain had cleared.

In December 1940 he was promoted General Officer Commanding-in-Chief of Southern Command, with the rank of Lieutenant-General, in succession to Auchinleck who was posted as Commander-in-Chief to India.

Alexander was now among the half-dozen most senior officers in the Army. Churchill was in despair at the shortage of great Generals, and his contempt could be immediate and withering. But for Alexander he felt regard and affection. He was moved by his legend, and saw in him a man who was always in complete control, ready to face any emergency, even disaster, confidently, happily and with poise. There was an attractive mixture in Alexander's character of the artist and soldier, of humility and dignity, of simplicity and greatness, of maturity and a certain boyishness which he retained from the years of the First War. He was the man who everybody would wish to be, the coolest of soldiers, the most civilized, the most charming, 'an officers' officer' as General Omar Bradley was to call him, a general's general, and a soldier's general. Churchill warmed to these qualities as they drove together through the north-east and now through southern England. Alexander was not in the least intimidated by his titanic companion; he was not intimidated by anybody. He never tried to impress, never seized the opportunity to plead with the Prime Minister his special needs, never joked about the serious nor pontificated about the trivial. Instinctively in Churchill's company he found the perfect balance between deference and an attitude of shared responsibility. He was flexible, natural, friendly and wise. An American journalist, Alfred

Wagg, once said of him that he was one of the few great men whose vanity didn't need the boost of being told he was. All this was immediately recognized by those directly above or below him, and soon by everyone in his Command who may not even have set eyes upon him. They were aware of Alexander in a way that they were not aware of their brigade or divisional commanders. He did not court popularity. He was not even very easy for a junior officer to talk to. He could still seem aloof in messes and at conferences. He never imposed his will, but assumed that other people would do it. His very appearance, his tailored good looks, his rows of medals (which by this time formed on his chest a whole paragraph compared to the single sentences of his contemporaries), his gentle manner of speaking and his light laugh, purged all meanness and frailty in his company. Nobody was ever jealous of Alexander. He never made a personal enemy. Such criticism of him as could be made was best put by Captain Liddell Hart in 1946:

He had a good intelligence and an exceptionally open mind, but success came so quickly and continually that there was no compelling pressure to set him to the grindstone of hard application that sharpens the edge. He was a born leader, but the ease with which he had always won men's confidence provided no incentive to increase his magnetism by applying the arts of leadership. But beyond that he had an innate reluctance to exert more power over others than the minimum necessary for the performance of his task, and sometimes it was not enough for the purpose. Eminent as his record was, he might have been a greater commander if he had not been so nice a man, and so deeply a gentleman.

We shall see some examples of this in his later career when formidable personalities crossed his path. But in Southern Command in 1941, even though one of his corps was for a short while commanded by Montgomery, there was no hint of it.

His headquarters could not have been more fittingly chosen for a commander of such aristocratic outlook. It was at Wilton House, Salisbury, the home of the Herberts, Earls of Pembroke, since the sixteenth century. Splendid as the Tudor house undoubtedly was and as the surviving parts attest, the 4th Earl pulled much of it down in 1630 and with the advice of Inigo Jones erected in its place a façade and a set of rooms that have no rival for their period in the whole of England. The Army did not tamely put the staterooms under dust-sheets and occupy lesser rooms and outhouses. Their main office was the Double Cube Room, the most glorious room in Britain, sixty feet long by thirty wide and thirty high, and there they placed their operational maps alongside the magnificent Van Dycks framed by carved and gilded swags of fruit and flowers. Alexander's own office was in the Corner Room, which had a warmth and intimacy rare in great houses of the seventeenth century, and from its windows he could look across the lawn to the Palladian bridge, a sublime structure which manages to create simultaneously a mood of exhilaration and repose. His private quarters were not in Wilton itself but in an estate house a little way up the hill from the entrance gates, where he lived with his ADC and a small staff.

It was at Wilton that Alexander first met Edward Seago, the painter, who was to become the closest friend of his middle and later years. Seago was then a Major in charge of a corps camouflage section, and Alexander, who admired his paintings and owned one of them, sent for him a few days after his arrival. For an hour they talked about nothing except painting, and found so much in common that during 1941 they frequently went on painting expeditions together, setting up their easels side by side. Alexander wore the uniform of a Lieutenant-General on these expeditions until Seago protested that it embarrassed the soldiers whom they met in the countryside, and then he wore plain clothes. Sometimes they would have supper in Seago's cottage, sometimes they would go to The Vale, a small Regency house on the edge of Windsor Great Park which the Alexanders bought late in 1940. As Seago's friendship was to mean as much to Alexander as the pleasure in painting which they shared, this is a suitable moment, when there is no narrative of active operations to interrupt, to describe, mostly in Seago's own words, his attitude to it.

Alexander's interest in painting was not scholarly but profound. On 9 June 1969, a few days before his death, he wrote to Seago:

I don't know if you saw the Monet exhibition at the Le Fèvre Gallery. What interested me was that in some of his pictures he gets a wonderful sparkling light, and yet it is apparently not done by the juxtaposition of light colours against dark colours, but colours against colours. To this you must know the answer, and I wish that I knew it too. What a fascinating problem this all is! Successful businessmen and soldiers have to depend upon others to achieve results, but the painter is alone with only his colours.

Undoubtedly the main influence upon him was French Impressionism. He rarely looked at pictures earlier in date. He painted in oil, usually on hardboard, never in water colour, and his subjects, with few exceptions, were landscapes. He was interested in the techniques of brush and oil, and would peer closely at pictures in exhibitions to see how other painters had achieved their effects. He always worked in the open air, but afterwards would sometimes make four or five versions of a scene from a sketch made on the spot. Seago said:

If Alex had chosen to devote his whole time to painting he would have become a very good painter. I think he had all the instincts of a painter inside him. The amateur painter is somebody who is very often pleased with something he's done. The professional is always disappointed. Churchill, to my mind, was the amateur of all amateurs. He thought he could do it, and he did it. He never explored; he never questioned; he never observed. He painted a house if it were there, and if it had a red roof, right, here's the red paint; if there was a green field beneath it, right, here's the green paint. It never occurred to him to ask how red is the red, how green is the green, and by putting the green against the red, does the red look brighter or turn the grass grey? This never entered his head. But with Alex it did all the time. How did he get his colours? Not by one colour mixed with another, but by one colour placed against another.

He had the attitude of a painter. What he lacked was time. You need years of practice before you can control your brush. You can't give it up for six months. You've got to go on and on. But his attitude was that of a professional. And he found painting the perfect relaxation, because when you're painting, you can't think of anything else but the picture, unlike gardening or driving, when you think about other things. If I said to some other amateurs, "This is out of tone", they wouldn't know what I was talking about, and so I wouldn't say it. It would spoil their fun. But Alex would.'

You would criticize his paintings as if he were a professional?

Yes, up to a certain point. I might say, "You're not getting anywhere with this picture. Scrub it." I would criticize his pictures in painter's language, which he would understand.

Was your relationship that of master and pupil?

Not at all. He would ask me sometimes when he came home in the evening, "Where have I gone wrong?", and I would tell him what I thought. But I was never his tutor.

I notice a strong influence of your own style on his?

Yes, that's bound to be, because Alex didn't have many painter friends. I was painting landscape in a manner which was the manner he liked to paint in himself.

He painted all his life. There seems to have been a period of satiety in the 1920s, for no pictures by him survive from his years in Constantinople and Gibraltar or on his return to England, when he had ample leisure and subjects, but he certainly painted in India, and whenever he had the opportunity, throughout the Second War. After the war, in Canada, and then in retirement at home, he was at his most productive, and three times exhibited at the Royal Academy. The revival, or intensification, of his interest was presumably due to Edward Seago, and the days they spent together in the south of England, the Major and the Lieutenant-General, but now two painters on a river bank, were among the happiest which he experienced.

Southern Command stretched from Portsmouth to Land's End, northwards to include Bristol and southwards the Isle of Wight. In it were six divisions divided into two corps, and many independent garrisons and camps like Gloucester and Bulford. The danger of invasion had abated, and once again Alexander's Command did not extend to the most threatened area, the south-east, which Montgomery took over in April 1941, first as a Corps Commander, and in December as GOC South Eastern Command. During the winter of 1940–1 the coast from Hampshire to Cornwall was handed over to county divisions in order to release the regular divisions for training, and Alexander spent most days of the week in long trips by car to inspect the defences or watch the training, much as he had done in the north-east, but now on the much larger scale of his new responsibilities. He was as insistent as Brooke, then Commander-in-Chief of all the forces in the United Kingdom, that training should be much tougher than previously, in preparation for the mobile operations overseas which both foresaw. Brigades should be prepared to go straight into action after an advance of 200 miles in transport or forty miles on foot. Some of these exercises were week-long and on an inter-Command scale, like 'Bumper', when Alexander commanded the home army against Laurence Carr, GOC Eastern Command, who represented the invading enemy. Montgomery was chief umpire, and earned more praise than Alexander, whose handling of the armoured divisions Brooke described at the post-Bumper conference as 'disappointing', but Brooke was tetchy and Alexander loyally made no reply. At the opposite extreme, we hear of him in the Isle of Wight inspecting an ammunition dump. The Commanding Officer was worried that he did not have enough troops to guard it. 'Nobody has enough troops', replied Alexander. 'There is a single division defending the whole of Cornwall. All you need here are two men with bicycles and a whistle.' 'He had a way of melting problems', the Colonel said in recalling this episode. It is a good description of Alexander's method. Why antagonize your Commander-in-Chief, and cause possible loss of confidence in his judgement, by protesting when you think yourself unfairly criticized? Why not relieve a subordinate's worries by minimizing them, even when you know them to be justified but beyond practical remedy?

In addition to Southern Command Alexander was made the commander-designate of 110 Force. This was a miniature army, established on paper but never fully mobilized, which Churchill regarded as the potential expeditionary force for any purpose that might arise. There were many such projects. Alan Brooke, on succeeding Dill as CIGS in December 1941, was 'appalled ... to find the lack of a definite policy for the prosecution of the war. We worked from day to day a hand-to-mouth existence ... that swung us like a weathercock.' The extension of the war to Russia in June 1941 and to the Far East in December stirred the Prime Minister to impress on the Americans, Russians and Japanese that Britain too had the power to operate on a continental and oceanic scale. One of Brooke's first tasks was to steer Churchill away from a major campaign in northern Norway, and later from a premature attack on Tripoli, for which wise advice he was rewarded by charges of lethargy and timidity. The very existence of 110 Force suggested to the Prime Minister other schemes. During 1941 four operations were proposed for it: the Azores, the Canaries, Sicily and French North Africa. For each in turn, and sometimes simultaneously, Alexander and his staff made detailed plans, and staged elaborate and highly secret rehearsals in Scotland for the units of 110 Force which could be spared from other duties. The proposal to capture the Azores was dropped to avoid offending the Portuguese, who later made a present of bases on the islands to the Allies. But the other three operations were seriously entertained, and cancelled only a short time before the appointed days.

The most ambitious were the assaults on the Canaries (*Pilgrim*) and Sicily (*Whipcord*). The Spanish islands were needed as an alternative naval and refuelling base in case Gibraltar should be lost to a German advance through Spain. Some 24,000 troops were to be under Alexander's command, and the operation was to be carried out 'without parley or ultimatum', even at the risk of involving Spain in war against us. *Pilgrim* was not finally abandoned until the end of 1941, and its later planning stages overlapped with *Whipcord*. This was an even larger operation. Alexander was given three divisions and several Brigade Groups for the capture of Sicily, an army of 60,000 men who would have required seventy-five sea-going ships to transport them and their vehicles, apart from assault-craft. Half the force would have landed at Catania, and half at Palermo, and having captured the island they were to hold it indefinitely. The object was to relieve the siege of Malta, open the Mediterranean to our shipping, and cut the communications of the Axis armies in Libya. It was timed to take place in December 1941, but was cancelled at the end of October because the defence of Sicily against certain counter-attack would have immobilized more troops than we could spare, and in any case the Germans could as easily block the Mediterranean from Crete, or from Spain or French North Africa, which *Pilgrim* might have forced them to invade. 'It would be a false move simply for the sake of making a move of some kind', the Chiefs of Staff decided, 'and it would expend our meagre resources prematurely and at the wrong place.'

The next plan for 110 Force was *Gymnast*, and then, with the Americans, *Super-Gymnast*, a descent on French North Africa. By this time Mountbatten had become Chief of Combined Operations, in succession to Roger Keyes, and he advised the Chiefs of Staff to nominate Alexander as the 'potential commander of amphibious operations' (or some equivalent title), whose staff would work in close association with Mountbatten's own staff in order to prevent the duplication and confusion that had arisen in the past.

At that moment Alexander was sent to Burma.

He was visiting coast-defences in the Isle of Wight on 19 February 1942 when he received a message to report immediately to the CIGS. Brooke told him that evening that he was to assume command of the army in Burma as soon as possible. The first person whom he consulted was Lord Mountbatten, who has given the author this account of their conversation:

Alex rang me up and said, "I'm very sorry, but I must see you urgently, because I've been taken away." So we lunched together at the Ritz next day. Alex said, "Winston sent for me personally, and said there's a terrible mess in Burma, and he thinks I'm the only person who can stem the rot." I said, "Alex, I've been watching the Burma situation carefully, and nobody can stem the rot at this stage. It cannot be stemmed until the Japanese have reached the borders of India, when they will have outrun their communications. When we've built up against them, the tide can be turned," (having no idea that the job was eventually going to fall to me). "But there's one thing you must insist on before you go out, and this I beg you to do. You must tell Winston that you will go out to Burma and fight as hard as you can, but that in your opinion there is no way of halting this advance until it has petered out at the gateway to India. He must then withdraw you, and immediately give you another worthwhile command. Because if he doesn't, he will waste one of our best generals. If they regard this as a defeat for which you are responsible, it will damage you irretrievably." He thanked me for that and said, "I hadn't thought of making that clear." "You must", I said, "you must".

Whether Alexander took Mountbatten's advice we do not know. What is certain is that others, including Brooke and Mountbatten himself, made the point for him, and Churchill needed no prompting. Alexander was to save Burma if he could, and if he couldn't, he was to save its army, and then return. Having for the last nine months been at the head of the finest and best-equipped expeditionary force which Britain could muster, he was now undertaking the rescue of a couple of harassed divisions in a desperate situation on the far side of the world. 'No troops in our control could reach Rangoon in time to save it', Churchill wrote in *The Hinge of Fate*. 'But if we could not send an army we could at any rate send a man.' Then he went on to describe, with his great gift for recalling and recreating an atmosphere, the simple meal at which he said goodbye to Alexander:

He dined at the Annexe with me and my wife. I remember the evening well, for never have I taken the responsibility for sending a general on a more forlorn hope. Alexander was, as usual, calm and good-humoured. He said he was delighted to go. In the First Great War in years of fighting as a regimental officer with the Guards Division he was reputed to bear a charmed life, and under any heavy fire men were glad to follow exactly in his footsteps. Confidence spread around him, whether as a lieutenant or in supreme command. He was the last British commander at Dunkirk. Nothing ever disturbed or rattled him, and duty was a full satisfaction in itself, especially if it seemed perilous and hard. But all this was combined with so gay and easy a manner that the pleasure and honour of his friendship were prized by all those who enjoyed it, among whom I could count myself. For this reason I must admit that at our dinner I found it difficult to emulate his composure.

To give him his full title at the outset of the three most strenuous years of his life, he was now Lieutenant-General Sir Harold Alexander KCB, CSI, DSO, MC. He had been knighted in the New Year's honours.

8

BURMA

It was not the most desperate – for the three Allies thought themselves in combination ultimately invincible – but the most heart-breaking moment of the war. The new enemy, Japan, had achieved by preparation and surprise successes which surpassed Hitler's. A list of names with dates attached is sufficient to recall them: Pearl Harbour (7 December 1941), Siam (8 December), *Prince of Wales* and *Repulse* (10 December), Hong Kong (25 December), Malaya (31 January 1942), Singapore (15 February), Dutch East Indies (8 March). All that were left of our strategic bases east of India were Australia and Burma. Both were exposed to invasion by the destruction of almost all our naval power at the battle of the Java Sea. The one British division available for reinforcement had been sent to Singapore and lost, and the Australian Government understandably refused to divert to Burma their divisions returning from the Middle East to defend their homeland. But Burma must be held. Churchill thought it 'even more essential than Singapore', and for the three reasons which Wavell, the Supreme Allied Commander in the area, put to the Chiefs of Staff on 7 March:

(a) To maintain connection with China.
(b) To protect north-eastern India with its war-industries.
(c) As an essential air-base from which Japanese air-bases can be attacked and aircraft passed through to China to attack Japan itself.

For a part of the British Empire of such strategic importance, singularly little had been done to prepare its defences before the Japanese war broke out. Until a few days after Pearl Harbour, Burma had been under Far Eastern Command, who regarded it as little more than a naval and air staging-post for the supply and reinforcement of Malaya and Singapore. It was thought inconceivable that Burma would be exposed to attack, unless Singapore were lost, which was itself inconceivable. Now both had happened. The southern tail of Burma was invaded in December, and by mid-February two Japanese divisions were advancing north to seize Rangoon, opposed only by the raw and incomplete 17th Indian Division. In the northern part of the country was the 1st Burma Division, of even lower calibre. The army commander was Lieutenant-General H. J. Hutton, formerly Chief of Staff to Wavell, whom Wavell himself had appointed in December, with orders to halt the Japanese and above all to save Rangoon. When Hutton lost the confidence of Churchill and Wavell that he was capable of doing either, Alexander took his place.

Hutton, like Auchinleck after him, did not deserve the censure that was heaped upon him. It was more the result of cumulative disappointment at home and the inadequacy of the means allotted to him than of his own shortcomings. The Official History is unusually frank: 'Wavell was still remote from the hard practical facts of the situation in Burma. The authorities in London and India, blaming the local commander for a course of events for which they themselves were largely responsible, decided to swop horses in mid-stream.' It is true that Hutton was a more brilliant staff officer than commander, and tried to compensate for what he lacked in inspiration by interference with the detailed decisions of his subordinates. But his divisional commander, Major-General Sir John Smyth VC, who suffered most from Hutton, has written, 'No one could have made a success of the job of trying to defeat the first Japanese invasion of Burma with such tools as were available.'[1] While Wavell pressed Hutton, and Hutton pressed Smyth, to hold and counter-attack in southern Burma, Smyth withdrew, river by river, to the angle formed by the junction between the long tail of the country and its body, wishing to concentrate his forces instead of leaving them to be 'eaten up in penny packets without ever being able to fight a real battle at all'. He had his eye on the broad swift Sittang river, sixty miles east of Rangoon. That was where he would make his stand, and in this decision he was quite justified. The 17th Division therefore fought a series of rearguard actions, to the mounting dismay of Wavell and Churchill, whose anger focussed upon Hutton as the man responsible. Even the Viceroy, Lord Linlithgow, joined in the clamour by signalling to Churchill in mid-February, 'Our troops in

Burma are not fighting with proper spirit. I have not the least doubt that this is in great part due to lack of drive and inspiration from the top', and went on to name Hutton as the chief culprit. Churchill forwarded the telegram to Wavell with the suggestion that if Wavell agreed with the Viceroy, Alexander should be sent out immediately to replace Hutton. Wavell replied on 18 February, with a hesitation attributable to his own choice of Hutton for the command so short a time before, 'I have no reason to think otherwise but agree that Alexander's forceful personality might act as a stimulus to the troops. I am reluctant to make a change, but it would help me to decide if you would inform me . . . how quickly could Alexander reach Burma after a decision is made. It should be within a week if possible.' Without waiting for Wavell's second thoughts, Churchill signalled on the 20th, 'We are sending Alexander as fast as possible', and his message crossed with one from Wavell, now further disillusioned by a hint from Hutton that Rangoon might be lost, firmly recommending the same action.

A disaster occurred between Alexander's appointment and his arrival in Burma, which confirmed Wavell's doubts of Hutton's capabilities. The 17th Division withdrew, as Smyth had wished, to the Sittang river, but had been delayed by Hutton's orders and was so closely followed by the Japanese that there was no time to organize the orderly withdrawal of the division across its single bridge. One brigade got across, and some of the divisional troops, but two brigades were still on the east bank, strongly pressed by the Japanese, and the bridge itself was in imminent danger of capture. During the night 22/23 February the Brigadier considered that if the Japanese attacked next day the bridgehead could not be held. Smyth was faced with the terrible choice between isolating his two brigades by blowing up the bridge or risking its capture intact, which would have left the road to Rangoon wide open to the Japanese. Thinking no doubt that a bridgeless river was a better obstacle than two exhausted brigades, who would in any case become prisoners if the bridge were captured behind them, he gave orders that the bridge should be destroyed. Some 2,000 men from the two brigades escaped by swimming the river or improvising rafts, but many more fell into Japanese hands, and all the heavy equipment. On 24 February the 17th Division could muster only 3,400 men, of whom 2,000 did not have even rifles. Such was the weakness and disorganization of the force that the west bank of the Sittang, Smyth's intended stop-line, could not be held. The survivors were concentrated round Waw and Pegu, twenty to thirty miles further back, nearly half-way to Rangoon. Fortunately the Japanese, themselves exhausted and awaiting equipment to cross the river, paused on its far bank for a week. This respite enabled reinforcements to be landed at Rangoon, notably the 7th Armoured Brigade and the 63rd Indian Brigade, but when Alexander arrived, the key battle of the Burma campaign had already been lost.

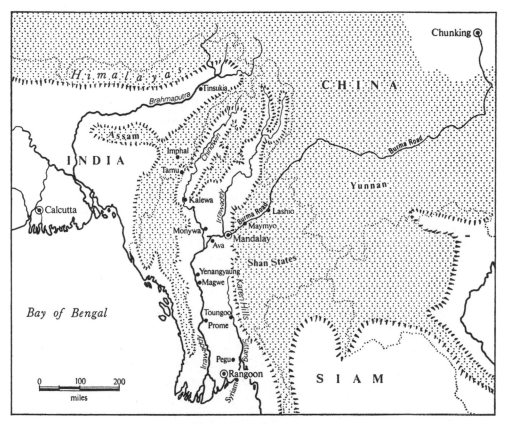

Map 6 Burma in 1942

All this time Alexander had been waiting in England. Day after day, with his ADC Rupert Clarke, he motored from his house near Windsor to Hurn airport in Hampshire, but on seven successive evenings was obliged to return home, since the weather was too bad to fly the long first leg to Egypt over occupied France and Italy. On the eighth evening, 27 February, he at last took off in a Liberator, and flew all night in such bitter cold that icicles formed on his oxygen mask. They spent twenty-four hours in the British Embassy in Cairo, and then flew on in another aircraft to India. Now engine trouble forced them to land in the Persian Gulf. Alexander was quite unruffled by these delays, refusing to abuse weather or machinery, or to waste nervous energy on a mishap when he must conserve it for a disaster, and for several hours sheltered from the intense heat under the wing of the 'plane and helped the mechanic with his repairs. They reached Delhi on 2 March, and continued next day to Calcutta, where they met Wavell and Smyth at the airport.

He learnt from Wavell that Smyth, a sick man, was returning to England, but Hutton was to remain in Burma as Alexander's Chief of Staff. The face-saving explanation was that the Burma army was now increasing to a size which demanded a more senior commander, and Hutton remained with Alexander until April, when he was replaced by General T. J. W. Winterton for the remainder of the campaign.

Wavell now gave Alexander his orders:

The retention of Rangoon is a matter of vital importance to our position in the Far East and every effort must be made to hold it. If, however, that is not possible, the British force must not be allowed to be cut off and destroyed, but must be withdrawn from the Rangoon area for the defence of Upper Burma. This must be held as long as possible in order to safeguard the oilfields at Yenangyaung, keep contact with the Chinese and protect the construction of the road from Assam to Burma.

This, concisely but not without ambiguity, told Alexander what he was expected to do. As regards Rangoon, he was expected to fight for it, and not, as Hutton had hinted, yield it tamely to ensure his army's escape. But how hard must he fight? At the risk of crippling his force, at the risk of encirclement? If the battle went against him, then Alexander was to defend Upper Burma for 'as long as possible'. Again it was not specified whether the security of the army was paramount. Was his task to conduct a slow retreat to the Indian border, or fight to the last in order to save Burma for its strategic value? It may be thought that only circumstances and Alexander's own judgement could decide the answers. In fact, the importance of Rangoon immediately, and of Burma ultimately, compared to the safety of the army, was never clear in Wavell's own mind, and the ambiguity of his instructions was twice to lead Alexander to the verge of total disaster. Wavell had already lost one great Asian base. He did not want to lose another. He did not think it necessary. He despised the Japanese army. Throughout the retreat to the Sittang he had seen no reason why the 17th Division should not face up to them and hit back, and made no allowance for the fact that the division was ill-equipped and half-trained. 'He never appreciated the tactical factors of this campaign in Burma', wrote Smyth. 'He regarded the tough, ruthless Japanese, who at this stage of the war were by far the best-trained and equipped jungle fighters in the world, as something akin to the Italians, whom earlier on he had defeated so spectacularly in North Africa.' During his visits to the Burmese front Wavell's attitude had distressed experienced officers who knew the truth, and they could not understand why the disasters in Malaya and Singapore had not taught Wavell the same lesson. Eventually he came to acknowledge his error. In 1946 he told General H. L. Davies, Hutton's chief staff officer, 'I was mistaken about the Japs. I didn't appreciate what fine, brave and ruthless soldiers they were.' But at Calcutta airport he conveyed to Alexander the opposite impression. One hard blow could save Rangoon. In a cable to the CIGS that night he summed up their talk in these words: 'Have issued instructions that Rangoon is not to be given up without a battle as aggressive as our resources will permit.' Alexander did not arrive 'too late to save Rangoon', as Arthur Bryant wrote. There had never been in Burma the resources with which any General could have saved it. The verdict should be rephrased: 'He arrived in time to save the army', not only from the Japanese, but from the over-confidence of the Supreme Allied Commander.

He flew to Magwe in central Burma next day, and landed at Rangoon at noon on 5 March, the last aircraft to do so. Rangoon was in a terrible state. The Governor of Burma, Sir Reginald Dorman-Smith, had given orders for its evacuation several days before, and demolitions had already begun, although the destruction of the port and oil-installations had been held up pending Alexander's decision. General Davies thus describes the conditions:

Air-raids against the city began on December 25th 1941, and an immediate result was the disappearance of most of the Indian dock labour.... With the Japanese advance beginning to threaten the city, the civil police disintegrated. Prisons and lunatic asylums were opened, and the inmates loosed on the unhappy town. This resulted immediately in looting and arson on a grand scale, together with armed attacks on civilians and troops alike which rendered necessary the imposition of martial law.

The city was overhung by a permanent dense pall of smoke from burning buildings. . . . The Zoo was cleared, and attempts, not always successful, were made to destroy the more dangerous animals. A large Orang Utang escaped in a wounded condition and lurked in the darkness attacking unsuspecting passers-by.[2]

Alexander spent an hour at the army headquarters in Rangoon, and then went to the front some forty miles north-east, where he found Hutton. Since his talk with Wavell at Calcutta the situation had further deteriorated. The Japanese had crossed the Sittang unopposed and were advancing in two divisional columns, one directed through Pegu towards Rangoon, the other moving cross-country to cut the roads leading north and surprise Rangoon by a turning-movement from the north-west. The road north and south of Pegu was already blocked, and Hutton, correctly guessing the enemy's plan, had given orders to withdraw from Pegu and concentrate north of Rangoon. Alexander immediately cancelled these orders. With barely a moment to think, knowing neither his troops nor the enemy nor the ground, he acted instinctively in response to Wavell's parting words. He must fight for Rangoon. Hutton and the staff begged him not to. The 17th Division was in no fit state for an offensive, the 63rd Brigade had only just landed, and his only striking force was the 7th Armoured Brigade which would be badly needed later on. There was no sense, they argued, in pitting this shaken, under-equipped force against two first-class Japanese divisions which were about to encircle them. But Alexander insisted that they must attempt to re-establish the line covering Rangoon by linking up with the 1st Burma Division whose southernmost troops were some forty miles to the north. The gap must be closed by attacking simultaneously from the south northwards and from the north southwards.

Hutton was right. The British attacks petered out. The 1st Burma Division never moved. The 63rd Brigade was crippled at the very start of its first battle by the loss of its Brigadier and all three battalion commanders in an ambush. The Japanese lost, and then regained, their road-blocks. The 'offensive' turned within a few hours into a fighting withdrawal, and it was only with great difficulty that they escaped the trap which Pegu had by then become. Meanwhile the Japanese, to whom this fighting had been little more than a local skirmish by a small part of their forces, continued to advance in strength westwards through the jungle to encircle Rangoon, and sent by sea a small force of Burmese nationalists to land near the oil-refineries at Syriam.

Alexander now abandoned all hope of saving the city. He had done his best to carry out Wavell's instructions, and in the middle of the night 6/7 March gave orders to evacuate Rangoon, destroy its installations, and retreat to the north. The vast oil-refinery was blown up next day, and a cloud of smoke hung 23,000 feet above the abandoned city. The remaining population, civilian and military, streamed northwards.

It is evident from what we know about Japanese intentions that Wavell's order to stand and fight for Rangoon nearly destroyed the army in Burma. If Alexander had persisted twenty-four hours longer, his retreat would have been cut off, for the main body of the enemy was already many miles behind him. On the night of 7 March he escaped what John Connell, Wavell's biographer, has described as 'the most perilous strait of Alexander's whole career'. No doubt Alexander had personally been nearer death or capture several times in the First War, (and indeed he said to his ADC, 'I've been in tighter spots than this'), but never was he in greater danger of losing the entire force under his command. When he withdrew from Rangoon on 7 March he found the road blocked by the Japanese ahead of him. Two successive attacks in battalion strength failed to dislodge them. That night an entire Japanese division was in a position to cut off his retreat. The column of British vehicles, including the army headquarters, the army commander himself, and two-thirds of his fighting troops, stretched twenty miles back to the outskirts of Rangoon. Alexander ordered a brigade attack at dawn, but just before it was due to start, the road-block was reported unoccupied and the road clear. The Japanese general had established it as a temporary flank-protection until all his troops had crossed the road on their way to attack Rangoon, which he believed to be still defended. Not wishing to divert his force from his main object, nor signal his intentions by too great a show of force while on the march, nor surrender to the rival Divisional Commander in the south the honour of capturing Rangoon, he abandoned the barrier which could have ended the Burma campaign then and there. Against a whole division trained in jungle warfare Alexander could not have forced a way through for his unwieldy convoy. In his Memoirs he wrote, 'If we could not have broken through the road-block, I was prepared to order units, groups and individuals to save themselves by fighting their way out, or by working through the jungle.' But, even if some had succeeded, they would have lost all their transport and heavy equipment, and the disaster, far greater than that on the Sittang, would have ended Alexander's career if not his life. He owed his predicament to Wavell's orders, his escape to luck.

Wavell was not pleased when he heard the news. He telegraphed to Alexander: 'Understand from naval authorities decision taken to evacuate Rangoon. Cable most immediate reasons for this very grave step, which affects whole course of war in East. Has battle taken place?' Alexander's reply began: 'The directive given was to hold Rangoon as long as possible but not to allow my force to be shut up there and be destroyed. This has been accomplished, but by a very small margin.' Wavell had the grace to send back the message: 'Well done. Responsibility for position in which you and your troops were placed was wholly mine, and I congratulate you all on determination with which you have extricated yourselves.'[3]

The battles near Rangoon were the only occasions in Burma when Alexander took direct control of troops in action. The 17th Division and the 7th Armoured Brigade were only part of his force. There were also the 1st Burma Division, not so far engaged, and the two Chinese armies, later reinforced by a third, which were beginning to assemble in east-central Burma, all of which were to come under his command. His function as Army Commander was strategic, administrative and political, and can best be described in that order.

Burma is split down the middle by the valley of the Irrawaddy, one of the great rivers of the world, which rises in the far north and empties into the sea west of Rangoon. Flowing parallel to it and nearer the Siamese border is the Sittang. The two valleys are separated by jungle-covered hills until they join at Mandalay in the very centre of the country. From near Mandalay the Irrawaddy's tributary, the Chindwin, flows close to the Indian frontier. The mountains between the Irrawaddy and the sea were impenetrable by armies and disregarded by both sides, but those on the Siamese border, in the district known as the Shan States, became increasingly important, since they were crossed by roads leading into China, of which the most famous was the Burma Road from Mandalay to Chunking. Alexander's plan was to hold the floor of the Irrawaddy valley with his British forces, and the Sittang valley and Shan States with the Chinese, both covering Mandalay. He first deployed them on a line between Prome and Toungoo, and in April fell back on a second line further north protecting the oil-fields at Yenangyaung, which was one of the vital points mentioned in Wavell's Calcutta directive.

With the loss of Rangoon the importance of Burma had already diminished. Once Burma's only major port had gone, there was no method of supplying the Chinese up the Burma road from Mandalay to Chunking, because no supplies could reach Mandalay. The oil, rice and timber, Burma's main products, were important to the Burmese and Japanese, but no longer to the British, since there was no means of shipping them out of the country. As an air-base Burma was now useless, its airfields destroyed by the Japanese or occupied by them. Only as a military barrier to north-east India and as a political link with China did it retain any strategic significance, apart from British hopes to see a Japanese army at last defeated and a fragment of our Empire in the East salvaged from the universal wreck.

It is strange that in these circumstances Alexander was sent no further directives from Delhi or London. 'We did not know', wrote General Slim, his Corps Commander, 'what was the over-riding object of the campaign until the last stages.' So long as Rangoon was safe, the object had been clear – to hold it. But now there was no longer a sufficient reason to maintain in Burma an army whose communications were cut, and whose life must therefore be short. Alexander was never ordered to evacuate the country: he did so because the Japanese and his supply-situation forced him to. Wavell did not face the consequences of the loss of Rangoon. On 7 March, the day it was abandoned, he cabled the Chiefs of Staff, 'I will do everything possible to maintain a hold on Burma', and in his despatch he repeated, 'I hoped that we might still manage to retain a hold on Upper Burma', but he never explained how the army was to be supplied once its stores were exhausted. Continued resistance in central Burma could only have been justified by the hope of an early recapture of Rangoon, and of that there was no question, because we were far too weak in the air and on the ground to take the offensive, because the Japanese could reinforce at will and we could not reinforce at all, and south of Mandalay the whole eastern flank was open to fresh Japanese incursions from Siam. Alexander's own view (which he kept to himself at the time) was more realistic. 'As the campaign progressed', he wrote in his Memoirs, 'it became increasingly clear that we were not strong enough to do more than slow down the enemy's advance, and that eventually, to save the army, I should have to get it back to India. If I could delay the Japanese until the monsoon broke in mid-May, time would be gained for the Indian forces to man the frontier.' This was an intelligible strategy, and the one which was eventually adopted, not by Wavell's intention or order, but by force of circumstance and Alexander's own decision.

Before Alexander arrived, Hutton had had the foresight to ship back to depots in and around Mandalay three-quarters of the stores from the bursting warehouses of Rangoon. The army lived off these depots for two-and-half months, and at no time were they short of food, petrol or ammunition, the essentials on which any army lives and fights. When the oil-fields were overrun in April, it was estimated that the petrol reserves would last no more than two months, and other stores little longer. Throughout the second half of the campaign no supplies of any kind reached the army from outside, and no reinforcements apart from a single British battalion which was flown in. Nothing could come from China; on the contrary, the British were obliged to undertake the maintenance, and even the pay, of all 70,000 men in the Chinese divisions, which added greatly to their administrative burden. Nothing could come by sea, for no ports were left to them in the south, and roadless mountains shut off the Irrawaddy valley from the west coast. Very little could come by air once the Japanese obtained air-superiority, and the shortage of suitable aircraft in India was desperate. And nothing could come overland from India because there was no road. 50,000 men were working on the construction of a road sixty miles long from Imphal in Assam to Tamu on the Burmese border, and it was finished, for fair-weather use only, by mid-May, just in time for the army to retreat along it, but the hundred-mile stretch onwards to Kalewa on the Chindwin was never developed into anything more than a rough cart-track. For the six wet months of the year these routes would have been quite impassable to wheeled traffic. The army in Burma was therefore beleaguered. 'In view of their isolation', wrote General Davies, 'it was impossible for anyone to visualise, with any certainty, any future for the army. The most probable alternatives seemed to be starvation in the jungles of North Burma or a prisoner-of-war camp. Neither was a pleasant prospect.'

In addition to his constant worries about supply, Alexander was disturbed by the many signs of deteriorating morale among his troops. His force was mainly Asiatic – Indians, Burmese and Chinese. The 17th Indian Division had been intended for service in the western desert, and though it might be supposed that Gurkhas would take more naturally to jungles and mountains than deserts, this was not so, for they had had no jungle training and their transport was entirely mechanized, confining them to the roads in a country where roads were few and closely bordered by jungles of which the enemy were masters. The 1st Burma Division was fighting in its own territory, but this was a disadvantage, for the proximity of their homes was an enticement to desert, and desertion was a wasting and contagious disease which the retreat aggravated. The army was desperately short of artillery, but it did have tanks. The all-British 7th Armoured Brigade, in the opinion of every survivor of the campaign, was the solid core of the defence. 'Always on the spot, ready to bring support or break through Japanese road-blocks . . . if one thing saved the army in Burma, it was this formation', wrote General Davies.

From shortly after the fall of Rangoon until the end of the campaign, they had no air support at all. The remaining fighters and fighter airfields were wiped out by the Japanese in two devastating raids, and the RAF withdrew to India. Thenceforward every 'plane in the sky was an enemy. They attacked not only troops on the ground, but the cities and communications behind them. The civilian crews of the railways and river transport abandoned their posts under air-attack, and the already congested roads were blocked by refugees. The population were indifferent or hostile to the British, more worried about their own safety and their rice-fields than the replacement of one governing power by another. They had no love for the Japanese, little for the British. 'It is definitely disappointing', wrote Dorman-Smith to Wavell on 8 March, 'that after all our years of occupation . . . we have not been able to create that loyalty which is generally associated with our subject races.' His very choice of words perhaps explains why. In southern Burma at that moment there was a young teacher and journalist called U Thant, and others like him, who never forgot how it felt to be a member of a subject race.

The hostility of the Burmese, the lack of any certain role or destination, the knowledge that they were cut off, the memory of the Sittang, reports of Japanese brutality to their prisoners, the withdrawal of all air-support, the intense heat, the prevalence of malaria and even cholera in their ranks, all contributed to the loss of morale which became one of Alexander's main anxieties. General Davies adds some other reasons:

The complete severance of all contact with homes and families bore very hardly on the spirits of the men. There was no post. Not a man in the army received a letter of any sort from the time Rangoon was evacuated until he emerged, months later, in Assam. . . .

The conditions in which the troops were fighting and living were exceptionally tough. There were no tents nor any shelter from the elements. There were no replacements of clothing or equipment. The men slept on the ground. If it rained, they got wet – and stayed wet until their clothes dried on them. There were no amenities of any sort. Nothing to read, nothing to drink, nothing to smoke. Essentials were also lacking. For instance there was a lamentable absence of salt – all the salt-bearing areas were on the South Burma coast. Men died for the lack of this simple commodity.

Spirits gradually rose as the weaker elements in the divisions were eliminated by death, capture or desertion, and the arrival of General Slim in the middle of March to command the British Corps was a turning-point. Slim, until then an unknown divisional commander in Iraq, was probably the finest British soldier to emerge from the Second War ('the greatest general we've ever had' was Mountbatten's tribute to him), and he relieved Alexander of much of his responsibility by his skilful and inspiring conduct of the retreat. Such was the confidence that Alexander reposed in him that he rarely interfered with Slim's dispositions. Alexander's headquarters was far from the front, in another Flagstaff House, at Maymyo, thirty miles north-east of Mandalay on the Burma road, the hot-weather retreat of the British Government in Burma, a Burmese Simla, where he was well placed to be within reach of the Chinese in the east and Slim's corps in the south. He visited the southern front once or twice a week, and on those occasions displayed his usual equanimity and courage. Slim in his book gives two instances of it:

I took General Alexander with me when I visited both divisional head-quarters . . . We were machine-gunned from the air . . . and he refused to take shelter in a trench, as I did very briskly, preferring to stand upright behind a tree. I was very annoyed with him for this, not only because it was a foolhardy thing to do, but because we had been trying to stop the men doing it. . . . This was not the only time I found the Army Commander's courage above my standard. . . . Returning that afternoon, the enemy were shelling a bridge over which we had to pass, so I whistled up a couple of light tanks that were standing by and suggested to General Alexander that he got into one and I into the other to cross the bridge. 'What about my car and driver?' he asked at once. 'Oh, he'll have to stand on the gas and chance it,' I replied. 'But it'll be just as dangerous for him as it would be for me!' 'Yes, but he's not the Army Commander.' 'All right,' said Alexander, 'you go in a tank. I'm staying in the car.' So, of course, we both went in the car.[4]

By far the most important of Alexander's many roles in Burma was his responsibility for cooperation with the Chinese. Here his difficulties were practical, political and human. The three Chinese armies (each equivalent in size to a British division) arrived in Burma with no artillery, tanks or lorries, and with only one rifle between three men. 'They had no administrative services', records the Official History. 'There were no engineers, medical, ordnance, supply or transport corps. . . . Most of the Chinese commanders regarded administration as unworthy of the consideration of a fighting soldier. . . . They had very few reserves of ammunition, clothing or equipment.' They depended for almost everything on the British. Moreover, they were ill-disciplined, unreliable as allies, unwilling to concert plans, and given to sudden bursts of despair, when nothing could move them. They would assent courteously, but no action followed. Still they were there, 70,000 of them, prepared to fight close to the borders of their own country in defence of it, and when given time and proper support, proved themselves on several occasions tenacious soldiers whom we were glad to have on our side.

The question of command remained in doubt until the end of March. Nominally Alexander was in command of all the British, Burmese and Chinese forces in Burma, but two men were at first unwilling, for reasons of prestige, to accept it. One was Major-General J. W. Stilwell, US Army; the other, the Generalissimo, Chiang Kai-shek.

Stilwell had been sent to China by Roosevelt as his personal representative, and landed in Chunking on the same day as Alexander reached Rangoon, 5 March. The two men had never met, but each by coincidence had been designated commander of their respective national forces in *Super-Gymnast*, the proposed occupation of French North Africa, and were simultaneously snatched from their desks in Washington and London to carry out side by side the defence of Burma. Stilwell was chosen for this role, though he was nearly sixty years old and blind in one eye, because he was the American officer who knew most about China, having served there for many years between the wars and learnt to speak Chinese perfectly. Of all the foreign Generals whom Alexander was to command during the war, Stilwell and Patton were the most eccentric in their methods and most outspoken in their dislike of the British, and it could have been unfortunate for Anglo-American relations that the first to come under his command was Stilwell, and the second Patton. But Alexander grew to like Stilwell, as he admired Patton. There was much that was engaging in his character. The diary which he kept in Burma, later published in *The Stilwell Papers* (1949), reveals that below his abusive, explosive, contemptuous manner was an ultimate willingness to cooperate, great fortitude and courage, and a certain simplicity and even modesty. For instance, there is no mention in his diary of the occasion in April when he personally led a Chinese battalion in a counter-attack against the Japanese in the Shan States, nor (for different reasons) of the bribe of 50,000 rupees which induced his men to follow him. His anti-British prejudices had no known cause, but they had been building up for many years before they came to a head in Burma. He always referred to the British as 'Limeys', a designation intended to be pejorative. Even their accent irritated him. He imagined that their one purpose was to off-load every dangerous mission on to American shoulders. The Limeys would not fight. They were totally unreliable. 'God damn them', he wrote in his diary, 'they left Rangoon and didn't even tell the liaison officer.' 'The bastards have promised us gas for the trucks and haven't delivered.' It was in his nature to be disrespectful of all authority, and to assume that anyone, American, British or Chinese, who thwarted his wishes was doing so out of personal malice towards him, or stupidity. It was not the British, but his own countrymen, who nicknamed him Vinegar Joe. When he met Roosevelt before leaving Washington for China, he found the President 'very unimpressive . . . just a lot of wind, frothy'. Chiang Kai-shek soon becomes 'Peanut' in the diary. He always lets one down, he is a fumbling strategist, 'he has been boss so long and has so many yes-men around him that he has the idea he is infallible on any subject. He is however determined and forceful, and wants to get on with the war. He is not mentally stable, and he will say many things to your face that he doesn't mean fully or exactly.' Of his Chinese divisional commanders he wrote, 'As usual they are dogging it. Full of excuses as usual. . . . It's all a bunch of crap. By Jesus, I'm about fed up.' 'Crap!' was his invariable retort. To be in the same room with Stilwell was like cohabiting with a jaguar.

It is scarcely surprising that Stilwell's first meeting with Alexander on 13 March went very badly:

Alexander arrived. Very cautious. Long sharp nose. Rather brusque and *yang ch'i* [standoffish]. Lets me stand around while waiting for Shang Chen to come. Uninterested when Shang did come. Astonished to find ME – mere me, a goddam American – in command of Chinese troops. 'Extrawdinery!' Looked me over as if I had just crawled out from under a rock.

Later, relations between the two men improved, but Alexander never won Stilwell's complete confidence. Their backgrounds and outlook were too far apart for a meeting of minds. But Alexander was adept at dealing with difficult men, never losing his temper, softening gritty encounters with a joke, always listening to, and, what is more, understanding, a different point of view and explaining carefully when he could not agree with it. Under this treatment Stilwell's references to Alexander in his diary gradually became more moderate. Within a week he is 'Alex'. '*March 22nd*. He's o.k. now. Took everything nicely.' And once: 'Good old Slim.' But at the slightest provocation the old manner would return: '*April 15th*. Did Alex have the wind-up! Disaster and gloom. No fight left in the British.' When, after the retreat into India, Stilwell heard the BBC describe Alexander as 'a bold and resourceful commander who has fought one of the great defensive battles of the war', his comment was short and inevitable: 'Crap!'

The main difficulty was that the Chinese armies did not look upon either Alexander or Stilwell as their real commander, but referred every order to the Generalissimo or his aides who would often countermand it. It had been impossible to settle the question of command at a political level. Stilwell had understood from Roosevelt that he was to command, under the Generalissimo, all the American forces in China (one detachment of air-force volunteers!) and such Chinese forces as might be assigned to him: if those forces operated in Burma with the British, Wavell would be their supreme commander, a command which he would clearly be incapable of exercising from his distant base in Delhi. Then Chiang proposed to Roosevelt that Stilwell should command the joint force, Chinese and British, and threatened to remove his divisions from Burma if his suggestion were refused. Changing his mind, he next proposed that Stilwell should be the independent commander of the Chinese, and Alexander of the British, and that they should 'cooperate', a proposal that Stilwell put to Alexander on 14 March, with the following reaction:

He was shocked. 'That makes my position impossible from the start.' So I gave him a dirty look, and said that I wasn't exactly on a bed of roses myself. He just stared blankly at me, as much as to say, 'I wonder what the bounder means.'

There was only one way of settling the dispute. Alexander must talk to Chiang Kai-shek in person. He flew to Chunking on 24 March, and reported to the CIGS the results of his mission:

Arrived Chunking 24th, left 27th. Had three interviews with General-issimo and dined with him. Purpose of visit was (1) to pay respects to Generalissimo; (2) to explain situation in Burma and our firm determination not only to hold Burma but to get back Rangoon; (3) to ensure he was satisfied with maintenance arrangements of his troops in Burma.
I particularly avoided asking for anything. I was completely frank with him on all points discussed. He in return was most friendly and cooperative, and stated definitely that in order to ensure unity of command, and pending decision in London and Washington, all Chinese forces in Burma will be under my command. Met a number of Chinese officers of high rank, and hope and think laid foundation of mutual confidence and friendship.

Stilwell took the decision very well. There was no outburst, not even in the diary; simply: 'Saw Alexander. Alex said Chiang Kai-shek agreed to command by British.' In the words of the Official History, 'Stilwell, while retaining command of the Chinese armies under Alexander's general direction, accepted this arrangement, and the two continued to work together loyally and amicably.'[5] The same cannot be said of Chiang Kai-shek. At later meetings with Alexander he and his formidable wife were courteous, but outspoken in their reproaches. Dorman-Smith (who was still Governor of Burma, and shared Alexander's headquarters at Maymyo) reported to London on 7 April:

Chiang Kai-shek and Madame dined last night. He was in good form, but she made some quite fruity remarks on the subject of air-support and of Britain's 'selfish policy of over-concentration on defence of her own island'. Alexander did his best to explain, but she is a tenacious lady. She said that perhaps soon China would be forced to reconsider her position. With an assured supply of arms and air-support she would fight on, but if those were denied her, then how could she continue?

And Chiang Kai-shek cabled to Wavell:

In all my life of long military experience, I have seen nothing to compare with the deplorable unprepared state, confusion and degradation in the war-area of Burma. . . . The Chinese forces went to Burma in the belief that they would be afforded Allied air protection. They have been astonished to find nothing of the sort, and the general conditions under which they have to fight are even inferior to those on the front in China. . . . If no vigorous action is taken in Burma to change the attitude of the masses . . . then defeat in Burma will become inevitable. If Burma is lost, the enemy will be able to develop his offensive to East or West at will.

Chiang had a good grasp of the strategic importance of Burma, but not of the impossibility of reinforcing it with 'planes and troops, nor of the more immediate problem of halting the Japanese advance. When the Allied line in central Burma collapsed in mid-April, it was on the Chinese part of the front that the break came. Slim's corps, with the help of the best of the Chinese divisions, remained intact in the Irrawaddy valley, although they lost the oil-fields, but in the Sittang valley the Japanese overran the Chinese and advanced rapidly through the Shan States to cut the Burma road at Lashio, far to the north-east of Mandalay. 'Jesus,' wrote Stilwell, 'this may screw us completely.' It did. The Chinese armies began to disintegrate and made their way back to China as best they could. Alexander took the only possible decision. He must surrender Mandalay, and withdraw his force from Burma.

He was determined that the Japanese should not pin his British corps against the bend of the Irrawaddy south-west of Mandalay, as Hutton had allowed himself to be pinned against the Sittang. The two situations were not unalike – the same superior and victorious enemy, two open flanks, and a huge river with only one bridge across it. Alexander had the bridge (at Ava) prepared for demolition, broke contact quickly on the southern front, and when the last of his troops were across, blew up the bridge at midnight on 30 April, 'a signal', Slim wrote, 'that we had lost Burma'. The ruins of Mandalay were occupied unopposed by the enemy next day.

Alexander's intention was now firm, though he still had no direct orders from Wavell. He hoped that he could withdraw quickly enough to escape the enemy, and that the monsoon would be delayed long enough for the mountain-tracks to be passable, but not so long that the

Japanese could use the same tracks in pursuit. He wished to impose between himself and them not only mountains and rivers but a sheet of rain. Morale in the corps immediately rose when this clear policy was announced, with the hope it gave of reunion with their families. But Alexander was disturbed by two problems: the first was pressure from home to send part of his force to China; and the second the logistics of the terrible march ahead of them.

The British, and particularly the Americans, attached great importance to the retention of China in the war. No excuse must be given to Chiang to complain that he had been abandoned. The main routes out of North Burma led to China, not India, and escape might be easier that way. When Wavell visited Alexander at Maymyo at the beginning of April, they had therefore discussed the possibility of a retreat to China, more as a political gesture than for any military advantage, and Churchill said definitely that he expected Alexander 'to fall back into China with the Chinese armies'. Alexander knew that this policy would create consternation among his British and Indian troops, and put forward the compromise that only part of them, a token force, would retreat with the Chinese. He nominated for this sacrificial role Slim's headquarters, the 7th Armoured Brigade and the 48th Gurkha Brigade, in fact the best. Slim strongly disagreed. His men would resent what amounted to internment in China after their long campaign, and there was no means of supplying them there or tending their wounded. The nearest Chinese province of Yunnan was known to be in a state of famine. The men would starve, and serve no useful purpose at a time when they were badly needed in India. Besides, the Burma Corps was now reduced to so low a state in equipment and fighting strength that they would be a poor advertisement for the Allies, and their presence in China might do more political harm than good. Alexander did not need to be told this. He saw it all too clearly, and Slim, trusting him, did not press the point. Political pressure from London and Delhi conflicted with Alexander's own common sense. He took his decision even before the Burma Road was cut. On 23 April he telegraphed to Wavell that 'owing to the supply situation' the Chinese would retreat to China, the British to India. If he had not made this decision, says Davies, who was present, 'I think it would have resulted in a serious situation between Slim and Alexander.' No British withdrew to China, but some Chinese did withdraw to India. Two of their divisions, including that which had given us much help in the battle

for the oilfields, succeeded in making their way over the mountains into
Assam. The rest dispersed north-east, and Alexander had no further
control over them nor responsibility for their fate.

Now everything depended upon the rate of the Japanese advance,
the beginning of the rains, and the state of the jungle-tracks. From
the Ava bridge to Imphal, the nearest base in India, is a distance,
across two broad mountain chains and one major river, the Chindwin,
of more than 300 miles. Work on the road had made the route barely
motorable in good weather, impassable in bad, and there was no
bridge over the Chindwin. The monsoon was expected to begin about
15 May. They had no more than a fortnight to get home. The Japanese
followed up quickly. They captured Monywa on the lower Chindwin,
forcing the army to use a single more northern route, and then severely
harassed them at the ferry-crossing of the Chindwin just south of
Kalewa. Alexander remained with the corps, having sent a large part of
his headquarters staff by air to India, wishing to share whatever fate
awaited them and because he was deeply concerned with the plight of
the refugees, Indian, Burmese and some British, who were intermingled
with the retreating convoys. Dorman-Smith had handed over to him
on 21 April all civilian affairs, 'because', he reported to Wavell,
'Alexander has shown himself quite excellent in dealing with civilian
officers and concerns'. He allotted all spare places on the lorries to the
refugees. The troops marched. When they reached the Chindwin,
Slim and Davies pleaded with him to withdraw his small tactical headquarters to the far bank, as the Japanese were pressing up the river very
fast from Monywa. He did so, just in time. The Chindwin crossing was
defended only long enough for the troops to escape, but they were
obliged to leave behind on the east bank much of their transport and all
their remaining tanks. Fortunately, it was their last battle in Burma.
Alexander appealed to Wavell to send a brigade forward from India
to help them on the last stage of their journey, but Wavell replied that
he had none to spare.

From Kalewa to Tamu, the nearest point to which India could stretch
out a hand to help them, was 100 miles through dense jungle. The rains
began on 12 May, and intensified during the next week. The road,
which had been stocked with sufficient food for the march, although the
troops were put on half-rations as a precaution, was just usable by the
ninety lorries which remained to carry the sick and wounded, and the
able-bodied men, who now numbered about 36,000, retreated on foot

through 'Death Valley', so-named because it was highly malarious, and so did the refugees:

There were hundreds of thousands of them. They died as they walked along this Via Dolorosa. They died of smallpox, of cholera, of weakness and starvation, or simply of old age – and where they died they lay. No one buried them, they were just pushed off the road into the verges of the encroaching forest, or down the steep banks of the lush ravines below.

The stench was terrible. Never for one moment of that last horrible month was it absent from the nostrils of the troops. . . . Everyone realised, from the humblest private soldier, that within the first few days of the initial heavy downpours, the road to Assam, the lifeline of the army, would disintegrate into an impassable morass. There was a dreadful tension in the air. Would the weather hold? Sickness took an increasing toll of the troops. The army had entered the area of cerebral malaria. Men would get the malarial shivers one night, and be dead by the morning.[6]

Alexander himself was ordered home. On 3 May Churchill had told Wavell:

I am anxious about Alexander. There is no sense in his remaining to command a force reduced to little more than a brigade. He is needed for very important business. Whenever you consider that his command has fallen to the level of a division or less, and that no important military advantage can be gained by his retention of it, you should order him to return to India by air, leaving him no option. This is what we did to Gort before Dunkirk.

He remained with the army until 16 May, and then flew from Assam to Simla, where he had a week's rest, and began to write his Burma despatch. He returned to Assam on 23 May, and when Stilwell, who with a few companions had made an adventurous escape on foot across the northern mountains, reached Tinsukia in the Brahmaputra valley on that day, Alexander and Wavell were there to meet him. The last men of the Burma army had struggled into Imphal on 20 May, and Alexander's command came officially to an end. By that time the heavy rains had removed all danger of a Japanese pursuit. The army was saved.

At a press-conference in Delhi on 25 May Stilwell told the world, 'We got a hell of a beating. We got run out of Burma, and it is as humiliating as hell. I think we ought to find out what caused it, and go back and retake it.' Wavell wrote in his despatch: 'It has been from a strategical point of view our most serious reverse of the Japanese war.' Of Alexander's own role he said: 'He took over an extremely difficult situation and a somewhat shaken and disorganised army. By his cool and inspiring leadership he did everything possible during the remainder of the campaign to check the Japanese advance and to keep the army together.' Mountbatten's summing-up was: 'He should never have been sent out. I think the miracle is that he did not lose his prestige through this unmitigated disaster, a hopeless defeat, which was in no sense whatever his fault.' And Churchill's: 'In this his first experience of independent command, though it ended in stark defeat, he showed all those qualities of military skill, imperturbability and wise judgement that brought him later into the first rank of Allied war leaders.'

What exactly had he achieved? To put the debit side first, he had not been able to prevent the Japanese from gaining their primary object. 'Burma', he wrote in his Memoirs, 'was a complete military defeat'; and Slim, in his, rubbed in the point more harshly: 'We had been outmanoeuvred, out-fought and out-generalled.' He had lost 13,500 men of the British corps alone and most of their equipment, while the Japanese had conquered Burma in three-and-a-half months, from the extreme south to the extreme north, at a cost of 4,500 casualties. But Alexander had denied them the satisfaction of forcing his capitulation. During a retreat of 700 miles he had survived all attempts to encircle him. As at Dunkirk, he had saved a beaten army by a combination of forethought, perseverance, example and good luck.

He was lucky three times: at the road-block north of Rangoon, in the appointment of Slim, and in beating the Japanese in the race for the Chindwin crossing. Three strokes of good-fortune are a reasonable compensation for so much ill-fortune in other ways. He was unfortunate in the timing of his take-over at the crisis of the whole campaign; in the loss of air-support; in the inadequacy of his troops and their equipment; in his poor communications; in his confrontation with so prickly a subordinate as Stilwell, so unpredictable an ally as Chiang Kai-shek; in the almost unprecedented isolation of a British army from all outside help; in the handicap of weather, the extreme heat and then the menace of extreme rain; in the disease, and the refugees, and the hostility of the population; and particularly in the lack of clear directives from his Commander-in-Chief. Seldom can a General have been faced by so catastrophic a combination of disadvantages. Yet he won through. He owed much to Slim, and he acknowledged that he owed to Stilwell the most effective contribution which the Chinese troops were capable of making. Of his own decisions, four stand out as decisive: to abandon Rangoon, when he knew that Wavell thought it at that moment unnecessary; to retreat across the Irrawaddy and surrender Mandalay without a fight; to withdraw his force to India without orders before the monsoon cut him off; and to ignore his instructions to send part of it to China. Some might add a fifth: his resistance to the pressure put upon him by Stilwell and Chiang Kai-shek to counter-attack southwards to throw the enemy off-balance, an offensive which was quite beyond their power and would have ended in disaster.

For these decisions, and for the example of calm courage which he set, Alexander can be said to have saved the army when another General might have lost it. He emerged from the campaign with heightened prestige. Two defeats in succession, Dunkirk and Burma, might have ended his effective career, as the first ended Gort's, and the second Hutton's and Smyth's. But even before the campaign was over and his army safe, Churchill had destined him for still higher command in a 'very important business', and it can only be because the character of the man had once again been proved equal to extreme adversity, and Churchill loved him for it, tacitly acknowledging that he had imposed on the British army in Burma a task beyond their powers.

9

THE WESTERN DESERT

Having written his Burma despatch during a recuperative month at Simla and Delhi, Alexander flew home in early July 1942. En route he spent three days in Cairo where he met Auchinleck for the first time since they had held parallel commands on the North West Frontier, but was careful to avoid any involvement in the controversy about the immediate past and future of Eighth Army, which was then building up to the climax of Auchinleck's replacement as Commander-in-Chief, Middle East, by Alexander himself. From Cairo he and his ADC flew to Lisbon and thence to Shannon in Ireland, a 'neutral' flight which obliged them to travel in civilian clothes and under pseudonyms, Alexander choosing to be listed as a mechanical engineer and Rupert Clarke as a student. The intrepid pair passed through unrecognized. On his arrival Lady Alexander noticed that he was still visibly affected by his ordeal in Burma, having lost several pounds in weight, and it took him some weeks fully to recover. Fortunately he was able to spend the first fortnight at home.

His next appointment, Churchill's 'very important business', was to command the British First Amy in *Torch*, the Anglo-American invasion of French North Africa, which had been much enlarged in size and scope since *Super-Gymnast*. The invasion was at that time set for 7 October and Alexander's American opposite-number was to be Patton in place of Stilwell, and both were to come under the supreme command of Eisenhower. Alex and Ike, as they were soon to become to each other, met for the first time in London on 4 August 1942. The meeting is described in the diary of Harry Butcher, Eisenhower's naval ADC:

This was an important luncheon, for with Ike junior to Alexander in rank, with no actual battle experience, with his appointment as C. in C. not yet confirmed by the President, with Alexander having commanded at Dunkirk during the evacuation and more recently in Burma, there was a touchy question of how acceptable Ike might be to Alexander. I was in Ike's office . . . when he returned from lunch. His first comment was: 'That guy's good! He ought to be Commander-in-Chief instead of me!' This evening I asked Ike how he felt they could click. 'Fine', he said. 'The last thing Alexander said as we were going out of the door after lunch was "You're off to a good start." ' Ike construed this as approval of him, which is important.[1]

Torch and *Lightfoot* (the coming offensive in the western desert) were two parts of the same strategic conception. The Allied purpose, pending the gathering of their full strength for the bound across the English Channel, was to win the whole southern shore of the Mediterranean, as a base for future operations in southern Europe, as protection for their shipping-routes, and (strategically most important) as an immense glacis to defend their sources of oil in the Middle East. 'The Suez Canal', Ferdinand de Lesseps had prophesied in 1884, 'will be a gateway to the oceans. Everybody will compete for its possession. You have thus marked the site of a great future battlefield.' But the battle of Egypt was much more than a struggle for possession of a waterway. If Egypt had fallen, the hinge of three continents would have snapped. 'A million square miles of territory lie behind the thin barrier at Alamein', Rommel wrote exultingly, and went on to despair of the shortsightedness of his political leaders in refusing him the means of seizing so rich a strategic prize. If he managed to skewer with his armoured divisions the British army which lay across the sixty miles of desert between Alamein and the Nile, Palestine and Syria would be exposed to his further thrusts, then Iraq and Persia, then the oil-fields of the Gulf, and ultimately a new route to the southern German flank in Russia. The possibility that the Caucasus front might break first, and German armies pour southwards through Persia before the Alamein battle had been fought, was a prospect so appalling that it was not seriously considered by the Allies, who had their own huge pincer-movement centrally in their thoughts, the battle in Egypt and the hand which would reach out to it from Algeria and Tunis.

Auchinleck was both Commander-in-Chief Middle East and temporarily in command of Eighth Army after his belated relief of Ritchie, the General responsible for the loss of Tobruk. Auchinleck himself had

not escaped some share of the blame for this disaster, and his achievement in halting Rommel on the Alamein line did not compensate in
Churchill's eyes for the loss of so many hundreds of miles of hard-won
desert. Churchill saw Tobruk as another Singapore. It assumed for him
an emotional and political significance out of proportion to its military
importance, but Rommel's capture of 33,000 prisoners and a vast
quantity of supplies by a single lightning manoeuvre was an under-
standable blow to Churchill's hopes and prestige when the news reached
him in Washington. 'Defeat is one thing,' he said, 'disgrace another.'
Auchinleck himself was deeply depressed, and two days later, 23 June,
offered the CIGS his resignation, adding, 'It occurred to me that you
might want to use Alexander', who was then due to arrive in Cairo
on his way back from Burma. Brooke replied reaffirming his own and
Churchill's confidence, and Auchinleck fought Rommel to a halt at
Alamein in a series of stabbing counter-attacks in July. Their effect can
be summed up in Rommel's own words: 'Our attack came to a halt
and our strength failed. . . . We were met by greatly superior British
armoured formations thrusting against our front. Our chance . . . was
irretrievably gone.'[2]

Churchill did not see the first battle of Alamein as a great victory.
His mind was still full of his earlier disappointment, he was challenged
in Parliament on his overall conduct of the war, and he regarded
Auchinleck's achievement in stopping Rommel as little more than a
failure to drive him back, and began to piece together from hints, and a
vivid imagination fed by his own oratory, the picture of a despondent
Eighth Army, not only punchless but punch-drunk, ignoring that their
performance in the July battles was one of which a dispirited army
would not have been capable. When Auchinleck cabled home that the
offensive could not be renewed until mid-September, Churchill made
up his mind that he must go to Egypt himself to see what was wrong.
He had wanted to go earlier, but Eden told him that he would only be
in the way. 'You mean like a great blue-bottle buzzing over a huge
cowpat?' 'That's just what I do mean.'[3]

When Churchill reached Cairo on 3 August, he was as high-spirited
as a schoolboy released for the holidays. He had once written that war
and preparation for war create 'the tremendous situations', and this
was undoubtedly a tremendous situation. He was sped on his way by a
vote of confidence in the House of Commons, and was surrounded by
Generals, Admirals and Air-Marshals who saw in him, as he saw

himself, more a Supreme Commander than a Prime Minister. The enthusiastic greeting of the troops whenever he appeared, the climate, the bathing, the exciting proximity of Cairo to the front-line, all combined to inspire him to dramatic measures, without which his visit would have ended in anti-climax. He had not left London with the intention of sacking Auchinleck. At that stage he thought only of appointing a new commander for Eighth Army, and the man on whom he had fixed his eye was Gott, of whom he had heard good reports from Eden, though Brooke thought Gott exhausted by his years of desert-fighting and already favoured Montgomery for the command. Churchill's change of mind about Auchinleck was due partly to trivial causes like the 'wire-netted cube, full of flies and important military personages' where he was offered breakfast at Auchinleck's desert headquarters, and the slighting remarks about the Commander-in-Chief made to him by the RAF at luncheon that same day, a luncheon which they had had the good sense to order in advance from Shepherd's Hotel in Cairo. Nor was Churchill impressed by Auchinleck's dour nature and lack of verbal fire (for to Churchill an idea expressed with animation always seemed sounder than a better idea stated more modestly), and when Auchinleck reiterated his conviction that no major attack could be launched before 15 September, Churchill, hungry for victory, compared him mentally to Rommel, and Auchinleck suffered from the comparison. The doubts which were seeded when Tobruk was lost now germinated. Auchinleck must go.

The question is not so much whether Churchill was wrong to relieve him of his command when he lost confidence in him, but whether he was wrong to lose confidence. Even John Connell, Auchinleck's biographer and eloquent champion, surprisingly ended his long analysis of the question with the conclusion that 'it is not to be disputed that a change in command was desirable', although he thought Churchill's methods shabby and unfair. Many senior officers in the Middle East agreed then, and agree now, that Churchill was right. Among them was General (later Field Marshal) John Harding, who with Dorman-Smith, brother of the Governor of Burma, was one of the two Deputies under General Corbett, the Chief of Staff:

Do you think that Churchill was right to relieve Auchinleck?

Yes, I'm absolutely certain.

You don't think he had a hard deal?

Well no, I don't.

But he'd done very well in the preceding month by stopping Rommel. Would you say that the whole of the July fighting had been a failure?

Yes. It had stopped Rommel, but more by courage than skill. The Auk tried to regain the initiative by limited attacks on various fronts, by committing armoured formations to battle without proper experience or training. Dorman-Smith held the view that it was quite ridiculous to remain regimental-minded or even formation-minded – the whole thing should be flexible. Well, I wouldn't disagree with him in principle, but to try and impose that philosophy in the middle of a crucial battle is insane. The Auk swallowed his advice. Morale was high in good regiments up to brigade level, but low all round. It was a chaotic situation. The Army was in a state of confusion.

Churchill made up his mind on 6 August, and offered the Middle East command to the CIGS, who was with him in Cairo. Brooke declined, believing that he had a greater duty to remain at Churchill's side, and recommended Alexander, who heard of his appointment in London early next day. Auchinleck was told of his relief on the 8th, and refused the compensating offer of the new Persia-Iraq command on the grounds that a General who has been declared unsuccessful ceases to exert any authority. Montgomery was to succeed Alexander in *Torch*, Gott was to command Eighth Army, Corbett and Dorman-Smith were both to be replaced at the head of the Cairo staff. There was a certain splendour in this wholesale slaughter and elevation of Generals, but Churchill's magnanimity sublimated his ruthlessness when he was faced by the actual process of telling Auchinleck that he was relieved. 'You know,' he said to Alexander a few days later, 'it was like killing a magnificent stag.' The future pattern was still not complete. Gott was shot down over the desert and killed before he had taken command of Eighth Army, and Montgomery, as Brooke had always wanted, was sent for to take his place. Anderson, the third commander whom First Army had seen in a week, replaced Montgomery.

Alexander flew to Cairo on 8 August and arrived at breakfast-time next morning. His meeting with Brooke and Churchill was invested with comedy, since each of them wished to have the first word with him:

We were expecting Alexander [Brooke's diary records] and I badly wanted to see him before the P.M. got hold of him, and had instructed for him to be brought round to my room. Unfortunately he arrived while I was having breakfast on the verandah. The P.M.'s flag-lieutenant whispered in my ear that he had arrived, but the P.M. overheard and had then to be told that Alex had gone off to the lavatory! Finally I got an opportunity and dashed out to see him. I wanted to warn him as regards the P.M.'s conception of the Command of the Middle East as opposed to that of the Eighth Army which he mixes together. I then brought Alex in to the P.M. and we had a long talk, after which I had a long go with Alex by himself.

Alexander was not to take over actual command until 15 August, and he had time to walk round Cairo and visit the desert army with Harding to form his first impressions. The soldiers appeared to him tough and fit enough, but lacking in cheerfulness and confidence. One sign of it was that his car was rarely saluted, and he considered whether he should issue a disciplinary order as soon as he had the authority, but decided that it was wiser not to, since whatever was wrong needed profounder treatment which an initial schoolmasterish approach would have depreciated. In the interval he toured the Alamein front to fix the topographical features in his mind, and set up his own simple camp close by the Pyramids, where he would be within reach of the vast main headquarters in Cairo but detached from its bustling atmosphere. On the evening of 10 August he saw Churchill again, and it was at the conclusion of that meeting that the Prime Minister drew towards him a small blue sheet of Embassy notepaper, and wrote on it in his own hand:

Directive to General Alexander
Commander in Chief in the Middle East

1. Your prime and main duty will be to take or destroy at the earliest opportunity the German-Italian Army commanded by Field Marshal Rommel together with all its supplies and establishments in Egypt and Libya.

2. You will discharge or cause to be discharged such other duties as pertain to your Command without prejudice to the task described in paragraph 1, which must be considered paramount in His Majesty's interests.

W.S.C. 10.viii.42.

The order was also initialled by Brooke. It must be one of the few military directives in modern times to mention the opposing commander by name, and it is curious in the light of what happened, and was known to be about to happen, that Alexander's horizon was confined by this famous order to Egypt and Libya alone, and that it contained no reference, even by implication, to the help which *Lightfoot* could give to *Torch*, or the synchronization of the two operations.

That night Churchill flew on to meet Stalin in Moscow, and on 12 August Montgomery landed at Cairo, three days after Alexander. Harding has given me this account of his first meeting with the two of them:

The first I knew of the changes in command was one afternoon [12 August] when my orderly came in and said, "The Commander-in-Chief wishes to see you." So I said, "Who is the Commander-in-Chief?" I went along to the C. in C.'s room, and there, sitting at the desk, was Monty: and sitting on the desk, drumming his heels against it, was Alex. I didn't know what their respective appointments were. Nobody had told me. Monty introduced me to Alex: "You know General Alexander?" It was the first time I'd ever met him, but I knew all about him of course. Monty said, "Well, John, you've been out here a long time. Tell me everything", and then he put me through a catechism for about an hour, with Alex not taking any real part in the discussion, and I was quizzed on all the formation commanders down to brigades. At the end he said, "From all this muckage, can you organize for me two desert-trained armoured divisions and a mobile infantry division?" I asked, "And hold the front too, presumably?" "Yes, of course." "Yes, I think I can."

By that evening Harding had produced a plan for the *Corps de Chasse* which Montgomery had been creating in his head as he flew from London to Cairo. It was the first decision he made, and his method of making it, with Alexander present but not interfering, foreshadowed the relationship which they both desired.

Together (for there is no purpose in disputing the priority of their orders, as they were entirely of one mind on the matter) they made it immediately clear that there would be no retreat from the Alamein position. In his Memoirs Montgomery made much of this order and the reasons for it, with the effect of placing Auchinleck's past decisions in the gloomiest light, so heightening the contrast with his own brilliance. He relates that Auchinleck had explained to him that 'at all costs the Eighth Army was to be preserved in being. . . . If Rommel attacked in strength, as was expected soon, the Eighth Army would fall back on the Delta. . . . I listened in amazement to this exposition of his plans.' That he had formulated this travesty of the facts very early on, and convinced himself of its truth, is shown by a note he made before the battle of Alamein: 'The Army plan of battle was that if Rommel attacked, a withdrawal to rear lines *would* take place [Montgomery's italics], and orders to this effect had been issued. . . . If changes in the high command had not been made early in August, we would have lost Egypt. . . . I changed the plan completely, and Rommel was seen off.'

In fact there was no such order. Nor was there a 'complete' change of plan. Auchinleck intended to withdraw only in the last resort, to save what was left of his army after a lost battle; not to withdraw if Rommel attacked. Arrangements had certainly been made to fortify the Delta as a delaying-line in case Rommel should break through, and these defences were not merely approved by Alexander but hurried forward by him. It was only sensible that both Auchinleck and Alexander should make these preparations, but that they implied an intention to retreat as soon as Rommel began his offensive was no more true of one than of the other. Both saw the defence of the Delta as independent of the battle which Eighth Army must fight at Alamein if the attack came. The difference in their attitude, which was of greater psychological than military importance, might be summarized like this: Auchinleck had said in effect, 'Eighth Army will fight as long and as fiercely as possible on the Alamein line, but in the last resort, rather than allow itself to be broken up in the open desert, it will move back to join the Delta garrison.' Alexander and Montgomery said, 'Eighth Army will never retreat from Alamein. If it is overwhelmed, the Delta defences may provide a temporary delaying-line, but the campaign will be over. Rommel will have won. Therefore Alamein will be defended to the last. It must be clearly understood that this is our final line.' European armies never fight literally to the last man. In either case there would have been survivors if Rommel had broken through, many of whom would have found their way back to join the Delta garrison. In the Auchinleck plan they would have been in semi-organized units; in the Alexander-Montgomery plan they would have taken their chance individually. But neither Auchinleck nor Alexander imagined that there was any real hope of saving Egypt if the line broke at Alamein. Auchinleck thought that part of the army might survive in a cohesive state; Alexander did not even think that. Harding, who left Cairo in late August to take command of 7th Armoured Division in the desert, was well placed to foresee the consequences of defeat:

If Rommel had broken through at Alamein, there was really no fall-back position. You could say that it was a good idea to have a skeleton plan for conducting operations in order to delay Rommel's entry into Cairo. But in my opinion, if he had broken through, the time-factor, the topography, and the effect on the general political and social situation in the Delta would have been such that nothing could have stopped him from entering Cairo.

Was it Auchinleck's intention to fight a last-ditch battle on the Alamein line?

Yes, in a sense, but with a plan to withdraw if in his judgement the destruction of Eighth Army was at risk. In that case he intended to impose delay on Rommel in the Delta, and to extricate the bulk of his force south of Cairo, and then over the Suez Canal into Palestine.

Why then did Alexander and Montgomery alter this plan? It sounds sensible – to fight the main battle, and if it went very badly, to have some line of retreat?

It got known, of course, that there was a plan to withdraw in the last resort. Monty and Alex (Monty primarily, but Alex in full support) said that there would be no retreat.

In any circumstances?

In any circumstances. If you were realistic, you had to admit to yourself that if the Alamein position became untenable through penetration and subsequent exploitation by Rommel, there was no other place in which you could fight an effective battle.

Does this mean that the Army would have been lost if the Alamein position had gone?

I think the greater part of it. The really good and brave would have got away. But it would have been a rabble. It was the realism with which Monty and Alex saw this situation that led them to decide that the only way of dealing with it was to make it quite clear to everybody that they fought and died at Alamein. It was impossible to fight in Cairo. This had a tremendous moral effect on the army. They were both absolutely justified.

The practical demonstration that they meant what they said, and a good example of the interpenetration of Auchinleck's plans with Montgomery's, came with the battle of Alam Halfa in the first week of September. The controversy over the Alam Halfa plan is of less importance than that over the 'retreat' order, though historically it has generated even more heat. It has been said that Montgomery took credit for Auchinleck's plan to make this ridge, which lay a few miles in rear of the southern part of the British line, a nodal point of the defences. Both guessed correctly that Rommel would attack in this sector, and both realized the importance of the ridge, which indeed declared itself by its very prominence above the desert. Both garrisoned it, Auchinleck by a brigade, Montgomery by a whole division. There the similarity in the two plans ends. Auchinleck had ordered on 30 July that the essence of the defence plan was fluidity and mobility, which implied, however indirectly, the possibility of retreat. Montgomery said that there would be no retreat, and Alam Halfa must be held as securely as a fortress, not as the fulcrum of a mobile battle. The way in which the battle was fought and won was of Montgomery's own devising, and he deserves for it historically the credit which he received overwhelmingly from his troops at the time.

The battles of Alam Halfa and Alamein, as Alexander always insisted, were Montgomery's battles. Rather than retell the detailed story of them, it is more useful in a biography of Alexander to assess what contribution he made to Montgomery's victories, to define the complex relationship between the two men, and to discuss whether Alexander might have ruled Montgomery with a firmer hand.

Alexander's responsibilities in the Middle East, outside Egypt, included Syria, Palestine, Transjordan, the Lebanon, the Sudan, Eritrea, Cyprus and guerilla activities in the Balkans and Aegean. Apart from the latter, all these territories were militarily quiescent. Alexander visited their small garrisons when he found time. He flew to Jerusalem and Syria before the battle of Alamein, and after it to Cyprus, Eritrea and the Sudan. He was also responsible for the huge administrative base in Egypt, which employed, including contracted labour, over two million men. He was the military member of the Middle East Defence Committee, on which Tedder and Admiral Harwood represented the other services. He was constantly in touch with the Resident Minister (Casey) on the political affairs of his command. The role of the Middle East Air Force was under his ultimate direction, and as a member of the Defence Committee he was consulted about the movements of naval units, the precarious situation of Malta, and the French fleet which remained neutralized in Alexandria harbour. In spite of the great range and geographical extent of his responsibilities, they were less than Auchinleck's had been, for Iraq and Persia were now in a separate command under Maitland Wilson (though administered from the Delta), and Auchinleck had in addition assumed control of Eighth Army after dismissing Ritchie. Alexander, as he wrote in his despatch, 'was free therefore to concentrate all my attention on the threat to Egypt from the west', and the despatch is concerned almost exclusively with it.

Such was the paramount importance of this front that Churchill considered that everything else could be left to 'quartermasters' and the Minister of State. Brooke had the greatest difficulty in preventing him from urging Alexander to take personal command in the desert. Churchill himself quotes with apparent approval an entry from the diary of his military assistant, Colonel Jacob:

The Prime Minister's mind is entirely fixed on the defeat of Rommel, and on getting General Alexander into complete charge of the operations in the Western Desert. He does not understand how a man can remain in Cairo while great events are occurring in the desert, and leave the conduct of them to someone else. He strode up and down declaiming on this point, and he means to have his way. 'Rommel, Rommel, Rommel, Rommel!' he cried. 'What else matters but beating him?'

The date of this entry in Jacob's diary is 8 August, the day after Alexander's appointment. Had Alexander taken this advice, or had he not been protected from it by Brooke, the strain upon his relations with Montgomery would have become intolerable, and it was partly because Brooke knew that Alexander would not interfere with Montgomery that he so strongly recommended his appointment, and was reconciled to the dismissal of Auchinleck because an Auchinleck-Montgomery partnership would have been calamitous. Alexander saw his role quite clearly. Having gone over the ground, he agreed with Montgomery the general plans, first of defence and then of attack, and left him to elaborate and execute them. He protected Montgomery's rear, first in the limited military sense, secondly in the far more important administrative sense, and thirdly in the political sense. He mastered very quickly the intricacies of the Middle East base, and saw to it by personal inspection that the new divisions arriving and the old divisions refitting were equipped and trained as efficiently as possible, and the whole base geared to support a major battle and the thousand-mile pursuit which must follow victory. In this task he received from McCreery, his Chief of Staff, wise advice and energetic support. Politically he interposed himself between the Army Commander and the Prime Minister's impatience. A prime cause of Auchinleck's fall from favour had been his admission that he could not renew the offensive until the middle of September. Now Alexander had to persuade the Prime Minister that it must be delayed until the last week of October. There were two reasons for this. The new men and new weapons arriving in Egypt could not be put into battle straight from the docks. Between 1 August and 23 October, 41,000 men joined Eighth Army and over 300 Sherman tanks which were now to be employed in battle for the first time in any theatre of war. Men and tanks must be properly prepared. Secondly, there was the timing of *Lightfoot* in relation to *Torch*, a matter (strangely, as it now seems) which was left to Alexander and not decided or even influenced by the Chiefs of Staff. General Al Gruenther, then planning *Torch* in London, has said to me: 'We hadn't time to think about Alamein. We Americans didn't even know where Alamein was.' In his despatch, Alexander gave his reasons for leaving an interval of a fortnight between the opening of the Alamein offensive and D Day for *Torch*, which was now fixed for 8 November:

I was convinced that this was the best interval that could be looked for in the circumstances. It would be long enough to destroy the greater part of the Axis army facing us. but on the other hand it would be too short for the enemy to start reinforcing Africa on any significant scale. Both these facts would be likely to have a strong effect on the French attitude. The decisive factor was that I was certain that to attack before I was ready would be to risk failure if not to court disaster.

With these arguments he successfully fended off Churchill's pressure for an earlier date. The battle of Alam Halfa, in the best way possible, lost any remaining chance that Auchinleck's September date could be adhered to, and at the same time strengthened Alexander's hand in his argument with the Prime Minister, since it was difficult for Churchill to maintain after one resounding victory that his Generals in Egypt were incompetent to decide the timing of the next. The actual date was determined by the phases of the moon. A near-full moon was required throughout the battle so that the sappers could see their way to clear the minefields. The October moon came on the 24th. Montgomery said that he would attack on the night of 23 October, and Alexander backed him up. After further grumbling, Churchill accepted it. Thus all things came together: the strategy, the administration, the tactical needs, and the unwavering agreement between the two men most responsible, Alexander and Montgomery, respectively the producer and director of the biggest desert drama the world had yet seen.

The solidarity of their partnership could fairly be said to be due more to

Alexander than to Montgomery. Like an understanding husband in a difficult marriage, he knew that idiosyncrasy must be accepted because it is valuable and unalterable, and that the marriage must be rooted first on the assumption, and then on the habit, of success. He must never allow himself to quarrel with Montgomery, for what would be gained? Intermittent demonstrations of his authority would only cause double damage to Montgomery's confidence, in himself and in his Commander-in-Chief. Any orders countermanding Montgomery's, or which forced him to take a line of action which he had discarded or not considered, would, he felt, provoke him to protest or disobey. For Alexander to antagonize Montgomery would mean antagonizing Eighth Army, and self-effacement, so long as things went right, was a small price to pay for amity. Alexander adopted this attitude not out of modesty or from lack of will-power, but as a deliberate act of policy, based on his own careful assessment of a particularly difficult and gifted man.

Montgomery was a General who must either be left unpinioned, or his neck wrung. As his neck could not be wrung unless he failed, and as he did not fail, he could not be pinioned. Alexander had the highest respect for Montgomery as a battle-fighter, and saw that there was no room on that narrow front for two top-ranking Generals. Had their roles been reversed, Montgomery would have been incapable of the self-control which Alexander constantly displayed. No previous Commander-in-Chief in the Middle East, neither Wavell nor Auchinleck, had taken second place to their Army Commander in demonstrable decision and public acclaim. Now the Middle East outside Egypt was reduced to a huge geographical area garrisoned by a handful of troops. It contained only one proper army, the Eighth, one front, Alamein, and one enemy, Rommel – and Montgomery had all three well in hand. The public did not hear of Alexander's wider responsibilities and would not have been much interested in them if they had, sharing the view of Churchill and of the Chinese Generals whom Alexander had known in Burma that administration is below the dignity of a true commander. The Commander-in-Chief did not even retain in his hands a strategic reserve. All reinforcements were fed forward to the Army as soon as they were ready, not always at Alexander's initiative. Harding gives this example:

One day de Guingand [Montgomery's Chief of Staff] rang me up and said, "The Army Commander wants you to send up the 44th Division tomorrow. He wants it to bolster his front while he builds up his plans for the offensive." Then Monty came on the line. I told him that the division was not ready because it was not properly equipped. I would have to ask Alex first. I found him talking to Miles Lampson [the British Ambassador in Cairo]. "Is that what Monty wants?" he asked. "Yes." "Well, do it."

This situation, and this Commander-in-Chief, ideally suited Montgomery. In his Memoirs he wrote: 'He never bothered me, never fussed me, never suggested what I ought to do, and gave me at once everything I asked for', a statement which could be read either as a tribute or as a description of a successful brush-off. For among the things which Alexander gave him was Eighth Army. 'He let me run this private war in my own way. . . . He was content to leave well alone.' Montgomery's version of their relationship, for all its outward sweetness, was intended to indicate that he had no rival in the desert, and Alexander unconsciously gave him every help to propagate this view. His visits to Eighth Army were deliberately pitched in so low a key that even some of the Corps Commanders scarcely knew him – like Horrocks, to whom Alexander appeared 'remote from the battle . . . as if he lived in a world of his own which few others were encouraged to enter'.[4] De Guingand, who admired Alexander greatly, wrote of him unwittingly in terms which suggest a wholesaler's routine calls on the manager of Fortnum and Mason's: 'I often used to sit in the Army Commander's caravan when Alexander paid his visits to Eighth Army before the battle of Alamein. Monty would rattle out his requests – troops, commanders, equipment, whatever it might be. His Commander-in-Chief took short notes, and with the greatest rapidity these requirements became accomplished facts.'[5]

None of these officers would ever have shown disrespect towards Alexander, for they certainly felt none. It was simply that Montgomery took advantage of Alexander's modesty to make Eighth Army wholly his own, not mainly out of personal vanity, but because he knew that soldiers would follow a single leader who was unmistakable. There is no doubt that his methods played a critical part in the defeat of Rommel. He took pains to emphasize that Eighth Army was quite different from any other army which happened to have had the same name. When it came to awarding the Africa Star, no man who had not campaigned with Montgomery was permitted to wear it, though Africa had been the battlefield of Eighth Army for three years before Alamein and it had suffered 80,000 casualties. As he once wrote, the commander must be 'not only a master, but a mascot'. So he focussed attention upon himself, first by curious headgear and cavalier behaviour, then by winning a dramatic series of victories, and most subtly by throwing Alexander into the shade.

None of his staff ever knew the other side of their relationship. Montgomery would constantly write to Alexander private letters in manuscript about the facts of his situation, his hopes and worries. Perhaps they saw Alexander's replies, full of encouragement, giving him the wider news, sometimes offering counsel and always help. There was never anything personal in these letters, but they do indicate better than any subsequent Memoirs or Official History the professional sympathy which existed between them during the desert war, and dispel any suspicion that Alexander was no more than Montgomery's Quartermaster General. Here are samples:

November 18th 1942. Dear Alex, Once I have secured the El Agheila position, any advance by me into Tripolitania would be an immense problem and could not be undertaken for a considerable time. This time would be very considerable if the enemy were still able to use Tripoli. It is clear that a very great deal depends upon the effective neutralisation of Tripoli. We should start this at once.

It is essential that we should be supplied immediately with the following information from U.K.: (a) Details as to the *real* progress of events in North Africa in general, and in Tunisia in particular; (b) the immediate, and distant, objectives of the 'Western Army'; (c) the dates by which Malta, and air-forces based upon Algiers-Tunisia, will be in a position to begin large-scale neutralisation of the enemy shipping to North Africa, and of the port of Tripoli itself.

It is most important that the Chiefs of Staff should be left in no doubt as to the problem facing Eighth Army in an advance into Tripolitania. The real way to take Tripoli is from the west. If however the Western Army is likely to be seen off by the Germans, then we should have to do something about it; but it would take time, owing to the need for building up stocks. It is so important to find out the real situation of the Western Army, what it is doing, what it hopes to do, its condition and its resources etc etc that I suggest someone should fly over and see them. You could fly there in one night in a Liberator. If this were done, we could find out the whole situation for ourselves.

Yours ever,

Monty

To this letter Alexander replied:

What you suggest in your letter is being done. There is a tendency that the West want to leave Tripoli to us. I have already sent a strong wire to the Prime Minister and the CIGS stressing our difficulties and urging the paramount importance of, first of all, clearing the whole North African coast before embarking on other ventures. I followed this yesterday by a Commanders-in-Chief letter to the Chiefs of Staff reinforcing this view and pressing Eisenhower to operate against Tripoli by sea, land and air at earliest possible. We have asked for a forecast of Eisenhower's target dates. So far his communiqués have been very meagre. People at home have been left in no doubt of the tremendous difficulties facing us.

It is sad to record that this easy, if rather impersonal, relationship appeared later to be soured by Montgomery's mounting egotism. The differences between the two men were accentuated by their joint success. Montgomery enjoyed adulation; Alexander was surprised and embarrassed by it. Once, when he was at the height of his fame, he was walking down a London street with Edward Seago, when a man stopped him and said, 'May I have the honour of shaking you by the hand, sir?' Seago walked slowly on. When Alexander rejoined him, he said, 'What a nice man. He was telling me about his service in the First War, but I don't know who he is and I can't think who he imagines I am, because we served in different divisions. He must be muddling me up with someone else.' But Montgomery, when on leave, would attend the theatre in full uniform, thus exciting (or as he would say, gratifying) the public's admiration.

In the field he made it clear that nobody existed for him except the troops of his own army. I retain in my mind a sharp picture of his arrival on the plains of Kairouan in Tunisia where Eighth and First Armies joined hands, both of them then under Alexander's command. We in First Army had won our own small battle at Fondouk and had every right to pursue the enemy across the poppy-fields, but they happened to lie in the path of Eighth Army's advance from the south. Montgomery drove up in an open staff-car like a Roman consul, his knuckles showing white on the rim of the windscreen as he raised himself to bellow, 'Out of my way! Out of my way!' accompanying his words with dismissive sweeps of his arm, as if First Army were a bag of refuse which a garbage-truck had accidentally dropped on his doorstep. The joy of the occasion, the pleasure of setting eyes upon this famous man, and momentarily the unity of the two armies, were simultaneously shattered.

He could be uncompassionate. In his addresses to troops he did not seem to weigh the effect of his words upon men about to go into action. 'When I give a party', he said to a Grenadier battalion before Mareth, 'it is a good party. And this is going to be a good party.' 200 men did not leave that party alive. He wrote to Alexander after his first meeting with Eisenhower before the battle of Akarit: 'I liked Eisenhower. But I could not stand him about the place for long; his high-pitched accent and loud talking would drive me mad. I should say that he is good probably on the political line; but he obviously knows nothing about fighting.' It is not difficult to imagine how that party went.

What de Guingand called affectionately 'his streak of boyish devilment' could seem to others insensitive and rude. With Alexander he became increasingly off-hand. With disarming self-knowledge he once wrote: 'We had totally different personalities. I ruffled people's feelings. Alex smoothed them down.' At the end of the African campaign he told Alexander that he was going on leave to England. 'Sure you'll be able to get on all right while I'm away?' 'I expect so, Monty.'

During the war Alexander never complained of Montgomery's ingratitude. But in his Memoirs he allowed himself to show that he had noticed it:

Monty has a lot of personal charm – I always like him best when I am with him. Yet he is unwise, I think, to take all the credit for his great success as a commander entirely to himself. His prestige, which is very high, could be higher still if he had given a little credit to those who had made his victories possible, and there are those besides his own fighting men to whom he owes something.

Alexander gave Montgomery only one order during the desert campaign: defeat Rommel. At the start of the battle of Alam Halfa he moved his tactical headquarters close behind the threatened part of the line, but made no comment of any kind, except to congratulate Montgomery when it was over. At Alamein it was almost the same. Montgomery did not fight the battle as Alexander would have fought it, for the concentration of tanks and infantry against so narrow a sector of the German-Italian line was alien to Alexander's favourite tactic of the two-fisted assault. In spite of the great importance which Montgomery had always attached to the orderly deployment of corps and divisions,

Alamein was as untidy and costly a battle as any previously fought in the desert. The *Corps de Chasse* which he had begun to assemble on the day of his arrival in Egypt never operated as such, because its tanks were used as battering-rams (Ronald Lewin's description) instead of spears, intermingled and congested with the infantry to the annoyance of both. 'The name of the armour', McCreery wrote in his diary after the first assault had ended, 'is mud.' At one moment the battle seemed lost. But it was won.

The question must be asked whether Alexander should have intervened. There were two occasions when he might have done so. The first was when the battle began to go wrong. A hole had been gnawed out of the German defences but it did not extend to their full depth, and the troops who had made it were exhausted. Realizing that his offensive was on the wane, Montgomery withdrew part of his force for a fresh attempt, and decided to make it in the extreme north. It would be just another slogging match, he told Tedder. On that day, 29 October, Alexander visited Montgomery's headquarters with Casey and his Chief of Staff, McCreery. McCreery suggested that the new attack should go in further south, against the line of junction between an Italian and a German division and away from the new concentration of Rommel's reserves. This change of axis, which Montgomery accepted, was in Alexander's opinion 'the key decision of the Alamein battle', for it was by this attack that the breach was at last made. Why then did he not suggest it himself? If he felt it right that his Chief of Staff should intervene in a detail, however important, of a battle actually in progress, why would it have been wrong for the Commander-in-Chief to comment before the battle began on the narrowness of the selected front and the proposed use of armour? 'There is no doubt in my mind', wrote McCreery, 'that the armour was not given a good directive in the early stages.'[6] He must have discussed this point with Alexander, who would himself certainly have been aware of the flaw. Yet he did not remedy it. He believed that on a matter of tactics he should never interfere, even by suggestion, with a commander of Montgomery's ability, because their mutual confidence, whether the advice was taken or not, whether it succeeded or not, would never be quite the same again.

The second instance is of even greater importance. It has already been said that the *Corps de Chasse* did not materialize. 7th Armoured Division was brought up from the south during the battle to provide

Montgomery with some sort of mobile reserve. As soon as a clean hole was driven to the full depth of the German defences, this division would strike through to the rear of Rommel's army and encircle him with his back to the sea. 'We have the chance of putting the whole Panzer Army in the bag, and we will do so', read Montgomery's message to his troops on 4 November, the day of the breakthrough. But no proper preparations had been made for this finishing blow. The situation which would follow victory had been incompletely thought out. The pursuit force was improvised, and it ran out of petrol before it was halted by a sudden downpour of rain. Besides, its attempts to cut off the retreating Germans were too shallow. They were strokes of a sickle instead of strokes of a scythe. They reached the coast to find the Germans gone. The verdict of the Official History is that 'the pursuit was poor and unambitious'. Liddell Hart reached the same conclusion:

After the event, the rain formed the main excuse for the failure to cut off Rommel's retreat. But in analysis, it becomes clear that the best opportunities had already been forfeited before the rain intervened – by too narrow moves, by too much caution, by too little sense of the time-factor, by unwillingness to push on in the dark, and by concentrating too closely on the battle to keep in mind the essential requirements of its decisive exploitation.[7]

It would be unreasonable to suggest that Alexander should have controlled the detailed movements of the armoured divisions after the breakthrough. But had he not placed such implicit trust in Montgomery, he might have done three things before the battle started. He could have retained in his own hands a GHQ reserve, and himself decided the moment and direction of its thrust. He could have insisted, as some of the armoured-division commanders had suggested, that at least one of their divisions should be fitted out to make it self-sufficient in fuel and other supplies for several days. And he could have laid down in advance an objective for the pursuit well in rear of Rommel's front. Although the battle had been planned two months ahead and the situation which developed at the end of it was foreseeable, he did none of these things. The relationship between a Commander-in-Chief and a single Army Commander is a delicate one. The former must not fight the latter's battles. But in the big movements he does have an overriding authority which lies halfway between the tactical and the strategic. Later we shall find Alexander as an Army Group Commander in Tunisia and Italy using that authority to control corps and even single divisions. But at Alamein he declined to exercise it over a whole army.

Once the long pursuit had started, it was certainly no business of the Commander-in-Chief to conduct it. Alexander visited Montgomery's headquarters several times, at first by car and then, as the distance lengthened, by 'plane. But only once do we hear of any attempt by him to influence the running battle. McCreery records it thus:

I well remember a conversation in Montgomery's caravan. Alex suggested that it might be possible to send a mobile force straight across the desert to cut off Rommel at El Agheila or Benghazi. Monty said, 'If anyone thinks I'm going to be such a fool as to get a bloody nose for the third time, they're very much mistaken.'[8]

The letters between Montgomery and Alexander already quoted illustrate the wider considerations which were in his mind. The landings in Morocco and Algeria on 8 November succeeded. The armies began to converge. Montgomery forced the Germans out of the El Agheila line on 17 December and the Buerat line on 15 January 1943. He entered Tripoli on 23 January, and it was there that Alexander met Churchill on 3 February. The Prime Minister said to him, 'Pray let me have a message which I can read in the House of Commons when I get back – and make it dramatic and colourful.' Alexander, who was sparing in colourful messages to the troops, rose to the occasion:

Sir, The orders you gave me on August 10th 1942 have been fulfilled. His Majesty's enemies together with their impedimenta have been completely eliminated from Egypt, Cyrenaica, Libya and Tripolitania. I now await your further instructions.

They must have chuckled over this last sentence, because his further instructions had already been given to him at the Casablanca Conference two weeks before.

10

ALEXANDER OF TUNIS

The Casablanca conference in January 1943 determined Alexander's role for the next six months. He was to take command of the two Allied armies, First and Eighth, and capture Tunis. Then he was to invade Sicily. His long-term role was not defined, because the Americans were doubtful about the future of the Mediterranean theatre, and even Churchill, embarrassed by his rash promise to Stalin that north-west Europe would be invaded in 1943, an operation which only Marshall still thought possible, would not commit himself to an attack on the Italian mainland after the conquest of Sicily. But Brooke was able to persuade the conference to maintain the Allied threat in the Mediterranean once the north African coast, with its great harbours from Alexandria to Oran, was in our hands, because the many options then open to us, even after Sicily had pointed to Italy as the most obvious, would oblige the enemy to disperse widely the divisions they so badly needed in Russia and France. As for north-west Europe, it was accepted that there would be only 'limited offensive operations' in 1943, unless Germany suddenly collapsed. If Stalin had been present at Casablanca it would not have been so simple. He had been invited but could not spare the time.

These were the main strategic conclusions of the conference, but in Alexander's career it had another significance. He became a commander of world rank. It was the first international meeting at the highest level which he had attended. Not only were the two leaders present, Churchill and Roosevelt, but Brooke and Marshall, Eisenhower and de Gaulle, Mountbatten and Admiral King, and the highest officers of the Allied navies and air forces. Alexander joined their company on 14 January, flying with Tedder from Cairo, and made an immediate and lasting impact. He started with the advantage that among all of them he alone could claim a victory – the capture of Tripoli was announced on the conference's last day – and his very appearance, in desert shorts, tunic open at the neck and rolled-up sleeves, marked him out from the others as a General with field command. When he addressed them on the prospects of the desert war, his manner was relaxed, confident, precise. Churchill wrote of him, 'He made a most favourable impression on the President, who was greatly attracted by him. ... His easy smiling grace won all hearts. His unspoken confidence was contagious.' He did not intervene in the higher issues of policy. As far as is known, he did not even take sides in the controversy whether Sicily or Sardinia should be the next objective, a decision which vitally affected him. Mountbatten remembers that 'he took our instructions in a very friendly manner, and just asked a few questions'. That was his way. At each stage of his career he was conscious of the exact degree of authority which his rank carried, and even as Army Group Commander accepted the strategic plans handed to him, protesting only twice, when his armies were whittled down after the capture of Rome, and when he was discouraged in the last months of the war from renewing the offensive in Italy.

Such was the impression which he made upon politicians and service chiefs alike, that it was simple for Churchill to propose to Roosevelt during the conference that Alexander should succeed Mark Clark (now posted to command Fifth Army) as Eisenhower's deputy in North Africa and take operational command of the two armies now about to unite in Tunisia. Roosevelt immediately agreed, and to Eisenhower the suggestion was 'extraordinarily pleasing'. Far from resenting the selection of three British officers to command the land, sea and air forces (for Cunningham and Tedder received the equivalent promotions), Eisenhower felt some embarrassment that Alexander should be subordinate to him, for he had never commanded in action any force larger than a battalion, and the Mediterranean was becoming mainly a British theatre. He told the President and Marshall, 'I would be delighted to serve under Alexander, if it should be decided to give him the supreme authority.' Brooke gives the British point of view:

By bringing Alexander over from the Middle East and appointing him as Deputy to Eisenhower, we were carrying out a move which could not help flattering and pleasing the Americans in so far as we were placing our senior and experienced commander to function under their commander who had no war experience. . . . We were pushing Eisenhower up into the stratosphere and rarified atmosphere of a Supreme Commander, where he would be free to devote his time to the political and inter-Allied problems, whilst we inserted under him one of our own commanders to deal with the military situations and to restore the necessary drive and coordination which had been so seriously lacking.[1]

Another reason was that the French forces in North Africa, enemies for two days at the outset of *Torch* but now allied, were unwilling to accept a British General as Supreme Commander because the action against the French fleet at Oran still rankled. Alexander's new status was a compromise which satisfied everyone.

Eisenhower and Alexander were perfectly matched. Alexander was the British Ike, Eisenhower the American Alex. Their similar temperaments, gracious but firm, smoothed the way to Allied cooperation when it could not be taken for granted. Both had difficult subordinates who did not naturally take to each other. Their fusing of the services, armies and nations was not accomplished by grace and charm alone, but by order, precept and example. The cracks were not papered over by these two at the top, but re-cemented. Each had natural tact, a way of imposing his will by suggestion and by assuming that people wish to help each other in wartime, a willingness to listen, a willingness to change his mind, a willingness to apologize, and a coolness in moments of crisis which became legendary of both. Alexander acquired his gift for high command by long experience of war at every level; Eisenhower developed his by its exercise. He was anxious to learn, and Marshall and Alexander were his tutors. His stance, however, was not a humble one. The publication of the Eisenhower Papers in 1971 revealed the positive side of his nature which had previously been underestimated. He was capable of strategic insight and clear exposition, though his diffidence often stood between his conception of a plan and its execution. His sweetness of nature and modest self-appraisal only enhanced the dignity of the man. With Alexander he never had a quarrel. Once he protested when King George VI sent a congratulatory message direct to Alexander instead of through him as Supreme Commander, and the reaction of each was typical. 'Eisenhower was very nice and tactful about the King's message', Alexander wrote to Churchill. 'He said that he only took it up on principle and not from any private feelings. It was stupid of me not to pass it on to him direct, but I have been my own boss for so long that it did not occur to me.' Once, as we shall see, he ordered Alexander to give the American troops in Tunisia a more purposeful role for the sake of public opinion in the United States, a decision in which he was quite justified. Otherwise he left Alexander, as had been intended at Casablanca, quite independent, and Alexander accepted Eisenhower's own estimate of himself as an innocent on the battlefield. Alexander reported to him, but did not ask his advice. Two tributes, one American and one British, show how he merited Eisenhower's trust. General Omar Bradley wrote:

He not only showed the shrewd tactical judgement that was to make him the outstanding general's general of the European war, but he was easily able to comport the nationally-minded and jealous Allied personalities of his command. . . . He was our only Army Group commander, and therefore our only experienced one. At the same time he had demonstrated an incomparable ability to fuse the efforts of two Allied armies into a single cohesive campaign. Had Alexander commanded the 21st Army Group in Europe, we could probably have avoided the petulance that later was to becloud our relationship with Montgomery. For in contrast to the rigid self-assurance of General Montgomery, Alexander brought to his command the reasonableness, patience and modesty of a great soldier. In each successive Mediterranean campaign he had won the adulation of his American subordinates.[2]

Harold Macmillan, then Resident Minister in Algiers, saw something of the methods by which Alexander earned Bradley's admiration, when he was invited to spend a few days at Alexander's headquarters at Ain Beida in March 1943:

It enabled me to learn something of the character of this very remarkable man. He has quite extraordinary charm. He has made simplicity the rule of his life. The whole atmosphere of the camp is dominated by his personality – modest, calm, confident. . . . I was particularly impressed by his methods. We stopped at the headquarters of General Omar Bradley, commander of the American Second Corps. He showed us upon the map how the battle was progressing, and there were certain dispositions and movements of troops of which I could see General Alexander did not altogether approve. By a brilliant piece of diplomacy, he suggested to his subordinate commander some moves which he might well make. He did not issue an order. He sold the American general the idea, and made him think that he had thought of it all himself. This system, which he invariably pursued, made Alexander particularly fit to command an Allied army. Later, when he found himself in the Italian campaign controlling the troops of many countries, he developed this method into a remarkable technique. If Montgomery was the Wellington, Alexander was certainly the Marlborough of this war.[3]

Alexander did not take over command of 18th Army Group (a designation which combined the titles of his two armies) until 19 February 1943. After Casablanca he was required to accompany Churchill to his meeting with President Inonu of Turkey at Adana, one of the oddest and least fruitful political encounters of the war, for the Turks were unwilling to be seduced from their neutrality. Then there was the celebration of Eighth Army's triumph at Tripoli. It happened therefore that Alexander became Army Group Commander in Tunisia some weeks after Eighth Army's first troops had crossed the frontier from Libya, and his arrival coincided with the climax of Rommel's spoiling attack against the southern flank of First Army.

After six months in Cairo as the master-organizer of Montgomery's victories, he now had two armies and the American corps under his direct command, and the task of welding their campaigns into one. The timing of his arrival in Tunisia was fortunate. The situation was about to be transformed by the sudden flood of new troops from the desert and from the United Kingdom, by the gaining of air-mastery, and by the perfection of the supply system from two firm bases in Tripoli and Algiers. Although he cannot have known it at the time, it was a further help to him that he assumed command at the very moment when Rommel's offensive passed its peak. Rommel had smashed through the American II Corps at Sidi Bou Zid and Kasserine in southern Tunisia to threaten a huge turning movement towards the Algerian frontier which could have cut Allied communications to the greater part of their front. By desperate improvisation, Anderson, commander of First Army, had sealed off the German attacks at Sbiba and Thala.

Those days in southern Tunisia, critical as they were, created more effervescence than anxiety. We in First Army were curiously flattered that Rommel should turn his attention to us, and in a cavalier mood we left our wet hills near Medjez-el-Bab for what seemed to us a desert, but was in fact tawny, stony country folded ridge after ridge, bare but marginally fertile, very open, very firm; gazelle-hunting country; tank country. We had scarcely met the Americans before. Their war seemed separate from our war, and now we saw them tragically in retreat, though not in despair. An isolated troop-carrier approached our little convoy of lorries, bristling with weapons and crammed with GIs. 'He's right behind us!' they shouted (and there was no need to specify who 'he' was): and then with that engaging curiosity of all American troops, they added: 'Between us and him there's nothing but genu-ine Bedou-ine A-rabs.' We went laughing on our way to meet them and him. The land was deserted. The Arabs had disappeared. Our column crawled at dusk into Thala. At that moment the place was dive-bombed, and Virginia Cowles, then a war-correspondent who had temporarily adopted us, intrepid and lovely as always, was the only one not to plunge for cover. We put our headquarters in the town's brothel, empty but heavy with cheap scent, and peeped (there is no word more suitable) round the southern block of houses. A battle was in progress. Rommel's tanks had gaily attached themselves in the growing darkness to the tail of the retreating British armoured column, and once inside our *laager*, let fly. We had no idea what was happening. On the outskirts of the town we dug makeshift trenches and waited for the dawn. When dawn came we gazed in astonishment at an empty horizon. Rommel had vanished. In *The Rommel Papers* we can now read why. He had crawled in person to within a few hundred yards of Thala and thought our position too strong to be worth mounting a new attack, so he retreated to Kasserine. Next day, with extreme caution, we followed him across the minefields which he had laid in the road-bed to trap us, and I saw (the image will never fade) the two halves of a British soldier, one each side of the road, blown apart by an exploding mine.

It was not a victory, but it was an escape from defeat. It gave Alexander the immediate chance to impose his authority in circumstances when everyone, British, American and French, looked to him for decision, and to weigh the quality of his subordinate commanders.

He was hard on Anderson, whose sheepish appearance concealed a strong will. He described in telegrams to Brooke and Montgomery a situation of confusion and planlessness which was less Anderson's fault than Eisenhower's, for Anderson had not been given the proper authority until too late nor enough troops, disadvantages from which Alexander himself did not suffer. Montgomery was not displeased by the implicit contrast between the performance of the two armies. 'From all I have heard from you and many others', he wrote to Alexander on

21 March, 'it is obvious that Anderson is completely unfit to command any army. He must be far above his ceiling, and I should say that a divisional command is probably his level.' Alexander asked him if he could spare Oliver Leese to take over from Anderson, but Montgomery could not. Anderson remained in command until the end of the campaign, watched closely by Alexander, and justifying his position if not adorning it.

Alexander was also hard on the Americans, whose first battle this had been. 'They are ignorant, ill-trained and rather at a loss, consequently not too happy', he reported to Brooke; and later he told Patton to his face that he found them 'mentally and physically soft, and very green'. When he visited II Corps headquarters, he was unfavourably impressed by its commander, Fredendall, whom he described as 'dithery' and with no ideas for improving the situation of his corps. This was awkward, for Alexander had never previously taken command of American troops and did not wish to start by relieving their senior field officer. Fortunately Eisenhower, who visited the front soon afterwards, came to the same conclusion after consulting Bradley, whom he had temporarily posted to the corps to report on its morale. When he asked Alexander for his opinion, Alexander tactfully replied, 'I'm sure you must have better men than that.' It was enough. Eisenhower ordered up Patton from Morocco to take over the command from Fredendall. Patton had no love for the British, declaring to Butcher when he heard the news of Kasserine, 'those mealy-mouthed Limeys couldn't have pushed me around', to say nothing of Rommel, and it was in that mood that he arrived. But Alexander immediately took to Patton, describing him as 'a dashing steed', excitable, ambitious, temperamental, but with a genius for inspiring troops by his combination of ruthlessness and sentimentality, profanity and deep moral sense. (Once he told Alexander how wrong and unwise it was for a soldier of high standing to have any intimate association with women during wartime.) They worked well together. Patton, whatever he might say or think privately, knew how to take orders and even advice. He made no protest to Alexander's first suggestion for improving American morale and training that he should form a II Corps school at which the majority of the instructors would be British officers from the two armies.

As soon as Rommel had withdrawn from Thala, Sbiba and Kasserine, Alexander disentangled American units from French, French from British, and gave each national formation its own sector, British in the

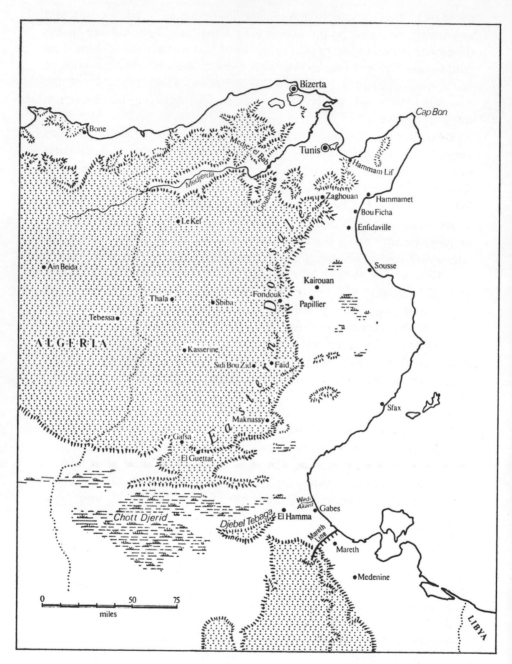

Map 7 Tunisia

north, French in the centre, and the American II Corps in the far south. He was also able to create a reserve corps under his own control. Now he had to decide a strategy for finishing the campaign.

The enemy's situation was hopeless. By his offensive against First Army, Rommel had succeeded only in destroying much American material, which was soon replaced, and in wounding American pride, which they were determined to recover. When he turned his armoured divisions against Eighth Army at Medenine on 6 March, he did not have even those consolations. He lost fifty tanks for no gain whatsoever. 'A great gloom settled over us all,' Rommel wrote later. 'For the Army Group to remain longer in Africa was now plain suicide.' Hitler ordered him to come home, but his armies to stay. There must be no retreat either from Tunisia or within Tunisia. The desert army must hold the Mareth line against the Eighth, and von Arnim's northern army the approaches to Tunis and Bizerta against the First. Whatever troops each could spare must hold the long mountain-range (the Eastern Dorsale) which linked them. The German-Italian dispositions therefore assumed the shape of a dumb-bell, big concentrations north and south and a long tenuous holding-grip between them. Alexander had two strategies open to him. He could either attempt to destroy the southern army where it stood, by breaking through the Dorsale to cut their escape route from the Mareth line, and then turn with his united strength to deal with von Arnim. Or he could order Eighth Army to break open the Mareth line and drive the enemy northwards across the plain of Sfax and Sousse. He chose the second method. The most interesting question of the Tunisian campaign is why he did so.

In his despatch Alexander did not even pose the alternatives:

The immediate problem was to get Eighth Army through the Gabes gap into the flat country where their armoured superiority would have full play and could be expected to carry them in one sweep to the beginning of the mountainous area at Enfidaville. With the enemy once back in a comparatively small perimeter round Tunis and Bizerta we should be able to establish a tight blockade by sea and air. This would mean that I had the enemy held in a complete stranglehold, and with full command of the initiative, could deliver the *coup de grâce* at the time and place of my choosing.

A few pages later he states that the key to the whole operation was Tunis itself, and defines the initial role of First Army as one of assistance to Eighth Army by limited attacks to draw off enemy reserves. In other words, he was planning to squeeze the two enemy armies together, instead of attempting to defeat each in detail. In early March he prepared an outline strategic map, sending a copy to Eisenhower, which illustrates this intention precisely. Eighth Army was to operate like a piston sliding up the cylinder formed by the Dorsale and the sea. There was to be no interruption to this movement by First Army, which would merely lubricate it.

That was how it was planned, and that was more or less how it was carried out. But at intervals before and during the operation, Eisenhower, Alexander and Montgomery had second thoughts. The first sign of this is a note of a conference between Eisenhower and Alexander on 7 March, published in the Eisenhower papers:

> The general plan for the Tunisian campaign will see the American forces making a thrust to the south to assist the Eighth Army into the open, and then will advance north and north-eastwards assisting Eighth Army forward by flanking movements.

That was in conformity with Alexander's plan. But then follows a sentence which contradicts it by proposing something much more ambitious:

> Every effort will be made to cut off the German garrisons in the south so that they cannot get into the Bizerta-Sousse bridgehead.

If this idea was in Alexander's mind, it was squashed by a letter from Montgomery which reached him next day:

> I suggest that II US Corps should limit the scope of its operations to 1. Securing Gafsa. 2. Holding it very firmly. 3. Building up and maintaining there petrol for me. Having got Gafsa, they could *demonstrate* down the Gabes road. If I can count on a dump of petrol at Gafsa, I could drive on towards Sousse without a pause at Sfax. Don't let them be too ambitious and ruin the show.

On 11 March Montgomery was still insisting that he needed only limited help in his attack on the Mareth line. He repeated that II Corps' main task must be to seize Gafsa, stock it with petrol for Eighth Army, and guard the dump. He went on:

> Then a strong thrust from Gafsa towards Gabes would help me enormously. The American troops must open the road, lift all mines and mend all demolitions: in fact get the road ready for me to use. . . . After Eighth Army is through the Gabes gap, I think we want to be careful not to get all bogged up

with each other. I suggest that the general line Papillier [south-west of Kairouan] – Maknassy should be kept clear for me. The American and French troops should keep to the west of that line, unless asked by me to act otherwise. If my operations to break through the Mareth line are successful, I shall go pretty fast once I am through the gap. . . . I do *not* want the Americans getting in the way.

Alexander replied on 14 March agreeing to everything which Montgomery proposed:

If Gafsa is captured, it will be strongly held. Having taken Gafsa, II US Corps will try and capture the defile at El Guettar, and will send strong reconnaissance units and sappers down the road towards Gabes to clear mines and mend demolitions, but no strong force will operate south-east of El Guettar. . . . A clear boundary will be laid down east of which no US or French troops will operate, the boundary being generally the line of the hills Maknassy to Faid, thence the eastern Dorsale to Fondouk.

Accordingly, on 16 March, Patton began his limited advance. He captured Gafsa, and continued south-east as far as El Guettar, which was lightly held by the enemy. There he stopped, in obedience to his orders that he must not operate in strength any further, for to break through the defile would mean mounting a major attack. Montgomery started his main assault on the Mareth line on 20 March, and finding stronger opposition than he expected at the coastal end of the line, appealed to Alexander on the 21st for American help:

Enemy obviously intends to stand and fight, and I am preparing dogfight battle in Mareth area which may last several days. Strong eastward thrust of the US armoured division through Maknassy to cut Sfax-Gabes road would have very good results.

Next day, he saw such a move not only as helpful but decisive:

If II US Corps could move south-east and sit tight in gap about fifteen miles north-west of Gabes [the Wadi Akarit line], none, repeat none, of the enemy army facing us could get out of the net. It is worth making a great effort to achieve this desirable end. No, repeat no, enemy could possibly escape. What can you do about this?

Alexander replied at 10 pm on the same day, 22 March:

The role you suggest for II US Corps is too ambitious at the moment. It is not sufficiently trained, and maintenance so close to Gabes would be difficult because 10 Panzer Division, believed now on the move, might attack their rear.

Montgomery accepted this decision without protest, and indeed with gratitude, because Alexander's last prediction was immediately fulfilled. On 23 March 10th Panzer Division left Montgomery's front and attacked Patton at El Guettar. Patton held them off by a brilliant action which seemed like a rehearsal for its re-enactment in the film of his life-story, only less tidy, and with more extras on both sides. Montgomery then switched the weight of his attack to his left flank, and sent his reserve corps to join the New Zealanders in their long march through the desert to outflank the Mareth line at El Hamma. Approaching as stealthily as a huge mechanised column can approach across a desert, they confronted the Germans in the mouth of the pass, and blasted their way through by moonlight, the low-flying fighters preceding the infantry and tanks by perilous margins. It was the most famous manoeuvre in the whole history of the desert war.

Alexander now decided that Patton might, after all, do more to help Montgomery. On 25 March he signalled to Eighth Army:

Saw Patton today, and decided to employ 9th Infantry Division with 1st Infantry Division on axis Gafsa-Gabes. As soon as these divisions have firmly secured defile of El Guettar, I hope to pass 1st US Armoured Division through for strong thrust to Djebel Tebaga.

Montgomery was delighted:

March 26th. Enemy reinforcing El Hamma. I understand Patton attacks with three divisions tomorrow, and a vigorous and determined thrust by this Corps down to Gabes would enable us to round up all this party.

Patton's attack started on the night of 26/27 March simultaneously with Montgomery's. Montgomery succeeded; Patton did not. 10th Panzer Division halted him in the defile, and his armoured division could not break through where his infantry divisions had failed.

Once the German-Italian army were forced out of the Mareth line, they withdrew to the Wadi Akarit north of Gabes, a very strong natural position, stronger, in Rommel's opinion, that the Mareth line itself. The same situation, and the same opportunity, was repeated. Eighth Army were obliged to mount another major attack, and Patton's corps were now even better placed to help them or, more ambitiously, to cut the enemy's line of retreat. He made another attempt on 30 March to force the El Guettar defile, and continued fighting there for a week, but again he failed. Alexander was now pressing him hard:

April 1st. My firm conviction, based on all sources of information, is that the enemy cannot stand further pressure in the El Guettar front, and will withdraw if you maintain pressure. I feel strongly that this is an opportunity which we must not miss. It may not occur again. My advice is to go on now.

The attack had one useful result. It drew 21st Panzer Division away from Eighth Army to join 10th Panzer in halting the Americans. The deadlock continued until Eighth Army broke through the Wadi Akarit on 5/6 April in one of the most brilliant of Montgomery's battles. The hills overlooking the dried stream-bed were attacked by six battalions of Tuker's 4th Indian Division, and in less than twelve hours' fighting, mostly with cold steel, the Gurkhas split the Axis army wide open. The campaign could have ended then and there, thought Tuker, had Eighth Army not shown themselves once again to be bad finishers. There was no *corps de chasse* on hand to exploit his victory.

Alexander again urged Patton that 'the big moment has now arrived for us to give a maximum of aid to the efforts of the British Eighth Army.' He did not succeed. In their own time, the Germans smoothly abandoned the Akarit and El Guettar positions, and fled north. On 7 April Eighth Army and II Corps joined hands in the plains south-west of Sfax, but the enemy had escaped. The same happened three days later at Fondouk, where Alexander's reserve corps broke through the Eastern Dorsale to capture Kairouan just ahead of Eighth Army. Apart from stragglers they caught nothing.

This story has been told in some detail, because it has not been told before by quotation from the contemporary messages, and because it illustrates General Jackson's contention (in a different context) that it was his soundness rather than his inspiration which carried Alexander to the forefront of the Allied commanders. The Tunisian campaign could have been shortened by several weeks if he had destroyed the enemy's southern army while they were held in the Mareth or Akarit positions, or by an earlier full-throttle attack through Fondouk to cut the coast-road at Sousse. The genesis of his uncertainty was his assumption that the campaign would end as it did end, with both Axis armies united in the north defending a wide perimeter round Tunis and Bizerta, where they could be, and were, destroyed. It appears from Eisenhower's note of the 7 March conference that the separate destruction of the southern army was at least considered at the planning stage. If it was, Alexander rejected the plan for two reasons. First because Montgomery did not then believe in it, wishing to have a clear run past Sfax and

Sousse to Enfidaville: 'I do *not* want the Americans getting in the way.' Secondly because Alexander thought the American corps too inexperienced for such a dangerous manoeuvre, for it was a long way, over eighty miles, from El Guettar to the sea across an open plain which the Panzer divisions could range at will. Then both Montgomery and Alexander changed their minds. Montgomery saw at the last moment an opportunity to round up 'all this party' by trapping them between his army and the American corps. Alexander, after a short hesitation, agreed. Patton, who had been riled by Alexander's order to halt his major forces after he had captured Gafsa and advanced to the defile, was now urged to break through it, after first one, and then a second, German armoured division had come up to oppose him. What the American official history calls 'the cautious restraint and frequent changes in instructions imposed by 18th Army Group' had robbed Patton of a chance which he had been eager to seize. Alexander's motives had been irreproachable – to save the Americans, without specifically telling them so, from a disaster greater than they had suffered at Sidi Bou Zid. But his later messages to Patton show that he thought that II Corps could and should break through in strength, even though the opposition had greatly stiffened in the interval. Their task was now much more than to draw off the enemy reserves: it was to fight a major battle in the plain and complete the encirclement of the Afrika Korps. What had happened to convince Alexander that the Americans were less green than he had supposed? There had been their successful battle against 10th Panzer Division in the defile, followed by the failure of their counter-attack. But more determinant were Montgomery's messages. If Montgomery wanted it, and if Patton was keen to try, Alexander would not veto the attempt: in fact he gave it every encouragement.

The possibility of forcing a major capitulation in the south had not been properly examined in advance, and the attempt to improvise the trap was a failure. With the troops at his disposal on other parts of the front, including his reserve corps, Alexander could have mounted a major breakthrough operation at El Guettar, Maknassy, Faid or Fondouk, coinciding with Montgomery's attack on Mareth or preferably on Wadi Akarit, all as part of a prepared plan. It is strange that the great exponent of the two-handed punch did not do so. Let the last word on this matter lie with the enemy. General Cramer, commanding the Afrika Korps, said in captivity that a maximum effort at Fondouk in early April would have shortened the campaign by a month, and added: 'Maximum effort only really starts in the brain of the man who gives his subordinates the time and means to accomplish a feasible and recognisable task.'[4]

Something happened to Alexander after the junction of the two armies. He now displayed a certainty of touch which had been missing during March and early April. 'He went to work', Alan Moorehead noticed, 'in a tornado of energy, as one who has suddenly seen the light.' There was the pressure of time, for at Casablanca he had promised to end the campaign by mid-May, so that the invasion of Sicily (*Husky*) could be mounted during fine weather, but he was also conscious that a climacteric moment in the war and in his own life had arrived. A German and Italian army of more than a quarter of a million men were surrounded in the small pocket round Tunis and Bizerta, which was all that remained of their African conquests. He had under his command the most experienced divisions of three nations, the unstinted aid of their navies and air forces, and abundant supplies. Nobody, not even the Germans, imagined any conclusion to the campaign other than a total Allied victory, but the thing must be done quickly and in style. This was an opportunity not to satisfy merely, but to exhilarate and amaze. Like a matador, he must fix the precise point to aim the sword, and time the thrust exactly, for if it hit bone, the execution would be clumsy and delayed. He must share the triumph fairly between those who had earned it, since a victory on so stupendous a scale must not be sullied by political recrimination, and it must provide a demonstration of Allied and inter-service unity which would serve as an example for the coming invasions of the European Continent. In perfect health, at the height of his powers, respected by all, loved by many, and enjoying the complete confidence of the two or three men in the world with the authority to command him, Alexander now bent his mind to the task of consummation.

He saw it in a wider context than the piercing of the Tunis defences by troops on the ground. The enemy must be denied supply and reinforcement, and prevented from escaping. From the middle of April a fine-meshed net was drawn round the coasts of northern Tunisia by naval and air forces. Between 20 April and 4 May only a single enemy merchant ship managed to cross the channel between Sicily and Africa, and that, says Tedder, was hit and lay aground off Bizerta. Allied submarines, destroyers and small craft harried the passage night and day, and Admiral Cunningham pays a deserved tribute to the Italian crews who continued to attempt it. The air offensive supplemented the navy's and became even more important when the Germans began to sneak through troop and cargo 'planes. The record of their perseverance is extraordinary. A few figures quoted by Tedder in his Memoirs will suffice to indicate its scale. On 11 April an entire air-convoy of twenty-one JU52s and five escort fighters were destroyed. Three days later the bag was 106 German air-transports. Late on the afternoon of 18 April a convoy of 100 Junkers was sighted, and seventy-three of them with sixteen of their fighter escort were brought down. During the whole operation the enemy lost 432 aircraft, apart from those destroyed on Sicilian and Tunisian airfields, at the cost of thirty-five Allied fighters. Even more ships were sunk in Italian ports by the Strategic Air Force than at sea by the Tactical Air Force. In May only 300 Germans got through by air, and none by sea. The result was that the Axis supply situation became desperate. They were so short of petrol that none could be spared even for moving to the front the tanks which had been repaired at base, and by the end of the campaign von Arnim (who had taken command of the Army Group when Rommel left) was incapable of manoeuvre. Nor was it possible, as it had been at Dunkirk, to send away the useless mouths (the *mangiatori*, as Warlimont calls them), since there were no ships or 'planes to lift them. Alexander was therefore confronted by an enemy whose dilemma was beyond remedy, but he could not know whether their last stand would be consequently more, or less, stubborn.

In deciding the disposition of his ground forces, he had several options. He could order his most experienced army, the Eighth, to make the main attack at Enfidaville where they lay. He could move Eighth Army round to the flatter ground east of Medjez-el-Bab in place of First Army. He could order First Army to make the attack. Or both could attack together. Montgomery says in his Memoirs that he wrote to Alexander on 10 April recommending that First Army should make the main effort at Medjez, and 'Alexander agreed'. To set the record straight, it is worth reproducing the actual messages that passed between them:

Montgomery to Alexander, 10 April 1943. I suggest a decision is required as to who is to play the major part in the final assaults on the enemy's last positions. There seem to be two alternatives:

A. Eighth Army does it. In this case I must move forward all my divisions and face up to a real battle on the Enfidaville position. In this case I would have to draw very heavily on Charles Miller [head of administration at 18th Army Group] and have at my disposal all the resources in northern Tunisia. Presumably this could be done, since First Army would merely sit tight and exert pressure.

B. First Army does it. In this case I would sit tight and merely exert pressure. I could do this on my own resources as far as maintenance goes.

I suggest to you that whoever is to do the business must be able to keep up a heavy and sustained effort. A very great quantity of artillery ammunition will be required. On no account must we split our effort and launch two or more thrusts none of which can be sustained.

Presumably you will decide if it is to be A or B.

Alexander to Montgomery, 11 April. Main effort in next phase of operations will be by First Army. Preparations already well advanced for attack, earliest date 22 April. Most suitable area for employment armour is in the plain west of Tunis, so require 1st Armoured Division and one armoured car regiment to join IX Corps from you as early as can be arranged. Hope you can develop maximum pressure possible against Enfidaville position to fit in with First Army attack.

The main assault was thus fixed by Alexander, and he gave Anderson his orders next day. But what should he do with the Americans? Their front in southern Tunisia had ceased to exist. They could be rested and retrained for *Husky* (Sicily), or squeezed in on the northern front for a share in the last act. At first, he decided to give them a token role by moving only one of their four divisions to the north, where it could 'help' the First Army capture Bizerta. He foresaw the difficulties of moving the whole of II Corps across First Army's lines of communications and of maintaining them in the northern mountains where there were few roads, but he was also still uncertain of their capabilities. He had not reckoned with American pride. Patton and Bradley were furious. They took the matter, as they were fully entitled to do, to Eisenhower, and Eisenhower insisted that the whole corps must be fitted in. He gives this account of it:

I had a personal interview with Alexander to insist upon the employment of the entire II Corps as a unit. For this I had several reasons. . . . Success would make the unit, and it would give a sense of accomplishment to the American people that they richly deserved in view of the strenuous efforts they had made thus far in the war. Out of victory participated in by both

countries on a significant scale would come a sense of partnership not otherwise obtainable. The soldiers themselves were entitled to engage in an
operation where for the first time conditions would favour instead of hamper
and impede them. A real victory would give them a great élan for the sterner
tests yet to come. Alexander instantly concurred.[5]

At about the same time Eisenhower handed over command of the corps
to Bradley, while Patton withdrew to plan *Husky*. The corps moved
north of the Medjerda river, still under Alexander's direct command,
and in his final orders they were given Bizerta as their objective. Bizerta
was not as famous a name as Tunis, but lying closer to Sicily, it was of
equal strategic importance. National pride was satisfied, and Alexander's plan was given an extra dimension.

There were preliminaries to the final assault, 'the crunch', as Churchill
described them, before 'the punch'. A compressing attack was launched
on 22 April along the whole 120-mile front, code-named *Vulcan*. It
might break through to Tunis from the west or south, but if it did not, it
would confuse the Germans as to the point of ultimate attack and
disperse their reserves. *Vulcan* had a limited success. Eighth Army made
little progress in mountains quite unsuited to their experience, though
First Army and II Corps gained important ground in the Medjerda
valley and in the north. But there was no breakthrough. Alexander had
attempted to exterminate the enemy by a bear's hug: now he would try
stabbing.

The final plan (Operation *Strike*) was put together very quickly, at
a conference with Montgomery on 30 April. Montgomery had fallen ill
following a visit to Cairo, and from his bed observed with some disdain
the efforts of First Army to finish off the campaign by *Vulcan*, although
his own army had made no significant contribution to its success.
Forgetting his earlier advice to Alexander that the attack should be
confined to a single front, he now proposed that Eighth Army should
renew its attempt to break through on the coast, and push three or
four divisions to Bou Ficha and Hammamet at the base of Cap Bon. But
Alexander had other ideas. He reported to the Prime Minister:

I had a long conference with Montgomery today, and have decided that
owing to the extreme difficulties of the ground and the fact that the enemy
has concentrated a strong force of guns against Eighth Army in the coastal
sector, his operations towards Bou Ficha would have been very costly in
casualties and were not certain of success. I have therefore cancelled his
large-scale operations, and Eighth Army will undertake active local action,

with the chief object of preventing the enemy transferring troops from their front to First Army front. 4th Indian Division, 7th Armoured Division and 201 Guards Brigade are moving over to First Army, starting tonight. A very strong attack with all available air and artillery support will be launched. . . on the axis Medjez-Tunis. I have every hope that this attack will lead to decisive results.

The Americans were to attack again towards Bizerta, the French towards Djebel Zaghouan. But the transfer of two divisions from Eighth Army to First was the key to the plan, which was all Alexander's own.

Operation *Strike* was his greatest victory, and it is wholly fitting that when he was invited to add a territorial designation to his title, he should have chosen Tunis. He did, it is true, have many advantages. He was attacking in overwhelming strength a weakened and beleaguered enemy, and the lie of the land favoured him. The Medjez-Tunis plain, the only route possible for a massive armoured attack, lay in the very centre of the enemy's front and led direct to their base at Tunis, only twenty-five miles away. Once Tunis was captured, the German-Italian army would be split in half, and he could turn north and south to complete their disintegration. So obvious was this route that von Arnim could not believe that Alexander would use it. When he observed dummy tanks at Goubellat further south, he deduced that this was a delicate double-bluff; he was intended to spot that they were dummies, move his armoured reserves to the Medjez plain, and then the attack would come at Goubellat: so he left his reserves at Goubellat. In fact the attack came from Medjez. Alexander was skilled at this sort of deception. It had been a main purpose of *Vulcan* to demonstrate that he could operate in great strength against every part of the front simultaneously. Now he would attack in two main places only – with his armoured corps in the Medjez plain headed for Tunis, and with the Americans in the north headed for Bizerta. The third element in the plan was the secret transfer of the two divisions from Eighth Army, and the order to Eighth Army that they must remain quiet, for Alexander knew that the Germans would never expect him to leave his most famous army unemployed in his most famous battle. Finally, for the first time a British General was using *blitzkrieg* tactics, by selecting a front of only 3,000 yards for a massed air attack followed by the assault of two infantry divisions and two armoured divisions which would burst through the gap without worrying about their flanks and make straight for Tunis. In this respect *Strike* was an improved version of *Lightfoot*. Alexander's plan, which seemed so obvious, was in fact one of the most subtle which he devised. It was simple for his own troops to understand, puzzling for an enemy. And everything worked out exactly as he intended.

The great assault began at 3 am on 6 May. The muzzle flashes lit up the gun-pits with a dancing yellow light, and the shells, tearing overhead at the rate of five or six hundred a minute, burst a few seconds later on the opposite slope like the flowering of a field of ruby tulips. When dawn came we could see through our field-glasses the infantry swarming over the hills and the Churchill tanks lurching up behind them. The attack was very successful. The Germans ran, throwing away their rifles, and the British armoured divisions were set in motion as early as 8 o'clock that morning. It was not easy for the convoys to make their way forward. The main road to Tunis could not yet be used because it was under fire, and the vehicles were confined to two narrow tracks, from which the surface dust, six inches deep, was whirled aloft by the strong breeze and churning tank-tracks. A map-board would soon become too thickly coated to be legible, and every sunburnt face turned pallid white. The congestion was appalling. Battalions took ten hours to cover as many miles, and when darkness came it was almost impossible to find the correct route among the maze of tracks and the litter of the morning's battlefield.

Next day, as the tanks and armoured cars raced towards Tunis almost unopposed, the lorried infantry took to the fields, and with carriers and small patrols searched the *wadis* to make sure that the flanks were not menaced. The expected German reserves did not appear. Some of them had been drawn off by *Vulcan*; others had never been given clear orders. The elaborate perimeter defences of Tunis were never manned. The anti-aircraft guns from the city's airports were rushed to the outskirts and their crews ordered to shoot at tanks, a role for which they were quite untrained. At 4 pm on 7 May Tunis fell to the Derbyshire Yeomanry. They found German officers sitting outside the cafés with their girl-friends, sipping gin. When the BBC broadcast at 6 pm the news that Bizerta had fallen to the Americans in the same hour, there was great rejoicing.

Alexander had no need to give further orders, for the battle was following precisely its allotted course. In his open desert car (which can be seen today in the Army Museum at Ottawa) he drove to all parts of the front, picking up the news from his radio-link and from the many headquarters which he visited. Sometimes he left the car to push through the heavy traffic more quickly in a jeep. Alan Moorehead saw him on the outskirts of Tunis 'travelling at almost reckless speed, both his hands tight on the wheel and his face whitened like a baker's boy with white dust'. Later that afternoon Alexander reported to Churchill:

Everything has gone better than I could have hoped. I had grouped to give the Americans Bizerta for themselves, and as you know, they entered it at the same hour as the First Army took Tunis. This will put the US Army right on the map and give them the confidence they badly needed. I have sent a French regiment into Tunis to take over the guards and run up the Tricolour. Our deception plan to mislead the enemy into thinking the blow was in the south worked well, as they sent the majority of their tanks and a number of their 88 mm guns down opposite 1st British Armoured Division, leaving the front facing IX Corps weak. IX Corps attacked with a huge weight of arms and armour, supported by practically the entire Air Force. It was a real thunderbolt. The Axis front line completely disintegrated and collapsed. . . .

Coningham [the commander of the Tactical Air Force] and I have just returned from Tunis where the population greeted us enthusiastically. We then went to IX Corps front, where 26th Armoured Brigade were attacking Hammam Lif.

It required five more days to end the campaign officially, but only three to put the result beyond doubt. At Hammam Lif the tanks of 26th Armoured Brigade drove along the beach, its left-hand squadron through the very surf, to outflank the last serious attempt to halt the advance. Thereafter it was a matter of finding the Germans and Italians to accept their surrender, and sparing enough troops to guard them. Two days later I wrote home this description:

You must imagine a fertile valley, with the corn standing about three feet high and speckled with poppies. The sun shines brilliantly, turning the little farms into islands of dazzling white and the sea into a vast bowl of wine. The background is therefore agricultural and Mediterranean. On to this you must impose, in the forward areas, one or two columns of smoke rising from vehicles which the Germans have destroyed in their retreat, a column of prisoners dressed in the drab uniforms of the Africa Korps, and the odd 88 mm gun, camouflaged with sheaves of corn, its crew lying dead around it.

Our armoured cars edge slowly forwards. At every small ridge they halt, and the commander scans the country ahead through his binoculars.

Behind them the great Sherman tanks, regularly spaced in diamond patterns, move heavily through the corn. They avoid the roads and surround each farm with the greatest precaution. The rate of progress is about a mile an hour.

Behind them come the infantry in lorries, and then the country begins to wear a far more military look. The supply trains, the ambulances, the repair-shops, the tank transporters and the huge bridging lorries all begin to flood into the plain, and there is a mass of vehicles where only an hour before the armoured cars broke fresh ground.

One by one the Allied divisions dropped off as they were no longer needed, and in the end it was left to 1st Guards Brigade, on the after-noon of 12 May, to meet the advanced patrols of Eighth Army at Bou Ficha, where the Afrika Korps had already raised their flags of sur-render. On the previous day the last of the German troops around Bizerta gave themselves up to Bradley. They all surrendered with strange unconcern, almost gaily, like the defeated team in a hard-fought rugger match, demanding baths and a celebration tea. Perhaps the love of drama among Germans and Italians is so strong that a capitulation on this scale seemed almost as magnificent as a great victory. The Official History gives the total of prisoners as 238,243. Very few got away. Neither the Italian fleet nor the German air force made any attempt to rescue them, and German records show that only a few hundred succeeded in reaching Sicily, some of them riding sawn-off telegraph-poles astride.

Among the prisoners were all the senior Generals. Alexander received von Arnim at his headquarters near Le Kef on 13 May. He treated him with courtesy, giving him supper and a tent for the night. 'I felt he was expecting me to say what a splendid fight he and his men had put up, but I'm afraid I disappointed him', wrote Alexander afterwards. 'However, looking back, I think it would have been a little more generous of me if I had been more chivalrous.' Instead, he sent a telegram to the Prime Minister:

Sir, it is my duty to report that the Tunisian campaign is over. All enemy resistance has ceased. We are masters of the North African shores.

11

SICILY

After Tunis there was no relaxation for Alexander as there was for most of his men, since he must prepare immediately for his next campaign, Sicily. But there were celebrations, and he enjoyed greater comfort. In Tunis on 30 May 1943 the Allies staged a victory parade, at which the salute was taken by Eisenhower, who placed Giraud beside him (since Tunisia, after all, was still a French possession) and behind him the three commanders who had won his victory, Alexander, Cunningham and Tedder. Everyone present thought their own national contingent the smartest, the most confident and the tallest in spirit if not in stature, and in the crowd were Italian prisoners who had begged leave to watch the parade and were among the most delighted, the most vociferous, of all. Later there were visits by Churchill, who in the Roman theatre at Carthage promised more glory to the sunburnt victors; and by King George VI, who in his demurer style distributed congratulations, encouragement and awards. Alexander was the constant companion of each.

By this time he had acquired two new headquarters, one in a pinewood near Algiers, the other the villa of the former British Consul at La Marsa, just outside Tunis, where tents were pitched in the garden to supplement the Consul's modest rooms. Here a frequent visitor, the only civilian member of the Mess, was Harold Macmillan. He conceived for Alexander an esteem and affection which made him the hero of his wartime volume of memoirs. He saw in him all the qualities which he most admired, and many of which he shared, chivalry, ease, firmness, an unshakable faith in victory, a patrician use of great power, a capacity to set worry aside and accept the enormous wastage of political and military debate, allowing controversy to flow round him like traffic until the moment came to halt it by decision. The portrait of Alexander which emerges from Macmillan's pages is the most attractive ever drawn of him, coloured by the recollection of the drama of those years of victory, of their bathes together in the early morning off Tunisian beaches, of finding among all those polite officers a man to whom he could talk as an equal in prestige. In a letter which reveals as much of Macmillan's character as Alexander's, he thus described the atmosphere of the La Marsa mess when the Sicilian campaign was approaching its climax:

It is rather like a large country house. You come to meals and otherwise attend to your own business. There is plenty of quiet amusement available – sightseeing, bathing or just agreeable conversation with the other guests. A cloudless sky, a dark and lovely sea, a slight breeze, a perfect August day, a cool night. No fuss, no worry – and a great battle in progress! This is never referred to but is understood to be going on satisfactorily. . . . Very occasionally, an officer comes in with a message for the 'Chief'. After pausing sufficiently out of politeness for the conversation in hand – the campaign of Belisarius, or the advantages of classical over Gothic architecture, or the right way to drive pheasants in flat country to show them well, or whatever it may be–General Alex will ask permission to open his message, read it, put it into his pocket, continue the original discussion for a few more minutes and then, perhaps, if the message should call for any action, unobtrusively retire, as a man might leave his smoking-room or library after the ladies have gone to bed, to say a word to his butler, fetch a pipe or the like. I have never enjoyed so much the English capacity for restraint and understatement.[1]

For all his outward placidity, Alexander was torn between the conflicting demands of the military, naval and air commanders. The Sicilian campaign appears on the face of it to have been a great success: an island of 10,000 square miles and four million inhabitants was captured by the largest amphibious operation ever launched (larger in its initial stages than *Overlord* a year later) and by a subsequent campaign which lasted only thirty-eight days. But under analysis, *Husky* cannot be ranked among Alexander's greatest achievements. The plan was fashioned by compromise, wholly acceptable to only one commander, Montgomery, who devised it, and in execution it was muddled by the failure to think more than one battle ahead and its glory tarnished by allowing the Germans to escape. One reason was Eisenhower's reluctance

to exercise his supreme power because he was over-conscious of his
lack of battle experience. It was for him to reconcile the divergent
views of the three services, to decide upon a far-sighted plan acceptable
by its logic to all of them, but he did not do so. Nor did Alexander, his
deputy, now designated Commander-in-Chief of the 15th Army
Group. In the Mediterranean there was only one commander of
inflexible will, Montgomery, but he was two removes from supreme
command. By a manoeuvre which one must admire and enjoy for its
political dexterity he altered the original plan to suit his own convenience, usurping the functions of both Eisenhower and Alexander,
but because he lacked ultimate responsibility, he was indifferent to its
effect upon other commanders and contemptuous of the fury which it
aroused. He secured for his own army a concentrated base in Sicily,
first pulling Patton's Seventh Army towards him for protection, then
pushing it away to give him room. It was a brilliant gambit, but its
selfishness led to uncertainty and created resentments which harmed
Anglo-American relations for the remainder of the war.

The point at issue can be stated quite simply. The original intention,
a modification of the plan which Alexander had prepared for 110
Force in 1941, was that the American Seventh Army would capture
Palermo in the north-west of Sicily while the British Eighth Army
captured Catania in the east. From these two strong bases they would
both advance to Messina. Montgomery told Alexander in April that this
plan was quite unacceptable to him. The Germans and Italians, who
could be expected to fight even harder for Sicily than they were fighting
for Tunisia, would be able to defeat each army in detail. He was prepared to land in the south-east as planned, but Patton must abandon
the quick capture of Palermo and land on the south coast alongside
him. Tedder protested that this would leave the Palermo airfields in
enemy hands, Cunningham that it would mean too great a concentration of shipping in one narrow sector, the administrative staff that it
would deny Patton a proper port for his supplies, and Patton, who was
barely consulted, that it would give Montgomery a firm base while he
had none and the opportunity to advance up the east coast of Sicily,
capturing famous towns like Syracuse, Catania and Messina, while
Seventh Army had the thankless task of protecting Montgomery's
flank.

In face of all these angry objections it is remarkable that Montgomery got his way. His first move was to win over Eisenhower's

Chief of Staff, Bedell Smith, by a brief talk (so Montgomery relates in his Memoirs) in the lavatory at Allied Force Headquarters in Algiers. Next he persuaded Bedell Smith to summon a staff-conference on 2 May in the absence of Eisenhower, Alexander, Tedder and Cunningham, and sold them the idea that they should present his plan as 'an agreed plan' to the four senior commanders next day. Montgomery was

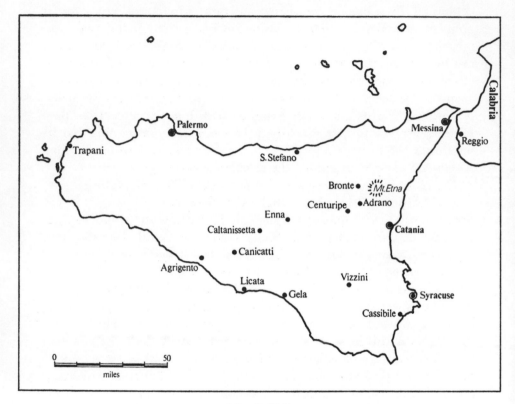

Map 8 Sicily

careful to sugar it to meet the objections which he foresaw. The American front would be extended slightly westwards to capture the airfields round Gela, and the Americans' supply problem could be eased by the use of DUKWs (large amphibious trucks) to maintain them over the open beaches. Next day all the commanders fell into line: Tedder agreed ungraciously, claiming afterwards, 'There was nothing new in it; it was a plan that had been examined weeks before. Personally I had always favoured it', when he certainly had not; Cunningham reluctantly; Alexander resignedly. Eisenhower agreed with the others. Even Patton raised no open objection, telling Alexander, 'General, I don't plan; I only obey orders.'

Montgomery's dialectical victory annoyed Alexander least of all the top commanders. He was too generous a man, in a way too innocent, to suspect an ulterior motive, and in any case his was the final decision. In his despatch on the Sicily campaign he was able to sum up the controversy, quite justifiably, in the words, 'I therefore decided to recast the whole plan. I took the decision on May 3rd, based n a conference on May 2nd which I had been prevented from attending by impossible flying weather.' As it turned out, Alexander's plan would have worked even better than Montgomery's, for a separation of the American from the British army would have been tactically, administratively and psychologically more advantageous. In fairness to Montgomery it must be said that nobody could have foreseen that the Italians would fight so feebly (they were in the main recruited from Sicilian peasants), nor that the Air Force would be successful in putting all but two of the enemy airfields out of action before D Day, nor that Mussolini would fall from power in the middle of the campaign. His plan, for all its disadvantages, had the merit of concentration within the range of fighter cover from Malta and northern Tunisia, and this was the decisive argument.

Its psychological effect was that because the plan was Montgomery's and not Alexander's, it lowered Alexander's authority and wounded Patton's pride. Earlier Alexander had considered a variant of the plan, but discarded it when Tedder and Cunningham objected. Now Montgomery was revealed as the master-planner and master-diplomatist, the two fields in which Alexander excelled, and was encouraged by his success to act with increasing disregard for his orders, to do what he wished and then inform Alexander that he had done it. When the campaign was over Patton complained to Montgomery about the 'injustice' of one of Alexander's directives. 'Monty looked at him for a moment', Bradley remembers. ' "George," he said, "let me give you some advice. If you get an order from Army Group that you don't like, why, just ignore it. That's what I do." ' His attitude to Alexander did not pass unnoticed by Brooke, who wrote in his diaries, 'Montgomery wants guiding and watching continually, and I do not think Alex is sufficiently strong and rough with him'; nor by Cunningham, who complained to the First Sea Lord, 'Montgomery seems to think that all he has to do is to say what is to be done and everyone will dance to the tune of his piping. Alexander appears quite unable to keep him in order'; nor by Tedder, who spoke of Alexander's 'sudden *volte-face*' over the *Husky* plan. Of course it was not so simple. Montgomery was a superb tactician, and in whatever he attempted, he succeeded. Alexander had the insight to ride him on a loose rein, having a confidence in Eighth Army which he was not yet prepared to concede to Patton's Seventh.

The planning for *Husky* proceeded in all its complicated detail, fitting together the huge number of pieces, as Churchill said, 'like a jewelled bracelet'. The target date, 'the July moon', was 10 July 1943. The invading forces were to converge on Sicily from every major port on the southern shore of the Mediterranean, the British from Tunis and all ports eastward, the Americans from those west. One complete division, the Canadians, sailed direct from the United Kingdom to land in Sicily without an intermediate stop. The two airborne divisions flew from the plain of Kairouan. Nine divisions were simultaneously afloat, two more than in *Overlord*. An elaborate cover-plan was devised to mislead the enemy into thinking that the attack would fall on Sardinia or Greece, and Alexander momentarily considered spreading the rumour just before D Day that Mussolini had sued for an armistice, an idea squashed by Churchill because 'it would not materially influence the battle and would rob victory of its fame'.

Eisenhower underplayed his hand in the planning and preparations to such an extent that Alexander cannot have known which decisions the Supreme Commander wished to reserve for himself. He was Eisenhower's deputy, but this gave him no authority over Tedder and Cunningham, with whom he was invited to 'coordinate' his plans. 'The Allied Commander-in-Chief,' Eisenhower wrote to Mountbatten when the latter was appointed Supreme Allied Commander in the Far East, 'must be self-effacing, quick to give credit, ready to meet the other fellow more than half-way, and must seek and absorb advice. . . . He is Chairman of a Board.'[2] This meant that the three services were not directed by the only man with the authority to do so.

The only operation which Eisenhower personally controlled was the capture of Pantelleria, a tiny island which lay in the Sicilian narrows. The operation had a marginal strategic purpose, to capture an important airfield, but it was more a demonstration of what Allied air-power could achieve and a test of Italian morale. It was startlingly successful. After days of air bombardment the Italian garrison of 10,000 men surrendered on 11 June as the first troops were about to land, and this 'impregnable fortress', as Mussolini had described it, this Italian Malta, was occupied without a fight. Next day a British battalion landed on the neighbouring islands of Lampedusa and Linosa. To the author, who accompanied the little expedition, the surrendered Italians demonstrated with pride how easily their coastal guns could have blasted the circling destroyers out of the water. 'Then why didn't you do so?' 'Because we were sheltering from the bombs!' they replied laughing. When I told the garrison-commander of Lampedusa that Linosa, a minute Mediterranean speck, had fallen to the assault of 500 bombers, he raised his hands in disbelief, admiration and despair: '*Cinquecento aeroplani sulla Linosa!*' I may have exaggerated the number, but the reaction was an indication of how fast Italian morale was ebbing.

A few days before 10 July Alexander moved his headquarters to Malta, where he and Eisenhower had offices in a tunnel so cold that they worked in overcoats though the temperature outside often exceeded 100 degrees. Here John Gunther, the American writer and journalist, met Alexander for the first time, and put into words the impression which he made upon so many:

> He looks a little like W. S. Maugham, with an uptilted chin, a beautifully poised head, neat brown moustache and an aware upward look, that might be called supercilious if it were not so serene. His voice, quiet and cultivated; his manner, tactful, wise, intelligent.[3]

Gunther noticed that while everyone referred to Montgomery as 'Monty', Alexander was always 'General Alex'.

On the evening of 9 July the wind began to rise and the sea became suddenly choppy. The invasion fleet was already approaching Sicily and the landing could not have been postponed without causing the utmost confusion. Alexander, with Eisenhower and Tedder, remained awake most of the night in great anxiety, but although the storm did not subside before the assault craft touched down at dawn next morning, it gave them two advantages: the Italians considered that nobody would dare land in such weather, and went to bed; and the heavy surf carried the craft over sand-bars where they might have grounded in a calm. The descent on the Eighth Army beaches was almost unopposed by the

Italian coastal division, and Syracuse was captured on the same evening. Patton's Seventh Army had much more trouble against the Germans at Licata and Gela, but after beating off an armoured attack, they too were firmly established ashore by the third day, and the British and American bridgeheads linked up securely.

The great disappointment was the airborne attack. Alexander's conception of modern war was the correlation of the three elements in which we live – land, air and water. The three services, he often said, must be a brotherhood. When each makes its separate contribution to a common goal, the air force by sweeping the skies, the navy the seas, there is no problem. But when they are intermingled in joint action, the navy putting the soldiers ashore, the air force dropping them inland, there is a risk of confusion and even disaster. Army-navy cooperation worked well in Sicily, because they already had some experience of amphibious operations. But for airborne landings there had been no Allied precedent, and this, their first experiment, was on the largest scale. In retrospect it seems extraordinary, in view of the long notice given for *Husky*, that combined training between soldiers and aircrew was limited to the last three weeks. The American airmen who were to tow the British gliders and drop the American parachutists did not arrive in North Africa until April, and had been trained for daylight operations only. None of them had seen action before. They were adding to the most difficult operation of war a hazard which the staffs in England and Africa should have foreseen.

Alexander watched the tandem pairs, tows and gliders, fly over Malta in the moonlight, and they seemed more certain of a fair landing than the little ships which he imagined storm-tossed off the Sicilian shore. But the formations which had set out so punctually and confidently from Kairouan broke up as they approached Sicily. Fifteen per cent of the pilots could not face the anti-aircraft fire and turned back; another sixty per cent failed to find their targets. The American airborne troops were scattered in small parties over an area of fifty miles along the southern hinterland, and only 250 out of the 3,400 were dropped in the right place. In the British sector it was even worse. Seventy of their 134 gliders were released too soon and came down in the sea, others fell at random in south-east Sicily, and only twelve landed in the correct area. The force which actually reached the bridge south of Syracuse which was their objective numbered eight officers and sixty-five men out of the 2,075 who had emplaned at Kairouan.

They achieved very little, for although they fought hard for the bridge, Syracuse was entered by Eighth Army virtually unopposed, and these two thousand men could have been landed much less wastefully from the sea. The sacrifice of the most highly trained soldiers in both armies by entrusting them to inexperienced aircrews still seems unpardonable. Their quiet graves in the military cemetery at Catania, with headstones recording euphemistically that drowned men were killed in action, are a silent reproach, and to their sons and daughters the only memorials of fathers whom they scarely knew.

The main interest of the Sicilian campaign for students of Alexander's generalship is his handling of the two armies once they were firmly lodged ashore. The island, it might be thought, was large enough to allow both Montgomery and Patton full freedom of manoeuvre. The British could overrun the east, the Americans the west. As the eastern sector was blocked by the huge volcanic mass of Etna, and led to Messina, the base essential to the Germans for supply and reinforcement, it was natural that the more experienced of the two armies should be given the more difficult task. Eighth Army had two corps, XIII and XXX. They were to flow northwards, one each side of Etna, while Seventh Army acted as Montgomery's flank-guard in case the German armoured divisions in western Sicily turned back to protect their base. Alexander summarized his strategy in a message to the CIGS on 14 July:

Future operations envisage thrust towards Messina through Catania by XIII Corps. XXX Corps will drive to the north coast at San Stefano, then turn east to join up with XIII Corps at Messina. When the island is split in two from north to south, American Seventh Army will be directed towards Palermo and Trapani. Meanwhile they will hold Caltanissetta-Canicatti.

Eighth Army would therefore carry the main burden of the campaign, while Seventh Army would be awarded the consolation prize of Palermo only when it was certain that there would be little or no German opposition in that quarter. It was a plan which under-employed Patton's immense striking power, and further wounded his pride.

Even this humble role was reduced by Montgomery's unilateral action. Finding his XIII Corps blocked by strong German reinforcements south of Catania, he decided to give priority to his left-hand thrust, and for this he needed the road Vizzini-Enna which Alexander had allotted to the Americans. Without consulting Alexander, he took it, and then demanded that the inter-army boundary be altered to confirm the accomplished fact. Alexander agreed. The Americans were naturally incensed. When he heard of the order, Bradley (II US Corps, on the right flank of Seventh Army) said to Patton, 'This will raise hell with us. I had counted heavily on that road. Now if we've got to shift over, it'll slow up our entire advance.' Seventh Army were forced to take their front to pieces and re-shape it further west. Their distress could have been mitigated by allowing them to fight for more elbow-room against the Germans in the west, having been deprived of it by Montgomery in the east, but Patton was still held in check. Alexander permitted him to reconnoitre in the direction of Agrigento, but told him that he must not become involved in heavy fighting. Palermo was still forbidden territory. It was now that the flaw in Montgomery's plan became apparent. Only three good roads led northwards from the beaches, and Montgomery had taken two of them. Seventh Army were cramped for space, their strength only half used, and humiliated by this overt demonstration that they were not to be trusted with a major role.

During the next few days the relative missions of the two armies did not change. Eighth Army pushed up the two main routes in an attempt to encircle Etna as Alexander had planned, and Seventh Army conformed by occupying the centre of the island in the Enna-Caltanissetta triangle. They were still forbidden to strike for Palermo, although by this time there was not even the excuse that Eighth Army required them as a flank-guard, for all German formations had moved eastwards. When Alexander told him that he must wait until Eighth Army had secured their base (presumably Catania), Patton drew himself up and replied, 'Yes, General.' At Army headquarters, comment was less restrained. Bradley later wrote that Alexander's directive 'confirmed my earlier suspicion – only Montgomery was to be turned against Messina. . . . Except for Palermo there was little to be gained in the west. Certainly there was no glory in the capture of hills, docile peasants and spiritless soldiers.'[4] One of Patton's staff put it more forcefully: 'When we reach the north coast, we can sit comfortably on our prats, while Monty finishes the goddam war.' It is to Patton's credit that he wished not merely to capture 'real estate in the empty west', but share in the real fighting for Messina; not just to look good on maps, but to excel. His restlessness at last became vocal. On 17 July he flew to see

Alexander in Tunis, and won his consent first to an immediate advance on Palermo, and then to a large share in the attack on Messina. When Patton expressed bluntly the disappointment which he had hitherto only muttered privately, Alexander took his point at once and gave him his liberty without argument. His later career has made it difficult to associate Patton with reticence, but there is no doubt that even American members of Alexander's staff were quite unaware that Seventh Army resented the role allotted to them in the invasion. It says much for Alexander's tact in repairing this damage that Patton bore him no grudge, and that Bradley could write of him in the passage previously quoted that he was 'the outstanding general's general of the European war'. General Lemnitzer, Alexander's American Deputy Chief of Staff, has confirmed to the author that whatever friction there may have been in the early stages of *Husky*, all was forgotten when Patton was given his head and Alexander realized for the first time what a thruster he had under his command.

In a remarkable campaign of six days Patton occupied the entire west of Sicily, entering Palermo on 22 July. Ladislas Farago, in his biography of Patton, describes this move as a 'disintegration of Alexander's strategic plan. . . . His job was so clearly to remain firm in the face of his two primadonnas. He let the campaign continue haphazardly, actually without a firm and purposeful design.' It is true that twice he had allowed Montgomery to have his way (in the change in the overall *Husky* plan, and in the switch of the inter-army boundary) and twice Patton (in releasing his army westwards, and allowing him to double back towards Messina), but in each case he was responding to circumstances, and the most that could be charged against him is that those circumstances might have been foreseen. What was his alternative? To dismiss the victor of Alamein, the hero of El Guettar? Far from relinquishing a purposeful strategy, the strategy only began to make sense when the two primadonnas were ranged side by side on the approaches to Messina. Montgomery's summing-up of the campaign is also less than just: 'There was no master plan. . . . The army commanders developed their own ideas of how to proceed, and then "informed" higher authority. The Seventh US Army, once on shore, was allowed to wheel west towards Palermo. It thereby missed the opportunity to direct its main thrust-line northwards in order to cut the island in two.' It is this sort of mangling of history which makes one suspect Montgomery's loyalty to his chief. In Alexander's original orders, Eighth Army, not Seventh, was to cut the island in two, but it was the Seventh who did so. Patton was not allowed to wheel west 'once on shore': for a whole week he was kept on a tight leash. The only army commander who acted first and told Alexander afterwards was Montgomery himself. The overrunning of the west was a necessary part of the campaign, to provide Patton with a port instead of the open beaches to which Montgomery's plan had restricted him. It was an independent operation which had no effect upon the cutting of the island in two.

Patton and Montgomery were each determined to be the first into Messina, and Alexander, with an amusement that can be presumed, saw no reason to dampen their rivalry for such a prize. Side by side east and then north of Etna their divisions stormed the successive ridges, and the fighting for such places as Centuripe and Adrano (Eighth Army) and Troina (Seventh Army) was very fierce. The Germans, having given up hope of effective help from their ally, were holding tenaciously. 'This small bridgehead', wrote Warlimont, viewing it from the Führer's headquarters, 'had become a vital point, decisive for the fate of the Mediterranean theatre, the future of the Axis, and perhaps much more besides.' When Mussolini fell from power on 25 July, Sicily became less important as a symbol, and on the same day Hitler decided to withdraw the entire force slowly through Messina, although the actual withdrawal did not start until three weeks later. On 28 July, having heard the news of the Duce's downfall, Churchill telegraphed to Alexander:

The only thing that really matters at this moment is the great battle you are about to fight as head of 15th Army Group. Important as the battle would have been in ordinary circumstances, its effect will be redoubled now. No one can tell what its consequences far beyond the battlefield may be. This is a decisive moment in the war and your armies may strike a resounding blow. I thank God you are there and that all is in your hands. Strike hard and home.

On that day Alexander moved his headquarters from Tunis to Cassibile, south of Syracuse, a dusty but well-concealed site in an almond grove, where they pitched their tents around a white farm-house which became the operational centre for the elimination of Italy from the war.

Pressure was maintained until the end along the whole front, by feints against Catania and heavy attacks by both Americans and British in the north. On 2 August Alexander signalled to Churchill:

I have just returned from a visit to General Patton who is in great heart. The Seventh US Army have done a grand job of work and are fighting really well. The Canadians have made a very satisfactory debut. Progress may be slow, but the country must be seen to be believed. Only a few mountain roads which pass through gorges and round cliffs, which are easily defended and easier demolished.

The whole of that countryside is dominated by Mount Etna, a stupendous mountain occupying the corner of the island with its flounced crinolines and forked trains flowing from them. The faint streamer of smoke drifting from the summit is just distinguishable from a cloud because it is continually spiralling upwards. The fields are seared by past eruptions, overburdened by lava which will take centuries to break down into fertile soil, and twisted into grotesque shapes like the heads and claws of antediluvian monsters. Beyond the limits of the lava the country is ridged by bare brown mountains like the Valladolid district of northern Spain, sun-baked and muscular, a country more suited to guerillas than armoured warfare. This was the scene of the final battles, a cone tapering to a point at Messina, and Alexander was in every part of the front, motoring in the extreme heat of mid-summer up the winding roads, and pausing for an hour's rest in such lovely castellos as Maniace near Bronte, built as a fortress-monastery by eleventh-century Normans and presented to Nelson with its dukedom. Here he added his signature in the visitors' book immediately below Kesselring's, whose temporary headquarters it had been.

He was also Governor of Sicily, responsible for law and order and for feeding the population. He proclaimed to the Sicilian people that the purpose of the Allied occupation was to deliver them from the Fascist régime which had led them into such misery, and restore to them the freedom which they deserved. Our temporary rule, he said, would be benevolent. 'Civilian hostility was nowhere to be seen', declares the Official History.[5] 'On the contrary, the genuine friendliness with which the Allied troops were everywhere greeted, in spite of the immense amount of suffering caused by Allied bombardments, was astonishing to many of those who had arrived, as they supposed, in the capacity of enemies.' If the civilians felt like that, how could their soldiers fight? Fascism had never been popular in Sicily and under the stress of defeat it had become odious. Even Fascist officials cooperated with their conquerors. In spite of acute shortages there was no starvation because fruit and vegetables were everywhere plentiful, and the main problem was the shuttling of refugees from town to country and back again. Alexander showed greater sympathy towards them than many of his subordinates. He ordered that their requisitioned lorries should be restored to them, and helped the recovery of the island's economy by employing thousands of Sicilians on the reconstruction of the roads and harbours.

The fighting in the north-east tip was the responsibility of the army commanders, since their objective, Messina, and the boundary between them, were no longer in dispute. Alexander's function was to finish the campaign neatly, and plan for the next. His immediate task was to prevent the Germans from escaping. In this he did not succeed, and it is worth analysing why, as an illustration of his reluctance to act outside the range of his direct orders even when his Supreme Commander showed no eagerness to intervene.

The fundamental reason why the Tunisian capitulation was not repeated on a smaller scale at Messina was that there was no agreement at the highest political level whether *Husky* should be followed by the invasion of Italy. The Germans could only be prevented from escaping across the Messina straits by occupying the toe of Italy behind them, and agreement to overlap the end of one campaign by the beginning of the next was not reached in time. In January at Casablanca not even Churchill had committed himself to an Italian campaign. By the time of the Trident conference in Washington in mid-May he had made up his mind in favour of it, and argued the case with great eloquence. The Americans were lukewarm. At one point their Chiefs of Staff spoke of Sardinia as 'the sole remaining objective in the Mediterranean', because the whole Allied effort must be switched to *Overlord*. At the end of May Churchill carried the debate to Algiers, taking Marshall with him, 'determined to obtain before leaving Africa the decision to invade Italy'. Eisenhower was reserved, Marshall cryptic. But some progress was made. Eisenhower was induced by argument to affirm that if *Husky* went well, 'say within a week', he would at once cross the straits and establish a bridgehead in Calabria, but in his final conference with Churchill, he was less confident. He said it would be better to decide what to do after *Husky* had started. At this meeting Alexander made what Churchill called 'an extremely impressive speech', suggesting that before the conquest of Sicily was complete, the Allies should 'cross the straits and secure a foothold on the opposite shore. . . . Securing a bridgehead on the Italian mainland should be considered as part of the plan.' If this suggestion had been adopted by Eisenhower and Marshall as warmly as it was supported by Churchill, the Sicilian campaign would have ended in a triumph. But there was no decision to trap the Germans in Sicily: it was left to Eisenhower to exploit a Sicilian victory as he thought best. This might be a subsequent landing on the mainland; it might only mean Sardinia.

Husky was therefore launched with no clear idea where the Allies should go next. As soon as it became obvious that the Germans intended to fight with or without the Italians, for the Messina triangle, Alexander again raised with Churchill the possibility of moving into the Italian toe. On 22 July he told the Prime Minister that 'we are prepared to jump a bridgehead on to the mainland at the first opportunity'. He was clearly hampered by the lack of enthusiasm shown by his operational chief at Algiers. If he had known that Eisenhower himself had begun to doubt his own judgement on the matter, he might have put his case more strongly. On 14 August Eisenhower said to Harry Butcher that it was a mistake not to 'have made simultaneous landings on both sides of the Messina strait, thus cutting off all Sicily and obtaining wholesale surrender'. It was now too late for such second thoughts. The Germans had begun their evacuation on 11 August. Even a few weeks earlier, in late July, a landing on the far side could have been improvised. The narrowing of the bridgehead and the pacification of western Sicily released several Allied divisions. More were left idle in North Africa. There were landing-craft available, as Cunningham has confirmed, wondering why they were not used. Allied air superiority was complete. The toe was barely defended except by coastal guns. A single corps could have advanced across the narrow peninsula to seize the ferry terminals north of Reggio, and the campaign extended during its last two weeks to both sides of the straits. It does not appear that at any level of command the possibility was seriously discussed. There is no mention of it in Alexander's Memoirs or despatch. The plan which he had put forward in late May was doubly relevant two months later when Mussolini fell, and if there had been firmer decision at the political and military summits, Alexander would certainly have been eager to try.

The Air Force claimed (as Goering had done at Dunkirk) that almost singlehanded they could prevent the Germans crossing the straits. They would harass them by day and bomb the ferry-terminals by night, and the Navy would help by sending light craft into the narrows. Their joint efforts were not enough. Every day from 11 August onwards the Germans moved 8,000 men across the straits, and by the time Patton occupied Messina late on the 16th, a triumphant few hours ahead of Montgomery, they had succeeded in evacuating the entire force of 40,000 Germans and 62,000 Italians, together with ninety-seven guns, forty-seven tanks and 17,000 tons of ammunition.[6] During the last few days they accomplished this feat in broad daylight. The air forces pleaded the intensity of anti-aircraft fire and the difficulty of intercepting fast craft on a passage of only a few miles. The Navy were prevented by the massing of heavy coastal guns on both shores from moving their bigger ships within range. But a more fundamental reason for their failure was put by Stephen Roskill, the Navy's official historian:

At no stage did the three Allied Commanders-in-Chief represent to the Supreme Commander that an emergency, such as would justify the diversion of all available air-strength, had arisen. The enemy later expressed his astonishment that the Allies had not used their overwhelming air-superiority to greater effect. . . . Even when the enemy's intention was plain, the action taken suffered from lack of inter-service coordination. The naval effort made was weak, and the air effort lacked concentration. . . . It was, in fact, from the Allied point of view, a combined operation in reverse; and if that view be accepted, it may reasonably be asked why the Supreme Commander took no steps to bring his service commanders together with the object of quickly producing a joint plan.

Roskill reached this significant conclusion:

The only way in which the trap might have been firmly closed on the enemy was by making a new landing on the southern shore of the Calabrian peninsula. . . . Had the Supreme Commander and the service leaders agreed on such a strategy in the middle of July . . . the Navies could have assembled the ships and craft needed to carry it out in early August; and that would have been in time to stop the withdrawal of the major part of the Axis armies across the Messina Straits.[7]

One reason why it did not happen was that the headquarters of the main commanders were far apart: Alexander was in Sicily, Tedder near Tunis, Cunningham in Malta, and Eisenhower in Algiers. Another was that Eisenhower would take no initiative. Alexander, as well as commanding the land forces, was his deputy. Could he have seized the opportunity with both hands, and presented his superior with a decision which he would have been unlikely to challenge, given the magnitude of the prize? Alexander seemed once or twice on the point of doing so, but his lack of supreme authority and his natural diffidence prevented him from insisting on a strategy which he knew to be right. Certainly his enemy expected it. 'A secondary attack on Calabria', Kesselring wrote, 'would have enabled the Sicily landing to be developed into an overwhelming Allied victory.'

Husky did, however, unseat Mussolini, and led six weeks later to Italy's capitulation. Badoglio announced publicly that Italy would remain Germany's ally, but in early August approached the Allies through the British Embassies in Lisbon and Madrid with the suggestion that she should change sides. Direct negotiations began the day after Messina fell, but by the time Alexander became personally involved there were only ten days to go before the landing at Salerno. It was necessary to persuade the Italians, without making specific promises, that the term 'unconditional surrender' meant no more than 'honourable capitulation', to be followed soon afterwards by some form of co-belligerency. It was also necessary to assure them that if they publicly changed sides the Allies would be able to protect them against German reprisals. The diplomatic and military problems were unprecedented. The Allies could not welcome the Italians as comrades-in-arms without shocking opinion in the armies and at home, while the Italians considered that they had already proved their good faith by deposing their Duce. Eisenhower and Alexander could not reveal to them their plans for landing in Italy without exposing their weakness and risking a leakage of their secrets, but until an assurance was given that the Allies would land in strength, the Italians declared that they could make no public move. There was an *impasse*. It was essential to obtain the Italian signature before 9 September, the day of the Salerno landing, but the Italians could not be hurried by advance notice of it. Italy was not bound to capitulate. Her new leaders wished to, but as no part of the country except Sicily was occupied by the Allies, she could fight on for months if the terms were not satisfactory.

At the beginning of September the negotiations were transferred to Alexander's camp at Cassibile, the very place, he may have reflected, where the Athenians surrendered to the Syracusans in 413 BC. Harold Macmillan and Robert Murphy, the American representative, conducted the political argument, and Bedell Smith and Alexander took charge of the military. The Italian plenipotentiary was General Castellano. In order to stiffen the new Italian Government, Alexander proposed that the Allies should drop an entire American airborne division on the airfields outside Rome and cooperate with five Italian divisions to defend the capital against the Germans when the capitulation was announced. With this proposal, and armistice terms which were not too severe, Castellano flew to Rome. On 2 September he returned to Cassibile not, as expected, with authority from Badoglio to sign, but merely to continue negotiations on its military aspects.

Macmillan suggested to Alexander that the moment had come for a display of firmness. Alexander drove to the camp in his shiniest car, dressed, as Macmillan remembers, 'in a well-pressed tunic, beautifully cut breeches, highly polished boots with gold spurs, and a gold-peaked cap'. He sent for the Italians, and according to his own account in a postwar interview, he said: 'Good morning. I have come to be introduced to the General. I understand that he has signed an instrument of surrender', knowing quite well that he had done no such thing. When told with mock-sadness that Castellano had not signed, he flew into simulated rage, as prearranged with Macmillan. 'There must be some mistake. Only this morning I saw Badoglio's telegram to Eisenhower stating that General Castellano was to sign. In that case he must be a spy.' Alexander then withdrew, leaving the Italians to confer. Macmillan's account continues:

The General [Alexander] was as eager as all the rest of us to hear the result. The Italians retired to their tent for consultation. Our tent was behind it. But the only way by which the General could reach us, unseen by the Italians, and preserving the sense of angry indignation which he had affected, was – after leaving the orchard at the far end – to creep round outside the wall till he could climb over it to join us. This he did with schoolboy delight. But the circuit was very long, and it was very hot; and his boots, although very smart, were very tight. Finally he reached us, and together we awaited anxiously the result. The Italians continued for some time to discuss their problem with eager volubility. At last they requested a further meeting with the Chief of Staff [Bedell Smith]. They formally announced their decision to ask immediately for authority to sign, and to meet all General Alexander's demands.[8]

Authorization arrived from Rome next day, 3 September. At dawn Eighth Army had landed on the far side of the Messina straits. Eisenhower flew to Cassibile for the final ceremony at 5.15 pm. There were only two signatures on the document, Bedell Smith's, on behalf of Eisenhower, and Castellano's, on behalf of Badoglio. The instrument of surrender, in fact an armistice, was also implicitly an instrument of alliance, for it presupposed Italian help against the Germans and Allied help for the Italians. It was kept a strict secret for six further days, until a few hours before the Salerno landings, for fear that if the Germans got wind of it, they would immediately take prisoner the Italian soldiers and statesmen on whom we relied, and disarm Italian troops in the field. In fact, although Badoglio and the King of Italy escaped in time, the larger part of the Italian army found itself surrendering twice in quick succession, first to the Allies and then to the Germans. If Badoglio had known that the Allies could land no more than three divisions at Salerno initially, he would probably not have authorized Castellano to sign. Even the air-drop on Rome was cancelled, because the Germans were in possession of the airfields and had deprived the Italian divisions of almost all their petrol and ammunition.

The most tangible immediate gain was the surrender of the Italian fleet, which sailed for Malta after dark on 8 September. The Italian soldiers, by now indifferent to both sides, were anxious to disperse to their homes. It was at first only a handful who were willing to fight against the Germans. As Alexander said privately to David Hunt, a member of his Intelligence staff, there seemed no logical reason why they should be a greater menace to the Germans in Italy than they had been to us in Sicily. They did not even declare war on Germany until 13 October. Still, the Italian capitulation was a great Allied achievement. The gradual erosion of Italian pride and power which had been begun by Wavell in the western desert and Abyssinia was completed by Alexander in Tunisia and Sicily. The Mediterranean strategy for which he and Brooke had fought so hard was vindicated at Cassibile exactly four years to the day after the start of the Second War.

12

SALERNO AND ANZIO

The decision to invade Italy was reached quite suddenly. The turning-point of the long debate came on 18 July 1943, a week before the fall of Mussolini, when Eisenhower signalled to Marshall his recommendation that the end of the Sicilian campaign should immediately be followed by the crossing of the straits of Messina, and Marshall, to Brooke's surprise, agreed. This decision, though final, was still cautious. A few days later the American Chiefs of Staff made it clear that an Italian campaign must not be allowed to harm the major operation in north-west Europe (*Overlord*). Seven divisions must be withdrawn from Alexander's command in the autumn and returned to England, together with the bulk of the landing craft and three heavy bomber groups. Alexander must do whatever he could with what he had left. 'Marshall absolutely fails to realise the strategic treasures that lie at our feet in the Mediterranean,' wrote Brooke in his diary: 'He admits that our object must be to eliminate Italy and yet is always afraid of facing the consequences of doing so.'

Brooke's exasperated running-commentary must not be allowed to stand as a verdict. Even after the withdrawal of the seven divisions there were still a score left in the Mediterranean and Near East with which Alexander completed the conquest of Italy twenty months later, and Allied naval and air supremacy remained unchallenged to the end. The Americans consented to an Italian campaign partly in order to put an end to an irritating argument which was beginning to harm their relations with the British, but also because they agreed that there were some advantages in it. In the summer of 1943 they doubted whether Alexander could achieve more than the conquest of southern Italy, and they saw the Foggia airfields and the port of Naples, possibly Rome, as the main prizes that could be expected. Italy would then become primarily an air-base for the Strategic Air Force and a military base for the invasion of southern France. The Russians could not be allowed to bear the whole weight of the war for the ten remaining months before *Overlord* was due. The two western Allies must fight somewhere, and the Mediterranean was the only possible place. The Italians might be knocked out of the war, and German reserves would be drawn away from the two vital fronts. The campaign would give support to the partisans fighting in Yugoslavia.

The Anglo-American disagreement was therefore less deep than it appeared: it was concerned with the scale of future operations in the Mediterranean, not with the need for any operations at all. Both allies were convinced that the war could not be won there: it would be won by the convergence in central Europe of the Russian offensive from the east and the Allied offensive from the west. Let it be once more stated (for the opposite legend is as persistent as a dye) that Churchill did not wish to shirk the cross-Channel invasion; that he did not wish to open a southern front in the Balkans: and that the Americans did not wish to abandon the Mediterranean theatre completely. The disagreement on what should be done with Alexander's armies once they had achieved their first strategic objectives had barely begun to emerge.

The debate was carried on at the highest levels, between the Combined Chiefs of Staff in Washington and between Roosevelt and Churchill in Quebec, two removes above Alexander, but his views were sought and given. He was strongly in favour of an Italian campaign. Sardinia and Corsica he regarded as objectives too insignificant for his large and experienced force. While the capture of the islands might pose a new threat, it would not by itself force Italy's surrender. The Balkans he considered more seriously, but only momentarily; the country was unsuited to mechanized warfare, and led nowhere. When the Italians opened negotiations for an armistice, there could be no further argument: their country must be occupied, and if the Germans chose to contest the occupation, the campaign would serve its purpose equally well, as a diversion for *Overlord* on the largest scale. The breadth of the peninsula was commensurate with the forces that Alexander could deploy and the number of enemy divisions which he could expect to contain, and its two long sea-coasts would give him opportunities for using Allied naval power to best effect. The main disadvantages were the rugged mountains and the rivers flowing from them east and west across the line of his advance.

The strategy was now beyond dispute. Less certain were the tactics. A plan was hammered out at a series of conferences between Eisenhower, Alexander, Tedder and Cunningham, usually at Carthage. When an Italian capitulation became probable they were all agreed that a landing in the toe of Italy would by itself be too tame a response to the opportunity. There must also be a main assault further north, and the twenty-mile arc of sand between Salerno and Paestum was ideally situated, because it was within the range of fighter cover from Sicily and would impress the Italians that a serious campaign was intended, with Naples as its first obvious objective. It was a bold plan, for there were only craft enough to lift three divisions for the assault and two more to follow up, and there were known to be eighteen German divisions in Italy, all of which might sooner or later be drawn into the battle. The caution of *Husky* was not repeated in *Avalanche*, the name given to the Salerno operation. It is therefore surprising that it was still thought necessary to stage a preliminary landing with two divisions of Eighth Army in the extreme south, across the straits from Messina, where they would be 300 miles from Salerno and confined to a mountainous peninsula where they might well be trapped. But Montgomery's first reaction to the role allotted to him was not that it was too meagre but that it was too risky. On 19 August he wrote petulantly to Alexander:

As things stand at present, I have been ordered to invade the mainland of the Continent of Europe on the night 30th–31st August. We must assume that strong resistance will be offered by the enemy. I have been given no clear object for the operation, but assume the object to be to secure the straits for the Navy and to act as a diversion for *Avalanche*. The craft and naval personnel allotted to me at present make any invasion of Europe with the above object, and assuming opposition, quite impossible. . . . Therefore I can only carry out a major raid across the straits. . . . I fully realise that *Avalanche* must have first priority but I presume you do not want *Avalanche* to be preceded by a disaster here. I request definite instructions as to the timing and object of any operation I am to carry out across the straits.

Alexander replied that Eighth Army's role was 'to secure a bridgehead in the toe of Italy to enable our naval forces to operate through the straits of Messina. In the event of the enemy withdrawing from the toe you will follow them up with such force as you can make available, bearing in mind that the greater the extent to which you can engage

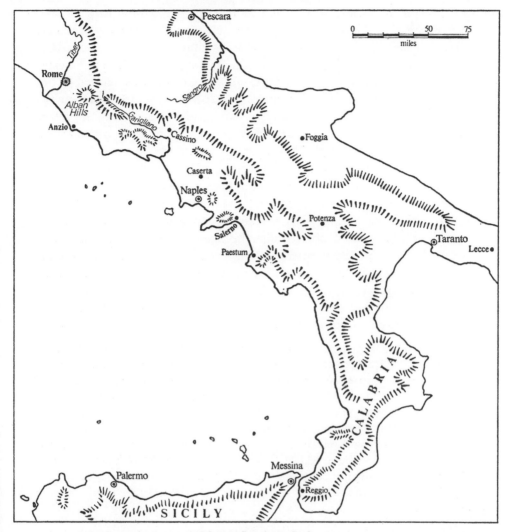

Map 9 Southern Italy

enemy forces in the southern tip of Italy, the more assistance you will be giving to *Avalanche*.' This was something a little more than a diversion, but a little less than the southern claw of a pincer movement. Montgomery's operation (*Baytown*) was separate from *Avalanche* though marginally helpful to it. It had been decided upon in July as a natural first step after the conquest of Sicily, primarily to clear the Messina straits for Allied shipping. When the whole situation was transformed by

215

the Italian armistice, and *Avalanche* was hurriedly mounted to take advantage of it, the role of *Baytown* was not stepped up correspondingly, although its original purpose had now become almost irrelevant. If it was impossible to put Eighth Army ashore alongside the Fifth at Salerno where they would have been most useful, they could have landed in the instep or at Taranto, with Potenza as their objective, and both operations merged into one. 'The toe', wrote Liddell Hart, 'was the worst possible place for creating an effective distraction.' Montgomery is justified in his comment, 'No attempt was made to coordinate my operations with those of the Fifth Army', but the main reason was his own insistence that a two-divisional landing across the straits was likely to end in disaster. How then could Alexander order him to land further north without provoking a serious conflict with his subordinate?

The decision was all the stranger because a landing at Taranto was improvised at the last moment, when it was thought that the Italians might help. Alexander's new initiative was as bold as *Avalanche* itself, an implied rebuke to Montgomery's caution. He cabled Brooke on 4 September, the day after the signature of the armistice at Cassibile and Eighth Army's landing in the toe:

The whole of last night was spent in military talks with the Italian party. I have made it quite clear to them that once the armistice is official we cease to be enemies but we are not allies. However, the greater their assistance to us the shorter time Italy will remain a battlefield and the better for them. I have given them specific action which will help us in the sabotage line – sit-down strikes, forming guerilla bands etc., also the seizure of ports and key points which will paralyse the enemy and open the door to us. I am mounting an operation to secure Taranto and build up V Corps in that area. Shipping is the difficulty, and it will probably have to be done by destroyers and naval units. It is vital at this stage to show a stronger front than we actually possess.

In fact the Italians did nothing. There was no sabotage, no resistance to the Germans, no immediate aid to the Allies. It was only because Eisenhower himself announced the armistice as the convoys were approaching the Salerno beaches on the evening of 9 September that Badoglio was obliged to confirm it an hour later 'in a depressed and subdued voice', as Alexander states in his despatch, which gave no encouragement to the Italian troops to change sides. The German takeover of the Italian defences, which had been planned months ahead, was successful in every place where they had the power to impose it, in-

cluding Rome, including Salerno. But not at Taranto. There a force of
Allied cruisers carrying 3,000 men of the 1st Airborne Division berthed
on 9 September unopposed, and the whole heel of Italy from Lecce to
Foggia lay open to Allied occupation. But the parachutists had landed
without tanks, with little artillery and inadequate transport, and could
not exploit their sudden advantage. The troops who could have done so
were inching up the toe.

Montgomery's misgivings were shown to have been unfounded.
Eighth Army crossed the straits of Messina under a triumphal arch of
shellfire, all of which was wasted because the mainland shore was found
undefended, and the most serious opposition came from a puma and a
monkey which escaped from Reggio zoo to attack some Canadian
soldiers. Even if Montgomery had been allowed, as he wanted, to use
both his corps, his progress northwards would have been little faster.
There were only two winding roads up the Calabrian peninsula, where
today the spider-thin viaducts of the autostrada reach from peak to
peak, and both were blocked by heavy demolitions every few miles. The
peninsula is mountainous throughout its length, in proportion comparable to the Highlands of Scotland, threaded by valleys which lift
suddenly into high passes. It was a contest between engineers, the
Germans testing with explosives the British ingenuity for bridging and
makeshift repairs. The advance, says de Guingand, 'was a veritable
calvary. . . . I felt most dissatisfied about this expenditure of effort and
valuable resources. Where was it getting us? Was it necessary?'

It certainly began to seem necessary on 10 September, when Alexander first urged Montgomery to make every effort to hurry to the relief
of Salerno, a role which had not been foreseen in his original orders.
Even now it was not clear whether his intention was to fuse *Baytown*
with *Avalanche*. His message ran: 'It is of the utmost importance that you
maintain pressure upon the Germans so that they cannot remove forces
from your front and concentrate them against *Avalanche*.' But pressure
would have exactly that result: the more quickly Eighth Army advanced
the sooner the German forces in Calabria would unite with those at
Salerno. It was not until 13 September, when Mark Clark's Fifth Army
at Salerno was in desperate straits, that Alexander gave Montgomery a
definite order to intervene in the northern battlefield. 'The situation on
Fifth Army's front', he signalled, 'is not favourable. The earlier you can
threaten the forces opposite Fifth Army the better. The next few days
are critical.' Although the Germans offered little resistance in Calabria

except by demolitions, the distance was so great that the crisis was over before Montgomery could come near enough to help. General Clark has described to the author the remote influence which one operation had upon the other:

At that time the only news we got was from the BBC. We'd get the picture that the Eighth Army was coming to our rescue. I remember sending Monty a message that we needed help. The faster he could get, and the nearer he could get, the very momentum of his Army coming up was a deterrent to the enemy and a boost to us. But there wasn't any physical joining of hands to the extent that any British came to intervene in the battle. Monty sent me some sort of personal message saying that we had joined hands, and I said, 'Well I haven't felt the grip of your hand yet.'

Fifth Army had run into very serious trouble. Instead of finding welcoming Italian hands on the beaches, they found German tanks. Their craft were fired upon as they were lowered from their mother-ships. There were two British and one American division under Clark's command and they fought their way inland far enough to create a salient but well short of the amphitheatre of hills which gave the Germans observation over the whole plain where the Allies were halted. If Rommel had sent down his eight divisions in the north of Italy to join Kesselring's in the south, the beachhead could not have survived. As it was, a strong German counter-attack penetrated to within a mile of the beaches at the junction of the American and British corps, and for three days there was acute anxiety.

When they advanced inland through the close network of lanes they found their way blocked by tanks and infantry, and the casualties began to mount. The optimism with which they had landed soon wavered. A front line of some sort was formed but the Germans began to probe it for points of weakness, and soon found them. The only way to stop their infiltration through the thick tobacco crops was by blocking every yard with men standing shoulder to shoulder, but though platoons were closely knit entities, there were gaps between platoons, bigger gaps between companies and battalions, and between the divisions and the two corps, wide open spaces. The Germans operated with small battle-groups of thirty men and a few tanks which would join up in rear of our positions, always on the move and always striking from a new direction. Salerno was a dusty, bloody, terrifying battle. The bombardment was incessant. The malarial heat cooled off for a few hours at night, but the darkness increased the dangers and men's fear, and no rest was possible. Almost every battalion destroyed at least once all its marked maps and codes as a precaution against capture, and Red Cross flags were hung out everywhere to protect the wounded. On 13 September a single battalion was attacked by an entire Panzer division, and held them off by firing 55,000 bullets at close range, while the artillery shelled the German concentrations for ninety minutes without pause. Prisoners captured on that occasion said that there were fifty tanks behind them waiting to break through to the beaches. The incident was typical of the Allies' extreme peril.

It was then that Alexander displayed his superb qualities as a fighting commander. The dangers which he had survived in his earlier career had given him a composure which few could emulate in a crisis. To him victory, to others disaster, was always just around the corner. If a miscalculation had been made about the role of Eighth Army and the vigour of the German reaction, it was remedied as the battle developed. The air forces, the naval forces and army reserves were moved forward from Africa and Sicily like additional fuel from pit-heads to generating stations to avert a power-cut. It was the steadiness with which he achieved this rescue-operation, his soundly based optimism, his quick decision, and the confidence which he showed and inspired when he visited the beachhead, that justify General Jackson's tribute, 'If any individual can ever be said to win a battle, Alexander won Salerno.'

At almost daily meetings with Cunningham and Tedder, equals to him in rank, his was the dominating mind. With Cunningham he had a particularly sympathetic relationship. Stewart Perowne has written of him: 'There was about him a kind of quiet power, a sort of perpetual movement of spirit, which showed from his bright kind eyes.' Tedder was less of a natural gentleman. But all three had a profound knowledge of what each could do to help the other, and their mutual understanding was so perfect, their organization so flexible, that great movements of air and naval fleets could be extemporized at his will. The battleships *Warspite* and *Valiant* joined the cruisers off Salerno to saturate the German troop-concentrations in heavy shellfire, and the Strategic Air Force switched from its distant roles to attack the same targets. The German air force was wiped from the skies. When Alexander urgently requested the return of the three groups of heavy bombers from the United Kingdom, and the bombing of German communications from bases in England, both requests were granted the same day. He advanced the rate of reinforcement by air and sea, flying in nearly 2,000 American parachutists to drop on the actual battlefield, and bringing 1,500 British infantry in cruisers from North Africa. Another American division was summoned from Sicily. Eighteen tank-carrying ships *en route* through the Mediterranean to India were made available for Salerno at Alexander's suggestion. Having arranged all this from his headquarters near Tunis he embarked on a destroyer at Palermo for the beachhead, where he spent the decisive day of the battle, 15 September.

The seriousness of the crisis, and his personal contribution to its alleviation, can be judged by his daily messages to Churchill and Brooke:

13 September. I consider the situation critical.

14 September. I am not satisfied with the position of *Avalanche*. I have instructed Eighth Army to push ahead with all speed.

15 September. I am here [at Salerno] with Fifth Army. Everything possible is being done to make *Avalanche* a success. Its fate will be decided in the next few days.

16 September. I have just returned from an extensive tour of Fifth Army's front. I saw both Corps commanders, all divisional commanders and several front-line brigades. Although I am not entirely happy about the situation, I am happier than I was twenty-four hours ago, for the following reasons. The Germans have not put in a serious attack since the night of the 13th. This has given us time to improve our position somewhat, rest some very exhausted troops and get some reinforcements of men and materials in. Eighth Army are also drawing nearer. I have also been able to cheer them up and issue certain directions, of which the following are the most important. Hold what we have gained at all costs. Consolidate key positions by digging in, wiring and mining. Reorganise scattered and mixed units and formations. Form local reserves, and as strong a mobile reserve as possible. Inform troops of the rapid approach of Eighth Army and the flow of reinforcements now arriving day and night. Our present weakness is due to the fact that the Germans have been able to concentrate strong forces quicker than we have been able to build up sufficient forces to hold what we had gained at the first rush. The Germans hold most of the dominating features and overlook us on to the beaches. Our troops are tired. There is very little depth anywhere. We have temporarily lost the initiative. . . . The whole of the air forces are concentrated in the battle area. We shall regain the initiative and start to gain key points as soon as we are strong enough to do so. God's blessing on our enterprise and a little luck will assure success to our arms.

17 September. I do not wish to mislead you by being over-optimistic, but I am satisfied that we now have the situation in hand.

18 September. I can say with full confidence that the whole situation has changed in our favour and that the initiative has passed to us.

In none of these messages, nor in his despatch, did Alexander mention two of his decisions which greatly influenced the battle. The first was the relief of the commander of the American corps, General Dawley: the second the cancellation of a naval plan to evacuate at least part of the beachhead. General Mark Clark spoke to me about both incidents in 1970:

Dawley was a man greatly my superior at West Point, and several years my senior. He was the protégé of General Leslie McNair [Commander of the American Army Ground Forces, to whom Clark had been Chief of Staff]. McNair admired Dawley greatly. He always talked Dawley to me. When I got command of the Fifth Army, McNair said he hoped I would accept Dawley as one of my Corps Commanders. I discussed this with General Eisenhower, and we both had reservations. When Alex came to the beachhead, we went to see Dawley. It was apparent that he was nervous and distraught, and afterwards Alex said to me, 'Wayne, you've got a broken reed there.' I said, 'I know it.' Alex communicated his feelings to Ike, and Ike asked me about it when he came to the beachhead. I said: 'Ike, I'm thoroughly aware of the situation. I have put Ridgeway in as Deputy Corps Commander to assist him. I dread relieving him.' Nothing ever hurt me more, but I felt I had to do it.

Dawley lost his nerve when the Germans threatened to break through to the beaches. When Clark asked him what he intended to do about it, Dawley replied, 'Nothing. I have no reserves. All I've got is a prayer.'[1] Alexander had the authority to relieve him, but he preferred to do it by suggestion to Clark and Eisenhower than by direct action against an American General. On his return from the beachhead, he told Eisenhower that 'he was most favourably impressed by Clark's calmness and serenity under adverse circumstances, but was most unfavourably impressed by Dawley'.[2] Two days later Eisenhower went to the beachhead himself and replaced Dawley by General Lucas, reporting to Marshall, 'Dawley is a splendid character, earnest, faithful and well-informed ... but he cannot exercise high battle command when the going is rough. He grows extremely nervous and indecisive.'

The second incident was more important but the evidence is less clear.

In his Memoirs Alexander wrote that during his visit to the beachhead on 15 September, 'I learnt of Mark Clark's quite impossible suggestion to transfer the American beachhead to the British sector.' According to the British Official History Clark ordered two emergency plans to be prepared, one to embark the British corps and land it in the American sector, and the other to embark the American corps and land it alongside the British, with the intention of consolidating his force when it appeared that it might be split in two. The British naval commander at Salerno protested that both operations were impracticable, perhaps suicidal. As soon as Alexander landed on the 15th, he was told of this intention and immediately put a stop to it. General Lemnitzer, who had joined Alexander in Sicily as his senior American staff officer, has given me this account:

Things were going pretty badly. We found out, on board the flag-ship of Admiral Hewitt [American senior naval commander] that they were putting together a withdrawal plan. This is one of the times when I saw General Alexander show his steel. He said that they must stop that immediately. The Navy were trying to make sure that if the Army had to withdraw, they at least had some kind of plan. But Alexander's view was that the news of this would spread like wildfire. If it were known among the troops ashore that they were even considering a withdrawal plan, it would be disastrous for morale. He issued instructions that all such planning would cease immediately. My guess would be that it was a naval initiative – the Navy were right to have a contingency plan.

I put the point to Mark Clark:

Did Alexander stop the Navy preparing an evacuation plan?

At the US Command and General Staff College, there was one lesson beat home to everybody, that in any amphibious operation you must have an alternative plan for evacuation. I thought of this possible eventuality and the possibility of having to shift troops either to or from the US and British sectors, should it become necessary. That is why Admiral Hewitt was asked to stand by.

Did you ever talk to Alexander about it?

I do not recall discussing this matter with Alex at the time, nor his having involved himself with this subject. Because the Germans had driven a wedge all the way to the Mediterranean between my British and American corps, it was prudent to have a re-embarkation capability of moving troops and supplies in either direction. The necessity never arose. The rumour started some time later that there might have been some plans to pull out. That was never the case. On the contrary, everyone fought harder to hold the Salerno bridgehead.

There was perhaps a tentative limited plan, discussed between Clark and some of his staff, which was repeated in garbled form to the Navy and assumed in their minds greater significance than he had intended. When Alexander arrived, the Navy were hard at work preparing a major operation, and he stopped them. It was a bold thing to do. If the American corps had been wiped out, the lack of any emergency plan to rescue them would have been severely criticized and blamed on him. Instead, Alexander said, as he had said at Alamein in August 1942, 'We stay here and we die here: we do not retreat.'

Kesselring attributed his failure to destroy the beachhead to naval gunfire and air bombardment. It was also due to Alexander's determination and calm, and to reinforcement much in excess of what had been planned. By 16 September Clark had the equivalent of seven divisions ashore, 170,000 men with 200 tanks, all landed over the open beaches. Eighth Army joined forces with their southern flank late on 15 September. The crisis was over. While Eighth Army filtered up the east coast and through the valleys of central Italy, Fifth Army broke through the ring of hills at Salerno and entered Naples on 1 October. There was talk of capturing Rome by the end of October.

It is unnecessary to follow in detail the fortunes of Fifth and Eighth Armies during the autumn and early winter months of 1943–4. They were fighting almost separate campaigns from river to river, divided by the central mass of the Abruzzi, slowed down by mud, mountains, supply difficulties and stiffening German resistance until at great cost and with diminishing elation they reached the line of the rivers Sangro on the east coast and Garigliano on the west. It was an unsatisfactory period of the campaign. It lacked a theme. No major use could be made of the open sea-flanks because sufficient landing-craft were not available. No decisive punch could be delivered at a single point because the Germans were numerically as strong as the Allies and confident that any local penetration of their line could be sealed off on another mountain, another river, further back. In one sense Alexander was fulfilling his main task by keeping the Germans engaged by the mere deployment of his own divisions opposite them. But a stalemate, even in mid-winter, did not suit his temperament or theirs. There must be continuous action. At first he considered it possible that if Montgomery could reach Pescara he could then swing west over the Apennines to converge with Fifth Army on Rome, but the plan came to nothing. Pescara was not captured until after the fall of Rome in June 1944. Meanwhile the two armies pursued their separate routes up each coast. It was a grim business. They became disheartened by what seemed to have become a battle of attrition in fearful conditions of weather and terrain. They were hardened, but very tired.

Alexander left the conduct of these battles largely to his army commanders, and bent his mind to the framing of a fresh concept of the campaign as a whole. Among his papers is a pencilled draft and sketch-map dated 21 October 1943, initialled 'H.R.A.', and headed 'How to work out a plan for the capture of the north of Italy'. It is a good example of the way in which he would talk to himself on paper and work out ideas which he would then test by discussion with his staff:

Our object is to drive the Germans out of the north of Italy so as to secure the valley of the Po for the following purpose: (a) as a base from which we can directly threaten the Balkans and the Brenner Pass with ground and air forces; (b) as a base from which we can launch an expedition into France to join up with a French seaborne force directed to the Marseilles area; (c) to secure airfields from which our strategic air forces can attack Germany.

The key to securing the valley of the Po is firstly to gain the gateway or exits over the Apennines between Rimini and Florence. Secondly, to secure bridgeheads over the Po river from the mouth to Mantua with a strongly held left flank from Mantua over the mountains to Spezia. Thirdly, a drive forward to secure the general line Venice-Verona-Spezia. The remainder of the Po can then be cleared and gates open into France.

Having cleared our minds what we want to do, we must now see how we can do it, because it is not unreasonable to suppose that the Germans will appreciate fairly correctly what our intentions are. Therefore, before we can plan in more detail, we must know the following: (a) what is the maximum number of divisions the enemy can maintain in northern Italy, assuming his main lines-of-communication are via Udine, the Brenner and from France, and taking into account what our air forces can do to hinder his flow of maintenance, the fact of a semi-hostile population, etc.; (b) assuming that the Germans guess our intentions, how and where will he locate his forces.

Alexander did not use this far-sighted concept of the Italian campaign in the major *exposé* of his aims which he presented three days later to a conference of the Mediterranean commanders at Carthage. Instead, he focussed attention on the immediate prospects in a document so 'masterly' (Churchill's description) that it was telegraphed verbatim to Roosevelt and Stalin. (It is reproduced in full in Churchill's *Closing the Ring*, pp. 216–20.) Alexander's contention was that 'a stabilised front south of Rome cannot be accepted, for the capital has a significance far greater than its strategic location, and sufficient depth must be gained before the Foggia airfields and the port of Naples can be regarded as secure.' He foresaw a 'slogging match' to capture Rome, and feared that German reinforcements might be used to snatch a quick victory when our own offensive was exhausted. Having thus gained general agreement that his armies must continue to advance, he began to elaborate his ideas in discussion with Eisenhower during the next few days. He persuaded him that it would be difficult to retain the initiative without landing-craft. Their 'slogging-match' northwards might turn at any moment into a German slogging-match southwards, and the way to forestall them was to land behind their front in the Adriatic and 'north-west of Rome'. This was the first seed of operation *Shingle*, which was to flower in January at Anzio. By early November it had become 'an amphibious assault south of the Tiber', and Eisenhower was reporting to Marshall, 'I am convinced that Alexander's plan is sound.' Alexander suppressed for the moment his notion of how the campaign might develop into northern Italy and beyond, wishing to lead Eisenhower to it by easy stages, and bearing in mind Brooke's private warning to him in a message of 18 October, 'My difficulty all along has been to persuade the Americans that our commitment in Italy would be a heavy one. They seem to have an ineradicable impression that our hearts are not in *Overlord*, and that we will take any opportunity of diverting to the Mediterranean resources which they consider should be concentrated in Great Britain.' Eisenhower wavered between the greater and the lesser plans. When he was with Churchill and Alexander at Malta in mid-November, he declared that the Po valley was a vital strategic area and must be seized; but when he was alone with his own people or writing privately to Marshall, he was advocating only that 'we should keep sufficient strength to hold what we have already gained and to force the Nazis to maintain sizeable forces in the area', and that 'if *Overlord* succeeds, it makes little difference what happens to us in Italy'.

While this uncertainty existed at the top level of command Alexander was unable to plan ahead, and it was unfortunate that when Churchill went from Malta to meet Roosevelt at Cairo, he was immobilized by jaundice and could not join them. His difficulty was increased by the decision that Eisenhower himself was to take command of *Overlord*. From that moment onwards Eisenhower viewed the Mediterranean mainly in terms of the help which it could afford him in his next campaign. He turned against *Shingle*. Italy must become a feeder for France, and the landing on the French Riviera across the Ligurian Sea (*Anvil*) assumed more importance in his eyes even than the capture of Rome.

Alexander had been considered as deputy for Eisenhower in *Overlord* and commander of ground forces. Eisenhower himself asked for him in preference to Montgomery 'because I had been so closely associated with him and had developed for him an admiration and friendship which have grown with the years. I regarded Alexander as Britain's outstanding soldier in the field of strategy. He was, moreover, a friendly and companionable type; Americans instinctively liked him.'[3] It was however considered inadvisable to strip the Mediterranean of its two senior commanders simultaneously, and if *Overlord* was to become a predominantly American operation, the Mediterranean, in a fair division of honours, should become British. Alexander was the natural choice in these circumstances to succeed Eisenhower as Supreme Allied Commander, but the appointment was given to General Maitland Wilson, Commander-in-Chief Middle East. Churchill, in whose hands the decision lay, explained to Roosevelt that it would be impossible for Alexander to act as Supreme Commander and at the same time fight the battle in Italy. He would be wasted as a political General far in the rear. A profounder reason may have been that Churchill knew that Alexander had more influence over the Americans than any other British officer and his continued presence in Italy, responsible for actual operations, would make ambitious plans for the Italian campaign more palatable to our allies.

Alexander showed no resentment at the choice of Maitland Wilson, an officer whose name was little known to the wider public and whose achievements could not match his own. When Churchill told Alexander of the decision, Brooke records, he was 'as always, quite charming to deal with, always ready to do what was required of him, never scheming or pulling strings. A soldier of the very highest principles.' Alexander betrayed no disappointment: it is doubtful whether he even felt it. He was deeply involved in the Italian campaign and wished to see it through to the end. He knew that the topmost appointment would remove him from the actual command of troops. He could handle

Wilson as he had handled Eisenhower, with tact and firmness but with even greater freedom because no conflict of loyalties could arise between them. Wilson would look after questions of reinforcement and supply, and the peripheral problems of the Mediterranean, including the Balkans. Alexander would fight the battle. At the same time it was announced that Montgomery would command all the land-forces at the outset of *Overlord*, that Tedder would become Eisenhower's deputy, and that Oliver Leese would succeed Montgomery in command of Eighth Army.

Churchill remained in the Mediterranean until the first weeks of 1944. After Cairo he went with Roosevelt to meet Stalin in Teheran, and then returned to Tunis, where he fell ill with pneumonia in mid-December. At no time, as 'fever flickered in and out', did he relinquish his direction of affairs, and foremost in his mind was Italy. 'Were we to leave it a stagnant pool from which we had drawn every fish we wanted?' He regarded a new offensive and the capture of Rome as the natural curtain-raiser to *Overlord*. Nothing more was to be gained by the slogging-match up each coast. He saw the stagnation of the campaign as 'scandalous', and in particular criticized the failure to make any use of sea-power, a failure which stemmed from the priority given in the Allied ship-building programme to cargo-ships at the expense of landing-craft and the diversion of nine-tenths of the existing craft to the Pacific and Far East. He therefore eagerly welcomed Brooke's suggestion that *Shingle* should be revived and strengthened, by a landing near the mouth of the Tiber which would coincide with a major push from the Garigliano-Cassino line, which Fifth Army were then about to reach. The necessary landing-craft must be obtained by delaying for a few weeks their return to the United Kingdom. His plan, and his excitement, built up quickly. He sent for Alexander, Wilson, Eisenhower and the other top commanders to visit him at Carthage. Their discussions round his sick-bed started on Christmas Eve and continued on Christmas Day. They then sat down to a magnificent Christmas lunch, with turkey, plum pudding and champagne, at which Churchill presided in a padded silk Chinese dressing-gown decorated with blue and gold dragons. A few days earlier he had been on the point of death.

They planned an amphibious assault by two divisions, and Churchill undertook to persuade the President and his Chiefs of Staff to retain in the Mediterranean enough craft to make it possible. The new *Shingle* would come under the command of Mark Clark. The Corps Commander would be General Lucas, who had succeeded Dawley at Salerno, and was in Alexander's opinion 'the best American Corps Commander', who also happened to be free with his VI Corps headquarters from current operations. Alexander was instructed by Churchill 'to give full weight to the importance of equality of hazards and sacrifice between British and American troops. I do not like the idea that the first and most risky operation undertaken in the Mediterranean under British command should fall exclusively on American forces.' After discussing the matter with Eisenhower and Clark, Alexander decided that each nation should contribute one division, with supporting troops in equal proportion. There was much unselfishness shown at Carthage, and great optimism.

In subsequent days and weeks the Christmas plan began to look less sound as new minds focussed upon its difficulties. Awkward but necessary questions were asked. Were two divisions enough? What would happen if the Germans brought down strong reinforcements from the north of Italy, France or the Balkans and isolated the beachhead without withdrawing from the Cassino front? In that case VI Corps might be overwhelmed, for the Carthage plan had allowed for no subsequent reinforcement, and supply for no more than eight days after landing, time enough, it had been assumed, for *Shingle* to achieve its purpose and the two fronts to unite.

Alexander's chief administrative officer, General Brian Robertson, flatly advised that the operation should be abandoned 'unless there is a reasonable prospect of a successful junction between *Shingle* and Fifth Army within one week of landing'. Mark Clark expected two or three German divisions to oppose him, and thought that fifteen days 'and probably longer' should be allowed between the landing and the junction. Alexander himself was having second thoughts. 'There can be no guarantee that operations will be over in eight days', he signalled Wilson on 31 December. 'It may even be necessary to support the initial forces with a further division under certain circumstances.' At Carthage, according to Alexander's own note of the conference, 'some discussion ensued on the question of whether the Germans would be able to reinforce quickly from the north. There was general agreement that this was unlikely, particularly in view of our air superiority.' Had that assumption been wise? He put to Churchill, now convalescing at Marrakesh, his doubts about the viability of the *Shingle* plan, but he did not press them very hard. He asked that some of the landing-craft should be retained for a further fortnight, but he did not raise the question whether two divisions were enough. Churchill persuaded the President to allow enough craft to remain to supply the force until the end of February, and suggested 'the elements of a third division' to follow up. As time passed, two divisions were alerted as reinforcements for the two assault divisions, including the American 1st Armoured Division. *Shingle* was becoming more realistic as D Day (22 January) approached. But the euphoria of Christmas Day lingered on to its detriment. How, with the experience of Salerno so recent, could they have fallen victims to such optimism?

The purpose of *Shingle* seemed clear enough. It was to force Kesselring to withdraw his XIV Corps from the Cassino front under the double pressure of frontal attack and the threat from Anzio to his communications. If it succeeded, Rome would fall as a result. Churchill and his commanders had agreed thus far at Carthage, but they had not defined the object more precisely. To Churchill the prize was Rome. To Alexander it was the threat to XIV Corps – the difference between a statesman's and a soldier's order of priority. So intent was each upon his own conception of the plan that Churchill had even misunderstood, after two days discussing it with maps spread over his counterpane and his commanders grouped around him, where exactly VI Corps was to land. On 4 January he signalled Alexander from Marrakesh:

All our talks [at Carthage] proceeded on the basis of landings north and south of the Tiber. Obviously Nettuno [the twin port of Anzio] is a much less ambitious movement. It may be a safer or a better operation, but it is certainly a different one. Think you should keep me informed about the reasons for the change.

There had been no change. A landing north of the Tiber had been firmly ruled out. Alexander replied:

My object in *Shingle* has always been to land a force in the most favourable area to get astride the enemy's lines-of-communication, and then to develop a threat against the rear of the German XIV Corps while it is being attacked frontally by Fifth Army. The best objective for this purpose is the Colli Laziali feature just south-east of Rome. If this operation is successful, it will undoubtedly force the enemy to withdraw, probably lead to the destruction of some of his divisions and certainly to the capture of Rome. Although there was some discussion at our conference about landing north of Rome,

I was clearly under the impression that an enlarged *Shingle* had been agreed to. Nettuno has always been one of the landing beaches for *Shingle* because it gives some sort of sheltered anchorage. Nettuno also gives the best access to a good road leading direct to the objective. To land north of the Tiber as well, with the forces at my disposal, would expose them to defeat in detail. It would also greatly increase the difficulties of maintenance which I have already stressed. The whole operation must depend upon the provision of the necessary craft to get the forces there and keep them going.

The idea of forcing the withdrawal of XIV Corps remained basic to Alexander's thinking, from the moment when he first conceived *Shingle* in October 1943 to its fruition in May 1944. He saw the Colli Laziali, or Alban Hills, as the place where he would cut the German communications, for it lay between the two main roads, Routes 6 and 7, leading from Naples to Rome. His operation instruction of 8 November for the first *Shingle* had stated this to be the objective, and in his despatch he wrote, 'I felt that provided that we got firmly on to the Alban Hills, and across Route 6, Kesselring would not dare to take the risk of retaining his positions at Cassino.' This November *Shingle* had been a force of one pivision only. In January he had two, and two more to follow up a few days later. His objective remained the same. In his orders of 12 January he stated, 'The objects of this operation will be to cut the enemy's main communications in the Colli Laziali area south-east of Rome, and to threaten the rear of the German XIV Corps.' Although there is no doubt that this is what he hoped would happen, he spoke with an uncertain voice to the commanders who alone could make it happen. He kept among his papers the notes of a discussion with Mark Clark on 9 January which show, at least implicitly, his hesitation about the object which he was to proclaim so confidently in his written order three days later:

Advance from bridgehead. Nomination, training and preparation of mobile hard-hitting force from a third division to operate as spearhead in advance from bridgehead. Suggest one or two Regimental Combat Teams with tanks and self-propelled artillery in close support all on lightest possible baggage and ration scale to increase mobility and reduce vehicles required. To be ready for loading D plus 3. *Fight for the bridgehead*: Rapid consolidation vital. Enemy counter-attacks. Take no chances. Keep a reserve. Build up striking force and have plan ready for its employment at first favourable opportunity. One main thrust by really mobile hard-hitting force. Steady pressure elsewhere.

The rest of the note is about the role of the main Fifth Army forces which were to attack across the Rapido south of Cassino two days before *Shingle* was launched. It is clear that Alexander was anxious that the bridgehead should be made secure before any advance was made from it. He was sounding a note of caution. The flying column, less than a division in strength, was not to be loaded until three days after the landing and was to operate independently from the main force which was to consolidate the bridgehead and then exert 'steady pressure'. No mention is made here of the Colli Laziali, a huge feature twenty-five miles from Anzio and sixty from Cassino, which would absorb two or three divisions if it was to be held against certain counter-attack from all sides. No 'mobile hard-hitting force' of this size could permanently cut German communications between Rome and Cassino. Its weakness would soon be revealed, and the force wiped out. It would scare the Germans, but not panic them into precipitate withdrawal. It was a raid, not a serious offensive, which Alexander was describing to Clark, in fact if not in name, and it threw doubt upon the purpose and viability of the whole operation.

When the two Allied divisions landed at Anzio some hours before dawn on 22 January 1944, the coast was found to be virtually un-defended, and Lucas was able to put his men ashore unharmed and occupy a bridgehead seven miles deep. Then he paused for three days to consolidate it, awaiting the arrival of his armoured division before he made any bold thrust towards the Alban Hills. This policy was entirely consistent with what Alexander had told Clark. If Alexander had altered his mind when he found that he had gained strategical surprise and decided to hazard a dash for Rome, he could have told Clark and Lucas to attempt it, for all three were together at Anzio on the morning of D Day. In his despatch he says that he considered at the time that Lucas could have been more adventurous, but on reflection he thought Lucas was right to consolidate his base before striking out: 'VI Corps, with the resources available to it, would have found it very difficult both to be secure on the Alban Hills and at the same time retain the absolutely necessary communications with the sea at Anzio. . . . The actual course of events was probably the most advantageous in the end.' Why then was it not foreseen? Why were different orders given?

There was no major offensive northwards from the bridgehead until 30 January, by which time Fifth Army's attack across the Rapido had failed and Kesselring had been able to bring up six divisions to seal off the bridgehead while still maintaining his front at Cassino. Although

Alexander was now numerically inferior to the Germans at Anzio, he still hoped to achieve his original purpose. He cabled to Churchill on 2 February that 'we shall soon be able to launch a general offensive to cut XIV Corps lines-of-communications, for which I have ordered plans to be prepared.' The offensive never started, for the Germans attacked first, with ten divisions against the Allied five. For a week the two armies fought each other to exhaustion and stalemate, and it was not until 20 February that the crisis was over and the line restabilized.

Shingle had led to an extremely successful defensive battle, but it had failed in its prime purpose. Looking back on the events a month after the landing, Alexander wrote to his army commanders, Clark and Leese:

After a careful study of the fighting during the past month, I have come to the very definite conclusion that one of the main reasons why the enemy has been able to foil us so far of victory in the battle for Rome is that he is quicker than we are: quicker at regrouping his forces, quicker at thinning out on a defensive front to provide troops to close gaps at decisive points, quicker in effecting reliefs, quicker at mounting attacks and counter-attacks, and above all quicker at reaching decisions on the battlefield. By comparison our methods are often slow and cumbersome, and this applies to all our troops, both British and American.

That was one candid reason for the failure. But it was not the main one. The operation was mounted in insufficient strength and with unjustifiable optimism; the objective was not feasible nor the method clear. Nobody down the chain of command specified in writing beforehand exactly what was to happen once the troops were ashore. Alexander seems to have doubted the validity of his instruction both to secure a firm base and seize an objective vital to the Germans twenty-five miles from it, and it became no more valid because the landing was unexpectedly easy. Fifth Army's two main efforts, at Anzio and at Cassino, were incapable of mutual support, and neither was powerful enough to do the job alone. It is possible that a daring raid launched on the first day might have penetrated to Rome, for there was nothing to stop it. Kesselring in his Memoirs wrote that the Allies 'missed a uniquely favourable chance of capturing Rome'. He must have known that this was untrue. For what would have happened? General (later Field Marshal) Sir Gerald Templer, then a Divisional Commander at Anzio, has given me his opinion:

I never understood how Anzio could possibly work. I am absolutely convinced that if Lucas had gone on (which he could have) he could have got to Rome, but within a week or fortnight there wouldn't have been a single British soldier left in the bridgehead. They would all have been killed or wounded or prisoners. We would have had a line-of-communications forty-five miles long from Anzio to Rome with absolutely open flanks. The Germans produced seven divisions in ten days, with plenty of armour, and we wouldn't have had a chance.

Mark Clark commented to me as follows in 1970:

We had a small and inadequate landing force. After experiencing the difficulties at Salerno, I had requested that we land at Anzio with three divisions. We landed with two – one British and one American, and the British division not in full strength. It was not possible that upon landing we could just move in and occupy the Alban Hills. The German reaction to our landing was swift. We had broken the German code and could read the messages from Hitler to 'drive us into the sea and drown us'. He also ordered several divisions from France, Germany, Yugoslavia and from other sectors of Italy to the bridgehead. Knowing of the impending onslaught, it was necessary to dig in, for had we advanced, we would have surely been defeated. Alex and I discussed these problems and decided to dig in and reinforce as rapidly as possible.

General Truscott, who commanded the first American division to land at Anzio, wrote in his book *Command Missions*:

Any reckless advance to the Colli Laziali without first establishing a firm base to protect our beaches would have been sheer madness and would almost certainly have resulted in the eventual destruction of the landing forces.

Thus the four generals in the best position to judge, Alexander, Clark, Truscott and Templer, agree that Lucas took the right decision. It was due to him that the bridgehead was strong enough to survive. Why then was he sacked? It is tempting to conclude that he was the scapegoat for everyone's disappointment, particularly Churchill's, but in fact he had been right by accident. Templer says:

I don't think he took the decision at all. I think he just failed to do anything else. He was absolutely full of inertia, and couldn't make up his mind. He had no qualities of any sort as a commander, absolutely no presence: he was the antithesis of everything that a fighting soldier and general should be.

Everyone who came into contact with Lucas felt the same. It was the

Dawley situation all over again. Alexander was reluctant to relieve him because he was an American, and Clark was hesitant on other grounds:

Lucas was another general officer highly regarded by General McNair. He, too, was several years my senior. Through his Chief of Staff, General Keiser, I learned that General Lucas was not well. I was not sure of his ability in that condition to fight off the German counterattack that was pending. Alexander also informed me that there were some differences between General Penney, commanding the 1st British Division, and General Lucas. I decided under the circumstances to order Lucas back to my Fifth Army Headquarters as Deputy Army Commander, and to put Truscott, commanding 3rd US Division, in as Corps Commander.

13

ROME

Alexander reached the climax of his career in the spring and early summer of 1944. He was to rise yet higher as Supreme Allied Commander in the Mediterranean, and directed two more major battles after the capture of Rome, the assault on the Gothic Line and the battle in the Po valley which ended in the capitulation of all the enemy forces opposed to him. But April to July 1944 was the period when his special gifts as a commander were demonstrated most vividly, and when his personality leapt into sharpest focus. It is therefore a good moment to summarize his character and method of command. His total achievement will be considered later.

The official tributes to him have followed a consistent pattern. It is said that he had modesty, courage, style and sweetness of nature; he was the finest product in the Second War of the British gentleman-soldier tradition. None of this was untrue, and it was widely recognized. So flawless indeed was the image that he presented that even a close friend like James Grigg, Permanent Under Secretary, and later Secretary of State for War, wondered whether it could be quite complete:

I have known him longer than I have known any other soldier, and I ought perhaps to know him better than I know any other soldier. In fact I sometimes wonder whether I really know him at all. I know all the externals – his athletic prowess, his fighting career, his military achievements. I know his good looks, his courtesy and charm. I know too his devotion to duty and his scrupulous loyalty to colleagues or subordinates. But there is something inscrutable about him which gives me the feeling that there is another life beyond all that, a life of his own into which very few are allowed to enter.[1]

Having questioned many who knew him best, I have come to doubt

235

whether that 'other life' existed. Alexander was no sphinx. Duplicity, moral or intellectual, was alien to him. To suppose another life is to suggest that in the privacy of his caravan he immersed himself in reading and contemplation which he was careful to keep private from his friends and even from his family, but there is no evidence for it in his subsequent writings or conversation, and over a lifetime an inner world of that kind would surely have become apparent. The explanation of his reserve is simpler. He believed that reticence increases a soldier's authority. A commander's privacy, like military security, should be graded from confidential to top secret, and his subordinates must be made aware that friendliness is something quite different from intimacy. Alexander's reticence emerged instinctively from his knowledge of how easily a chance word, even a glum or radiant expression, could cause dismay or exuberance, both unintended, and a slight air of mystery in his manner and pronouncements helped to keep open his options and enhance respect. It was also his nature. A gentleman does not utter everything he thinks. Vulgarity is a form of promiscuousness, and friendship, to be valued, must be rationed. To him war was an intensely serious profession, comparable only to the higher levels of politics. Lacking intellectual brilliance, and conscious of his duty and supreme responsibility, he thought of little but the business in hand, concentrating like a surgeon upon the 'operation', to the exclusion even of the basic causes and objects of the war, since they had already been defined and expounded by his political chiefs. Hence when he touched on deeper matters it was with restraint. He did not wish to be known too well, and perhaps there was not a great deal more to know. I have questioned two fellow Field Marshals about Alexander as a man. First Templer:

Did you feel you ever really got to know him?

No.

Did he ever have any intimate friends in the Army?

As far as I know, none.

You wouldn't call yourself one of them?

No.

Did you think him a very clever man?

He was obviously an extremely able man – extremely well educated as a soldier.

What was the secret of his magnetism?

His career, his courage. He had great panache. He was a *beau sabreur*. He had chic, but he never showed off. He had the aristocratic gift. He could be fun. He was always prepared to be kind and amusing, and had excellent manners. His supreme quality was that he was so transparently honest. All his foibles, frailties and strength of character combined into a man for whom anybody who met him would willingly die.

And Harding, his Chief of Staff:

You probably had a longer and more intimate association with him than anybody. Did you feel you knew the inner Alexander?

I think so. I say that deliberately. He was a character whom it was extremely difficult to know. I was continually being surprised by some new facet of his character or some new thinking of his.

Did he ever talk to you about his family, or his political or religious convictions?

No. He would occasionally mention his family, but never deeply. He never talked about religion, and about politics only in terms of what was happening at the time. He also talked about his ambitions, how he would have liked to have won the VC or become a rugger international.

Was he ambitious, or did he just carry out the jobs he was given?

He was ambitious in the sense that he wanted very earnestly to excel in his chosen profession, not so much for his own advancement, but to show that he was a genuine, sincere, dedicated soldier.

Did he have compassion? Did he mind deeply the deaths in battle of his soldiers and friends?

He certainly had sympathy. It was evident in the way in which he would talk to soldiers. They were able to understand each other, because he had commanded everything. But I wouldn't use the word compassion. He was certainly not ruthless, or regardless of loss of life. But he looked upon casualties in a professional not personal light. He thought, 'What will be the effect of heavy casualties on morale? How will they affect my ability to continue the operation?'

Did you find him rather stiff in his manner?

He was a little aloof. It took us quite a long time to get on terms when I could express my own views freely, and know that he was responding to what I was saying. He had a sort of detachment.

Did you call him Alex?

Only when we were alone.

Could he be gay?

He was very cheerful. He was a happy man. He had a streak of vanity in him, which came out in his dress, his demeanour, his way of walking. It was no more than that. His appearance was dignified, erect and calm.

At the beginning of this book I asked myself the questions how it was that Alexander, so gentle and temperate a man, came to choose so violent a profession as a soldier's, and how he managed to rise to supreme command when he was naturally unassuming and avoided any challenging display of his authority. The answer to the first question must be that he discovered that he had a natural gift for soldiering, and became interested in its technicalities and in human nature under stress. He responded to its excitement and virility. It demanded skill, knowledge, experience and courage. It was homicide on a scale which transformed it into a crusade and an art, dignified by its difficulties and risks, by its political motivation, and by the knowledge that great men of all nations and all ages have thus engaged their talents. Alexander could understand the pacifist's case, but he would have thought it supine, unrealistic, the feebleness of a man who protests against the method but is happy to benefit by the result. He once remarked, 'War is horrible, but it is often necessary. It will probably always be necessary. If I see a fly, I do not crush it but let it out of the window. But if I see an enemy army, my whole purpose is to destroy it. There are certain things which are evil, in a way that a fly is not evil, and we must fight those things, first by argument, then if argument fails, by war.' Professional soldiers are as essential to a nation as its statesmen, one to identify the evil, the other to defeat it. It was enough for him that the evil be convincingly designated, and then the task took precedence in his mind over the motive, which was eventually almost forgotten because it was unquestioned.

The second puzzle is more difficult to resolve. Alexander could have ended his career as the best Brigadier in the British Army, and it is arguable that at Nowshera he reached his professional peak because there he could do no wrong, being poised equidistant between what he understood best, the mentality of the private soldier and the execution of given orders. The limitations of his ability began to appear when the forces under his command became so huge that their manipulation required weeks and months of forethought, not hours or days. He was

Alexander at Simla, May 1942, immediately after his return from the Burma campaign

Commander-in-Chief, Middle East, August 1942

(*above*) In Sicily, August 1943. Left to right: Montgomery, Alexander, Bedell Smith, Patton

(*below*) Salerno, 15 September 1944. Left to right: Alexander, Clark, McCreery

An Army Commanders
Conference in Italy
before *Diadem*. Left to
right: Harding, Leese,
Lemnitzer, Alexander,
Clark

In Central Italy

Churchill's visit to the Italian front. Left to right: Leese, Churchill, Alexander

Outside Rome, 7 June 1944

The Alexanders leaving the Parliament buildings, Ottawa, after his installation as Governor-General of Canada on 12 April 1946

(*above*) A painting by Alexander of Ottawa from near Government House, 1950

(*below*) Eisenhower visits Alexander in Ottawa

Field-Marshal Earl Alexander of Tunis as Governor-General of Canada

not by nature an originator. He was an executive. Mountbatten said to me:

He had almost every quality you could wish to have, except that he had the average brain of an average English gentleman. He lacked that little extra cubic centimetre which produces genius. If you recognise that, it's perhaps a greater tribute to what he did achieve by leadership, courage and inspiring devotion in those who served under him.

Promotion generates its own momentum. Alexander had never failed to deliver the required result. He reached high command when its pickings were greatest, when victory was most dramatic. He became identified with success. As one campaign followed another his prestige among the Allies grew to the point where there was no substitute for him, and with his success, seen to be qualified only in retrospect, he gained in confidence and authority, and became the Supreme Commander in personality as well as in title.

He remained modest because that was his nature, and he knew that a wrong decision could mean the death of ten thousand men and that he was capable of wrong decisions. In a sense truer of him than of any other commander in the Second War he was the servant of his soldiers. Once when a senior General met him at an airport, he found a posse of motorcycle outriders ready to escort his car. When he asked why they were there, he was told 'To clear the road.' Alexander replied, 'Would you mind dismissing them. I have a marked objection to clearing my own troops off the road for me.' He commanded their complete respect because he understood frailty though he did not share it, and because he imparted to his troops something of his own dignity. The army in Italy never felt itself to be a forgotten army, poor cousins of the huge forces in north-west Europe. On the contrary, it considered itself an élite, and this was largely due to Alexander's own high concept of its role. He not only commanded his men but represented them. He was one of them. When he visited a headquarters near the front line, as he did almost daily, it was never to reproach nor bestow extravagant praise. He came to inform and enquire and discuss, to encourage and to sympathize. One felt that he was capable at any moment of changing places with a subaltern.

His method of command was less by order than by influence and persuasion. His instinct for the higher conduct of war was based upon a feminine intuition for what was or was not possible, and for what was thought to be possible by those whose duty it was to carry it out. He was dealing daily with Generals who had pride in their commands, who were themselves accustomed to respect, each with characteristics which must be weighed and used. Some army Commanders, like Leese, must be injected with a little ginger because they were too methodical and deliberate. Others like Patton and Mark Clark were pushers who must sometimes be restrained. Montgomery must be humoured. Anders comforted. Juin praised. It took much tact to nudge such disparate men into a team. Alexander would try to win them over to his plan by asking for their opinions. If they had good reasons for objecting to it, he would modify the plan. He dropped a suggestion here and there, knowing that sooner or later it would come back to him with their label upon it. He realized that a General who had survived so far was a man of mettle and determination, with confidence in his own judgement, and that to force upon him a plan with which he disagreed would mean that it was executed with reluctance.

Here are two examples of the impression he made upon Americans. The first was a journalist, who met him during the last phase in Tunisia:

He was covered with dust, yet he glowed. His personal staff, though many were in fact in front of him, swept like a train behind him. His manner, however, is not imperial. He chatters. He turns quickly from side to side, recognising people because he remembers that he once knew and liked them, and not because he felt he ought to be polite. When he moves, a sort of lambent hollow remains behind him, and everyone follows wondering what he will say next, what he will do next, where he will choose to go. He wears an aura compared to Anderson, who peers about him like a tourist, and few of his soldiers recognise or salute him. That would be quite impossible with Alexander. People would know that he was coming when he was still five miles away.

The second was Mark Clark:

Knowing of Alex's long experience in combat, of his fine leadership, I was naturally hoping as a new American commander, who had never commanded a large force in combat, that we would get along. That's the way it developed, from the start. I had implicit confidence in Alex's judgement, above all in his fairness, and in his willingness to lay the cards right on the table. We could discuss frankly differences of opinion. I have never met a man who was a finer leader.

Do you think he had an original mind as a soldier?

No question about it. He would come and see me, and we would go over the map and ponder all courses of action open to us; and he would pick my brain to see how I thought it ought to be done. In almost every case where I had strong opinions, he was very quick to agree. Sometimes he didn't agree. But he was able to put his ideas over in a gentle way, so that you liked to take orders from him. The only time that Alex and I really disagreed was when we approached Rome.

From what you say, I understand that to you Alexander was not a General of the type of Patton or Montgomery, who imposed his will upon his subordinates. It was really decision by discussion?

Exactly. In every case he was gentle and understanding.

Do you think he was sometimes too gentle?

No, I don't think so. He commanded respect. He was a thoroughly professional soldier. I would never accuse Alex of being wishy-washy or straddling an issue. He'd say exactly what he wanted, and oftentimes that's the way we'd do it.

'Oftentimes', in this context, is a significant word.

Alexander never sought publicity, giving press conferences only rarely and preferring off-the-record talks with a few journalists like Alan Moorehead or Mrs Luce, whom he could trust. Fame came to him more slowly than to Montgomery, and was therefore more truthful to his real nature. He was an acquired taste. 'Alexander is respected and admired', wrote Harold Nicolson to his sons in April 1943, 'but Monty is the chap for the people. You can imagine how this irritates me. But Alex is the darling of the Cabinet. They think him wonderful.' Later Alexander's reputation seeped back to England in letters and press-reports from the front, creating an authentic picture of his imperturbability and charm, and what can best be defined as his generosity. He never ceased to be a patriot. To an American who told him that the US Marines had never lost a battle he gave the sharp reply, 'Then they can never have fought the British.' But when he watched an American film of their army's exploits in North Africa which gave them all the credit for victory, and a member of his party protested, Alexander cooled him down: 'No, you're quite wrong. They did a lot, and it's necessary for home-consumption in the United States that they should imagine that they did it all.' General Lemnitzer, his American Deputy Chief of Staff, has given me this other instance of his attitude:

It was my duty through the Italian campaign (and an onerous one) to prepare the communiqué each evening. In doing this, I would rely on our operations people at the headquarters, and then I would get on the telephone to General Gruenther or Freddy de Guingand. It was always a tug of war. When I read out my draft of what I proposed to say, the Army that wasn't given emphasis would protest. Then we would have a terrible argument.

One evening I got very irked about this. A typical comment had come from one of them: 'Why do we have to say so much about Fifth (or Eighth) Army? All they had to do was to lean forward; there was no resistance in their sector.' So I said to General Alexander, 'Our system is all wrong. Why are we always talking about General Clark's Fifth Army or General Montgomery's Eighth Army? We ought to be talking about General Alexander's 15th Army Group.' Well, I saw a smile cross his face, and he said, 'Listen, Lem. The Army Group, its C-in-C and its staff, exist only to assist the armies which are doing the fighting. If we are winning there is glory enough to go all the way round; and if we're losing, it doesn't make any difference.' That was his philosophy. He was a very selfless individual.

He owed much to Lemnitzer, but even more to Harding, who became his Chief of Staff shortly before the landing at Anzio. Harding's knowledge of war was almost as great as Alexander's, for he had begun his battle experience by commanding a platoon at Gallipoli. Their personalities were complementary: if Alexander attracted attention and despite himself was invested with glamour, Harding was thoughtful and profound. There has been much speculation about the credit due to each of them for the major strategic concepts of the Italian campaign in 1944, and much should go to Harding. Until he joined Alexander, there was an uncertainty of aim, a lack of concentration. The campaign was developing into a battle of attrition. Harding, in constant discussion with his chief and by written memoranda, began to question the validity of Alexander's strategy, particularly the unending process of hammering at varying points of the Cassino sector. He suspected that Alexander was allowing his dedication to cloud his tactical and strategical judgement. Alexander was intent upon keeping up pressure on the Germans as long as he had any reserves. Harding gradually persuaded him, once Anzio was secure, to rethink the operation and concentrate his forces for a complete breakthrough in the spring. One of the conclusions which they jointly reached was that in spite of the great superiority which the Allies enjoyed in the air, in armour and artillery, they must create a three-to-one superiority in infantry at the decisive point, and that point could only be the Liri valley, where the mountains fell suddenly away to create a broad strip suitable for armoured operations in the direction of Anzio and Rome. A dozen divisions must be assembled between Cassino and the sea, thinning out Eighth Army on the Adriatic coast to provide them. This was the germ of *Diadem*, the offensive of May 1944.

Meanwhile the terrible battles around Cassino continued, in the hope, naturally, of sudden success, but also for the sake of emphasizing the importance which the Allies attached to the Italian campaign and nailing German divisions to the spot.

Imagine a tossing mass of hills of about the same height and same degree of ruggedness as the English Lake District. Their steep slopes were covered by chutes of small, grey stones, between which you would sometimes find a shy Alpine plant, but more often the rusting splinter of a high-explosive shell. Although it was less than three miles to the front-line trenches from the nearest point approachable on wheels, the steep climb would take a fully laden man as much as four hours. If he were wounded near the summit, the stretcher-bearers could not bring him down to an ambulance in less than five hours, sometimes eight, and many died. The tracks followed the easiest gradients, and though their foundations had been well laid by generations of Italian peasants, and widened and revetted by our engineers, a four-inch covering of liquid mud would overlie the solid stone after every shower of rain. Day and night the stores of food, water and ammunition were carried into these remote mountains, for the first part of the journey by strings of mules and then doggedly handled beyond the point where shellfire made the tracks impassable to every animal but man.

Cassino town itself had been in peacetime a place of great prosperity, a market for the rich countryside and a resort of pilgrim-tourists who for centuries came here to visit the monastery where St Benedict had founded his order. Under the Fascist régime the main buildings had been reconstructed in a more palatial style, and for that reason survived to some degree the heaviest pounding by bomb and shell which any place has endured in the history of war. This is no exaggeration. There was scarcely a square yard in the centre of the town which was not pitted by a bomb-crater, there was not a single roof left intact, and many of the smaller houses had been obliterated, the rubble from their walls spread over a wide area or sunk beneath the mud. Where once the streets had opened into ornamental piazzas, now there was nothing but interlocking craters, deep cauldrons of black water. Yet Cassino in its ruins did not appear shabby; it glistened in the sunlight from its veil of powdered marble, and from between the fallen blocks of stone began to spring a carpet of grass and flowers. A haze of smoke hung over the town. From only a mile outside, the most powerful field-glasses could not detect a single human movement. Yet there were 1,500 men hidden among the ruins, half of them German parachutists, and half their enemies. There were no civilians. The soldiers lived in shored-up cellars of the houses, a platoon to each house. The Germans were at most 150 yards away; at least, in the next-door room.

The Monastery of St Benedict, standing 1,700 feet above the town, became the symbol of the whole campaign, and because it was the symbol, it was allowed to become the key. In retrospect, and from an examination of the ground impossible under battle conditions except to platoon commanders, it can now be seen that the monastery did not deserve to become such a military focus. In his despatch Alexander described it as 'a bastion defending the gate, for from it the Germans could command the whole floor of the Liri valley'. But dominant though it was, it was not the highest point of the German Cassino line, and it was impregnable, the route to the foot of its walls lying across gorges strewn with broken rock and interlaced with wiry brambles. It was never taken by storm. It was abandoned to the Poles when they had by-passed it to the north. It drew attention because it was a building and not a mountain-top. Its occupation by the Germans was taken for granted. When Alexander was urged by his subordinates to destroy it by air-bombardment, he did not hesitate, and his decision, almost incidental at the time, aroused a controversy which surprised him. As an illustration of the pressures to which a Commander-in-Chief is subject the sequence of events is worth examination.

The demand that the monastery be destroyed originated with the 4th Indian Division who were about to attack it. The Divisional Commander, Francis Tuker, claimed that 'Montecassino is a modern fortress and must be dealt with by modern methods'. Whether the Germans were in occupation of it or not made no difference, for in the last resort they would be bound to take refuge within its walls, and use it as a rallying point for sorties and wounded. It was impossible to make a tactical distinction between a strongly fortified mountain and the building which crowned its summit. The monastery was an integral part of the German defence-system. So he insisted that his division

244

could not undertake the attack until the monastery had been softened up.

Tuker's request rapidly escalated the chain of command. His Corps Commander, Freyberg, who endorsed it, put it to Clark, and Clark to Alexander. Alexander replied that if Freyberg was convinced of the military necessity, the monastery must be bombed, regrettable though that would be. Clark urged him to think again, but Alexander was adamant. 'When soldiers are fighting for a just cause', he wrote in his Memoirs, 'and are prepared to suffer death and mutilation in the process, bricks and mortar, no matter how venerable, cannot be allowed to weigh against human lives. In the context of the Cassino battle, how could a structure which dominated the fighting field be allowed to stand? The monastery had to be destroyed.' He said much the same when he visited our brigade a few weeks after Cassino fell. 'A commander, if faced by the choice between risking a single soldier's life and destroying a work of art, even a religious symbol like Monte-cassino, can only make one decision.' He said this with a sincerity that was impressive.

We know now that the Germans were not occupying the monastery. Their fortifications were on the hill around it, but no closer than 200 yards from its walls, and they posted sentries outside the main gate to prevent any troops entering the precincts. The German Corps Commander, General von Senger, had informed the Vatican that Monte-cassino would not be occupied by his troops. Unfortunately the version of this declaration which reached the Allies was that 'no considerable body of troops' was in the 'immediate vicinity' of the building, which left the matter in doubt. The Allies could scarcely believe that any commander could resist making use of so formidable a fortress in the very centre of his line. Von Senger, however, saw it differently. Apart from his strong personal feelings about the sanctity of the place (he was a Catholic from Bavaria), he was unwilling to bottle up troops in so obvious a target, when they could occupy the shell-proof emplacements which he had prepared on the surrounding hillside during the previous three months. To the Allies looking up from the valley it seemed that a German observer must be stationed behind each of the monastery's thousand windows. But the upper part of the hill below the walls afforded the Germans even better observation, because it was un-restricted and concealed. Indeed, from the monastery itself the bulk of Cassino town is shielded from view by the convex slope of the hill: the view improves as the observer descends. To add fifty feet to a hill already 1,700 feet high gave them no extra advantage. 'Even under normal conditions', von Senger wrote in his autobiography, 'Montecassino would never have been occupied by artillery spotters. So conspicuous a landmark would have been quite unsuitable.'

Fred Majdalany, in his book on the Cassino battles, argues that it was irrelevant whether the Germans occupied the monastery. He calls the question 'the great red-herring'. The troops who were to attack it thought that it was occupied, and that was all that mattered. But was the question so irrelevant? If the monastery were destroyed, and the Germans could prove afterwards (as they did, by the widely publicized statements of the Abbot) that they had respected its neutrality, there would be four results. The bombing would be wasted, since no enemy soldiers would be killed by it and no military installations destroyed. The ruins would make an even more formidable strongpoint than the intact building. The Germans would then have the pretext to occupy it immediately. And world Catholic opinion would be deeply shocked.

This is just what happened. The German occupation of the ruins ('a far finer defence position than it would have been before its destruction', wrote von Senger) made the Allies' task more difficult. Only the upperworks were destroyed, leaving almost intact the loopholed glacis. The bombing boosted German more than Allied morale, after the first impact had passed. There had been insufficient coordination between the air attack and the ground attack, for the assault troops had been warned to expect the bombing a day later and were not ready. So, in Majdalany's summing-up of the tactical consequences, 'The bombing expended its fury in a vacuum, tragically and wastefully. It achieved nothing, it helped nobody except the Germans. To them it seemed nothing more than a petulant gesture by the Allies in compensation for their previous failures to capture the position.'

The bombing of Montecassino on 15 February 1944, like the later bombing of Dresden, worried the Allied conscience at the time, and still worries it. Mark Clark wrote after the war that he considered it not only a psychological mistake 'but a tactical military mistake of the first magnitude'. All other Allied commanders, supported by Churchill, have defended the decision in retrospect, and so have the majority of historians. My own view is that it was a blunder but not a crime. The question of German occupation was highly relevant, but it was treated as secondary, and the evidence for it was based upon chance observations from ground and air, not on specific enquiries through the Vatican, which in such a matter could have afforded an exceptional channel of communication between enemies. Nor was it fair to leave the decision to Alexander. The monastery headed the list of historic buildings which the Allies had undertaken to save from damage if it were possible, and the decision should have been taken at the highest political level. If the troops had known that only the Abbot, five monks and some hundreds of peasant refugees were within the walls, the monastery could have been neutralized in their minds as well as on the ground. It was possible to fight the battle around the hill, as indeed it was fought, without damaging the monastery by more than a stray shell. The bombing was not a crime because these facts were not certainly known at the time, and Alexander could not risk the reproof that the failure of the ground attack was due to his greater compassion for 'bricks and mortar' than for flesh and blood.

Diadem was launched on 11 May 1944 by an assault along the whole line from Cassino to the sea, followed twelve days later by the breakout from the Anzio bridgehead. The story of the offensive has been told so often – the unforeseen success of the French corps in advancing across the southern mountains, the pinching-out of the Cassino position by the Poles from the hills and the British from the plain, the exploitation of their success by the Canadians who overran the Hitler line before the Germans could man it properly – that the details need not be repeated here. Alexander's decision had been taken months before. Several times he had climbed the slopes of Monte Trocchio which faces Cassino from a mile away, and contemplated the ground below him, pondering one of the major strategic decisions of his life. Immediately below ran the ribbon of the River Rapido, little wider than a country lane, which divided his unseen troops from their unseen foe. Beyond stretched the Liri valley, the classical route to Rome, gently rising and falling in meadows and vineyards, the only corridor in the whole width of Italy where he could bring his full strength to bear. The most obvious route was the only one. The pass must be taken by storm.

The Liri valley was fought over with an intensity that left scars which thirty years later have still not entirely disappeared. The little villages were reduced by bomb and shell to rows of decaying molars. In the ruins of one house a gun-team would rig a tarpaulin over roofless walls, cooking their supper with the sticks of furniture that remained. In the next, where only the cellar was intact, a wretched peasant family looked up from the earthen floor, crouching all day on their haunches, refusing to leave. From any house where a few rooms remained undamaged, there was a glow of hurricane-lamps at night, the buzz of field-telephones. The constant traffic of heavy lorries ground the decent civilian life out of the place, and we reflected that this was probably all that the Italian peasants would ever know of the British and Americans. After a day or two we pressed on to shatter and occupy another village. There was great urgency. We knew that Alexander had not only his reserves behind us, but seven whole divisions lodged firmly on the enemy's flank at Anzio. The failure of January had produced a bonus in May.

Alexander reserved for himself the decision when to release VI Corps at Anzio to join in the fight. The timing and direction of the two offensives was the only major way in which the Commander-in-Chief could influence the battle once it had begun, and he gave to the problem his most careful consideration. Initially he had planned to strike first from Anzio, to draw the German reserves away from the main front, but later gave priority to the attack north and south of Cassino when he learnt that Kesselring expected it to begin in the bridgehead, and because a failure at Anzio, where he had fewer reserves, would be less remediable. The two attacks could not be launched simultaneously because each in turn needed the full weight of Allied air support. His plan was to judge the moment when success at Cassino was beyond doubt, and then direct VI Corps to intercept the German retreat. The objective was Rome, but the method was to destroy the right wing of the German army before they could rally to Rome's defence. He planned not a mere loosening of the front, but a trap.

At a conference of his Army Commanders at Caserta on 2 April he made it quite clear that Route 6 was allotted to Eighth Army until just short of Rome, where the boundary turned sharply north, leaving Rome indisputably within the sector of Fifth Army. This was confirmed by his written order of 5 May. It was not only that Alexander considered that for political reasons the glory of capturing Rome should fall to the Americans, but he was anxious to save at least one of his armies from becoming involved in possible street-fighting in the city itself.

The key-paragraph of his written order read: 'Fifth Army will launch an attack from the Anzio bridgehead on the general axis Cori-Valmontone to cut Route 6 in the Valmontone area, and thereby prevent the supply and withdrawal of the troops of the German Tenth Army.' These were crucial words. 'Our objective', he telegraphed to Churchill on the morning of 11 May, 'is the destruction of the enemy south of Rome, and we have every hope and every intention of doing that.' Churchill agreed: 'At this distance it seems much more important to cut their line of retreat than anything else. . . . A cop is much more important than Rome, which would anyhow come as its consequence. The cop is the one thing that matters.'

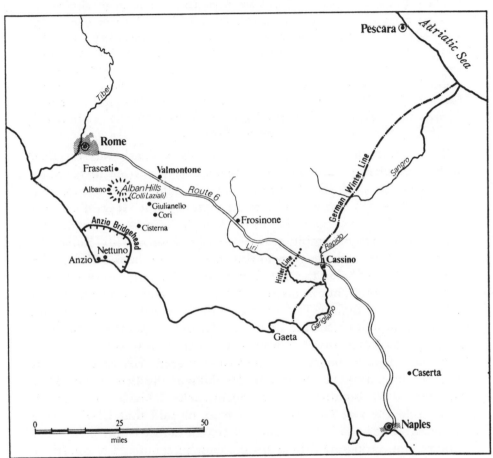

Map 10 Operation *Diadem*, May–June 1944

Alexander ordered Clark to begin his offensive from Anzio on 23 May, when Cassino had fallen and the Germans were in flight up the Liri valley. The manoeuvre was precisely timed. Both attacks made good progress. The Canadians breached the Hitler line at the very moment when Truscott's VI Corps were entering Cori. There was now no doubt that the two Allied fronts would shortly merge, but more important, each claw of the pincer-movement was biting, as Alexander planned, towards Valmontone. Then, on 25 May, Mark Clark diverged from the agreed plan. General Jackson, in *The Battle for Rome*, summarizes in scathing words what happened:

Mark Clark now held a firm base from Cisterna through Giulianello to Cori from which he could develop his attack on Valmontone to cut Vietinghoff's [Tenth Army] line of retreat. There was very little that von Mackensen [Fourteenth Army] could do to stop him. The Americans were tired but elated by victory and had plenty of reserves in hand. May 26th could have been the decisive day of *Diadem*. Mark Clark, and not von Mackensen or Truscott, decided otherwise. It can be said that overnight he threw away the chance of destroying the right wing of von Vietinghoff's Tenth Army for the honour of entering Rome first.

This verdict may be thought unfair. Mark Clark was certainly ambitious, slightly vain, slightly Anglophobe. He wrote in his autobiography, *Calculated Risk*, 'We not only wanted the honour of capturing Rome, but we felt that we had more than deserved it.' It is difficult not to read 'I' for 'we'; impossible to disentangle his personal longing for glory from a natural ambition to reward his soldiers with 'Rome, the Great Prize' (the title he gives to this chapter of his book). He coveted the distinction of being the first General since Belisarius to capture the city from the south, but he also felt strongly that Fifth Army deserved it more than the Eighth, just as they had 'deserved' Naples, but his reasoning did not pretend to be logical. He did not want Eighth Army slipping into Rome ahead of him by a side-gate, with the excuse that they happened to be more conveniently placed. His ambition was matched by a ruthless patriotism. He thought the British soft. They lacked his dash. Eighth Army was lagging behind, leaving it to Americans to do the real fighting. But it must be said that Clark always achieved what he said he would achieve. Alexander came to like and admire him, proposing him as his successor in command of the Army Group only five months after their clash of wills in the outskirts of Rome.

On the evening of 25 May Clark ordered Truscott to switch the weight of his attack north-west to capture the Alban Hills, although at that moment only the reconnaissance elements of one German division lay between him and Route 6. Next day the offensive was reopened on the new line, leaving only one of Clark's seven divisions to pursue the manoeuvre which Alexander had ordered. The Germans reacted quickly to protect their escape-route against this slender threat, and held Valmontone long enough to allow Tenth Army to get away.

There are two points at issue. Did Mark Clark disobey Alexander's orders? And was Alexander too weak with his subordinate?

I discussed the first point at length with Mark Clark in Charleston, South Carolina, in March 1970:

From my reading of the story, General, it does seem that Alexander was very definite in his order that the breakout should be in the direction of Valmontone?

Let's get this straight. I had been assigned the mission of capturing Rome. When Alex came to see me before the battle, he said: 'Wayne, I have drawn the boundaries between Fifth and Eighth Armies and you see I have given you Rome.' He joked a bit, and added: 'If you don't take it, I will bring up some more troops and we will take it.'

I had been told by General Marshall the approximate dates for the Normandy landings. It was important that we take Rome before D Day [5 June, postponed to 6 June]. The British Eighth Army was far in rear of the Fifth Army. I am sure, when Alexander proposed we attack to the east, it was for the combined purpose to hit the flank of the Germans and to cut them off, and at the same time to facilitate the advance of Eighth Army. The Fifth Army had already suffered heavy casualties in this spring offensive so far. These were all things at the back of my mind.

Now, whoever held the Alban Hills held Rome. Warfare is fighting for observation. So I didn't feel that I could start out with my main effort going across the low ground with the Alban Hills remaining in the enemy's hands on my left flank. We discussed this thing, and there was no difference of opinion on my Fifth Army staff. We had to go to Valmontone; but we also had to secure the Alban Hills. To my mind it was militarily unsound to leave the Alban Hills alone, to forget all about Rome, and put my whole effort into attacking the rear of the German forces opposing Eighth Army.

To cut their line of retreat?

I don't think there was any possibility of my doing it. There were other access roads out of the Valmontone area which the Germans could have taken. There was no possibility of my surrounding them.

Nevertheless, General, this was your senior commander's plan and order, was it not?

No, no. I never violated his orders. I told him, and he agreed, that I would simultaneously advance on Rome and send a task force to Valmontone. He wanted it. He never overruled me. Can you find any place where he said that I directly violated his orders?

No, he certainly never said that. But he was clearly disappointed that you made your main thrust towards the Alban Hills and not to Valmontone.

If he had wanted me to do it differently he could have issued the order, and I would have carried it out. But he finally agreed to my method.

He agreed to your doing both simultaneously?

That is correct.

And he had no comment to make on the relative strength of the two thrusts?

Yes, he did. As I pointed out to you earlier, this was our big disagreement. I told Alex that I would send a column to Valmontone. I did send a column. If I had taken the entire army and pushed it against Route 6, the Germans would have had the opportunity to debouch from the mountains and attack my left flank. That is why I attacked the Alban Hills. To censure me for thinking only of the glory of capturing Rome is sheer nonsense. I know Alex didn't like the way I was doing it, but he issued no ultimatum to me to make me do it differently. He left it to me. I told him exactly what I was going to do, and he acquiesced.

It will be noted that Mark Clark did not deny that his plan occasioned the 'big disagreement' between himself and Alexander. When on 23 May Lemnitzer delivered Alexander's orders, Clark and Gruenther were 'very unhappy about it' Lemnitzer told me, 'because they had their own plans, you see, and there was a considerable difference of opinion as to what the objective should be'. Alexander was 'pretty upset', particularly since the Valmontone plan was not a last-minute manoeuvre but had been thought up months before and discussed in detail with the Army Commanders and confirmed in writing. When Clark says that Alexander 'acquiesced', he can only mean that he acquiesced *post factum*. He visited Clark in the bridgehead on 27 May, and by that time it was too late to switch back to the original line of advance. The Americans were swarming over the Alban Hills. It was a remarkable and decisive feat of arms. To recall them was unthinkable, because the opportunity to cut Route 6 had now passed, and the resulting confusion and controversy would have damaged Anglo-American relations irreparably.

Moreover, there is some validity in Clark's argument. A flank-march under the noses of a strongly entrenched enemy is one of the riskiest operations of war, and if Clark had adhered to Alexander's plan, the Germans might well have escaped up subsidiary routes through the mountains. A main effort directed away from Rome could have delayed the capture of the city by several days. As it was, the city fell only a few hours before the time originally set for *Overlord*. Clark's mistake was that he did not argue his case with Alexander long before the offensive began. Instead, he paid lip service to the Army Group's plan by sending a mere 'column' in the required direction, and until the last minute kept to himself an intention of which he knew that Alexander would disapprove.

In his daily messages to the Prime Minister, Alexander showed no trace of his annoyance, although Churchill was pressing him hard to carry out his original plan. 'Surely half your armour could be used, and indeed used up', he telegraphed on 28 May, 'in making a scythe-like movement cutting off the enemy's retreat. . . . I would feel myself wanting in comradeship if I did not let you know now that the glory of this battle, already great, will be measured not by the capture of Rome or juncture with the bridgehead but by the number of German divisions cut off.' Alexander replied evasively. He said not a word which could be interpreted as a reproach to Mark Clark. Nor did he even refer to the matter in his despatches. It was only years later, in his Memoirs, that he allowed his disappointment muted expression:

When the final battle for Rome was launched, the role of the Anzio force was to break out and at Valmontone get across the German main line of supply to their troops in Cassino. But for some inexplicable reason General Clark's Anglo-American forces never reached their objectives, though, according to my information later, there was nothing to prevent their being gained. Instead, Mark Clark switched his point of attack north to the Alban Hills, in the direction of Rome. If he had succeeded in carrying out my plan the disaster to the enemy would have been much greater; indeed, most of the German forces would have been destroyed. True, the battle ended in a decisive victory for us, but it was not as complete as might have been. . . . I can only assume that the immediate lure of Rome for its publicity value persuaded Mark Clark to switch the direction of his advance.

Fifth Army's storming of the Alban Hills was generously acknowledged by Alexander in his message to the CIGS at 6.30 pm on 4 June. As it was the culminating moment of his career, and throws so fine a light on his character, the message deserves to be put on record:

I do not think there is much doubt but that we have got a fair cop. The broad picture is that we have blown a large hole between Albano and Palestrina. This is a brilliant success for Fifth Army, who have pushed rapidly forward to the outskirts of Rome. Fighting has continued all day in the suburbs of the city and in the area between the Colli Laziali and the Tiber. The Germans are obviously struggling hard to keep a corridor through Rome, but they are greatly disorganised and in grave difficulties. There was a report this morning that one of our reconnaissance regiments was in Rome at 0800 hours. If this is true, they will seize the bridges over the Tiber to prevent the enemy using them or blowing them up. I hope this victory has come at just the right moment. If so, then our timing has been very good.

Even more characteristic was his suggestion to Churchill: 'I am considering the advisability of only mentioning the capture of Rome in my military communiqué amongst other inhabited localities taken by my armies in their stride from day to day.' Churchill exploded: 'The capture of Rome is a vast, world-wide event and should not be minimised.' It was not. But when Alexander entered the 'inhabited locality' on 5 June, he did not do so in triumph. He drove himself around the city in a jeep, sight-seeing.

I4

SUPREME COMMANDER

After the fall of Rome, the mood of the Allied armies in Italy became euphoric. Nothing seemed beyond their scope. Scarcely pausing to survey the rich prize which they had gained, the two armies fanned northwards, forming each side of the Tiber tributaries to the river where no tributaries existed, channelling up the major and minor valleys. Alexander gave them broad directives: Eighth Army were to make for Florence by Terni and Perugia, the Fifth for Pisa, Lucca and Pistoia. If these cities could be captured ahead of the bulk of the German troops, the Allies would have achieved the intention of *Diadem*.

At first it seemed impossible that the enemy could regain cohesion, but Kesselring achieved it by refusing to stand upon a single line which would expose him to another breakthrough, and ordered his divisions to impose increasing delays by demolitions and small rearguard actions, absorbing and checking the Allied advance in the manner of a hydraulic buffer. All the ingenuity of their engineers contributed to these tactics. Every bridge and culvert was blown up, and where the roads ran for some distance over unbroken ground the tarmac was torn up by patterns of small craters. Branch-tracks and buildings were systematic-ally mined, trees felled across the roads, the railways cut by charges of gun-cotton and the sleepers split by a great steel hook mounted on the back of the last waggon to pass over them. The tanks of the armoured divisions kept to the roads where the surface was intact, shouldering their way through the hedges when an impassable obstacle was en-countered. When no way round could be found, a team of bulldozers would shear a channel for the tanks, and the infantry moved forward to shield the engineers or extend by a night advance the gains which the armour had made during the day.

The troops had hitherto had little chance to discover how warm and serene Italy can be. On their remote mountain crests or in sodden, battered villages they had found during the winter little to excite their admiration. But now as they passed into undamaged Tuscany and sheltered Umbria, they came upon the Italy of white oxen lumbering along a lane, of little hill-top towns, of cypresses, olive-groves and tall poplars on a river bank. To an armoured troop or platoon of men in the vanguard the countryside looked quite deserted, untouched, sunny, sleepy and almost welcoming. They were sent to attack green hills with cows grazing on them, or villages where the women were still hanging out their washing. The material damage done by their gyrations was little more than the ravages of a herd of cattle running amok among the corn. It was not the country but the people who suffered most. The war which the armies had been following for years burst upon them in the middle of an afternoon. The familiar names of their villages would for the space of a few hours be circled upon the maps of rival commanders, mispronounced upon a score of wireless-sets, and lifted from obscurity into the communiqués which the world would read next day. A sloping field, which to the farmer had been merely an awkward piece of ground to plough, would be reconnoitred by a German subaltern, occupied by a tired dozen of his men, shelled, attacked, captured. The armies could have no respect for private property. They imposed themselves upon the country like a plague. No door was closed to them, and while they brought with them every resource of civilization, the peasants dug up the empty ration tins for scraps of food, and when they were wounded (lacking the experience to judge the feathery shuffle of a mortar bomb) crawled to Allied aid-posts for their charity and skill. Patient of their hardships, they came forward to meet the leading troops with baskets of cherries, a clutch of eggs or a bottle of wine.

The Italians who experienced the odd replacement of one army by another were immediately struck by the contrast between the two. Our men were confident, healthy, even rather languid; the Germans were tired, sick and nervous. The psychological effect of constant retreat and the hostility of the people, which grew, as summer advanced, into open partisan warfare, were added to the physical exhaustion imposed on the Germans by lack of transport and air-attacks which prevented the use in daylight of the few lorries they had salvaged. Not many of them, even in moments of greatest hopelessness, would take the ultimate step of desertion, but their attitude when taken prisoner was often one of gratitude to their captors, relief at finding themselves treated no more harshly than one of our own men under arrest. They never knew us as we knew them. They never saw a billet which their enemy had occupied the night before, nor handled our litter of abandoned belongings as we handled theirs. All they knew was that Allies' supplies and equipment were apparently inexhaustible, their initiative unchallengeable. For themselves they could see no rest, no destination.

Alexander shared the mood of his soldiers. He too was elated. As if to emphasize the urgency of his campaign and his utter involvement in its steady progress, he moved his tactical headquarters from the palatial setting of Caserta to Frascati outside Rome, then to a caravan camp on the shores of Lake Bolsena, and finally to the neighbourhood of Siena. Here he gathered round him the score of officers needed to direct the campaign and retain touch with his main staffs at Caserta – Harding, Lemnitzer, Brian Robertson (administration), Airey (Intelligence), signallers, air and naval liaison-officers, and two or three aides – to whom were added distinguished visitors, among them King George VI, Churchill, Brooke, Marshall, Smuts, and (a frequent guest) Harold Macmillan. The atmosphere of their Mess was pleasantly relaxed. Shop-talk was discouraged but not banned. They often talked about Italy. Alexander was interested in the country and liked the Italians, though he never learnt to speak their language fluently. He was constantly on the move, bringing back to the Mess each evening his experiences of the day.

At 9 am he held a short conference at which first the Intelligence picture would be presented, then the operations of the preceding day, followed by reports from the air and navy. He concerned himself little with administrative matters or civilian affairs, and these conferences were more for the purpose of sharing more widely information which he already possessed. He spoke but little, reserving his major planning sessions for an Inner Cabinet or for periodic meetings with his Army Commanders which could last all day. At 9.30 he set out for the front. Lemnitzer often accompanied him on these trips, and has given me this account of them:

We spent about three days of every week travelling down to battalion level. The rest of the time we would tour other headquarters, or make official or political visits. We drove in the open Ford car which he had specially made for him in North Africa, for he was averse to sitting in a car from which he couldn't see everything, especially in the days before we gained air-superiority. Under fire he was absolutely imperturbable. I never saw him excited. He never wore a helmet, always his red-banded hat. He had great courage, and a remarkable ability to talk to other ranks and extract information from them, gauge their morale, and give them information for which he knew they were hungry. When we were on tour, he would often turn aside to look at some place of historic interest or a battlefield. His curiosity was insatiable.

He devoted so much of his time to visiting forward troops because he knew the importance of a commander's physical presence, and because he wished to familiarize himself with the difficulties of a rapid advance through rugged country and to see the ground ahead. But the major question which occupied his mind was the future of the campaign as a whole. For the first time in his career he took the initiative in the strategic argument.

The choice was between exploiting the success of *Diadem* into north-east Italy and thence into Austria, or limiting the offensive to the line of the northern Apennines or the Alps for the sake of opening a new front on the Mediterranean coast of France. Alexander and Churchill favoured the first alternative, the Americans the second. The invasion of southern France (*Anvil*) had first been suggested at the Quebec con-ference of August 1943. *Overlord* was to be supported by the capture of Toulon and Marseilles in order to divert German reserves from the north-west and give the Allies new ports of entry into the main theatre. It was agreed that this manoeuvre was the logical end-product of the Mediterranean campaign. Having started as a major diversion, Italy was to become a base for air-operations against Central Europe and sea-borne operations in support of the French campaign, which in con-junction with the Russians would end the war. At Teheran in November 1943, Stalin was told of this plan and warmly approved it. Thus there was a British commitment to both their major allies to carry out *Anvil*, even at the cost of withdrawing troops and landing-craft from Italy. During the winter 1943-4, the British changed their minds, largely because Maitland Wilson, on taking over the Mediterranean command from Eisenhower, advised against it. He doubted whether a landing in the south of France would contain as many German divisions as a maintained offensive in Italy. A decision was postponed, but it was agreed that if *Anvil* was to take place at all, it could not coincide with

Overlord but must follow it by a few weeks or months. The postponement made possible the continuing supply of Anzio and the mounting of *Diadem*.

Shortly before the opening of the offensive in May 1944 Alexander visited London. His main purpose was to ensure an adequate supply of artillery ammunition to his command, but he took the opportunity to press the argument that *Anvil* was already having a distracting effect upon his forthcoming operation, and the withdrawal of divisions from Italy after the capture of Rome would spoil his chances of a complete victory. He told the Cabinet that he viewed *Anvil* 'with strong misgivings'. German troops could be held as easily in southern France by the threat of it as by its actual execution. He held out the hope of spectacular achievements if his armies, with the craft to lift them and the air forces to support them, could be left intact. Churchill was impressed, seeing in Italy the chance of a major success in which British arms would predominate and which would balance and complement *Overlord*, in which the Americans would be bound eventually to play the greater role.

Alexander returned to Italy, and for the next month was occupied wholly with *Diadem*. When Rome was captured he returned to the argument with increased urgency and authority, and now added to it a new dimension. On 19 June he addressed the following memorandum to Churchill:

As I see it, we are on the march to a great victory which has unlimited possibilities. Kesselring's Tenth and Fourteenth Armies are a beaten force but not yet eliminated from the field. The condition of his forces is one of extreme weakness in men and material and in a grave state of exhaustion. . . . It appears clear that they will try to stand on the Pisa-Rimini line [the Gothic Line], and I am praying that they will do so. By so doing they will commit their last divisions in Italy, the equivalent in fighting value of some ten to twelve divisions holding a 180 mile front.

If I can bring them to battle once more, provided that my armies are left intact, I can mass such a powerful force of fresh troops, guns, tanks and air against them that a great breakthrough into the Po valley should not only split them in half but finally eliminate Kesselring's two armies. There will then be nothing to stop us marching straight to Vienna, unless of course the Germans send at least ten or more fresh divisions from elsewhere to try to stop us, and I understand that such an enemy course of action is just what is most required to assist our other operations. I believe we have here now the opportunity of inflicting on the German army such a defeat that its repercussions will be unpredictable.

To Brooke he wrote: 'The morale of our own troops is irresistibly high . . . and the whole Army Group forms one closely articulated machine capable of carrying out assaults and rapid exploitation in the most difficult terrain. Neither the Apennines nor even the Alps should prove a serious obstacle to their enthusiasm and skill.'

He had a valuable ally in Smuts, who was then visiting him in Italy. On 23 June Smuts wrote to Churchill:

I have discussed the position with Alexander and Wilson. Neither favours *Anvil*. . . . They agree that there will be no difficulty in a breakthrough to the Po and thereafter swinging east towards Istria, Ljubljana and so to Austria. Alexander favours an advance by land and sea, while Wilson favours the latter and thinks three divisions with one or two airborne divisions will suffice and make possible the capture of Trieste by the beginning of September. Thereafter the advance would continue eastwards, gathering large partisan support and perhaps forcing the enemy out of the Balkans.

The argument, from a Commander-in-Chief who had fulfilled almost all his previous predictions, appeared to Churchill unanswerable. He urged it strongly on Roosevelt and Marshall, while Alexander in Italy won over Clark. Marshall was not convinced. He replied that Eisenhower needed the French ports to deploy more troops on a wider front, and that the Germans would be likely to withdraw from north Italy to the Alps as soon as Alexander attacked, where they could hold a shorter line with fewer divisions. Alexander's plan would prolong the fighting in Italy indefinitely, and make no contribution to the success of *Overlord* commensurate with *Anvil*.

Alexander lost the argument. The first breach in British solidarity for his plan came with the defection of Wilson, who was persuaded that the Allies would retain in Italy enough troops to complete its conquest even when seven divisions (four French, three American) had been withdrawn for *Anvil*, and that to look further than Italy was a pipe-dream. Nor was Brooke convinced of the plan's validity:

June 23rd. We had a long evening of listening to Winston's strategic arguments. In the main he was for supporting Alexander's advance on Vienna. I pointed out that, even on Alex's optimistic reckoning, the advance beyond the Pisa-Rimini line would not start till after September; namely we should embark on a campaign through the Alps in winter. It was hard to make him realise that if we took the season of the year and the topography of the country in league against us, we should have three enemies instead of one.[1]

But it was the strong American opposition to the plan which determined the issue. On political grounds, it would have been unwise to force the Americans to abandon a project dear to them and on which many of their calculations were based, and substitute for it one which would annoy the Russians. On military grounds, there was much to say for *Anvil* and less for Vienna. It is true that in the event *Anvil* made little contribution except in additional divisions to Eisenhower's campaign, but at the time when *Anvil* was conceived and detailed plans were made for its execution, it could not have been foreseen that the Normandy bridgehead would burst open before the landing in southern France took place. It was a sensible insurance policy. Alexander was on unsure ground in his assertion that 'troops which could overrun a brave and stubborn enemy such as we had met in the Apennine ranges north of Florence, would surely not be stopped by what we might find in Yugoslavia and beyond. It was a dazzling idea, this grand project of reaching Vienna before our Russian allies.'[2]

He believed that his seven lost divisions would have turned the balance, and that with them he could have broken the Gothic Line in August, crossed the Po in September, captured Venice and Trieste in October . . . but here the programme falters. Winter descends, the tortuous Alpine roads become impassable (even in the Ljubljana Gap, 2,000 feet high, on which he focussed his hopes of a breakthrough into Austria), and the administrative difficulties would have made it impossible to maintain more than three or four divisions on those heights, where they would easily have been held by twice that number of German divisions, still full of fight and more securely based. Before *Diadem* he had agreed with Harding that in mountainous country a three-to-one superiority in infantry was needed to penetrate German defences. How much more true it was of winter warfare in the high Alps. 'It seems hardly within the bounds of possibility', General Sixsmith has written,[3] 'that Alexander could have got into Austria that year.' Michael Howard concurs that *Anvil* was the better choice: 'It was thanks largely to the stubborn perseverance of the American military leaders that the strategy for better or worse was ultimately carried out as had been jointly planned. An effective case has still to be made that there could have been any more rapid or economical way of winning the war.'[4]

Harding still holds the opposite view. In his introduction to Shepperd's book on the Italian campaign he wrote: 'The diversion of troops from Italy to the south of France in the autumn of 1944 was, in my opinion, the biggest strategic blunder of the war.... Had the Allied armies in Italy not been weakened and their advance lost momentum by this diversion, it is not too much to claim that Vienna . . . would have fallen to Allied rather than Russian arms.' Clark in his autobiography uses almost identical words: 'The weakening of the campaign in Italy in order to invade southern France, instead of pushing on into the Balkans, was one of the outstanding political mistakes of the war.' Such certainty is impressive. But it is hard to resist the conclusion that Alexander, Harding and Clark dismissed the political and military difficulties too lightly.

One can admire their boldness while doubting their judgement, and make allowance for the circumstance that when the debate reached its climax, Alexander's armies, advancing ten miles a day up the spine of Italy, seemed unstoppable. To weaken such a triumphant force for the sake of an irrelevant back-door pounce on France seemed to them criminal.

The irrevocable decision to press ahead with *Anvil* was made on 2 July, and the operation was carried out on 15 August. Fifth Army fluttered forward to the Gothic Line with one wing broken. Clark had no more than five divisions left. Equally illustrative of their common disappointment and of Alexander's tactful method of command are these two messages exchanged between him and Clark about the employment of the French corps before the moment came when they must be withdrawn for *Anvil*:

July 16th. Personal for General Clark from General Alexander. Will you please convey to General Juin the following message from me: Whilst I am most sensible of the great contribution the French have made to the success of our operations in Italy, I shall be most grateful to General Juin if he can continue to keep up pressure on the enemy for the next few days so as to allow them no relaxation and to ensure that his front, when relieved by Eighth Army, will be taken over under the most favourable conditions.

Clark replied:

I have examined carefully the question of continued pressure by the French raised in your message to General Juin. I instructed Juin to release units specified by Allied Force Headquarters on dates prescribed, even if their withdrawal would force the French to adopt a defensive role. General Juin decided that the removal of these units, and the character of the resistance on the French front, made it necessary for him to assume the defensive, with provision for a follow-up of any enemy withdrawal with light forces. I consider that Juin is doing all he is capable of accomplishing.

Their heart had gone out of the offensive. Alexander wrote with some bitterness to Brooke that he had hoped that the impression would not be given at home that the Italian theatre had sunk to a level of secondary importance, for that would have a deplorable effect upon the morale of his troops. The CIGS could give him little consolation, imploring him not to work upon the Prime Minister's emotions for the sake of the Italian front at the expense of other fronts. Alexander, once again, must do what he could with what he had left.

IIe was obliged to attack the Gothic Line with twenty divisions against twenty-two German. He proposed that the two armies should attack the central part of the line side by side, for it was in the centre that they were both concentrated, and he did not wish to waste time. Leese argued strongly against this plan, claiming that Eighth Army's chances of success would be much greater if they switched their whole impetus to the Adriatic coast, where Kesselring was not expecting them, and where their tanks and artillery would be more effective on the lower ground. Clark, he said, could make his own dispositions unhampered by the need to coordinate them with Eighth Army's. Behind this diplomatic reasoning was the rivalry between Leese and Clark which dated from the Anzio breakout, and Alexander, true to his method, consented to the change, even though it meant the loss of three weeks in humping Eighth Army secretly and therefore slowly across the Apennines to the far coast. It permitted Leese to fight a battle which he considered he could win, and recreated the conditions of the two-handed punch which had become Alexander's trademark. He described the plan to Brooke: 'We shall be able to prevent Kesselring from shifting his reserves from one Army front to the other by keeping up a series of heavy blows by our two Armies in turn.'

Eighth Army were the first to attack. They broke through the coastal sector towards Rimini and were on the point of debouching into the Lombard plain when, at Coriano, the Germans stopped them. Then Alexander launched Fifth Army at the centre. Their experience was similar. After a dramatic initial success in capturing the Futa pass, the highest point of the Florence-Bologna road, they were halted on the

Map 11 The final offensive in Italy, 1945

mountain-ridges beyond. Both armies lacked the reserves to make the final bound. Alexander pointedly drew the melancholy conclusion that politics had robbed him of victory. But in his Memoirs he acknowledged by implication that even if they had reached the plain before winter, the subsequent battle would have been just as hard:

Success would not have been easy to exploit. It had been confidently expected that after breaking into the flat expanse of the Romagna, we should be able to stage a rapid advance to the Po. But the continuous water-lines of the Romagna and the Po Valley itself were to prove hardly less serious obstacles than the mountains over which we had fought. Soon the rushing streams of summer were to become the raging torrents of an abominable autumn; and although by mid-October both Fifth and Eighth Armies were within a day or so's march of their goals – Bologna and Ravenna – it was shortly obvious that the final destruction of the German armies in Italy would have to be postponed until the spring of 1945.

I remember vividly a visit which Alexander paid at that time to the headquarters of 1st Guards Brigade in the mountains above the San-terno valley, one of a dozen such visits which he made that day. There was nothing higher than ourselves for miles around. We looked down upon the crumpled quilt of foothills, whitened by the first snow, and beyond them to the great northern plain of Italy, crossed diagonally by the Via Emilia on which the German lorries were clearly visible. We could see the villas and farmhouses in the plain which we still hoped to occupy before true winter arrived; and on the far horizon, a hundred miles from where we stood, with blue shadows down one side and sharp serrated edges, rose the Alps. Alexander arrived on foot with his ADC. This was his first sight of the Alps, for the day was exceptionally clear, and he was moved by it to reveal to us a little more of his strategic vision than he would normally confide to junior officers. Sketching with one hand imaginary lines across the plain as if a map were spread in front of him, he indicated how he intended the battle to develop, and then he said: 'Those mountains may stop us, but I don't think so. They are full of Italian partisans, only waiting for us to give the word, and they have the weapons. Beyond them lies Central Europe. We can't stop here. We're too good to waste, doing nothing. You want to go on. I want to go on. We *will* go on. Yes, it would be fun, I suppose; fun if we succeed, less fun if we don't.' He was now almost talking to himself. 'But what a pity it is to maul this beautiful country. I'll be glad when it's all over. I suppose they'll want me to govern some Dominion or other.

But all I shall want to do is to paint and fish.' Those were his exact words. I wrote them down as soon as he had left. We were surprised by the alternation between his exhilaration and melancholy, but his mood matched our own. The armies were tired, and the Alps seemed very high and very far away.

The reason why the offensive was halted in December was not, as was widely rumoured, a shortage of artillery ammunition, nor even the difficulty of the muddied mountains, but the need to rest the troops. Alexander had taken the unusual step of appealing direct to Eisenhower for help:

October 10th. I know you realise and appreciate what we have done and are doing here to keep German divisions from being transferred to the Western front. But the time has arrived when my armies will not be able to continue the offensive much longer. This is mostly due to the fact that all divisions are very tired and completely lack fresh replacements. . . . My last chance is to appeal to you personally. Anything you can do to help Clark will be to our mutual advantage.

Eisenhower could do no more than transfer to Italy 3,000 American reinforcements destined for France. 'You are a real friend', signalled Alexander in reply, but both knew that these green GIs could make little difference.

At the end of October Alexander summoned his Army Commanders to Siena and put the facts bluntly to them. They would maintain the offensive for a few more weeks, and then, whether Bologna and Ravenna were captured or not, they would halt to rest and retrain for a major operation in the New Year. He outlined his plans, without any apparent loss of optimism. What he had failed to do in 1944 he would achieve in 1945:

A two-handed punch [ran his notes for the conference] one each side of the Adriatic, developing a pincer movement converging on Trieste, designed to destroy Kesselring's armies. (a) An unopposed landing by Eighth Army through Split, Sibenik and Zader, followed by a rapid advance on Zagreb, Ljubljana and Fiume in cooperation with Yugoslav partisans, and collaborating with the Russians; (b) A major offensive by Fifth Army to join up with them. D Day to be no later than February 20th.

The early date is surprising. The campaign was to start in mid-winter.

While outline plans were being made for this ambitious operation, Alexander was doubly promoted. He was awarded his Field Marshal's baton and supreme command of the Mediterranean theatre. He had been privately warned by Churchill in early September that Maitland Wilson was taking Dill's place as head of the British Military Mission in Washington, and that he, Alexander, was to succeed him. 'I am arranging that when the time comes, as it will very soon, I will promote you to Field Marshal. The appointment will date from the capture of Rome, so as to preserve your existing seniority over Montgomery.' It had been necessary to promote Montgomery earlier to the highest army rank because of his vast responsibilities in north-west Europe. On 12 December 1944 Alexander became Supreme Commander, and Clark succeeded him in command of the Army Group. Truscott was posted back to Italy to command Fifth Army, and Oliver Leese (who had gone to Burma to command Fourteenth Army) was succeeded by McCreery in command of the Eighth. In the New Year General Sir William Morgan was brought in as Alexander's Chief of Staff instead of Harding, who achieved his wartime ambition to command a corps.

When Maitland Wilson had succeeded Eisenhower as Supreme Commander a year earlier, Churchill had made it clear to Alexander at Marrakesh that Wilson was to handle political and administrative questions, leaving Alexander in complete control of the strategy and tactics. Although this arrangement was never put in writing, Alexander assumed that the Prime Minister had repeated it to Wilson, and made his own operational plans, keeping Wilson informed 'out of politeness', as he later said, but without any real regard for Wilson's seniority. Wilson did not accept this position, and on more than one occasion attempted to assert his authority. When, for instance, in June 1944 he received his copy of Alexander's memorandum to the Prime Minister advocating an advance to Vienna, he protested against this bypassing of the chain of command and ordered Alexander to refrain from sending to London 'anything but purely operational reports'. He complained with some acerbity: 'Any reference to future policy puts me in an impossible position with the Americans. You must remember that I am the servant of the Chiefs of Staff, and that the Americans are sticklers for the correct channels. Further, they regard direct communication between you and London with the greatest suspicion, as an attempt to influence the British Chiefs of Staff as opposed to an Allied expression of opinion.' Alexander paid no attention to this rebuff, since it was not repeated by Brooke or Churchill, both of whom continued to correspond with Alexander almost daily, and expected his direct replies. Wilson was undoubtedly piqued, and the incident may explain in part his with-drawal of support for Alexander in the *Anvil* argument.

When Alexander himself became Supreme Commander he assumed the responsibilities which he had denied to Wilson. His was the brain behind the Mediterranean strategy, his the guiding hand in the final offensive. Without allowing Clark's feelings to be ruffled, he virtually combined during the last months of the war the roles of Supreme Com-mander and Commander-in-Chief. It was seen retrospectively that Wilson's position had been redundant. There was even less need in the Mediterranean for a two-tiered higher command than there was in France, where Eisenhower commanded much greater forces in the dual role, and resented, as we shall shortly see, any suggestion that a land-force commander should be interposed between him and his Army Groups.

In Wilson's year, few major decisions had been required of him out-side the context of the Italian campaign. Alexander's responsibilities were broader. There was the problem of the Poles, the problem of Tito, the problem of liaison with the advancing Russians, and the problem of Greece.

It was fortunate that the Greek crisis reached its climax at a moment when there was a lull in Italy, but less fortunate for Alexander that it coincided with his assumption of the supreme command. The escalation of the crisis during 1944 was due to the Allied policy of support for the Greek guerillas without consideration of what the political consequences might be after victory. It was not realized until too late that ELAS (the main body of Greek partisans) was a Communist front, and although Stalin and Roosevelt had both agreed that Greece was a British sphere of influence, support for the partisans might lead to a civil war when the Germans withdrew, a conflict in which Britain was bound to back the legitimate Government against the Communists. 'We were speaking with two voices', wrote Sir Reginald Leeper, the British Ambassador appointed to Athens; 'the political voice, which was giving full support to King George of Greece, and the military voice, which was giving support with arms and gold sovereigns to the King's worst enemies in the Greek mountains.'[5]

On 4 October 1944 British troops under General Scobie began to follow up the German withdrawal and on the 15th they entered Athens. The British saw themselves as liberators and providers of immediate succour for a starving population. ELAS saw them as an alien army attempting to impose on Greece a king whom they no longer wanted. At first the British troops were acclaimed, but within a few days they found themselves involved in civil strife in defence of the Government of Papandreou against bands of ELAS partisans and their sympathizers in Athens, freedom-fighters turned revolutionaries. Civil war broke out on 3 December. 'Do not hesitate to act as if you were in a conquered city where a local rebellion is in progress', cabled Churchill to Scobie. 'We have to hold and dominate Athens.'

Alexander was then in London being briefed for his new responsibilities, but the situation in Greece was the main topic of his discussions with the War Cabinet, who gave him a free hand to restore order. On 10 December he flew with Macmillan to Caserta, and next day continued to Athens. They found the British troops in a state of siege. Scobie held the centre of the city, but the rebels were in control of the inner and outer suburbs and blocked the entrance to the Piraeus. The route from the airport to Scobie's headquarters in Athens was under such pressure by the partisans that Alexander and Macmillan were forced to make the six-mile journey in armoured cars which were spattered with bullets as they drove. Having assessed the situation with Scobie, Alexander sent back his first report to the Prime Minister:

December 11th. The military situation is more serious than I had thought from the information which we had in London. The initiative is not wholly with us. The British forces are in fact beleaguered in the heart of the city. Even the various ordnance dumps and stores are not within the perimeter of our protection. We control less of the city than I had been led to believe. The aerodrome itself is not too secure. More serious is the condition of the port of Piraeus. We are not in complete possession of the harbour and unable therefore to unload our ships there. Port Heracles is not in our possession, nor is the electric power station and other important dumps in that area. There are only six days rations and three days ammunition reserves available at the present rate of expenditure for the troops in the central area of Athens. The most urgent step therefore is to reinforce from the dumps available at the aerodrome, and then to maintain the supply from Italy. I have, therefore, ordered the following:

The leading Brigade of 4th Infantry Divisions which starts to land by air tomorrow to be employed with tank support in opening and keeping open the lines of communication between the aerodrome and the city centre. In addition to the 4th Infantry Division, one armoured car regiment, thirty-six Sherman tanks and various necessary stores to be despatched from Italy forthwith. All the above will probably have to be landed over the open beach at Phaleron.

When sufficient force is available, the following plan will be put into effect. The port of Piraeus to be cleared and occupied so as to establish a firm base for operations. Then to clear the road from Piraeus to Athens so as to ensure a safe line-of-communication from the port to the central area of Athens, which is now held by our troops. Having linked up securely both ends of the dumbbell, to undertake the necessary operations to clear the whole of Athens and Piraeus. Speed and energy in execution of the above plan is all important, and I have given orders accordingly.

He also gave instructions that any rebels found armed but dressed in civilian clothes should be shot, and certain areas should be entirely evacuated of the civilian population to permit the use of naval gunfire and air-bombing. Finally, he sent one of his best Divisional Commanders, General Hawkesworth, to take command of the ground operations under Scobie's overall control.

In twenty-four hours Alexander had transformed the military situation in Athens, assuming as Supreme Commander (designate by one day) control of a force little larger than a brigade. He immediately appreciated that the security of his communications by air and sea must have priority, and that Athens could not be held without urgent reinforcements. 'As soon as this was achieved', he wrote in his despatch, 'the force would be firmly based, both tactically and administratively, and the clearing of Athens would follow as a straightforward military operation.' It was a situation in which Alexander excelled and even revelled. The danger to himself and his troops, the concern of his Prime Minister, who could think, according to Brooke, of little else during those anxious days, the stimulating companionship of Macmillan, the historical associations of the scene, evoked all his greatest qualities as a soldier. Having taken these immediate measures, he showed himself to his troops and the people of Athens by walking down the main street in animated conversation with the head of the Russian military mission, and crawling with Scobie over the rippled tiles of neighbouring houses to obtain a better view of the fighting.

With Macmillan he began simultaneously to examine possible political solutions to the crisis, sending joint cables to Churchill, to which Alexander contributed the military paragraphs, Macmillan the political. On that very first day they endorsed Leeper's suggestion that Archbishop Damaskinos should be appointed Regent of Greece. He alone could open negotiations with the insurgents, who trusted him for his record of resistance during the German occupation. He alone could dismiss Papandreou and appoint a new Prime Minister in his place. He alone could succeed in persuading ELAS to lay down their arms. 'In this way', they said, 'a proper measure of responsibility can be restored to the head of the Greek state, and the most powerful cry against us, foreign intervention, effectively answered.' Churchill was reluctant to accept the plan. 'To appoint a Regency against the King's wishes,' he replied, 'would be an act of constitutional violence', and the King, then in London, refused, protesting that such a measure would be taken to mean that the monarchy was written off before his people had been consulted. For Damaskinos he felt 'personal distrust'. He might accept him as Prime Minister, but never as Regent. Churchill sympathized. 'If we force Damaskinos on Greece, we should be punishing the King for obeying his constitutional oath and be ourselves setting up a Dictator.' Alexander and Macmillan replied that even if they managed to clear Athens and Piraeus of the rebels, they had not the strength to control the rest of the country. Further troops could not be diverted from Italy except at the cost of sabotaging our campaign and risking a major confrontation with Russia, and even with the United States – which at this period was ostentatiously neutral – not to mention liberals at home. We should not allow ourselves to be dragged into a long war from one end of Greece to the other, with the object of exterminating the Communist party. A political solution must be found, and none existed better than that which they had proposed.

The telegrams came and went several times a day, but Alexander could not remain in Athens indefinitely. He returned to Caserta on 12 December to take up his command, leaving Macmillan in Athens, besieged in the British Embassy with the Ambassador and a staff which included Harold Caccia and Osbert Lancaster. The ELAS snipers were only 2,000 yards away across the Ilissus. 'It was a fine house,' wrote Macmillan, 'admirable for entertainment, and not altogether unsuitable for a siege.' When bullets flew into the bedrooms, they pulled their mattresses into the corridors. There was no heat, no light, and no water, but they had filled the baths before the civil war began. A corner of the garden – 'the prison-yard' they called it – was sheltered enough for occasional exercise, and the spirit of their company is illustrated by Osbert Lancaster's story that as he crouched beneath the garden wall under a hail of bullets, the Ambassadress called from the window, 'Oh, Osbert, do be careful with the wall-flowers!'

The process of clearing the capital and its approaches was very diffi-cult, and the fighting was bitter. Gradually the British began to gain the upper hand. By 18 December Allied ships were able to discharge in the southern basin of the Piraeus, and the dumps and airport were secure. But Alexander reiterated to the Prime Minister on 21 December that the stripping of troops from Italy for Greece was highly dangerous, as the Germans might attack our weakened front, and 'it is my opinion that the Greek problem cannot be solved by military measures'. It was on the receipt of this message that Churchill decided that he must visit Athens himself, taking Eden with him. The news of his imminent arrival was brought to Athens by Alexander himself, who reached Piraeus by destroyer on Christmas morning. Churchill came by air that same afternoon, and Alexander, Macmillan and Leeper discussed the situation with him for three hours in his aircraft, as it was too cold and too dangerous for him to leave it immediately. Then he moved to quarters in HMS *Ajax* lying off Piraeus, and there, that night, he met the Archbishop for the first time. One of the best passages in Alexander's Memoirs describes the scene:

Churchill was sitting on a sofa when the Archbishop was ushered into the room. I think that the Prime Minister had in his mind that he was going to meet a politically sleek cleric and a man of little real importance. I happened to be in the room at the time and I watched the encounter with fascination. Winston, slumped on the sofa, looked bored and obviously dubious about the prospects of the meeting. Then a magnificent figure of a man appeared in the doorway – strong, virile, well over six feet, with his black beard and his great head-dress which made him look like a giant.

Churchill rose in astonishment, obviously immensely impressed by the appearance of his guest. They sat down together and started a discussion which had to be interpreted. I recollect that the Prime Minister said some-thing to which the Archbishop objected, and from that moment it was never in doubt that his Beatitude had very strong views of his own. Winston, in short, had found his man.

Next day they held a conference at the Greek Foreign Office, attended by Churchill, Eden, Macmillan, Alexander, Damaskinos, represent-atives of ELAS, and observers from the American, Russian and French missions. Alexander sat between the Archbishop and Macmillan. Churchill began by saying that his role was that of convener, and it must be for the Greeks themselves to decide their future. Alexander added, 'Instead of putting my brigades into Greece, I should like to see Greek brigades coming to help me in Italy against our common enemy.' The British then left the conference, and heard only next day of its success. All had agreed to request the King to accept Damaskinos as Regent. Papandreou resigned his office, and was replaced by a new Government under Plastiras. ('I hope', said Churchill when he first heard the name, 'that this doesn't mean he has feet of clay.') The King would not return to Greece until a plebiscite had decided in his favour, and he was eventually persuaded to agree by Churchill on his return to London.

It was not quite the end of the Greek incident. Fighting continued in the streets of Athens for several weeks more, but a truce became effective on 15 January 1945. When Alexander revisited the city soon afterwards, he was able to walk round the sunlit streets with Macmillan, acknowledging the salutes of the soldiers and the plaudits of the crowd. 'It was quite extraordinary', wrote Macmillan of this occasion, 'to see the delight of the people in what had now come to be called the Second Liberation.' On their return from Yalta in February, Churchill and Eden, again accompanied by Alexander and Macmillan, were greeted by a moving acclamation by the Athenians. 'I have had great moments in my life', said Churchill to Harold Nicolson ten days later in the House of Commons, 'but never as when faced by that half-million crowd in Constitution Square.' Two British divisions remained in Greece until the end of the war, and their absence marginally weakened Alexander's last offensive. But 22,000 Germans were cut off in Crete and the Aegean islands, so that the balance was to some extent restored.

Alexander was now free to plan the contribution of his armies to final victory. Momentarily, however, he was distracted by the suggestion that he should give up his new command within two months of assuming it, in order to replace Tedder as deputy to Eisenhower in north-west Europe, and take control of the land-battle. The idea originated with Montgomery's dissatisfaction with the chain of command in France, but it was also strongly urged by Churchill, who was beginning to lose interest in the Italian campaign and thought it too subordinate a position for his favourite general. On 1 March he wrote to Alexander as if the matter were already decided: 'I have written privately to Eisenhower to tell him that you will be replacing Tedder as Deputy Supreme Commander about the middle of this month and that I propose

Tedder shall replace you in the Mediterranean.' Eisenhower and Brooke were in favour of it, and so was Montgomery, who thought it 'might go some way to putting matters straight'. The proposal lapsed when Roosevelt expressed the fear that it might seem that Alexander was 'being put in to support Eisenhower after a failure in the Ardennes', and Eisenhower, switching his ground, muttered to Tedder, 'I will have nobody standing between me and my Army Group commanders.' The cancellation of Churchill's offer caused Alexander no disappointment. 'I am well content to stay in Italy', he said. The reason was that it gave him the opportunity for his greatest exploit of the war. His last battle must rank with *Diadem* as a conception and with Tunis as an achievement.

It was all the more remarkable because he acted on his own strategic initiative. The Chiefs of Staff gave him no encouragement, and withdrew from Italy three further divisions, including the Canadian corps, to reinforce the north-west. Alexander was left with the equivalent of twenty divisions against twenty-three German, to which should be added on each side several Italian combat groups which Alexander found more useful than his opponent. But they were not so unequally matched as these figures suggest. The Fifth and Eighth Armies totalled some 536,000 men. The Germans had 491,000. Eighth Army had 1,220 pieces of artillery against 665, and 1,320 armoured vehicles to the German 400. Still more important was the Allies' absolute command of the air, and the help of 60,000 Italian partisans behind the German lines. These figures were of course known in London, but the conclusion was that Alexander could be expected to do no more than 'contain the German forces now in Italy and prevent their withdrawal to other fronts', a task which he could adequately carry out by 'limited offensive action' and 'the skilful use of cover and deception plans'. Instead, Alexander planned to force the capitulation of the entire German army facing him.

He cannot have conceived this grandiose plan out of vanity, for even if his campaign had ended tamely in the northern Apennines, his reputation as an aggressive and skilful commander was assured. He thought it wasteful for the finest Allied army to leave undefeated the finest German army, and he knew that his men would regard it as a matter for shame to stand idle while others fought. (I can bear personal witness to this, from my clear recollection of the elation with which the news of Alexander's intention was greeted in my own brigade.) Strategically he argued that if the German army in Italy were not broken up in the field, they could withdraw into the Alps to man Hitler's redoubt, which was then thought to have more reality than was later proved.

Knowing the scepticism in high places, he phrased his arguments carefully to win consent for his plan. Early in January 1945 he was telling the CIGS that only a loaded pistol could for certain keep the Germans on their present front. If it were seen to be unloaded, they would hold what remained to them of Italy by a skeleton force, and send the rest to France. He reloaded his pistol by resting and retraining his troops. Next he began to speak of the folly of leaving a loaded pistol undischarged, and to hint in his letters to Churchill of 'an all-out offensive'. Brooke was discouraging. 'From both the manpower and the ammunition situation', he wrote to Alexander on 11 January, 'it does not look as if we are in a position to stage spring offensives simultaneously both in France and Italy. We are going carefully into the matter, but I feel certain that we must concentrate on one main effort, and that main effort must be on the vital front, France.' Alexander knew that the time had come to make a more personal appeal. He sent Gruenther (now Chief of Staff, 15th Army Group) to London bearing a letter of which the import is contained in these sentences:

When a long line is held by few divisions, the advantage lies with the side that has the initiative and can attack. We hold that initiative because of our air and armoured superiority and above all our mobility. For lack of fuel the Germans have become extremely immobile. In consequence, I firmly believe we have a great opportunity of winning a first class victory on the Italian front.

In face of such confidence the Chiefs of Staff agreed. They cancelled the withdrawal of two further divisions from Italy, and wished Alexander luck. He discussed the plan with Mark Clark, left him to work out the details, and turned his attention to his two eastern allies, the Yugoslav partisans and the Russians.

Alexander had first met Tito after the fall of Rome, and had been much impressed by him. He met him again in February 1945. By that time Alexander had abandoned the plan for an amphibious operation through northern Yugoslavia in combination with a land offensive by Fifth Army, both directed on Trieste. When he went to Belgrade on 21 February, he was therefore able to assure Tito that he did not intend any large-scale operations through his territory, and asked only for facilities to use the Ljubljana pass for supplying his armies from Trieste.

Tito agreed, and further volunteered to exchange Intelligence information with the Allies and put under Alexander's command any Yugoslav
forces which might enter the Allied sector. In exchange for these
courtesies, Alexander promised Tito a million rations for his troops. He
wrote to the CIGS, 'I found Tito very friendly, sensible and cooperative.
He has agreed to all the proposals I put to him.'

From Belgrade he flew on to visit Marshal Tolbukhin in Hungary,
himself piloting the Russian aircraft for part of the way. At Yalta
Alexander had been able to make little progress in coordinating his
plans with the Soviet Union, and he hoped that by direct contact with
the commander of the Ukrainian armies to avoid confusion between the
Allies as their offensives developed towards each other. He reported to
Brooke that he had been well received, but on future Russian plans he
had been able to gain no information. Operations must develop as circumstances dictated, he was told, which meant that the Russians
would advance as far west as they could in competition with the Americans from France and with Alexander from Italy. One curious incident
helps to explain Alexander's reference to his good reception. He
revealed it in his Memoirs:

I was shown to my billet, a small and comfortable little house in the
village, where a Russian girl was detailed to look after me as a sort of female
valet, I suppose. She wore a dress or uniform vaguely reminiscent of that of a
hospital nurse. It appeared that she intended to sleep on the settee in my
room, but I didn't think that that was quite the thing, and she spent the
night outside the door.

As far as he had been able, he had now set the stage for 15th Army
Group's offensive of 9 April 1945. On the day of the attack he found
himself with time on his hands. To Edward Seago, whom he had attached
to his Mess as a companion and official war-artist, he suggested, 'Let's
go into the hills with a picnic lunch.'

So we went off [recalls Seago], found a lovely place by a stream, and goat-
boys came and shared our lunch. I couldn't keep quiet any longer. I said,
'Alex, I must know.' 'Know what?' 'But you *must* be thinking of what is going
on at this moment. And here we are, sitting by a stream, talking to a little
boy and eating grapes.' 'Of course I know what is going on.' 'But then
how can we be doing this?' 'Well, I've worked for days on it. I've planned
every bit of it. Now I've had to hand it to my generals, and they've got to
put it into action. I can't know anything more until the reports come in.
They'd much rather I was out of the way.' After we had finished our lunch,

he stretched out on the grass and went sound asleep. He woke up at about 4.30 and we drove back to Caserta, straight to the operations room, and he remained there the whole night.

The offensive was again double-fisted, and the deception plan (always endemic to Alexander's operations) misled von Vietinghoff, Kesselring's successor, to expect a major landing on the coast south of Venice. Instead, the only amphibious element of the operation was by DUKWs across Lake Comacchio on the right wing of Eighth Army's attack. The Senio was crossed, then the Santerno, and after an initial success which exceeded all their hopes, they widened their bridgeheads, overrunning one German defence line after another, to create within a few days a broad salient which welled over the plain like a limp mainsail suddenly filling with wind. At the moment when the Germans began to fear for their communications with their winter line in the Apennines, Fifth Army also attacked, heading for Bologna. The German line was at this stage under great pressure but there was no breach. They had exhausted all but their minimum reserves of ammunition in contesting the initial attacks, and if they could not stem the offensive immediately, or at least conduct a slow and orderly retreat, they would find their army cut into small pockets and their withdrawal across the Po a matter of great difficulty. All the bridges over the river had been demolished by air attack, and their elaborate system of ferries, adequate for supply traffic, could not stand the sudden strain of transporting their entire army from the south bank to the north – unless time was on their side.

This was the situation which Alexander had planned. It was the moment for the armoured divisions to slice behind the Germans and gain the banks of the Po before them. In this they succeeded. The Germans were in a state of utter confusion. Their supply trains were divorced from their fighting troops, their stragglers cut off in thousands by the branching columns of British tanks or waylaid by the ubiquitous Italian partisans. If they managed to reach the river, it was only to find the banks choked by earlier arrivals, and the actual passage could only be made under a rain of shells and bombs. The air was thick with the smoke of burning lorries, and the countryside strewn with their wrecks. Everywhere roamed packs of transport horses turned loose by the Germans on the river banks, and parties of weary soldiers trudged northwards to swim the river or give themselves up to the first Allied troops who appeared. One of their Corps Commanders, Graf von Schwerin, gave up the struggle and surrendered with his staff near

Ferrara, saying openly to his interrogator that the position was hopeless.

The battle almost ended on the Po on 24 April. It was completed a few days later on the Adige. I wrote home this account of the scene which Alexander himself had nearly witnessed, for he had left our head-quarters but an hour before:

At least a hundred enemy motor and horsed vehicles were collected on the southern floodbank of the Adige, frantically trying to disperse into the fields or edging slowly down to the pontoon bridge by which they hoped to make a last minute get-away. This was the last time our loyal friends the Ayrshire Yeomanry fired their guns. They concentrated their fire on the bridge itself, directed by an artillery spotting aircraft hovering over the river, and finally scored sufficient hits on it to cut the bridge in half. It floated downstream a blazing wreck, leaving on the south bank a vast quantity of material which could be dealt with at our leisure. The Germans who survived and could swim, jumped into the water and swam across. The remainder had no choice but to surrender.

The Allied armies raced through northern Italy, shedding divisions as fast as they became redundant, while the Italian partisans blocked the Alpine passes, killing Mussolini on his flight northwards towards Switzerland. The Americans sped north-west, the British north-east. The historic cities of the plain fell hour by hour. The remaining Germans gave themselves up in battalions. It was a total victory.

This is not the place to retell the complicated story of the negotiations with German representatives in Switzerland which preceded the final capitulation. Alexander was naturally informed of them, but pursued his battle regardless of their outcome. On 28 April the German pleni-potentiaries arrived at Caserta, and next day signed an instrument of unconditional surrender, involving a million men, to take effect at noon on 2 May. Alexander was not himself present at the signing, where the leading Allied representative was his Chief of Staff, General Morgan, who had been with him almost to the last on the mole at Dunkirk.

The victory was not unclouded. Tito, in breach of his agreement with Alexander in Belgrade, refused to put under Allied command his partisans who had penetrated into Venezia Giulia in north-east Italy and Carinthia in southern Austria. The two armies met, and almost collided. Churchill was as unremitting with his allies as with his defeated enemies. Tito must not be allowed to seize territory which was not his own. Alexander warned the Prime Minister that if this could not be prevented by diplomacy, it would be difficult to enforce by arms:

If I am ordered by the Chiefs of Staff to occupy the whole of Venezia Giulia by force if necessary, we shall certainly be committed to a fight with the Yugoslav army who will have the moral backing, at least, of the Russians. Before we are committed, I think it as well to consider the feelings of our own troops in this matter. They have a profound admiration for Tito's partisans, and a great sympathy for them in their struggle for freedom. We must be very careful therefore before we ask them to turn away from the common enemy to fight an ally.

Churchill replied with the sharpest rebuke that he ever addressed to Alexander:

The wide circulation given to your message has done much harm. I hope that in the changed circumstances produced by the President Truman's telegram ['If Tito takes hostile action and attacks our Allied forces anywhere, we would expect Field Marshal Alexander to use as many troops of all nationalities in his command as are necessary'], you will find it possible to give me the assurance that the Army under your command will obey your orders and its customary sense of duty and discipline. I have been much distressed by this paragraph of your message, and wish that, as far as the British troops are concerned, it had not been given such a wide circulation.

Alexander's message had in fact been marked 'personal for the Prime Minister, copy to the CIGS'. Nor can there be any doubt that he was correct in his assessment of the troops' reaction. On the reverse of the Prime Minister's telegram, Alexander scribbled: '(a) the necessity of weighing the morale factors when making a plan; (b) the Yugoslav partisans will fight fiercely for what they believe to be their freedom.' But in his official reply he took a more conciliatory line. The controversy fizzled out when Tito withdrew his men from the most sensitive areas of Italy and Austria.

At last Alexander was able to enjoy some leisure. He joined Churchill at the Potsdam conference, and stood alongside him with Montgomery on the rostrum at the Berlin victory-parade. He spent a few days leave in England at the end of June. At his suggestion Churchill came out to Italy after his election defeat and stayed a week or two in a villa on Lake Como which Alexander had put at his disposal, 'to have some sunshine', as Churchill wrote to his host in a letter of thanks, 'and develop a new interest in life. I have found this in painting.' The two men set up their easels side by side.

On 1 October 1945 Alexander handed over his command. At the airport to see him off there was a British band and an American band,

and detachments of the Army and Navy of both nations. His aircraft was escorted part of the way home by ten Spitfires and three Fortresses. It was the end of his military career.

Looking back on it, the magnitude of his achievement makes criticism of this or that decision seem petty and even insolent. He had advanced from Alamein to Austria. He twice forced the capitulation of an entire Army Group in the open field. He brought about the defeat of Italy. He won all his battles, except those in France and Burma which he salvaged. He won each of them in a manner which inspired confidence that he would win the next. His luck was an element of that confidence, but it was not seen at the time as luck, nor were his mistakes seen as mistakes. There was no moment when he aroused public criticism, and the esteem of his staff and commanders grew with each successive campaign. Such a reputation among those most competent to judge, men who saw him day by day in crisis or discussion, cannot be won by good fortune, nor by personal charm or integrity. It was put to the test again and again. Alexander never faltered. There has been no sentence in this narrative of his military career to suggest that he was ever at a loss or avoided a difficult decision. Sometimes he may have decided wrongly and sometimes he changed his mind, but a change of mind is among the most difficult military decisions of all. With few exceptions his orders were clear, and within the capacity of his troops, who knew that he knew what could be achieved. The ability to inspire this degree of trust came from his long experience of battle at all levels, and from his constant involvement in his operations. At a turning-point of his last offensive in Italy, he included a chance sentence in a message to Churchill which summarizes his gift: 'It is most important that I am on the spot to ensure that victory flows in the right direction.' Eisenhower or Maitland Wilson would have considered that the Supreme Commander had no business to be on the spot at all.

Yet no subordinate General was ever heard to complain that Alexander was breathing down his neck. In Italy self-contained units of a dozen nations served under him – British, Americans, French, Canadians, New Zealanders, South Africans, Indians, Poles, Brazilians, Italians, Greeks, Jews and American-Japanese. As Mark Clark has written, 'In the Italian campaign we had demonstrated how a polyglot army could be welded into a team of allies with the strength and unity and determination to prevail over formidable odds.' This was Alexander's achievement. An intense patriot, as his conduct at Dunkirk had proved, he could understand the different stresses to which other nations were subject, but knew that the stress of war itself was the universal experience by which they were all united. His sympathetic relations with Anders of the Polish Corps, for example, held together that superb formation when they considered themselves betrayed at Yalta. Among the Americans the 'Limey' sneer was never applied to Alexander, except by Stilwell until he came to know him better, for they appreciated his profound dedication, his aggressiveness towards the enemy which he never applied to themselves, his controlled optimism and his courage. Alexander's ruthlessness in pressing an attack had no counterpart in his dealings with his commanders. Although he had a hand in the dismissal of Dawley and Lucas, there is no record that he ever sacked a senior officer directly. Mountbatten put it this way to me:

He was essentially kind-hearted in every way. He was such a gentleman. He put up with insubordination. I never did. I fired senior officers or Governors if they crossed me and I was convinced they were in the wrong. I was well known for this. It meant that people jumped around, partly out of fear. I was far less popular than Alex for that very reason. People knew that I was ruthless. Alex was beloved by everybody because he had never harmed anybody.

If Alexander had been more insistent, he could not have sustained for long an attitude which conflicted with his nature. He was always aware that a clash of opinion at the crisis of a battle might shake the loyalty of a commander in preparing for the next. Able, ambitious men, he considered, did not require leading, still less driving, but cajoling, persuading, co-ordinating. His function was to indicate to them the direction and confines of their operations, and then adjust them as the battle developed, and in response to the elation or despair occasioned by triumph, jealousy or exhaustion. He shirked nothing, but he did sometimes smooth controversy by concessions to a stronger will.

As a tactician he had no rival, but as a strategist he lacked profound foresight. He often arrived at the final solution by a process of trial and error which wasted lives and missed opportunities, as in the central phase of the Tunisian campaign, in Sicily, in correlating Montgomery's operations in Calabria with Clark's at Salerno, at Cassino, and above all in the initial gambit at Anzio. The increased bite of his operations after Harding's arrival as his Chief of Staff shows that his grasp could gain by

281

association with a sharper mind. His estimate that his armies could reach Central Europe before the Russians was over-optimistic, and this was the only occasion, except one, when he questioned the directives given to him. The other was the last offensive in Italy, his most impressive exploit, for it was thought to be impossible. There he revealed most clearly his understanding of the essentials of war. In the last round the Brigadier showed that he was also a Supreme Commander.

15

CANADA

Alan Brooke was 'very very weary' when the war ended, and hoped that the rumour might be true that he was about to be offered the Governor-Generalship of Canada in succession to Lord Athlone. If he were allowed to retire from the Army, he told Churchill, the man who should succeed him as Chief of the Imperial General Staff was Alexander. In the event he remained CIGS for another full year, and it was Alexander who went to Canada.

The news was given to Alexander by Churchill at Potsdam, as they strolled together in the garden of his villa on 16 July 1945. 'I know that Brookie wants you to succeed him as CIGS', said Churchill, 'but Canada is a much more important post, and I hope you will accept it.' Alexander agreed at once, not only out of duty, but because the offer was most attractive to him for several reasons. It was a compliment to have been invited, first by the Canadians, then by Churchill. It was a job of which he thought he could make something. He had a feeling for the dignity of Empire, and the character of the people and the vast spaces of the Canadian north appealed to his romantic instinct. He would be assured of an income, and live in a great house which for the space of several years would become a home where he could unite his family and draw closer to his young children from whom the war had separated him for so long. Ottawa would certainly not be retirement. He did not want that. He was only fifty-four. But it would afford him a period of relief from major responsibilities, and an entirely new experience.

The motives of Mackenzie King, the Canadian Prime Minister, in submitting his name dovetailed with Alexander's own inclinations. Although there was no 'Alex' legend comparable to the 'Monty' legend, he was a wartime hero of the first rank for whom Canadians felt a special regard. His known personality suggested that he would never overstep the constitutional bounds of his office, and although he was an aristocrat by birth and temperament, he was not in any sense a stuffed shirt. The only doubt was whether Canadians might consider that the time had come to appoint a Canadian as the King's representative, and Alexander was in fact the last of the British Governor Generals. But Mackenzie King decided that a break with precedent was premature. He put forward three names to Buckingham Palace, preserving the King's right to decide between them, and said that any one of them would be most acceptable: Lord Airlie, Alexander, and G. M. Trevelyan. Lord Cranborne (later Salisbury), whom Mackenzie King consulted in London, considered that Alexander would be the best choice because he was 'a great soldier, but also a great diplomat, one who would be fond of going about the country to explore the recesses of Canada'.[1] King George VI came independently to the same decision. His private secretary's letter to Mackenzie King spoke of Alexander and his wife in the highest terms and referred to 'his great position as a world figure and as meriting so great a recognition'. Mackenzie King did not need persuasion. He had never met Alexander, but while the decision was still open, he saw in a newspaper a picture of the Alexanders with their son Brian in the garden at The Vale. 'As soon as I saw that picture', he wrote in his journal, 'it settled my mind at once as to his being the right person.' The appointment was announced on 31 July 1945, but Alexander did not assume office until the following April, when Lord Athlone retired.

He returned from Italy in October 1945. The next six months were very busy. The popular acclaim which he had discouraged during the war now found expression. In the New Year's Honours he was created a Viscount, 'of Tunis and Errigal', by which he linked his boyhood to a moment of supreme triumph. At Harrow school he was greeted by the boys with an ovation which they usually reserved for Churchill; and by the Irish Guards as their paragon. He was made a Freeman of the City of London at a ceremony which required him to drive through the streets in a coach loaned from the Royal Mews, to address a huge crowd from the balcony of the Mansion House, and later to speak at a banquet in the Guildhall attended by Attlee, Alanbrooke, Eden and Auchinleck. 'This is my farewell to arms', he said. 'The wartime enemies of the British way of life have gone. But our invincible enemies are fear, fatigue, selfishness, laziness and pessimism.' In the Albert Hall he welcomed the delegates to the first General Assembly of the United Nations with the words: 'We are a nation who hate and detest war, and no one hates it more than we soldiers who have seen at first hand the misery and degradation which it brings. . . . We are conscious of the utter waste of time and sheer stupidity that civilized men should try to resolve their problems by resorting to the laws of the jungle. . . . But at a time of great crisis, some of man's noblest qualities emerge: bravery, enterprise, discipline, self-sacrifice and comradeship.' These are the sentiments expected of veteran soldiers whether they have won or lost their battles. In Alexander's case they were not insincere. Although he had enjoyed the Second War, a feeling of satiety had overcome him which he had not experienced in 1918. War is an adventure and a duty of which, in the broadest terms, mankind must feel ashamed.

He began to prepare himself for Canada. A room in Canada House was set aside for him, and there he spent many hours reading Canadian history and current documents and newspapers, or in conversation with Vincent Massey, the High Commissioner. When Mackenzie King came to London in November, they met for the first time. Alexander impressed him 'as a very able man, not unlike Lord Byng in appearance at the side of his face, and his manner quick, thoughtful, but quite clearly a character welded together. He is rather shy. . . . It is quite clear that he desires to be as tactful a man as can be. Lady Margaret was very quiet. Seems most natural and friendly, of a kind nature. I am sure he will be a real success in Canada. As a man, he is one of the most manly men I have met, and clearly one of the best informed.'

The Alexanders sailed on 4 April 1946 in the *Aquitania* from Southampton, accompanied by their three children (Rose, thirteen, Shane, ten, and Brian, six), a Nanny, and three large sheepdogs. Their arrival at Halifax six days later coincided with one of the heaviest falls of snow which the Maritimes had experienced, but the warmth of their welcome was undiminished by it. Alexander, who disembarked in morning dress, told reporters that his main worry was that he would forget not to return a salute in a top-hat. The crowds were delighted by the immediate evidence of their easy manners. It was noted that among the luggage disembarked was a bundle of shooting-sticks, two cricket-bats, and a large picnic-hamper. For part of the way to Ottawa Alexander drove the special nine-car train, and at intervals they halted to speak to people gathered at country stations, and walk the dogs up and down the snow-covered tracks. When they reached Ottawa on 12 April, they were driven straight from the station to the Parliament buildings through flag-decked streets. There Alexander took his three oaths of office, as Governor General, Commander-in-Chief, and Keeper of the Great Seal of Canada. The speeches were as formal as the occasion. 'We are proud to recognise in Your Excellency', said Mackenzie King, 'one of the great military leaders of world history.' Alexander replied, 'Although I have now said farewell to arms, this does not mean rest and relaxation. On the contrary, there is lots of splendid constructive work to be done, and it will be my aim and privilege to devote myself whole-heartedly to the duties of my office.' The ceremony took only thirty minutes. They then drove to the Governor General's official residence, Rideau Hall, where (according to the *Toronto Telegram*) 'two lines of household servants waited quietly, hearts beating excitedly under crisp aprons and neatly pressed liveries'. A new role, and a totally new way of life, awaited them.

Alexander was Governor General of Canada for six years, 1946–52, as long a period as the entire course of the Second World War. Fortunately there is no need to describe it in as great detail, nor chronologically. What is important is his conception of the office and the totality of his achievement, and this can best be explained by grouping the experiences of these years into three main sections: his constitutional function, his other activities, including the writing of his war despatches, and his journeys through Canada and abroad.

Constitutionally the Governor General has the same relationship to his Ministers as the Sovereign bears to Ministers in the United Kingdom. In general he is bound to act on their advice, and this is a limitation on his initiative and responsibilities. His title of Commander-in-Chief means no more than the Queen's, and the fact that Alexander was also a Field Marshal gave him no more authority over Canada's armed services than if he had been a civilian. Politically he had the theoretical right to refuse assent to Bills, to the appointment of individual Senators or Ministers, and to the dissolution of Parliament. In fact the use of his prerogative was controlled by custom and the need to be seen to be above politics. The famous Byng crisis of 1926 (when the Governor General refused the Prime Minister's request for a dissolution) had sounded a warning to all his successors, although Byng's action had not been in itself unconstitutional. Alexander's function was formal. He

opened, prorogued and dissolved Parliament. He signed Bills and
Orders in Council. He assented to the appointment of leading political
and judicial figures in the State. He was not even the channel of communication between the Canadian and British Governments, a function
performed by their respective High Commissioners, Vincent Massey
and Sir Alexander Clutterbuck. He did not receive Cabinet minutes,
nor meet, except socially, any Ministers except the Prime Minister. He
wrote fortnightly letters to the King, but in them tendered political
comment, perhaps, but seldom political advice.

Alexander observed these mostly unwritten rules meticulously. His
nature was a-political, and he was a great respecter of tradition. He
realized that for a Governor General of little political experience to
oppose the wishes of a Cabinet of highly political men would be not
only improper but foolhardy. It is remarkable that a man who had
exerted such immense authority for six years should have been able to
make the transition to ceremonial powerlessness so quickly and
graciously. He did so because he grasped completely the nature of what
was expected of him. 'I am neither a Governor nor a General', he was
fond of saying. He was the King's representative, not of the King of
England specifically, but of the King in Canada, and he must act like a
sub-King. If he overstepped the mark inadvertently, he was immediately
made aware of it. There were two early instances. Before he left England,
he made the apparently innocuous remark to a journalist that he hoped
'still further to cement the friendship between Canada, Britain and the
United States', only to hear that its propriety had been challenged by
questions in the Canadian House of Commons on the grounds that the
Governor General had nothing to do with executive government. When,
a year later, in a speech to the Canadian Institute of Mining and
Metallurgy, Alexander proposed that the Canadian armed forces might
contribute to the development of Canada's empty regions, the secretary
of the Congress of Labour objected that 'statements of that kind should
come from the properly constituted Government department handling
defence matters'. The triviality of these isolated incidents is itself proof
of how carefully Alexander guarded his tongue, but it made the
necessarily frequent exercise of that tongue more difficult. On major
political issues which arose during his term, such as the incorporation of
Newfoundland as a province of Canada, or the question of a Canadian
citizenship distinct from British, both of which were clearly of concern
to the Crown, he made no public comment at all and was not even

consulted in private. Once only was he required to use his major prerogative, the appointment of a new Prime Minister, and this raised no problem, for Mackenzie King on his retirement in 1948 recommended St Laurent to succeed him, and the office was handed over by one to the other in Alexander's own study at Government House.

The Governor General was, however, frequently consulted by the Prime Minister on matters which were not subjects of immediate political controversy. With Mackenzie King he soon established a mutually respectful relationship. It was in no sense intimate, for King was always careful to observe the protocol, addressing Alexander as Your Excellency and writing 'Dear Governor General', while Alexander found his spiritualism difficult to understand. He wrote to his old friend Shane Leslie: 'I suppose that Mackenzie King's interest in spiritualism is due to the intense love and admiration he had for his mother. There is a picture of her in his sitting-room with a special light thrown on it, and a bowl of flowers always before it. I believe that this is a well-known complex, but I always feel it is somewhat unnatural and rather sinister.' But he found King a courteous man, who never failed to write a long manuscript letter of thanks for every small gesture of hospitality, and he admired his formidable political gifts, particularly his authority in the Cabinet, where he could end an acrimonious discussion by saying, 'Well, gentlemen, we are all agreed', when there had been no sign of an agreement until that moment, and provoke no murmur of dissent to his decisive summing-up.

The Prime Minister visited Alexander about once a fortnight, and their discussions were usually held alone. No minutes were made, and we should know very little of the advice which Alexander gave him were it not that Mackenzie King dictated a detailed daily journal from which Pickersgill has published long extracts since King's death. From these it is clear that Alexander exercised to the full his right to advise and warn, and that King derived much benefit from their talks. They rarely discussed domestic matters, but King consulted him on every aspect of foreign and defence policy. For example, on 9 May 1946, there had been a debate in Cabinet about American strategy in Alaska, and King had expressed to his colleagues the startling opinion that 'the long-range policy of the Americans was to absorb Canada ... and it might be inevitable for us to have to submit to it, being so few in numbers and no longer able to look to British power for protection'. Later that afternoon King outlined the discussion to Alexander:

The Governor General said to me the war has changed the whole problem of strategy. So far as this continent is concerned, the strategy must necessarily be one. The United States, inevitably to protect itself, must take many measures in Canada which Canada herself would not be able to take. This will go on, but in the meantime there will be developments in the world which perhaps before it is too late will result in a sort of US–UK–Canada federation or alliance. Each maintaining our own, but working cooperatively and effectively together. The atomic bomb has changed everything. It has made the north of Canada the vulnerable area of attack of this continent; even the industries of Pittsburgh, etc.

I was struck by the clear vision which he seemed to have of the whole situation.

In November of the same year they talked about a message from Attlee concerning the contribution which Canada might be expected to make towards the cost of Imperial and British defence, and British talks with the Americans on joint defence of the North American continent. 'I let His Excellency know', wrote Mackenzie King, 'how much I deplored this':

I found him very responsive. He spoke very nicely of Attlee's Government. He said he thought Attlee had done a damn good job; that he had a difficult position. No doubt these communications were put in his hand and he just sent them on. I said I knew all this and knew how these matters were done. I said that somebody had to be told that that was not the way our defence relations between the different nations were to be carried out. I told him I was simply discussing the matter with him in a very friendly way, and not with a view to making representations. He said to me he understood that, but he had his relations with the King and others. He thought he could be helpful in these matters; as G.G. it was part of his duty to help in any way he could. I said I was glad to have him to talk to as I could not talk to some of my colleagues on these matters. I found him so fair and reasonable in his attitude ... I returned home feeling much refreshed by the evening's conversation.

One further example must suffice. On 6 December 1947, Mackenzie King lunched at Government House and saw Alexander privately before and afterwards. They discussed the danger of war in Russia:

He said he thought it was better to take a stand at once than to allow things to go on indefinitely. If the latter course were followed, we should all be destroyed. He himself would rather be dead than deprived of his liberty at the instance of the Communists. . . . I much enjoyed my luncheon, and felt a certain freedom in the conversation both before and after luncheon, and at the table, than I have felt at any time.

One difficulty which Alexander was not required to face was the problem of French Canadian separatism. It had not yet arisen in an acute form. Politicians in Quebec would certainly talk of provincial autonomy and raise the cry of Quebec against the Federal power, but made no attempt to stir up racial conflict. Alexander was as well received in Quebec as in the rest of Canada, but he never emphasized his Englishness nor their Frenchness. Had he been less reticent, he could have provoked a crisis. He was careful to invite to Government House more French-speaking Canadians than had his predecessors, and at least once a year spent several weeks in residence in the Governor General's official quarters in the Quebec Citadel. He already spoke French quite well, and improved it by taking lessons from a tutor in Ottawa, Mother St Thomas of La Salle Academy, a lady who insisted that he do his homework, and examined him on it as sternly as a school-child when he returned. Speeches in the French language never came easily to him, and he would ask his French-speaking assistant-secretary, Frank Delaute, to transcribe his English into a French text within his capacity to deliver. In the car on the way to the meeting he would rehearse his speech out loud for the comments of his wife who spoke the language more fluently. 'Come, Alex,' she would say, 'you can do better than that', and he would try again.

Margaret Alexander was the Governor General's greatest asset. When she made her first public appearance in Canada, at the oath-taking ceremony in the Senate Chamber, she was greeted, according to a newspaper report, 'with a sigh of satisfaction', which soon became something much more. There had been Governor Generals before who had out-shone their wives, and wives who had outshone the Governor General, but the Alexanders made a happy balanced partnership, and their love for each other was all the more evident for being undemonstrative. She performed her semi-viceregal task to perfection. As a hostess she was considerate, calm, friendly and competent, the same qualities, indeed, which distinguished Alexander himself. Incapable of irritability, she was firm in her judgements and gracious in her instructions. She thought good manners not a mere convention of civilized life, but its very quality. She overcame her shyness, but never at the cost of her reserve. 'She was a lady whom all other women liked', one of Alexander's staff said to me, 'and that is not an easy thing to achieve in Canada.' She was admired for her successful adaptation to a role which comes naturally to few women, and the effort which it cost her never showed.

Government House, or Rideau Hall, stands in its own park near the Ottawa River, an agglomeration of buildings added to an original semi-Palladian mansion, and shapeless externally apart from its formal entrance porch. Inside, it is well adapted and decorated for its purpose. A hallway opens on the left to a ballroom in the grandest style, and on the right to its surprising contrast, a huge hall hung with canvas like a marquee, known as The Tent Room, which the Alexanders found useful for informal parties. Beyond, there is a large drawing-room which can seat forty or more, a dining-room, a library, a billiard-room, all hung with official portraits of royalty or past Governors. There is present everywhere the gold and vermilion of palaces, expressing official rather than personal taste, but the private apartments are charming, particularly the Governor General's panelled study at the far end of a corridor which dignifies by increasing intimacy and guarded admission the expected guest.

A building for the secretariat is attached to one side. There was necessarily a large staff. The head of it was Major-General H. F. G. Letson, formerly Canadian Adjutant-General and Chairman of the Canadian Joint Staff Mission to Washington. Under him was a French-speaking assistant secretary. There were two British ADCs (of whom one for a period was James Chichester-Clark, later Prime Minister of Northern Ireland), and at least two Canadians. Lady Alexander had as her lady-in-waiting Bridget Vesey and later Jennifer Bevan. The domestic staff, mostly brought from England, and under the Comptroller, Major Mark Milbank, included Wells, Alexander's driver at Dunkirk and throughout the Mediterranean campaigns. It was a household large enough to cater for dinner-parties of up to sixty people, who might include half-a-dozen guests staying in the house. The Alexanders insisted that proper regard be paid to protocol and ceremonial, for the Athlones had been very royal, and their successors did not wish to make too sharp a break with tradition. Formal parties remained formal. When all the guests were assembled, the Governor General and his wife would make an entrance, and Lady Alexander would curtsey to her husband when he arrived and left. There were certain people, Ambassadors, Ministers and other prominent men, who must be periodically invited to Government House with their wives, and they expected to find there a degree of decorum and grandeur which would have horrified them (and their host and hostess) anywhere else in Canada. It represented the 'dignified' part of the Governor General's function, to translate Bagehot's definition to the context of a dominion, in contrast to its 'efficient' part.

Outside these occasions, the Alexanders behaved with the simplicity most natural to them. Unless he was on tour, his life was fairly relaxed. After breakfasting alone with his family, he took a walk and read the newspapers. At 10.30 he saw Letson for half-an-hour, and then received any individuals or delegations who might have appointments. Whenever he could, he joined the garden staff for a glass of beer at noon. After lunch, at which the ADCs were invariably present, he painted or skied, and before dinner read for an hour, unless he had a French lesson.

It doesn't sound very hard work? I asked General Letson.

That's a question of definition. Lord Alexander made the decisions. I carried them out. It was a matter of delegation.

What was he like to work for?

He was always dignified, always friendly, always meticulous in regard to punctuality and so on. He was very easy to work for, if you did your job. You got clear decisions. His manner was that of a considerate Commanding Officer; a plain straightforward man. There were two sides to him: his extreme reserve, and his boyishness, which was a most attractive combination.

His recreations paradoxically were an important part of his activities. The memory which he has left behind in Canada is not that of a statesman in secret consultation with the Prime Minister, nor of a host at grand dinner-parties, nor of the central figure on ceremonial occasions. He is remembered for sharing the life and pleasures of the people. He won the hearts of Canadians by his obvious enjoyment of their country and their way of life. No previous Governor General had mingled with them so unostentatiously. Alexander would drive himself in a jeep to the lakes and mountains around Ottawa, with a pair of skis, his bathing-trunks, a fishing-rod and net, or his easel, tossed into the back. When he skied in the Gatineau hills, or in the Quebec Laurentians, it was in the company of anyone else who happened to be there. They noticed him, but he was not mobbed or photographed. When he painted, it was not in the guarded park of Rideau Hall (though he made a studio there, out of part of an old laundry) but in the open country. If he was invited to kick-off at a football match, he did not give the ball a ceremonial tap, but booted it further than any amateur had done before, having practised assiduously beforehand. A nation of sports-lovers soon came to recognize that he did these things not in the manner of a candidate for political office, but because he enjoyed them. He relished the rigours of the Canadian winter. He was always willing to try his hand at something which might make another man in his position seem ridiculous. Invited to bowl at the Montreal Legion Hall, he scored a strike with the first ball he had ever bowled, knocking all the pins over. At the Calgary stampede Letson found him standing by the pen from which the bulls were released, and he murmured, 'Harry, I think I'll jump on one of those', and was only dissuaded by Letson's reminder that he was due at the Veterans' club in half-an-hour and must not mess up his clothes. Newspaper-reports and photographs show him sliding down a fireman's pole, driving a Prairie harvester, sawing timber, tapping maple-trees, and helping to put out a fire under the orders of a farm-lad who had no idea who he was. His children contributed to his growing legend. Both boys went to Canadian schools, and Rose worked for a time as a secretary in an Ottawa insurance office before going to McGill University. The Alexanders added to their family an adopted baby, Susan, when she was a few weeks old. In the last years of his term he delighted the young people of Ottawa by becoming an addict of square-dancing, imported from Calgary; and expertise in this art, not social status, was the qualification for an invitation. In the winter there were skating-parties. The effect of all these activities is illustrated by an article in the *Ottawa Journal* in February 1949:

The current picture of Lord Alexander is of a highly successful and popular Governor General. We see photos of him in snowshoes and skis sharing our winter-sports and obviously loving it all. We see him entertaining a large group of visiting newspaper editors, cordial, keen, interested, well-informed. We read of his easy democracy, his friendly manner, his complete lack of pretentiousness and self-glorification, his unaffected interest in Canada and Canadians, and we say to ourselves the King is excellently served by so admirable a representative, and Canada too.

Official visitors to Canada were entertained and lodged at Government House, and Alexander found that he already knew the majority of them. Some were close friends. Among them were Churchill, President Truman, Eisenhower (before his Presidency), President Auriol of

France, Prince Bernhard of the Netherlands, Nehru, Wavell, the Duke and Duchess of Windsor, Mountbatten, Alanbrooke, Mark Clark, Montgomery. These guests put the Alexanders and their household to tests of tact and administration to which they were well accustomed, and they were never found wanting, even when Churchill (who in his old age became increasingly indifferent to the social courtesies) sent down a message shortly before dinner that he felt disinclined that night to sit between two women and wished his neighbours at the table to be Alexander and Mackenzie King. A more agreeable occasion was the visit of Princess Elizabeth and the Duke of Edinburgh in October 1951, a few months before the Queen's accession. Alexander held a barn-dance in their honour, to which he invited eighty other young people. The royal couple were apt pupils for this unfamiliar dance, and dressed to suit the occasion, the Princess in a short blue skirt and brown checkered blouse, the Duke in blue jeans. Alexander himself wore a vivid checked shirt and a buckskin jacket which he had been given at Calgary.

These events were well publicized. But one of Alexander's pre-occupations at Government House was quite unknown to the public. He was compiling his despatches on the African and Italian campaigns. He did not regard himself as a natural writer; his style was rather pedestrian, and easy as he had found it to dictate reasoned memoranda on higher strategy, the drama of the war had been staled by the lapse of time. The labour of rereading and arranging in narrative form the vast accumulation of wartime documents, all of which had been shipped to Ottawa, made no appeal to him. He was anxious that the record should be full, fair and accurate, but he needed help. He therefore invited David Hunt, who had served on his Intelligence staff in Africa and Italy, to join him for that purpose.

Hunt spent nearly a year at Government House, from June 1946 to May 1947. He wrote the drafts of the despatches, basing them on the documents, his own recollection and frequent discussions with Alexander himself. As the different sections were completed, he submitted them to the Field Marshal for his approval. Alexander made very few changes. He might occasionally comment to Hunt, 'You've been a bit hard on So-and-so', but on the main sequence of events and the evolution of his strategic plans he was in agreement with what Hunt had written, for Hunt used whenever possible the actual words of the orders and directives which Alexander had written at the time, and knew intimately the working of his Chief's mind.

A Commander-in-Chief's despatch is not autobiography, nor is it, as history, wholly objective. Alexander naturally did not wish to criticize his subordinates, even when he knew that they had been wrong, nor reveal in so official a document the occasions when strong disagreement had ruffled Allied unity. Nor would it be natural for him to admit in his despatch his own errors of judgement or retrospective thoughts on how this or that battle might have been more economically won. A despatch is a record of how he saw things at the time, why he took certain decisions, and what consequences flowed from them. His despatches are therefore not free from special pleading or slurring over mistakes, his own or other people's, and were not expected to be. Nevertheless they are among the great state-papers of our military history.

The despatches were not published in the precise form of the original drafts. The drafts were submitted for comment to various Government departments, including the other services and the Foreign Office, to ensure that no offence was given nor unmentionable secrets revealed. A long list of suggested amendments or modifications reached Alexander from these various quarters, including those of Montgomery, then CIGS, who confined himself to substituting in the pre-Alamein section of the Africa despatch the words 'General Montgomery decided' for Alexander's 'I decided', amendments which Alexander sometimes accepted and sometimes did not. For instance, the draft version dealing with the plan to defend Alam Halfa had run: 'I adopted this plan of defence in principle.' In the despatch as printed, it reads: 'General Montgomery accepted this plan in principle, to which I agreed.' One amendment from the Foreign Office was resisted: in describing Eighth Army's advance from Alamein to Tunisia, Hunt had written that it was equivalent to an advance from London to Moscow. The Foreign Office thought this comparison somewhat provocative. Hunt's offer to substitute 'an advance from Moscow to London' was not thought funny.

When the despatches were published in the early 1950s, the only criticism which they aroused was in Italy, where from sensational extracts published out of context it was assumed that Alexander had written indifferently about the contribution of the Italian partisans and anti-Fascist politicians. This was not so. As the full despatch shows, Alexander believed more than the Americans in the value of the resistance movements, and did most to support them. The controversy aroused by his despatch in Italy was fierce but short-lived.

One further echo of the immediate past reached Ottawa. It was announced in November 1946 that Kesselring was to be put on trial by a British War Tribunal for crimes against humanity, and his defence counsel asked Alexander for a testimonial which could be used to rebut the charge. Alexander, anxious to avoid involving his office in an acutely controversial matter, replied that he could not provide any statement to the defence or prosecution, but would be willing to give information if he were asked for it by the President of the Tribunal. No such request reached him, and Kesselring was condemned to death in April 1947. Churchill cabled to Alexander, 'Am concerned about Kesselring's death sentence, and propose to raise question in Parliament. Can you do anything?' Alexander answered: 'I too am concerned, and will do what I can. What do you suggest?' Churchill advised that he should make his views known to the Prime Minister, and Alexander did so. He cabled Attlee, 'I am unhappy about Kesselring's sentence. I hope it will be commuted. Personally, as his old opponent on the battlefield, I have no complaint against him. Kesselring and his soldiers fought hard but clean.' The message was passed to the Court of Appeal in Italy, and undeniably had an influence upon their decision to commute the death-sentence to one of imprisonment for twenty years.

As a change from his many activities in Ottawa, Alexander greatly looked forward to his journeys in other parts of Canada, seeing in them the civilian equivalent to his frequent wartime visits to the front, and wishing to undo the tradition that Government House was the focus of the Governor General's life and function. As these journeys were necessarily official, they were encumbered by many engagements which were arduous or repetitive. The same type of person received the Governor General's party at place after place, served them the same chicken and wine, demanded the same speeches and made much the same conversation. He was required to perform all the ceremonies familiar from accounts of royal tours – to open bridges, lay the foundation-stones of hospitals, receive honorary degrees, address veteran associations and distribute medals, show himself to crowds of schoolchildren. He performed these functions with energy and good grace. He was physically very fit, and Lady Alexander, who usually accompanied him, was young. He insisted, for instance, that no award of decorations should be skimped: the citation must be read out in full, for it was a great moment in a young man's life to have his merit recognized by the King's representative. Whenever he saw an opportunity to give more pleasure than offence, he broke the strict protocol of his visits, and descended among the crowds.

It was said by Canadians that he saw more of Canada than any of his sixteen predecessors, travelling 184,000 miles in Canada alone during the six years of his term. He sought out Canadians everywhere – in the cities, on the land and in the backwoods, in the Maritimes, in Quebec, in Ontario, in the prairie provinces, on the Pacific coast, in the north-west and in the Yukon. He penetrated far beyond the Arctic Circle to Aklavik, to Whitehorse, Yellow Knife, and Port Churchill on the Hudson Bay, flying over territories where the only signs of life were the camps of prospectors, fishermen and Government surveyors. The development of Canada was a subject which fascinated him, as it had his grandfather a hundred years before. Like him, too, he made friends with the Indians, who honoured him at Vancouver with the title of Chief Willie Scow at a full tribal ceremony never previously accorded to a white man. He encouraged by his visits the toil and enterprise of men who were discovering and extracting the wealth of Canada's rocks and soil. He read extensively about mining and industry. When the party was visiting, say, a paper-pulp region, he would ask Letson to give him a full brief beforehand, and the chairman of the company would be warned to bring his technical experts with him to answer questions beyond his competence, for Alexander was certain to ask them. At Leduc in Alberta he was present at the first strike of oil. At Sudbury, Ontario, both Alexanders went down a nickel mine. Examples could be multiplied, but let one account, in *Time* magazine of October 1946, stand for many other tributes to his energy:

The Dominion's most industrious gadabout was back again in Ottawa last week, cheerful as ever after a coast-to-coast tour. In fifteen weeks Alexander had travelled 15,000 miles, visited all nine provinces, made 52 speeches, decorated 400 war-veterans. He also collected 38 parchment scrolls of welcome, keys to Vancouver and Charlottetown, a silver trowel, six 30-lb salmon.

Alexander also went abroad, on official or private visits. Three times he was in the United States, first as the guest of President Truman in the White House, then privately in other parts of the country. Once in Hollywood he was invited to watch the making of a film about the Second War. Alexander happened to be wearing the full uniform of a Field Marshal, as he was due to inspect a guard of honour at San

Francisco later in the day, and an actor, mistaking him for an extra, slapped him on the back: 'Who's your dresser? He must be a genius. He's got your medals just as if they were real.' Such incidents were godsent material for yet another after-dinner speech. He inspected at Seattle Canadian troops about to embark for Korea; he gave an address at the University of California in Los Angeles; he was at West Point; and several times in New York. He was seen and recognized everywhere in the United States, and his presence gave people as much pleasure as their welcome gave him.

His most ambitious journey abroad was to Brazil in June 1948, in fulfilment of a promise given to President Dutra during the war to visit the veterans of the Brazilian division which came under his command in Italy. He flew there from Ottawa, in stages to suit the limited range of his special Dakota, first to Florida, then to Haiti and Trinidad, and so to Rio. His reception was overwhelming, beginning with showers of confetti from high buildings on the route from the airport to the guestpalace where the Alexanders were accommodated. Between banquets and his inspection of two whole divisions of Brazilian troops, he was taken to the races, where the main event was rechristened Grand Prix Viscomte Alexandre de Tunis. It was a six-day visit, the first ever paid by a Governor General of Canada to a South American country. The Alexanders loved it.

There were holidays. Three times Alexander returned to England, once for the Victory Parade in London. But usually they sought some remote retreat in Canada, where Alexander could fish and paint, and the children could bathe, such as Twin Islands off the coast of British Columbia, where they were not even in telephonic touch with Ottawa, or a shooting-lodge in Silver Valley not far from Vancouver, or in Prince Edward Island, or in the Jasper National Park, Alberta. They varied the pattern of their holidays year by year to explore different parts of Canada and let Canadians know that they considered themselves in every sense their compatriots.

His five-year term of office ending in 1951 was twice extended by a further six months and might well have been further prolonged had Churchill not invited Alexander to join his Cabinet as Minister of Defence. On 24 January 1952 the news of his retirement was made public and it was announced simultaneously that Vincent Massey was to succeed him. To mark his departure both countries added to his titular honours. He was already (1946) a Knight of the Garter. Now he was created an Earl, taking the designation 'of Ottawa and of Castle Derg, Co. Tyrone', and his elder son became Lord Rideau. As a signal mark of their esteem the Canadians made him a Privy Councillor, the first Governor General to be so honoured, but no constitutional means could be found to gratify his dearest wish, to hold Canadian as well as British citizenship. He formally gave up his post on 28 January 1952, and two weeks later sailed from Halifax to England, embarking at the same pier where he had landed six years earlier. The farewell celebrations were muted owing to the death of King George VI a week earlier, but Alexander broadcast to the Canadian nation:

It is not my personal wish to go before my term of office as your Governor General is ended, but I go because I believe it is my duty to take on other responsibilities which I have been asked to assume. Let me tell you that my wife and I have spent the happiest six years of our life among you, and that our children who have grown up as young Canadians love this country and its people as we do. For us Canada has become our second home. I have been intimately acquainted with the Canadian people both in war and peace, and I am proud to have had the privilege of witnessing at first hand the rise of a new nation, which is going to play an ever-growing role in the world's affairs.

Alexander's achievement was to make the Crown acceptable to Canadians, not by referring to it frequently (for he seldom did) but by his implicit reminder of its existence and by his own example. By his dignity and friendliness he represented the Sovereign to the people in the light that was most agreeable to them. During his tenure of office there was never any mention of ending the formal ties with the Crown. He felt this responsibility deeply. By his bearing he symbolized the respect of Crown for people, and of the people for the Crown. He had an amalgam of qualities, some of them intangible, which enabled him to combine informality off-duty with the capacity to assume the most dignified posture when required. One Canadian newspaper described his Governor-Generalship as 'a happy chapter in the history of Rideau Hall, unmarred by bitterness or error'. Another printed above their farewell message the simple headline, 'Goodbye Alex'. *The Times* of London commented: 'It has been a success of personality. While remaining completely British, Lord Alexander has identified himself with Canada to an extent rare, if not unique, in the long succession of

Governor Generals. Without seeking popularity, he has done the things that have made him popular.' We can see now that his achievement went a good deal further than mere popularity. His reputation and acclaim in the United States was of the greatest benefit to Canada. So was the experience which he could put at the service of his two Canadian Prime Ministers. His Governor-Generalship was not only a triumph of tact and charm, but of wisdom and an unwavering sense of duty.

16

MINISTER OF
DEFENCE

When his term as Governor General of Canada was drawing to a close, Alexander received a number of offers of fresh employment. At one time or another it was suggested, more or less officially, that he might go to Washington as British Ambassador, or to Australia, New Zealand or Northern Ireland as Governor General; that he might become Chairman of the Anglo-French Channel Tunnel Association; join the board of ICI or BSA; or become President of the British Legion. If he felt any inclination to accept one of these offers, it was dispelled by Churchill's own. He invited him to join his Government as Minister of Defence.

He put this suggestion to Alexander while he was his guest at Government House in Ottawa in January 1952. On the same occasion he asked Gerald Templer, then GOC Eastern Command, whom he had summoned to Canada, to take over command of British troops in Malaya. Templer has described the scene to me:

On the last day of Churchill's visit, I went to bed at 1 am and was fast asleep when Alex's ADC knocked on my door and told me that the Prime Minister wished to see me at once. I dressed and went downstairs to the study. When I came in, Alex was standing at the high marble mantelpiece with his arms folded across it, absolutely exhausted (for he was a man who liked to go to bed at 10 pm), and Churchill was lying full-length on a sofa, with a cigar in one hand and a brandy-and-soda in the other. He asked me to go to Malaya. I accepted . . . , and then the old man heaved himself up and went to bed.

I asked Alex to stay behind for a moment, and we briefly discussed Malaya. Then he said: 'But what about me? I've got the Ministry of Defence.' I said, 'But you didn't take it, did you?' 'Yes, of course I did. It's my duty.' I said,

'But, Alex, for heaven's sake don't. You'll make the most imperial nonsense of it. You'll get mixed up with all those politicians.' 'Oh no I won't,' he answered. 'I'll be in the House of Lords.' He really felt that as a peer, a Field Marshal, a Knight of the Garter, only going to Cabinet meetings and so on, he could avoid the rough and tumble of political life.

Lady Alexander says that he 'hated the very idea of the job' when it was offered to him. 'He did it because he thought he ought to. If they felt that he was the right man, he must do it. It was his duty.' To Seago he said, 'I can't get out of it. I simply can't refuse Winston.'

Churchill's motives are equally clear. When he became Prime Minister for the second time in October 1951 he at first decided to be his own Minister of Defence, as he was during the war, but soon found that with his advancing age and the press of other business, the two offices were more than he could manage in combination. He wanted someone to run the Ministry while he retained control of its policy, and he chose Alexander because he was an old friend with a leading reputation, who could be trusted not to challenge the Prime Minister's domination of a field which he had made his own. When the appointment was announced it did not escape criticism. Nobody said a word against Alexander himself nor his fitness for the job, but Labour Members questioned whether a Field Marshal would be able to form a judgement independent of the Chiefs of Staff, 'who would regard him as one of them'. *The Times* commented that there were already four 'non-political' peers in the Cabinet (Simonds, Ismay, Leathers and Cherwell), and 'leaders should absorb the art of politics in the only school where it may be learnt', by long service in the House of Commons. Alexander would be the first regular soldier to join the Cabinet since the Duke of Wellington, it was said (inaccurately, for Ismay was another), and the precedent was not considered a happy one.

Alexander arrived home on 26 February, dined with Churchill next night, was sworn in as a Privy Councillor, and on 29 February attended his first Cabinet meeting. On 5 March he listened from the Peers Gallery to Churchill's speech introducing the Defence White Paper. It was symptomatic of their future relationship.

Alexander suffered from two disadvantages as Minister of Defence. His powers were not clearly defined; and he was not by temperament a politician. Each disadvantage accentuated the other. Because he was a-political, he found it difficult to assert himself in Cabinet debates; and because he was seen to be unwilling or unable to shape his Ministry according to his own ideas, others were quick to take the initiative from him. Harold Macmillan has written that in those days the Minister of Defence was 'a coordinator, not a master'. There was no clear frontier drawn between his powers and those of the First Lord of the Admiralty (J. P. L. Thomas) and the Secretaries of State for War (Antony Head) and Air (Lord De L'Isle). None of the three was himself in the Cabinet, but all were members of the Cabinet Defence Committee, over which Churchill presided in person, and he turned naturally to each of them, and to their Chiefs of Staff, for comment and advice. The Minister of Defence was left in a void. A man of strong political will could have imposed his authority, but Alexander did not have that type of mind or ambition. He was content to let the others have not only their say but their way, and tended to respond to circumstances instead of moulding them. His Parliamentary Secretary, Nigel Birch (now Lord Rhyl), has described to me what happened:

I liked him very much. My personal relations with him could not have been better. You couldn't quarrel with him in any way. But it was terribly difficult to get anything done. He had no desire to control the Service Ministers, no wish to reform the system. He looked on himself as Chairman of a Committee. He didn't want to change anything. He knew that if he tried, it would mean a row, and his one wish was to cause as little trouble as possible by interfering as little as possible. I was younger then, and burning with energy, and used to put up my ideas to him, for instance on our nuclear policy or getting the Treasury to agree our estimates in outline three years ahead so that we could plan properly. But these ideas never got anywhere. Alex wasn't really interested. He hated reading long documents. On the other hand, he'd do anything that Winston wanted him to do. Often, when we'd agreed with the Service Ministers on a certain line of argument, and it came to the Cabinet Defence Committee, Alex would go back on what we'd agreed because Winston wanted something different. It was all very frustrating.

But during the war, and in Canada, he'd been used to handling problems of this sort, and dealing with powerful personalities. Why do you think he didn't exert himself more?

He'd had a pretty easy time in Canada, and he was no longer young. He had been a sort of king there, and people don't push you around when you're a king. Even a Field Marshal's life can be fairly sheltered, because he's surrounded by staff officers and seldom appears on his own at a conference. But when you're a Minister, you have to stand up in Parliament

303

alone, you have to appear in Cabinet alone. Alex didn't like that. He had no political feeling at all.

Was it simply that he didn't understand politics? Or did he actually despise it, and think politicians rather second-rate people?

I think that both are true up to a point. Occasionally I used to try to brief him for a Cabinet meeting. I'd say: 'This subject's coming up. A will say this, and B will say that. Perhaps your answer might be so-and-so.' He'd reply, 'Oh but surely they wouldn't say that, would they?' Of course they always did. He wasn't used to that rough world.

How did he get on in House of Lords debates?

All his speeches were written for him. He would take the office-brief pretty well straight. Occasionally he would add something of his own, but very rarely. Of course, you can read a brief well or you can read it badly, and Alex read his well. But he couldn't cope easily with unexpected interventions. In the Commons he would have had a terrible time. But they have better manners in the Lords, and of course he had tremendous prestige. Everybody loved him.

He had another advantage, that he already knew almost everybody. In the Cabinet were many of his close friends, like Churchill himself, Eden, Butler, Macmillan, Walter Monckton, Maxwell Fyfe, Oliver Lyttelton. The leading men in NATO when he assumed office were Eisenhower, Montgomery and Al Gruenther. Harding was CIGS. Alexander admitted that he enjoyed this partial re-creation of the war-time fraternity, and it stimulated him to be back once more in the centre of events. Yet the atmosphere was now wholly different. He was a member of a Conservative Government, answerable to Parliament, and ultimately to a vast Party organization outside with which he could never identify himself. He was shaken to discover that in politics deviousness was regarded as quite normal. When he said exactly what he thought on some subject which arose in a Cabinet discussion, Churchill commented, 'In all the years that I've been in the Cabinet, that's the first time I've ever heard anyone answer a question absolutely straight.' On another occasion (but the story may be apocryphal) Churchill turned to him with a question about Service pensions, and Alexander replied, 'I think we ought to do what is right.' 'Well,' said Churchill, 'that's the most subversive political doctrine that I've ever heard.' Alexander found political subterfuge not merely dishonest but highly confusing. Harding once accompanied him to a plenary meeting of the NATO Council in Paris:

At the end of the first morning's session I asked him what he made of it all. He replied that he 'Didn't like it, didn't like it at all', and in response to my question 'Why?', he replied that he'd been confused, and he didn't like being confused. He had found it difficult to follow the discussion, most of which had seemed to him irrelevant, or unconnected with the items on the Agenda – and at the same time the Foreign Secretary (Anthony Eden) had kept passing him notes on entirely different subjects. He could handle politicians effectively as an individual and on an objective basis, but his simple faith of duty and loyalty put him out of sympathy with their manoeuvres in the corridors of power.[1]

He thought politics, compared to soldiering, dirty. He was at a loss when confronted by intellectual brilliance and quick changes of tactics, and never appreciated the art and dexterity of political argument. He stigmatized as 'intrigue' the tactical processes, the checks and balances, the implicit bargaining element in debate, natural to men who hope to influence great decisions; and as 'plotting' the lobbying required to win assent for policies in which they deeply believed. To a soldier loyalty is the supreme virtue, superior even to courage: to a politician a colleague's obstruction is simply one of the hazards of office. Alexander thought it as dreadful to oppose your leader in an hour of crisis as to shoot the Colonel in the back as he leads you into battle. 'Fighting your own corner', which Churchill once described as among a Minister's chief functions, seemed to him ill-mannered and motivated by a lust for personal power. So he opted out of the political struggle, with the result that his uncomplicated niceness ceased to be effectual. He hated politics because he did not fit in.

Alexander was Minister of Defence for two and a half years, from March 1952 till October 1954. It was a period of great complexity in foreign and defence affairs, for Britain's importance in the world was declining, and she was reluctant to admit it. We were attempting to rearm with modern weapons which we could not afford without curtailing important domestic programmes like Macmillan's 300,000 new houses which had been an election pledge. We were refusing to become part of the new Europe except by 'association' with the abortive European Defence Community, because we still hoped to play a role on the worldwide stage. Our position in the Middle East and South-East Asia was challenged. There were the wars in Korea, Malaya and Indo-China, the problems of the Suez base, of Persian oil and the future of the Sudan. There was the continuing Berlin crisis, the question of German re-armament, the development of the H-bomb and the protests which it aroused at home. In the middle of Alexander's term Stalin died. In all these matters the responsibilities of the Foreign and Defence Ministers were intertwined, and when Alexander resigned his office, Eden wrote to him a generous letter which shows that their partnership, though unequal, was, on a day-to-day basis, a helpful one:

Defence and Foreign Affairs are intimately linked, and you have been so patient and understanding on many intractable problems. In particular, we could never have solved our Egyptian and Sudanese problems (if they are solved) without you, and in Buraimi, Germany and everywhere else, you helped us so much.

Until the contemporary state documents can be examined, it will be impossible to say exactly what Alexander's contribution was. No important initiative is publicly associated with his name, and the leading political Memoirs of the period, Eden's, Butler's and Mac-millan's, seldom mention it. It seems probable that Alexander carried out loyally the higher policy decided by more powerful Ministers, and gave his influential backing to proposals which he would not himself have originated. On only a few occasions did he figure prominently in the newspapers, and of these the most important was when he went with Selwyn Lloyd (Minister of State at the Foreign Office) to Korea in June 1952, within three months of assuming office. For the only time in his life he kept a diary of this journey, which supplements the published records of his mission.

Its main purpose was to see for himself the conditions of the Korean war and visit the Commonwealth Division, assess the chances of an armistice with the Chinese, and allay public disquiet in Britain about the intentions of the American command and the South Korean Govern-ment of Singman Rhee. There had been a number of incidents (martial law, imprisonment of political opponents) which created the suspicion that Singman Rhee was a dictator who denied to his own people the democratic rights for which the United Nations claimed to be fighting, and that his main purpose was to force the Americans to reconquer the whole country, even at the risk of precipitating a third World War. Armistice talks were in progress at Panmunjon, but local fighting continued, and it seemed possible that the talks would break down on the question of the repatriation of the thousands of Chinese prisoners-of-war who had declared themselves anti-Communist. The Chinese claimed their return; the United Nations refused. On 28 May 1952 the Prime Minister gave the House a depressing account of these events. The Communist forces numbered nearly a million, and if unlimited war were resumed, the consequences could be very grave. He announced that Alexander had received and accepted an invitation from General Mark Clark, Commander-in-Chief of the UN forces in Korea, to visit him. Alexander himself gave the same information to the House of Lords.

He and Lloyd left London on 6 June in the same aircraft which had brought the Queen home from Kenya after her father's death. They flew by stages to Delhi, where they breakfasted with Nehru and his sister Mrs Pandit, and then continued to Tokyo by Rangoon, Bangkok, Hong Kong and Okinawa, stopping at each place to refuel or spend the night. Alexander was seeing the Far East for the first time since his Burma campaign. In Tokyo they were extremely busy. They called on the Prime Minister, Shigeru Yoshida, whom Alexander found 'a man of intelligence and charm, and a gentleman', and told him that 'if Japan wanted friendship with the British, they must settle amicably the matter of the judicial and financial problems of British forces in Japan'. They then met the Emperor, who was 'shy and nervous. . . . When I asked him if he thought that the Chinese were genuinely wanting an armistice in Korea, he pointedly said that he could not answer that because he was not kept informed by his Ministers.' After talks with the Foreign Minister of Japan, they returned to Mark Clark's headquarters, and with him and the American Ambassador (Robert Murphy, an old friend from 1943 in North Africa) they raised one of the main questions which they had come to settle.

The British Ministers asked for a British representative to be attached both to the armistice delegation at Panmunjon and to Mark Clark's headquarters. 'We all agreed that a representative on the armistice talks had disadvantages as well as advantages,' wrote Alexander in his journal; but in his reminiscences, Mark Clark puts it much more strongly:

I knew the British were impatient for a truce, and upset over the prisoner-of-war situation and the measures we were taking to get matters under control. I welcomed the chance for two of their leaders to see at first hand what we were up against, but I was dead set against changing the composition of our truce team. A change such as that during the critical stage of negotiations would only be an indication of weakness and indecision to the Communists. It would give them hope that differences of opinion between America and Britain had become more acute. . . . I am sure our Government would never have agreed to British representation at Panmunjon. If nothing else, it would have raised the question of other United Nations participating in the talks. I convinced Alex of the inadvisability of such a move.[2]

On the second suggestion, that a British officer should be attached to his headquarters, Clark could be more accommodating. He agreed to the appointment of a British Deputy Chief of Staff, provided that General Omar Bradley (Chairman of the Joint Chiefs of Staff in Washington) also agreed. Thus it was arranged. Major-General S. N. Shoosmith, whom Clark had known in Italy, was sent to Korea in July, responsible to Clark and not in direct communication with London, and his presence at Clark's headquarters helped to quieten British fears that Korea was becoming almost exclusively an American theatre of war. It was the most tangible result of Alexander's visit.

Next day, 13 June, he flew to Korea itself and spent three days visiting Commonwealth and other troops in the front-line, and naval and air-bases behind it, as well as the main prisoner-of-war camp at Koje, where rioting had only recently subsided. He wrote in his diary:

I flew by helicopter just behind our front line, and had a wonderful view of No Man's Land and the Chinese positions. Our forward position is a naturally strong one, and commanding magnificent observation. . . . I am impressed by three things: (a) the lavish scale of first-class equipment and the efficiency of the whole set-up; (b) the immense organisation and equipment which seems necessary for modern war; (c) the good discipline and high morale.

Returning to Pusan on 16 June, he and Selwyn Lloyd called on Singman Rhee, the seventy-eight-year-old President of South Korea:

I found him a very charming and courteous old gentleman, much younger-looking than his years. I believe him to be a sincere patriot who believes that what he is doing is right and for the best, but his Asiatic manner of doing it is quite unlike what we think can or cannot be done in a European democracy. I told him something about the front which I had visited for three days, and said that I felt somewhat perturbed as a military man that the situation in the rear of the Armies was not quite as stable as it ought to be. I also told him that Parliament and people at home were disturbed at political events in South Korea. Mr Rhee said that he had been misrepresented and the British people had not been correctly informed of his good intentions.

I replied that this was his fault. He had put on martial law for no very apparent reason, and had kept it on for nearly a month although he had promised General van Fleet [GOC Eighth Army in Korea] some time ago that he was going to take it off soon. . . .

I said that it would help if he would give me a message for Mr Churchill which was satisfactory. His message was not a very clear-cut one, but amounted to his gratitude for the help and assistance he was receiving from the British, and that if Mr Churchill would have a little patience he would see that all would be well, and it would be shown that Mr Singman Rhee had been right and had taken the best course.

These were the main events of Alexander's visit. He flew from Tokyo to Canada on 18 June by the northern route through Alaska, and then south to Washington where he gave President Truman and General Bradley an account of his experiences. He also visited the UN Head-quarters in New York. He arrived back in London on 25 June, having completed the circuit of the globe in nineteen days.

That might have been the end of a successful mission but for two controversies which subsequently marred it. Soon after his return, Alexander found himself the victim of an error in Allied communications which was in no sense his fault, and of a slip of the tongue which certainly was.

While he was with Bradley in Washington on 23 June he was given the news that the Americans had bombed the huge hydro-electric works of Suiho on the Yalu river, the boundary between North Korea and Manchuria. It was the heaviest raid of the war. Clark's motive was to give teeth to the American negotiating position at Panmunjon, 'to bomb them where I could hurt the Communists worst', as he said to me in 1970, 'so that we could return to the conference-table where meaningful things could take place.' To the British it seemed that it was needlessly provocative to deliver such a damaging blow while armistice talks were in progress, and Attlee asked why, when our Minister of Defence had just been with General Clark in Korea and was at that very moment in Washington, we had not been consulted or even informed. Eden replied that Clark had obtained the approval of the Joint Chiefs of Staff before the bombing, but 'it was regrettable' that the British Government had not also been told. Clark's account of the affair was that 'although I would have informed Alexander of the Suiho bombing as a matter of courtesy, the authorization did not come from Washington until after he had gone'.[3] It would nevertheless have been wiser to tell him of the plan, for by this oversight it was made to appear that Alexander did not enjoy the complete confidence of his old friend and subordinate of the Italian campaign. He was not held to blame, but Aneurin Bevan made a ritual demand for his resignation on the strength of a press-report that Alexander had said in Washington, 'Personally I am in favour of the bombing, as the power-plants are undoubtedly military targets.' The incident passed off without further trouble. The plants were bombed several times again, but the Communists did not break off the talks in protest, and a truce was eventually signed in July 1953.

The second incident was, for Alexander, more unfortunate. On 1 July he made in the House of Lords a statement about his Korean visit, declaring that in his opinion a new Chinese offensive could be halted within a few miles of its start-line. That night he spoke in London at the Dominion Day dinner at the Canada Club. There were 500 people present, but he assumed that it was a private gathering, and qualified his earlier statement to Parliament by adding: 'There are weaknesses in Korea, one of which I did not like to mention to the House of Lords.' When someone shouted, 'Why not?', Alexander replied, 'Because it is a thing I was asked not to mention as a matter of secrecy', and then continued, 'I should be very much happier if General van Fleet had a little more reserve in his own hand.' There were press-reporters present. His remarks were on the wire within the hour, and the Tass Agency was one of those which picked them up. The news was stopped from appearing in the British press by Alexander's personal appeal, but it nevertheless became public knowledge next day. Churchill heard it at 3 am and telephoned at once to Alexander to ask for his explanation. That afternoon the House of Commons questioned the Prime Minister on the incident for a whole hour. Churchill reiterated that Alexander had thought he was speaking in private, and while the word 'secrecy' was no doubt unfortunately chosen, there had been no breach of military security, because it would be obvious to the Chinese that a military commander is never satisfied with the strength of his reserves. If Alexander had included the remark in his public statement, it would have passed without comment. It was only the 'secrecy' context which had given it undue prominence.

In the House of Lords they were kinder to Alexander than in the Commons. 'It is said that a good rider must have three falls', said Lord Jowitt. 'The same thing applies to a politician, who must have three indiscretions before he is condemned.' In fact Alexander was never in need of his third chance. The remainder of his term of office passed without reprimand from any quarter, but the experience of these terrible pitfalls of office did not endear him to his new role.

Among the many clichés with which the Ministry padded out his speeches was this specimen: 'I would not like to leave the impression that everything in the garden is rosy and that we have nothing to worry about. There is a long pull before we reach the top of the hill, which is still a long way off and will mean many sacrifices.' Alexander read out these flyblown sentences without a blush, because he was not a man who cared much for the niceties of style, and because the essence of them was true. He found a new problem on his desk every day. Always better at personal negotiations than in conference or on paper, he sought out privately the Defence Ministers of his NATO allies, and discussed with them what he understood best, the organization of a multinational force. With M. Pleven, for instance, his French opposite number, he worked out in detail the implication of the Eden Plan for British association with a European army – the training of EDC forces alongside the British, the cooperation of their air forces, a British liaison mission, the training of German army and air-force cadres in Britain, and the placing of the British Army on the Rhine under a European commander. He was also excellent at the set-piece exposition, as when he addressed the Commonwealth Prime Ministers on the distribution of British forces throughout the world. He much enjoyed his tours abroad as the official guest of other NATO countries, or to watch exercises in Germany, Holland and Scandinavia. Only once again as Minister of Defence did he revisit the United States and Canada, when in July 1954 he lunched with Eisenhower at the White House, inspected missile-bases, and opened the Commonwealth Games at Vancouver.

At home his official engagements included the Farnborough Air Display, taking the salute at the RMC (Sandhurst) and at the RAF College at Cranwell, unveiling war-memorials, opening the Motor Show, attending the Alamein reunion at the Albert Hall. He had little to do with the Conservative Party in or outside Parliament. Once he addressed the Party's annual conference at Scarborough, and once he spoke at a constituency meeting, for R. A. Butler at Saffron Walden.

Compared to other senior Ministers he had a politically easy time.

He would have thought it improper, even if he had had the knowledge, to speak up in Cabinet on matters outside his Department's responsibility, like Harold Macmillan, Minister of Housing, who pressed almost to the point of resignation his dismay at Britain's apparent indifference to the growing unity of Europe. Alexander cared about Britain's position in the world. He told Nigel Birch a few days after assuming office that he considered it his duty to arm the British people, not disarm them, but when it came to reconciling the cost of it with competitive claims from other departments, he did not 'fight his corner', and was prepared to accept the Treasury's arbitration and the advice of his civil servants, telling the Foreign Press Association, 'We cannot afford military security at the expense of national bankruptcy.' The expenditure of the Service Departments, however, still totalled £1,600 million a year. When the Americans tested their hydrogen bomb, Churchill, wildly excited, insisted that Britain must have one too. Alexander could not sustain an argument against it, and was in any case convinced that conventional forces must be replaced by nuclear deterrents 'awful in their character', as Churchill wrote to him, 'and largely beyond human control or even comprehension'. The deterrent made it easier for Alexander to agree to the proposed evacuation of the Suez base. 'It is right and wise', he said in Vancouver, 'since the nuclear bomb has made it needless to concentrate troops in a small area.' He was speaking as a soldier who had commanded the Canal zone for several critical months, but when he was asked by the Conservative Foreign Affairs Committee whether he thought evacuation a sound policy politically, he replied (as recorded in the opening pages of this book) that such decisions belonged to his colleagues, not to him. R. A. Butler, who was also present, intervened to lessen the consternation which this strange remark occasioned.

Alexander was not a failure as Minister of Defence. He just never tried very hard to be a great success. He was fortunate in the protection and advice of a solicitous staff, in having Service Ministers who knew their own minds, and a Parliament Secretary who relieved him of the chief burdens of political controversy, and most of all in the guidance, indeed instructions, of the triumvirate of Prime Minister, Foreign Secretary and Chancellor of the Exchequer. His public reputation was not enhanced by his years as a politician, but it was certainly not diminished. His two small errors of judgement were soon forgotten. But

Churchill perhaps came to realize that he had been mistaken to force so unpolitical a man into politics, and when Alexander, in the autumn of 1954, told him that 'for personal reasons' (which meant, in effect, that he was unhappy and rather bored) he would be glad to leave the Government at the Prime Minister's convenience, the offer was accepted. In the reshuffle of 18 October, Alexander was succeeded in the Ministry by Harold Macmillan. It was the end of his public career.

17

LAST YEARS (1954-69)

The last fifteen years of Alexander's life were not years of retirement except in the loosest sense that he had not one job to occupy him but a multiplicity. Often he had spoken as if the Second War, then Canada, and then the Ministry of Defence, were the last tasks that he would undertake, but when the end of his official career came in 1954, he found his enthusiasm for new experience unabated. He must earn money by business, and gladly accepted the appointments which his rank and reputation thrust upon him. For a man who so carefully guarded his privacy and loved his home-life it seems at first remarkable that Alexander should have allowed both to be eroded by the pressure of so many occupations, until one remembers that he found it difficult to refuse a friend (and these offers of work and requests for his patronage always came from friends), that he was responsible for his still young family and, most important, that he enjoyed constant and varied activity, grumbling occasionally at his lack of free time, but uneasy when he had too much of it. Besides, he was fond of ceremony, even a public dinner, and while nobody was less conceited or histrionic, he enjoyed dressing up for a great occasion, when an hour of pomp was followed or preceded by an hour's reunion with his friends. Reserve and conviviality, simplicity and display, were strangely intertwined in his character. He could wear with swagger the robes of an Earl or Knight of the Garter, the uniform of a Field Marshal or of an Elder Brother of Trinity House, but he ordered his suits from Montagu Burton. He was as contented attending dinners of the Irish Guards Old Comrades as speaking second only to Churchill at the Royal Academy banquet.

He remained essentially a happy man. He was an entrancing companion; he loved laughing and exchanging stories. His painting came to mean more and more to him. He had an agile brain, assimilated information quickly, and his memory was sharp, but he did not become contemplative in his older age. He read for enjoyment (mostly history and biography), not for study or reflection, and when he said his prayers, as he did every night, it was more in thankfulness than in contrition, for there was nothing with which he needed to reproach himself.

He assumed that everyone else must be as honest and dedicated as himself. Once when a soldier failed to salute him in uniform, his companion heard him mutter, 'Funny, he ought to *enjoy* being a soldier.' When his son Shane complained that a woodcutter had left his work unfinished and sent in a bill for £80, Alexander said, 'Oh, give him the money. He'll come back to finish the job.' Of course he never did. 'Well,' said Alexander, 'you'll always find one or two people like that.' Once in Belfast an old man asked him in the street for money. 'How much?' said Alexander. 'Five pounds, your honour.' Alexander gave it to him, and when asked why he gave so much, replied, 'Because he wanted it: he said so.' His naïveté was part of his unaffected modesty. He never seemed to realize that he had become a public figure. When he was cruising in the Thames with Seago on one of their painting-holidays, they put in at the Guards boat-club at Maidenhead. 'They may remember me here', he said to Seago. 'I used to be a member once.' When Seago went with the Alexanders to *My Fair Lady*, a man in the audience was seen to be staring intently in their direction. 'There's a man over there looking at you', said Lady Alexander. 'But I've no idea who he is', said Alexander, looking round. 'Don't be silly,' interrupted Seago, 'he recognizes you for what you are.' 'Oh, I don't think it can be that', he replied.

The simplicity of his attitude extended to his home-life. Having lived in various rented houses since their return from Canada (The Vale had been sold in 1946), they bought in 1959 Winkfield Lodge on the edge of Windsor Great Park, an old house to which an entrance-front had been added in the early part of this century. They pulled down a six-bedroom wing, and were left with a modest house of no special architectural distinction, but comfortable and secluded by shrubbery from the road, with a large garden behind. Above the garage Alexander made a studio, and in the garage he stacked in a filing-cabinet the priceless records of his campaigns, which were handed over to the Public Record Office after his death. To the garden he added two long brick walls which he built with his own hands when he was over seventy, and a small swimming-pool. He came to enjoy gardening, and today the garden is even more expressive of his taste and personality than the house, neat and varied, with a trace of romanticism.

Winkfield Lodge was the focus of his later years, the retreat of his leisure hours. They had a cook, and a Nanny for the children, Miss May Turner, who had been with them since the birth of Brian in 1939. They seldom entertained guests for more than a meal, and seldom accepted private invitations, for they were happiest when alone with each other or with their children. Once a year, for ten years in succession, they took a holiday in the Mediterranean, cruising in the Astors' yacht to the Aegean, to Istanbul or the Yugoslav coast, where Alexander once again met Tito. They spent another holiday in Portugal, where he and Auchinleck together toured the battlefields of the Peninsula War. Occasionally they went to Hever, and once to Chartwell. Alexander sometimes visited Caledon, where his brother Erik, still a bachelor, lived in seclusion until his death in 1968. His second brother, Herbrand, had died three years earlier, but William, the companion of his boyhood, remained close to him all his life, and survived him.

Alexander, as all his children agree, was the perfect father. He seldom scolded, he was always interested, always fun. With the girls, Rose and Susan, he developed a teasing, more overtly intimate, relationship than with the two boys. He could deny them nothing. When I asked them if he gave them advice, they said that he did so very seldom, for his advice was implicit in his own example, his good humour, his generosity of spirit. Remembering his own childhood at Caledon, he allowed them perfect freedom, which included the right occasionally to run wild. Only one of them, Rose, the eldest, was married during his lifetime, to Major Humphrey Crossman, and her children, David and Emma, were the only grandchildren whom he knew. Shane married Miss Hilary van Geest in 1971, and Susan married Andrew Hamilton in the previous year.

The Alexanders were adequately well off. Only in the last year of his life, when his aunt, Lady Norbury, left him a substantial legacy, was there money to spare. His father had left him £10,000 of which all but £3,000 was spent on his education, and his mother's estate produced £5,000, with which they bought The Vale. A Field Marshal's pension would go little way to meet the expense of private education for the children, and Alexander was obliged (even had he not welcomed the novelty of it) to supplement his income by directorships. Within a month of leaving the Ministry of Defence, hc was appointed to the boards of Barclay's Bank and the Phoenix Assurance, and later he joined the Thompson Foundation and became Governor of Securicor. In terms of time the most important of his directorships was Alcan, the Canadian company with worldwide interests in the extraction and processing of aluminium. He was invited to join their board partly owing to his connections with Canada, but also because he could represent the company in the United Kingdom, where Alcan had large investments but no resident director. Alexander became Chairman of Alcan's British company, and was diligent in his attention to its many ramifications. His directorship also took him frequently abroad. At least three times a year he attended board meetings of the parent company in Montreal or elsewhere, and flew on their behalf to Australia, New Zealand and Jamaica. He was not a cypher on the boards of these eminent companies. He was useful to them for his acquaintance with leading men in all parts of the world, he had an innate wisdom which outweighed his lack of business or financial experience, and he had acquired in Canada a knowledge of the problems of fast-developing countries. His fellow-directors speak, above all, of his happy manner with people, from factory-foremen and bank-clerks to senior Ministers in foreign countries, which helped to resolve diplomatic difficulties and create goodwill.

His honorary appointments were many. From August 1946 until his death he was Colonel of the Irish Guards, and paraded with them many times at the Trooping, on St Patrick's Day and other ceremonial occasions, and attended the annual dinners of the branches of the Irish Guards Association in Dublin, Belfast, Liverpool, London, Birmingham and Manchester. He visited the regiment's battalion in Aden. At the Queen's Coronation (while he was still Minister of Defence) he carried the Orb. He was Constable of the Tower of London from 1960 to 1965, which brought him an honorarium of £200 a year but no quarters in the Tower, and although he was generally responsible for its administration, the executive work was done by a deputy. From 1957 to 1965 he was Lieutenant of the County of London, and for a further year of Greater London, in succession to Lord Alanbrooke. The appointment involved him in attendance with the Queen at the arrival of state visitors, functions at County Hall and in different parts of London, and the signing of innumerable letters of a formal character. He was President of the MCC for one year, 1955, handing over the Presidency to Walter Monckton, his old partner in Fowler's match. He became Chancellor and then Grand Master of the Order of St Michael and St George, and an Elder Brother of Trinity House. He was a Freemason. He was a Governor of Harrow. He was first President of the British Heart Foundation. He accepted, in 1953, the chairmanship of the Anglo-German Association, for which his background and reputation particularly suited him, and he welcomed to London on their behalf Chancellor Adenauer and General Hans Speidel, Commander-in-Chief of the Allied Land Forces in Europe. All these activities, separately part-time but cumulatively onerous, kept him so busy that it was a rare day when he had no appointments, and then he would sit down to his private correspondence, writing by hand as many as thirty letters in a morning.

He was made a Freeman of many cities in addition to London, and received many honorary degrees. There was only one remaining national honour which could be awarded to him, the Order of Merit, and that he received in 1958 when he was lying seriously ill in Canada and was not expected to live. It is worth setting out the titles and distinctions which he held when his cup was full:

The 1st Earl Alexander of Tunis KG PC OM GCB GCMG CSI DSO MC and Baron Rideau of Ottawa and Castle Derg; also Viscount Alexander of Tunis, and of Errigal; Field Marshal in the Army; Grand Cross of the Legion of Honour, Legion of Merit and DSM (USA), Order of St Anne and Order of Suvorov (Russia), Grand Cross of George I and Order of the Redeemer (Greece), Virtuti Militari (Poland). . . .

but this is still not complete, for even Burke's *Peerage* ends its list, despairingly, ' . . . and many others'. The grandest of his awards were those that came to him most easily. Once when David Hunt was admiring his medals, Alexander reminded him of General Foy's remark on a similar occasion: 'Come into the garden, and let me take six shots at you from the range of a few feet, and if you survive, you can have all my medals, because that is what I had to do in order to win them.'

Alexander was not particularly interested in the past; he had too much to do in the present. 'The war', he said to Susan, 'is over.' His friends and many strangers sent him their Memoirs and War-Histories, but from their unmarked condition it seems that he put most of them into his bookshelves unread. He was generous to students who asked him for interviews about his campaigns, and at least one tape-recording (of a conversation with Major Verney of the Irish Guards) survives to show with what humour and sharp recollection he could recreate the atmosphere of a scene long past. Inevitably he was pressed by publishers to write his Memoirs, or at least to allow a biographer access to his papers. To the latter suggestion he replied, 'I don't want anything published until after my death.' To the former his reaction was at first fastidious. 'He stood aside from the often murky stream of martial reminiscences', said *The Times* approvingly. He had published his despatches, and had little more to say, and even less to answer, for during his lifetime no book had challenged his military capacity, and he was content to leave the final judgement to history. 'After all,' he said, 'I can't go back and do it all over again.'

In 1960 he was eventually persuaded by the *Sunday Times* (mainly, his widow believes, because he thought insufficient justice had been done to his troops) to allow his Memoirs to be ghost-written. His collaborator was a military historian, John North, 'who undertook', as he says in the Foreword, 'the task of committing my thoughts to paper'. The book was compiled in many interviews between Alexander and North, and he refreshed his memory by retracing in the autumn of 1960 the path of his armies' advance from Cairo to northern Italy, accompanied by North and two of his former Chiefs of Staff, McCreery and Harding. Lady Alexander joined them in Tunisia for the remainder of the trip.

His admirers found the book disappointing when it was published two years later. Liddell Hart said that the Memoirs 'provide double cause for regret. While contributing scarcely any fresh evidence, they do disservice to history by misleading treatment of the available evidence, and will react detrimentally upon the reputation of a soldier universally respected for his fairness.' The structure of the book was odd, following no rational or even chronological plan, and relegating to elongated footnotes the narrative of his campaigns, as if a soldier's problems and achievements were less important than his casual anecdotes. It was bare of documentation, and drew almost nothing from post-war publications. The book appeared to have been written primarily to entertain, not as his considered contribution to history, and it was thought unworthy of Alexander, as if he had not really wanted to take the trouble. They were not Memoirs. They were conversational reminiscences on the road. When they were published, a certain interest was mixed with the dismay, mainly because Alexander hinted for the first time at his opinion of Montgomery, and the Press revived the legend of a Monty-Alex rivalry which never existed at the time because both were too busy, and Alexander too understanding. Attention focussed once again on the Alam Halfa and Delta 'retreat' plan at the very outset of their partnership in Africa, an incident insignificant in comparison to what each later achieved. The unimportance of the controversy ('Did Monty alter Alex's despatches?') was a fair measure of the triviality of the book. The answer is that Monty did, and Alex accepted the alteration.

In October 1958 Alexander was in Ottawa on Alcan business when he had his first heart-attack. It was serious, and he spent six weeks in hospital. He flew home from Canada, apparently recovered, but on the day after his arrival he had a second attack, which put him back into hospital, at Windsor, for a further six weeks. This time his recovery was more permanent. He decided that he could regain his full strength by doing as much as possible to the point when he began to tire, and then he stopped. By 1960 his health was almost completely restored, and he gave up none of his directorships or other activities. His voice was un-slurred, his mind alert, his gait still buoyant. Thus he continued until 1967, when his heart began to flutter slightly, but the fluttering was stabilized by treatment, and he resumed his ordinary life.

In March 1969 he and his wife stayed for a few days with their old Canadian friends, the Letsons, on Grand Cayman Island in the Caribbean. There the news reached them that Eisenhower had died, and both were invited to his funeral, Alexander officially, his wife as a family friend. They had a difficult journey to Washington by Miami and Boston, and the lying-in-state and funeral were long ceremonies in bitter cold. It did not appear that Alexander was overtired by them, and he accepted an invitation from Pierre Trudeau to fly in his 'plane to Ottawa next day. After a day or two in Montreal on Alcan business, the Alexanders flew home. For two months he lived a normal life, and it is only in retrospect that the strain of those few days in North America can be suspected of having weakened him.

On 11 June he attended a meeting and dinner of Phoenix Assurance, from which he was retiring as a director, and responded to a toast by its Chairman, Lord De L'Isle, on whose breast he had pinned the VC after Anzio. Early next morning, he complained of nausea, but returned to Winkfield Lodge where his condition seemed to improve. Two days later, on Saturday 14 June he was able to come downstairs in a dressing-gown and watch the Trooping on television. On Sunday, it seemed, he was much the same. In the late afternoon he dressed and walked round the garden, and then returned to bed. A few minutes later his wife found him lying in excruciating pain. He was taken for X-rays to the Princess Christian Nursing Home in Windsor, and the doctors diagnosed a perforated aorta. They removed him at once to Wexham Park Hospital in Slough for an emergency operation, but his heart could not stand the strain. He died under the anaesthetic at about 3 am on Monday 16 June 1969. He was seventy-seven.

Many of his friends first heard the news later that morning at the Garter ceremony in St George's Chapel, Windsor Castle, when they saw his stall hung, as is the tradition, in black crêpe. Most appropriately it was there that his funeral service was held on 24 June. The streets were lined by men of the Irish Guards, and his coffin, borne on a gun-carriage, was escorted by eight pall-bearers: General Lord Robertson, Harold Macmillan, Field Marshal Sir Francis Festing (formerly CIGS), General Lemnitzer (US Army and retiring Supreme Allied Com-commander, NATO), Marshal of the RAF Sir Charles Elsworthy, Field Marshal Lord Harding, Lord Mountbatten, and Marshal of the RAF Lord Portal. As the coffin was carried into the Chapel, the steps were lined by men of the Royal Canadian Mounted Police. In the con-gregation were Field Marshals Montgomery and Slim. These men, and a thousand other men and women gathered in the Chapel and outside, had helped him weave the fabric of his life. The funeral was splendid in the colour and drama of its military perfection, but the burial was in keeping with the simplicity of his nature. His body was laid privately in the churchyard of Ridge, near Tyttenhanger, his family's Hertfordshire home. There you will find among the other graves a stone bearing affectionately at its head the single word ALEX: and below it his full name and titles, and the dates of his birth and death.

REFERENCES

2 The First World War
   1. Kipling, *The Irish Guards in the Great War*, Vol. **II**
   2. Hillson, *Alexander of Tunis*
   3. Quoted in Hillson, *op. cit.*

3 The Baltic
   1. Tallents, *Man and Boy*
   2. *Nachrichtenblatt of the Baltic Gentries*, Munich, December 1969.
      Quoted in Jackson, *Alexander of Tunis as Military Commander*
   3. Duranty, *I Write as I Please*

5 The 1st Division
   1. Bryant (*ed.*), *The Turn of the Tide*
   2. Colville, *Man of Valour*

6 Dunkirk
   1. Spears, *Prelude to Dunkirk*
   2. Mordal, *La Bataille de Dunkerque*
   3. Eden, *The Reckoning*
   4. Mordal, *op. cit.*

8 Burma
   1. Smyth, *Before the Dawn*
   2. Davies, *Army Quarterly*, January 1956
   3. Telegrams in Connell, *Wavell, Supreme Commander*, 1969
   4. Slim, *Defeat into Victory*
   5. Butler, *Grand Strategy*, Vol. III
   6. Davies, *op. cit.*

9 The Western Desert
   1. Butcher, *Three Years with Eisenhower*

2. Liddell Hart, *The Rommel Papers*
3. Eden, *The Reckoning*
4. Horrocks, *A Full Life*
5. de Guingand, *Operation Victory*
6. McCreery, 12*th Royal Lancers' Journal*, April 1959
7. Liddell Hart, *History of the Second World War*
8. McCreery, *op. cit.*

10 Alexander of Tunis

1. Bryant (*ed.*), *The Turn of the Tide*
2. Bradley, *A Soldier's Story*
3. Macmillan, *The Blast of War*
4. Quoted in Macksey, *The Crucible of Power*
5. Eisenhower, *Crusade in Europe*

11 Sicily

1. Macmillan, *The Blast of War*
2. *Eisenhower Papers*
3. Gunther, *D Day*
4. Bradley, *A Soldier's Story*
5. Harris, *Allied Military Administration of Italy*
6. Shepperd, *The Italian Campaign*
7. Roskill, *The War at Sea*, Vol. III, Part I
8. Macmillan, *op. cit.*

12 Salerno and Anzio

1. Clark, *Calculated Risk*
2. *Eisenhower Papers*
3. Eisenhower, *Crusade in Europe*

13 Rome

1. Grigg, *Prejudice and Judgement*

14 Supreme Commander

1. Bryant (*ed.*), *Triumph in the West*
2. Alexander, *Memoirs 1939–45*
3. Sixsmith, *Army Quarterly*, October 1969
4. Howard, *The Mediterranean Strategy in the Second World War*
5. Leeper, *When Greek Meets Greek*

15 Canada

1. Pickersgill (*ed.*), *The Mackenzie King Record*

16 Minister of Defence

1. *Sunday Times*, 22 June 1969
2. Clark, *From the Danube to the Yalu*
3. Clark, *op. cit.*

BIBLIOGRAPHY

Unpublished sources
The Alexander Papers dealing with the African and Mediterranean
Campaigns, and other official documents of the Second World War (Public
Record Office).
Alexander's letters, narratives and other personal papers in the possession
of Lady Alexander and the Earl of Caledon.

Despatches
Lord Gort's Despatch on the BEF 1939–40, including Appendix describing
    the last days at Dunkirk
General Wavell's despatch on Operations in Burma 1942
Alexander's despatch on the Burma campaign
Alexander's despatches on the Mediterranean campaigns:
    El Alamein to Tunis
    The Conquest of Sicily
    The Allied Armies in Italy, Sept. 1943 to Dec. 1944
    The Italian Campaign, Dec. 1944 to May 1945
    Greece, Dec. 1944 to May 1945

Official Histories
    The War in France and Flanders 1939–40, L. F. Ellis
    The Defence of the United Kingdom, Basil Collier
    The War against Japan, Vol. II, S. Woodburn Kirby
    The Mediterranean and Middle East, Vols. III, IV and V, I. S. O. Playfair
        and C. J. C. Molony
    Allied Military Administration of Italy, C. R. S. Harris
    Grand Strategy, Vols. II to VI, J. R. M. Butler and John Ehrman
    The War at Sea, Vol. III, Capt. S. W. Roskill

The US Army in World War II
> *Northwest Africa*
> *Stilwell's Mission to China*
> *Mediterranean Theatre of Operations*, (Sicily to the Surrender of Italy)
> *The History of the Fifth Army*

Published books

Adleman, Robert (and Col. George Walton), *Rome Fell Today.* 1968
Alexander of Tunis, Field Marshal, *Memoirs 1939–45*, (Ed. John North). 1962
> *The Battle of Tunis*, Basil Hicks lecture. 1957
Anders, Lt-Gen. W., *An Army in Exile.* 1949
Barnett, Corelli, *The Desert Generals.* 1960
Bennett, Geoffrey, *Cowan's War.* 1964
Birkenhead, Lord, *Walter Monckton.* 1969
Böhmler, Rudolf, *Monte Cassino, A German View.* 1964
Bradley, General Omar N., *A Soldier's Story.* 1951
Bryant, Arthur (*ed.*), *Lord Alanbrooke's Diaries, The Turn of the Tide.* 1957
> *Triumph in the West.* 1959
Buckley, Christopher, *Road to Rome.* 1945
Butcher, Harry C., *Three Years with Eisenhower.* 1946
Carew, Tim, *The Longest Retreat* (Burma Campaign 1942). 1969
Carpentier, Gen. Marcel, *Les Forces Alliées en Italie.* 1949
Churchill, Sir Winston S., *The Malakand Field Force.* 1898
> *The Second World War*, Vols. II–VI. 1945–54
Clark, Gen. Mark W., *Calculated Risk.* 1951
> *From the Danube to the Yalu.* 1954
Collier, Richard, *The Sands of Dunkirk*, 1961
Colville, J. R., *Man of Valour* (Lord Gort). 1972
Connell, John, *Auchinleck.* 1959
> *Wavell, Supreme Commander.* 1969
Cooper, Duff, *Haig.* 1935
Cunningham, Admiral of the Fleet, *A Sailor's Odyssey.* 1951
Dulles, Alan, *The Secret Surrender.* 1967
Duranty, Walter, *I Write as I Please.* 1935
Eden, Anthony (Earl of Avon), *Full Circle.* 1960
> *The Reckoning.* 1965
Eisenhower, General Dwight D., *Crusade in Europe.* 1948
> *The Papers of*, (*ed.* Alfred D. Chandler Jr.). 1970
Farago, Ladislas, *Patton.* 1963
Gaulle, Gen. Charles de, *Unity 1942–4.* 1956
Gough, Gen. Sir Hubert, *Soldiering On.* 1954

Grigg, Sir James, *Prejudice and Judgement.* 1948
Guingand, Gen. F. de, *Operation Victory.* 1947
Gunther, John, *D Day* (Sicily). 1944
Harington, Gen. Sir Charles. *Tim Harington Looks Back.* 1940
Higgins, Turnbull, *Soft Underbelly.* 1968
Hillson, Norman, *Alexander of Tunis.* 1952
Horrocks, Lt-Gen. Sir Brian, *A Full Life*, 1960
Howard, Michael, *The Mediterranean Strategy in the Second World War.* 1968
Hunt, David, *A Don at War.* 1966
Ismay, Gen. Lord, *Memoirs.* 1960
Jackson, Gen. W. G. F., *The Battle for Italy.* 1967
  The Battle for Rome. 1969
  Alexander of Tunis as Military Commander. 1971
Kesselring, Field Marshal, *Memoirs.* 1953
Kipling, Rudyard, *The Irish Guards in the Great War* (two vols.). 1923
Kippenberger, Gen. Sir Howard, *Infantry Brigadier.* 1949
Leeper, Sir Reginald, *When Greek Meets Greek.* 1950
Lewin, Ronald, *Montgomery as Military Commander.* 1971
Liddell Hart, Sir Basil, *The Rommel Papers.* 1953
  History of the First World War (new edition). 1970
  History of the Second World War. 1970
Linklater, Eric, *The Campaign in Italy.* 1945
Macksay, Kenneth, *The Crucible of Power.* 1969
Macmillan, Harold, *The Blast of War, 1939–45.* 1967
  Tides of Fortune, 1945–55. 1969
Majdalany, Fred, *Cassino: Portrait of a Battle.* 1957
Mallory, J. P., *The Structure of Canadian Government.* 1971
Montgomery, Field Marshal Earl, *El Alamein to the Sangro.* 1948
  Memoirs. 1958
Moorehead, Alan, *The End in Africa.* 1943
  The Desert War. 1965
  Montgomery. 1946
Mordal, Jacques, *La Bataille de Dunkerque.* 1948
Nicolson, Harold, *Diaries and Letters, 1939–45.* 1968
Patton, Gen. George, *War As I Knew It.* 1948
Perowne, Stewart, *The Siege within the Walls.* 1970
Pickersgill, J. W., (*ed.*), *The Mackenzie King Record*, Vols. II, III and IV.
  1968–70
Robinson, J. A., *Alexander.* 1946
Seago, Edward, *The Paintings of Earl Alexander of Tunis.* 1973
Senger und Etterlin, Gen. von, *Neither Fear nor Hope.* 1963
Shepperd, G. A., *The Italian Campaign.* 1968

Shirer, William L., *The Rise and Fall of the Third Reich.* 1960
Slim, Field Marshal Lord, *Defeat into Victory.* 1956
Smyth, Brig. Sir John, *Before the Dawn.* 1957
Spears, Gen. Sir Edward, *Prelude to Dunkirk.* 1954
Stilwell, Gen. Joseph W., *The Stilwell Papers.* 1949
Tallents, Sir Stephen, *Man and Boy.* 1943
Taylor, A. J. P., *English History, 1914–45.* 1965
Tedder, Marshal of the RAF Lord, *With Prejudice.* 1966
Truscott, Gen. Lucius, *Command Missions.* 1954
Tuker, Lt-Gen. Sir F., *Approach to Battle.* 1943
Verney, Peter, *The Micks: The Story of the Irish Guards.* 1970
Walder, David, *The Chanak Affair.* 1969
Warlimont, Gen. Walter, *Inside Hitler's Headquarters 1939–45.* 1964
Wheeler Bennett, John W., *King George VI: His Life and Reign.* 1958
Young, Desmond, *Rommel.* 1950

INDEX

329

NIGEL NICOLSON

Nigel Nicolson was born in 1917, the younger son of two writers, Sir Harold Nicolson (whose Diaries he edited) and V. Sackville-West. He was educated at Eton and Balliol College, Oxford, and served in the Grenadier Guards in North Africa and Italy during the Second World War. With Sir George Weidenfeld he founded the publishing firm of Weidenfeld & Nicolson Ltd. He entered Parliament as the Conservative MP for Bournemouth East in 1952, but lost his seat seven years later because he publicly opposed the Suez operation. He became Chairman of the British United Nations Association in 1961. He has written several books on politics, architecture, and social history.